Lecture Notes in Computer Science 10376

Commenced Publication in 1973
Founding and Former Series Editors:
Gerhard Goos, Juris Hartmanis, and Jan van Leeuwen

More information about this series at http://www.springer.com/series/7408

Anthony Anjorin · Huáscar Espinoza (Eds.)

Modelling Foundations and Applications

13th European Conference, ECMFA 2017
Held as Part of STAF 2017
Marburg, Germany, July 19–20, 2017
Proceedings

 Springer

Editors
Anthony Anjorin (iD)
University of Paderborn
Paderborn
Germany

Huáscar Espinoza
Tecnalia Research and Innovation
Derio
Spain

ISSN 0302-9743   ISSN 1611-3349   (electronic)
Lecture Notes in Computer Science
ISBN 978-3-319-61481-6   ISBN 978-3-319-61482-3   (eBook)
DOI 10.1007/978-3-319-61482-3

Library of Congress Control Number: 2017943853

LNCS Sublibrary: SL2 – Programming and Software Engineering

Printed on acid-free paper

This Springer imprint is published by Springer Nature
The registered company is Springer International Publishing AG
The registered company address is: Gewerbestrasse 11, 6330 Cham, Switzerland

Foreword

Software Technologies: Applications and Foundations (STAF) is a federation of leading conferences on software technologies. It provides a loose umbrella organization with a Steering Committee that ensures continuity. The STAF federated event takes place annually. The participating conferences may vary from year to year, but they all focus on foundational and practical advances in software technology. The conferences address all aspects of software technology, from object-oriented design, testing, mathematical approaches to modeling and verification, transformation, model-driven engineering, aspect-oriented techniques, and tools.

STAF 2017 took place in Marburg, Germany, during July 17–21, 2017, and hosted the four conferences ECMFA 2017, ICGT 2017, ICMT 2017, and TAP 2017, the transformation tool contest TTC 2017, six workshops, a doctoral symposium, and a projects showcase event. STAF 2017 featured four internationally renowned keynote speakers, and welcomed participants from around the world.

The STAF 2017 Organizing Committee would like to thank (a) all participants for submitting to and attending the event, (b) the Program Committees and Steering Committees of all the individual conferences and satellite events for their hard work, (c) the keynote speakers for their thoughtful, insightful, and inspiring talks, and (d) the Philipps-Universität, the city of Marburg, and all sponsors for their support. A special thanks goes to Christoph Bockisch (local chair), Barbara Dinklage, and the rest of the members of the Department of Mathematics and Computer Science of the Philipps-Universität, coping with all the foreseen and unforeseen work to prepare a memorable event.

July 2017   Gabriele Taentzer

Preface

The European Conference on Modeling Foundations and Applications (ECMFA) is dedicated to advancing the state of knowledge and fostering the industrial application of Model-Based Engineering (MBE) and related methods. MBE is an approach to software engineering that sets a primary focus on leveraging high-level and suitable abstractions (models) to enable computer-based automation and advanced analyses; MBE techniques promise a significant boost in both productivity and quality.

The 13th edition of ECMFA was held during July 19–20, 2017, in Marburg as part of the Software Technologies: Applications and Foundations (STAF) federation of conferences. The Program Committee received 48 submissions, each of which was reviewed by at least three Program Committee members. The committee decided to accept 18 papers, 13 papers for the Foundations Track and five papers for the Applications Track, resulting in an overall acceptance rate of 38%. Papers on a wide range of MBE aspects were accepted, including model-driven generative techniques, model consistency management and evolution, language engineering, and experience reports.

We thank Lionel Briand for his interesting talk on the current challenges of model-driven verification and testing of cyber-physical systems. We are grateful to all Program Committee members and additional reviewers for providing excellent reviews, participating actively in ensuing discussions, and providing constructive feedback for all submitted papers. We thank the STAF organization for providing an excellent framework in which ECMFA can continue to co-exist and profit from the synergy with other related conferences. Finally, we thank all authors who submitted papers to ECMFA 2017, making this conference possible.

July 2017

Anthony Anjorin
Huáscar Espinoza

Organization

Program Committee

Shaukat Ali	Simula Research Laboratory, Norway
Anthony Anjorin	Paderborn University, Germany
Colin Atkinson	University of Mannheim, Germany
Fabien Belmonte	Alstom, France
Reda Bendraou	UPMC-LIP6, France
Ruth Breu	Universität Innsbruck, Austria
Jean-Michel Bruel	IRIT, France
Daniela Cancila	CEA TECH, France
Eric Cariou	LIUPPA, Université de Pau, France
De-Jiu Chen	KTH Royal Institute of Technology, Sweden
Nancy Day	University of Waterloo, Canada
Zinovy Diskin	McMaster University, University of Waterloo, Canada
Maged Elaasar	JPL, USA
Romina Eramo	University of L'Aquila, Italy
Huáscar Espinoza	TECNALIA, Spain
Anne Etien	Université Lille 1, France
Madeleine Faugere	Thales, France
Lidia Fuentes	Universidad de Málaga, Spain
Sebastien Gerard	CEA, LIST, France
Susanne Graf	VERIMAG/CNRS, Université Grenoble Alpes, France
Esther Guerra	Universidad Autónoma de Madrid, Spain
Regina Hebig	Chalmers|Gothenburg University, Sweden
Philipp Helle	Airbus Group Innovations, Germany
C. Michael Holloway	NASA Langley Research Center, USA
Zhenjiang Hu	NII, Japan
Muhammad Zohaib Iqbal	Quest lab, FAST, National University of Computer and Emerging Sciences
Bernhard Kaiser	Berner&Mattner Systemtechnik GmbH, Germany
Jörg Kienzle	McGill University, Canada
Ekkart Kindler	Technical University of Denmark, DTU Compute, Denmark
Vinay Kulkarni	Tata Consultancy Services Research, India
Thomas Kühne	Victoria University of Wellington, New Zealand
Thierry Lecomte	ClearSy, France
Malte Lochau	TU Darmstadt, Real-Time Systems Lab/University of Passau, Germany
Ralf Lämmel	Universität Koblenz-Landau, Germany
Henrik Lönn	Volvo Group, Sweden

Model-Driven Verification and Testing of Cyber-Physical Systems: Tackling Scalability and Practicality Challenges (Invited Talk)

Lionel C. Briand

University of Luxembourg, Luxembourg City, Luxembourg

Abstract. Testing and verification problems in the software industry come in many different forms, due to significant differences across domains and contexts. But one common challenge in the context of cyber-physical systems is scalability; the capacity to test and verify increasingly large systems interacting with complex physical environments. Another concern relates to practicality. Can the inputs required by a given technique be realistically provided by engineers given their background and time constraints? This talk reports on ten years of research tackling the verification and testing of cyber-physical systems as a search and optimization problem, often but not always relying on abstractions and models of the system under test. This experience spans several application domains and organizations. Our observation is that most of the problems we faced could be effectively re-expressed so as to make use of appropriate search and optimization techniques to automate specific testing or verification strategies, targeting various categories of faults. However, to achieve scalability, such solutions had to be often complemented by machine learning to help the search focus on regions of the input space that were more likely to exhibit failures.

Contents

Meta-Modelling and Language Engineering

On the Automated Derivation
of Domain-Specific UML Profiles

Alexander Kraas[✉]

Software Technologies Research Group, University of Bamberg, Bamberg, Germany
Alexander.Kraas@swt-bamberg.de

Abstract. The model-driven engineering (MDE) of domain-specific languages (DSL) is becoming increasingly important. In this area, metamodels are the central artefacts, defining the syntax and semantics of DSLs.
Different technologies are available to create metamodels, with the Meta
Object Facility (MOF) being one of them. Apart from other uses, a
MOF-based metamodel can serve as input for an automated derivation
of a profile for the Unified Modeling Language (UML).

In this paper, we propose a novel mapping of redefined or subsetted
metaclass attributes, so that the values of their corresponding stereotype
attributes can be computed at runtime by employing the Object Constraint Language (OCL). This is achieved by an automatic introduction
of additional OCL expressions. A further contribution is the transfer of
the static semantics of a metamodel to its derived UML profile. This
transfer is realized by an automatic update of existing OCL constructs
in such a way that they can be utilized for a generated UML profile
without any modification.

Keywords: Metamodel · DSL · UML · Profile · Derivation · OCL

1 Introduction

The creation of metamodels is a key task in model-driven engineering (MDE),
because metamodels are used to define the syntax and semantics of domain-
specific languages (DSLs). Depending on the employed technology, a metamodel
can be based on the Ecore meta-metamodel of the Eclipse Modeling Framework
(EMF) [24], or – as considered in this paper – on the Meta Object Facility
(MOF) [17] that provides advanced language concepts for attributes, such as
subsetting or redefinition.

Although different kinds of artefacts (e.g., textual and graphical editors) can
be generated semi-automatically based on metamodels, some effort is required for
their completion. Hence, it can be preferable to reuse existing tools and frameworks for the Unified Modeling Language (UML) [19]. This can be achieved
by defining a UML profile for a DSL of interest, because UML profiles are a
standardized UML extension mechanism. Thanks to this mechanism, UML profiles usually can be used in UML editors without any additional implementation

© Springer International Publishing AG 2017
A. Anjorin and H. Espinoza (Eds.): ECMFA 2017, LNCS 10376, pp. 3–19, 2017.
DOI: 10.1007/978-3-319-61482-3_1

effort. Due to this reason, we prefer the utilization of UML profiles instead of implementing tools for DSLs from scratch.

However, in comparison to language concepts of the MOF, some restrictions exist for those concepts that are applicable for UML profiles. In particular, the stereotypes of a UML profile cannot inherit from UML metaclasses so that stereotype attributes cannot redefine or subset attributes of metaclasses.

As proposed in [5,6,26], a UML profile can be derived automatically based on an existing metamodel. However, these approaches have limitations concerning the mapping of subsetted or redefined attributes. Furthermore, no automatic transfer and update of the static semantics defined by the Object Constraint Language (OCL) is supported. To remedy this situation, we present here a novel approach for the automatic derivation of UML profiles from MOF-based metamodels. One key contribution is the automatic generation of OCL expressions for stereotype attributes that are derived from redefined or subsetted metamodel attributes. These OCL expressions enable the computation of stereotype attribute values at runtime. A second contribution is the automatic transfer of the static semantics of a metamodel towards its derived UML profile. For this purpose, all OCL constructs of a metamodel are updated and transferred to the UML profile in such a way that the static semantics can be validated based on a UML model. Otherwise, this model would have to be transformed into a corresponding domain model where the validation is then performed.

We have implemented and successfully applied our novel derivation approach for the generation of a UML profile [25] for the Specification and Description Language (SDL) [10]. SDL is employed in the telecommunication sector for many years, in particular for specifying communication protocols and distributed systems. Since the grammar of SDL is rather complex, we consider SDL as a good example to evaluate the results of our approach.

Related work. The most closely related approaches to ours are [5,6,22,26], which also derive a UML profile from an existing metamodel for a DSL. Their commonality is that, in addition to the metamodel, mapping rules have to be provided as input for the profile derivation. Depending on the approach, this is realized in terms of so called 'Integration Metamodels' or 'Mapping Models'. In contrast, our approach expects metamodels as input for the derivation of UML profiles, which make reuse of 'abstract concepts' as proposed in [4,23]. Since 'abstract concepts' are a subset of the metaclasses contained in the UML metamodel, not all aspects of a DSL have to be modelled from scratch. Furthermore, due to the correlation between 'abstract concepts' and UML metaclasses, no mapping rules must be explicitly defined in our approach. Equally important and in contrast to us, the related works do not treat the generation of OCL expressions and constraints for 'subsetted' or 'redefined' attributes, and do not address an automated transfer of the static semantics towards a UML profile.

Another category of existing works covers the derivation of metamodels based on existing UML profiles, as proposed in [13,14], which is exactly the opposite of our approach. The creation of a UML profile from scratch may be an option for a new DSL with low complexity, but for an existing DSL with higher complexity this could become difficult. This is because not only the static semantics of the DSL but also UML's static semantics have to be taken into account. Therefore, the manual creation of a metamodel followed by an automatic derivation of a UML profile should be preferred for more complex DSLs such as SDL [10]. This variant should also be chosen if the syntax rules for a DSL are given because, then, existing tools [7] (e.g., EMFText [8] or xText [2,3]) can be utilized for an automatic derivation of metamodels.

Structure of this paper. The next section introduces our approach at an abstract level, while our detailed derivation of a UML profile from a metamodel is presented in Sect. 3. The results of our approach are evaluated and discussed in Sects. 4, and 5 presents our conclusions and suggestions for future work.

2   Overall Approach and Running Example

According to our approach not only UML profiles but also model transformations and additional metaclasses can be automatically derived based on a single metamodel. Due to space restrictions, we focus on the first aspect in the remainder of this paper. This section presents an overview of our overall approach and illustrates it with a small running example.

Our overall approach. The central artefact for all derivations is a domain-specific metamodel MM_{Domain} (see Fig. 1), which is generated on the basis of syntax production rules of an existing computer language or DSL. To obtain a metamodel that does not require too much effort for further refinement, we reuse 'abstract concepts' that are defined by an existing metamodel (MM_{AC}) by inheritance, as proposed in [4,23]. For this purpose, syntax rules have to be enriched with particular annotations before a metamodel can be generated. In addition, an important prerequisite for our entire approach is that MM_{AC} has to 'match' with a subset of the UML metamodel, as is argued below. Otherwise, the UML profile (UP_{Domain}) and its associated Model-to-Model (M2M) transformations $T_{DM-to-UML}$ and $T_{UML-to-DM}$ cannot be derived.

After the generation of MM_{Domain} in step (A), a few manual refinements have to be made before it can be used as input for steps (B)–(E). In particular, OCL constraints have to be specified to meet the static semantics of the DSL. Thereafter, we can automatically derive UP_{Domain} and, if required, additional metaclasses (MM_{Add}) that extend the MM_{UML} in steps (B) and (C). The derivation of additional metaclasses may be an option if stereotypes cannot be employed due to their restrictions as defined by the UML [19]. For instance, such an approach is applied for the value and expression languages of the SDL-UML profile [11] and of the MARTE profile [20]. Since the input and output artefacts of steps (B) and (C) are models, we realize both derivations by two dedicated M2M transformations, which are implemented using the operational language of the Query/View/Transformation specification (QVT) [16].

In contrast to the aforementioned artefacts, we utilize two Model-to-Text (M2T) transformations to generate source code for the M2M transformations

$T_{DM\text{-}to\text{-}UML}$ (D) and $T_{UML\text{-}to\text{-}DM}$ (E). Both M2T transformations are implemented with the MOF M2T Language (MTL) [15], and the Acceleo [1] component of Eclipse is used for the execution. The source code of a generated M2M transformation is generated in terms of the operational language of QVT.

We have implemented our approach in terms of plug-ins for the *Model Development Tools (MDT)* edition of Eclipse[1]. Although we could generate an Ecore-based metamodel in Step (A), it is a design decision to use a UML-based representation; otherwise, we could not subset and redefine metaclass attributes, because the required language concepts are not supported by the Ecore. However, the code generators of Eclipse-MDT can handle both formats.

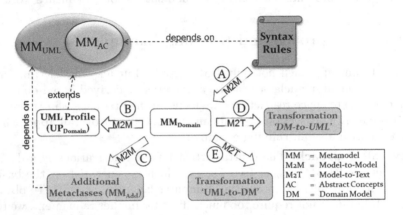

Fig. 1. Transformations and their derived artefacts.

The 'Abstract Concepts' metamodel. The metamodel MM_{AC} holds a key role for the entire derivation approach, because generated metaclasses of the metamodel MM_{Domain} inherit from 'abstract concepts' defined by MM_{AC}. An important prerequisite for MM_{AC} is that it has to 'match' with a subset of MM_{UML}. Otherwise, a straightforward mapping of MM_{Domain} to UP_{Domain} as presented here is impossible. A metamodel MM_{AC} is considered to be 'matching' with MM_{UML}, if the following constraints are fulfilled:

- For each metaclass MC of MM_{AC}, a corresponding metaclass MC' with an equal name shall be present in MM_{UML}. In addition, metaclass MC shall have an equal or lesser number of attributes than metaclass MC'.
- For each attribute a of a metaclass MC, a corresponding attribute a' with an equal name shall be present in metaclass MC'. In addition, attributes a and a' shall have the same properties, e.g. the same type and cardinality.
- A data type of MM_{AC} shall have a corresponding data type in MM_{UML}.

Different approaches could be applied to obtain MM_{AC}. Since MM_{AC} shall 'match' with MM_{UML}, we consider a creation of MM_{AC} from scratch to be

---

[1] https://eclipse.org/modeling/mdt/.

too error-prone and expensive. Another option is to use the MOF or the
UML Infrastructure Library [18]. Since their metaclasses are primarily used in
MM_{UML} to define its 'Kernel' package, they could also be reused to create a
MM_{AC} that only supports 'structural' language concepts (e.g. *'Classifier'*[2]).
Finally, also the reuse of parts of MM_{UML} could be considered if language concepts for behavioural specifications (e.g. *'StateMachines'*) are required.

Different kinds of metaclasses. Our derivation approach is based on the
assumption that metaclasses of a metamodel MM_{Domain} can be categorized into
three different groups. The first group consists of 'abstract concept' metaclasses
MC_{AC} that always have a 'matching' counterpart in MM_{UML}. The second group
embraces all MC_{St} metaclasses that map to *'Stereotypes'* of UP_{Domain}, and
which are marked with a «ToStereotype» stereotype. Finally, the third group
consists of the MC_{AMC} metaclasses that map to 'additional metaclasses' of
MM_{AMC}, and which have a «ToMetaclass» stereotype applied.

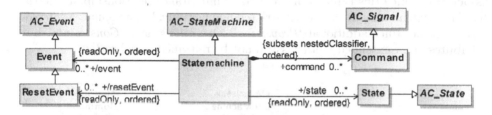

Fig. 2. Example of annotated syntax rules and their corresponding metaclasses for a
simple state machine DSL.

Running example. To discuss the derivation approach in more detail, we introduce a simple state machine DSL as a running example. The syntax rules and
their corresponding metaclasses of MM_{Domain} are shown in Fig. 2. The employed
textual notation is a variant of the Extended Backus-Naur Form (EBNF) and
based on the concrete syntax specified in [9]. In addition, our textual notation
includes different kinds of annotations (written in italic-style), which establish
associations to the 'abstract concepts'. The naming of the annotations is based on
the respective language concepts of the MOF, e.g., the annotation `generalized
class` introduces a *'Generalization'* relationship between two metaclasses.

The 'abstract concepts' used for the given example consist of metaclasses
contained in the 'StateMachine' package of the UML metamodel [19]. As shown
in Fig. 2, a `Statemachine` defined by the given DSL consists of an `Event` set,
a `ResetEvent` set, a `Command` set and the `State` set. Note that the example is
only employed by us to illustrate the different derivations; it cannot be used to
derive a syntactically complete metamodel.

---

[2] Names within quotation marks and written in italic style refer to UML elements or
attributes as specified by the UML Superstructure [18].

3   UML Profile Derivation

After generating and refining MM_{Domain}, it can be used as the source for deriving a corresponding UML profile (UP_{Domain}). However, the UML Superstructure [19] defines some constraints concerning the extension of UML metaclasses by stereotypes. Thus, we take the following constraints for *'Profile'* and *'Stereotype'* elements into account for our derivation approach:

- *"An element imported as a metaclassReference is not specialized or generalized in a Profile."* ([19]: Sec. 18.3.7 Profile – Constraint 1)
- *"A Stereotype may only generalize or specialize another Stereotype."* ([19]: Sec. 18.3.9 Stereotype – Constraint 1)

Due to the constraints cited above, a *'Stereotype'* is not permitted to inherit from a metaclass by a *'Generalization'* relationship. Instead of this, the extension of a particular UML metaclass by a *'Stereotype'* has to be defined by an *'Extension'* association. Since this is not equivalent to an inheritance relationship, a *'Stereotype'* can extend a metaclass in a restricted manner only. In particular, a *'Stereotype'* can introduce additional *'Properties'*, *'Operations'* and *'Constraints'*, but attributes of an extended metaclass cannot be redefined or subsetted.

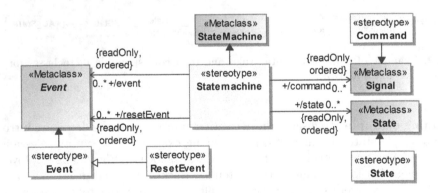

Fig. 3. «Statemachine» *'Stereotype'* derived from the running example.

3.1   Our Automated Derivation Approach

To ensure a proper derivation of a UML profile, we enrich the input metamodel MM_{Domain} with particular metadata, as discussed in the previous section. Hence, three different kinds of metaclasses (MC_{AC}, MC_{St} and MC_{AMC}) are present in MM_{Domain}. However, only the MC_{St} metaclasses are mapped to corresponding *'Stereotypes'* in UP_{Domain}. This fact is shown in Fig. 3, which contains *'Stereotypes'* that are derived based on our running example. For instance, the Statemachine MC_{St} is mapped to the «Statmachine» stereotype, whereas the

AC_StateMachine MC_{AC} is not mapped. Instead, the «Statmachine» stereo-type has an *'Extension'* to the 'matching' UML metaclass StateMachine. Due to this mapping, the MC_{AC} metaclasses of MM_{Domain} have not to be present in UP_{Domain} and, therefore, derived *'Stereotypes'* have not any kind of link to MC_{AC} metaclasses.

Mapping to 'Stereotypes'. A metaclass MC_{St} of MM_{Domain} is mapped to a corresponding *'Stereotype'* in UP_{Domain}. Due to the restrictions identified before, a *'Stereotype'* can inherit from another stereotype by a *'Generalization'*, whereas an *'Extension'* has to be used to establish a relationship between a UML meta-class and its extending *'Stereotype'* (see Fig. 4). Hence, we take the following two cases for the derivation of stereotypes into account:

Case A: A MC_{St} A that inherits from a MC_{AC} T_AC is mapped to a *'Stereotype'* A' that has an *'Extension'* to the UML metaclass T_AC'.
Case B: If a MC_{St} B inherits from a MC_{St} A, both metaclasses map to *'Stereo-types'* and stereotype B' has a *'Generalization'* to stereotype A'.

An example of Case A is shown in Fig. 3, where the «Statemachine» stereotype is generated for the corresponding metaclass MC_{St}. In addition, an *'Extension'* from *'Stereotype'* Statemachine to the StateMachine metaclass of MM_{UML} is introduced. The «ResetEvent» stereotype is an example for Case B, because it inherits from the «Event» stereotype.

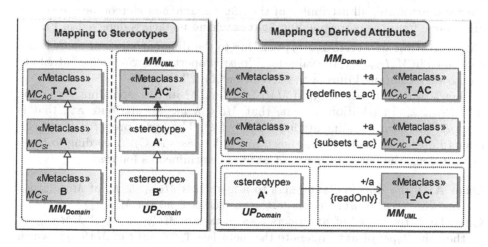

Fig. 4. Mapping to Stereotypes and mapping to derived attributes.

Mapping to stereotype attributes. The extension mechanism of *'Stereotypes'* must also be considered for the mapping of the attributes of a MC_{St}, because subsetting and redefinition of a stereotype attribute is only applicable as long as no attribute of a UML metaclass is involved. Hence, the rules discussed here apply to the derivation of stereotype attributes.

Derived and read-only stereotype attributes: If an attribute a of a MC_{St} A in MM_{Domain} redefines or subsets an attribute t_ac of MC_{AC}, then a is mapped to a derived and read-only attribute a' of *'Stereotype'* A' in UP_{Domain} (see Fig. 4). This mapping is required because MC_{AC} has a 'matching' metaclass in MM_{UML}; hence, the mapped attribute a' of A' would redefine/subset an attribute of a UML metaclass, which is not permitted. In addition, we generate an OCL expression and assign it to the *'defaultValue'* property of a mapped attribute. This OCL expression is used at runtime to compute the attribute value. More details on the generation of appropriate OCL expressions can be found in Sect. 3.2. For example, the command attribute of the MC_{St} Statemachine shown in Fig. 2 redefines the nestedClassifier attribute, whereas its corresponding mapped attribute (see Fig. 3) is specified to be derived and read-only.

Subsetted/redefined attribute: In contrast to the mapping discussed before, a redefinition or subsetting relationship can be preserved if an attribute a of a MC_{St} A redefines or subsets an attribute b of another MC_{St} B. In this case, the mapped stereotype attribute a' redefines or subsets the stereotype attribute b'. The mapping is possible because a' and b' are owned by *'Stereotypes'*.

Mapping of other attributes: We map all other attribute kinds of a MC_{St} one-to-one to corresponding stereotype attributes in UP_{Domain}, because no further restrictions apply for them. Due to the derivation approach, also an automatic update of existing OCL expressions that define the *'defaultValue'* of an attribute (see Sect. 3.3) is required. As shown in Fig. 3 and except for the command attribute, all attributes of the «Statemachine» stereotype are copied one-to-one from the corresponding Statemachine metaclass depicted in Fig. 2.

Computation of attribute types. Due to the different kinds of metaclasses contained in MM_{Domain}, the value for a *'type'* property of a *'Stereotype'* attribute has to be recomputed during the derivation of a UML profile.

Let A be a metaclass MC_{St} in MM_{Domain} and A' its corresponding stereotype in UP_{Domain}. In addition, assume that MC_{St} A has an attribute att that is mapped to a corresponding attribute att' of A'. The *'type'* property of att can refer to one of the metaclasses shown in Fig. 5 (Cases A–C). According to these assumptions, the *'type'* property of att' is determined as follows:

Case A: If the *'type'* of att refers to a metaclass MC_{AC} T_AC of MM_{Domain}, then the *'type'* of att' refers to the metaclass T_AC' of MM_{UML}.

Case B: If the *'type'* of att refers to a metaclass MC_{ST} T_ST of MM_{Domain}, then the *'type'* of att' refers to the metaclass T_STbase' of MM_{UML}, which is extended by stereotype T_ST'.

Case C: If the *'type'* of att refers to a metaclass MC_{AMC} T_AMC of MM_{Domain}, then the *'type'* of att' refers to metaclass T_AMC' of MM_{Add}.

All attributes of the stereotype «Statemachine» shown in Fig. 3 are an example of Case B, because instead of referring to stereotypes, the *'type'* properties of these attributes are recomputed to the extended metaclasses of MM_{UML}.

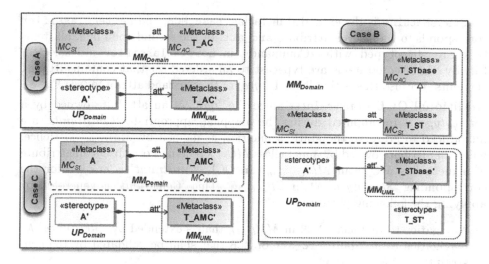

Fig. 5. Different kinds of metaclasses in MM_{Domain} used as attribute types and their corresponding mapping targets.

3.2 Introduction of Additional OCL Constructs

In addition to the OCL constructs already present in MM_{Domain}, further OCL constructs are introduced for UP_{Domain} as part of our UML profile derivation.

OCL expressions for derived attributes. When a redefined or subsetted attribute of a metaclass MC_{St} in MM_{Domain} is mapped to a read-only and derived attribute of a stereotype in UP_{Domain}, the value of such an attribute can be computed at runtime based on its *'defaultValue'*. Hence, an OCL expression is introduced for each of these attributes. All OCL expressions can be generated according to the same generation pattern that consists of the following parts:

- Navigation to metaclass MCB in MM_{UML} that is extended by *'Stereotype'* A;
- Navigation to attribute src_att of MCB that is used as source for the value computation;
- Selection of relevant items of attribute src_att depending on the applied stereotype or the element kind;
- Type-cast of the selected items in order to match the *'type'* and cardinality of the derived attribute src_att.

A generated OCL expression is constructed according to the following template:

```
base_MCB.src_att->select(/* applied ST A or element kind */)->type-cast
```

The example given below is used to calculate the value for the command attribute of the «Statemachine» stereotype shown in Fig. 3.

```
self.base_StateMachine.nestedClassifier->select(
isStrictStereotypedBy('Command')).oclAsType(uml::Signal)->asOrderedSet()
```

StateMachine is the extended metaclass base_MCB, and nestedClassifier corresponds to the source attribute src_att. In the second code line, all items that are stereotyped with «Command» in nestedClassifier are selected. Finally, the selected items are typecast to an ordered set that contains Signal elements, because this is the defined *'type'* of the command attribute (see Fig. 3).

Additional OCL constraints. Since the *'type'* of an attribute owned by a *'Stereotype'* is recomputed during the mapping, appropriate *'Constraints'* are introduced to preserve the static semantics, as defined by MM_{Domain}. Hence, when an attribute owned by a metaclass MC_{St} A redefines or subsets an attribute of a metaclass MC_{AC} in MM_{Domain}, an OCL *'Constraint'* is created for the corresponding *'Stereotype'* A' in UP_{Domain}. This *'Constraint'* is generated by applying the following pattern:

- Navigation to metaclass MCB in MM_{UML} that is extended by *'Stereotype'* A;
- Navigation to attribute src_att of MCB that shall be validated by the constraint;
- Determination of the set of valid elements VE that can be contained in att_src based on the applied stereotypes or the element kinds.

An OCL *'Constraint'* is constructed according to the following template:

```
base_MCB.src_att->notEmpty() implies base_MCB.src_att->forAll( VE )
```

The example below restricts the valid types of the nestedClassifier attribute of the «Statemachine» stereotype (see Fig. 3) according to the static semantics as defined by the originating metaclass (see Fig. 2). Hence, the shown *'Constraint'* restricts the elements that can be contained in nestedClassifier only to those elements that have the «Command» stereotype applied.

```
base_StateMachine.nestedClassifier->notEmpty() implies base_StateMachine
   .nestedClassifier->forAll(isStrictStereotypedBy('Command'))
```

3.3   Update of Existing OCL Constructs

A metamodel MM_{Domain} usually includes OCL constructs that define the static semantics. These constructs can be OCL *'Constraints'* or OCL expressions, which are used to define the behaviour of *'Operations'* or the *'defaultValue'* of attributes. To ensure that OCL constructs defined for a metaclass MC_{St} can be utilized for its *'Stereotype'*, an update has to be carried out at specific points.

Since OCL constructs of metamodels are only present as textual notations, they cannot be processed by the M2M-transformation that implements step (B) of the overall approach. Hence, we implement the update by using an OCL parser and a pretty printer. Before UP_{Domain} is derived from MM_{Domain}, an Abstract Syntax Tree (AST) is generated by the parser for each OCL construct in MM_{Domain}. This AST consists of different kinds of nested OCL expressions as specified in [21]. To perform the update, every OCL expression of an AST is visited by the pretty printer. During this visit, the AST is converted back to its textual notation and the update is performed as discussed below.

PropertyCallExp. This kind of OCL expression is used to navigate from a `source` expression to the `referredProperty`. According to the UML [19], a stereotype and its extended meataclass exist as separate instances in a model. Hence, the UML provides two different and implicitly defined properties to navigate between metaclass and stereotype instances. The '*extension_<stereotype>*' property is used to navigate from a metaclass to an applied stereotype, whereas the '*base_<metaclass>*' property is used for the opposite direction.

Referred property maps to a 'Stereotype' attribute: Due to the fact that stereotypes exist as separate instances, we introduce an '*extension_<stereotype>*' navigation (as shown below) for a PropertyCallExp, if its `source` expression has a result type that refers to a MC_{St} metaclass and its `referredProperty` is also owned by a MC_{St} metaclass.

```
input: source.referredProperty
result: source.extension_<stereotype>.referredProperty
```

Expression source is a 'self' variable: Another update for a PropertyCallExp occurs if its source expression is a 'self' VariableExp with a result type that refers to a MC_{St} metaclass and if its `referredProperty` is owned by a MC_{AC} metaclass. In this case, an additional '*base_<metaclass>*' navigation must be introduced because, in UP_{Domain}, the 'self' VariableExp refers to a stereotype instance from which a property of its extended UML metaclass is accessed:

```
input: self.referredProperty
result: self.base_<metaclass>.referredProperty
```

OperationCallExp. This kind of OCL expression is used to invoke a particular operation (the `referredOperation`) for a given `source` expression. The predefined OCL operations `oclIsTypeOf()` and `oclIsKindOf()` can be employed to determine whether the result type of a `source` expression directly or indirectly matches the expected type. If one of these operations is applied to a MC_{St} metaclass, an update of the OperationCallExp is required, because this kind of metaclass is mapped to a '*Stereotype*'. Due to this mapping, both operations are not usable in UP_{Domain}. Hence, they need to be replaced with the user-defined operations `isStrictStereotypedBy()` and `isStereotypedBy()`, which determine whether a specified stereotype is (directly or indirectly) applied to an element identified by the `source` expression.

```
input: (A) source.oclIsTypeOf(MCSt); (B) source.oclIsKindOf(MCSt)
result: (A) source.isStrictStereotypedBy(<qualified stereotype name>)
        (B) source.isStereotypedBy(<qualified stereotype name>)
```

TypeExp. This kind of OCL expression is used to refer to a particular type: a '*Class*' or '*DataType*'. Because MM_{Domain} contains three different kinds of metaclasses (e.g., MC_{AC}), a TypeExp of an OCL construct contained in MM_{Domain}

has to be updated. This is because, after deriving a UML profile, a referenced *'Type'* can be contained not only in UP_{Domain} but also in MM_{UML} or MM_{Add}. Hence, the fully qualified name of a *'Type'* is determined depending on its containing artefact, and then this name is used for updating the TypExp. For instance, the TypExp `AC_Element` is updated to `UML::Element`.

4   Evaluation and Discussion

We have successfully applied our approach to derive a UML profile for SDL [10], which we use here for evaluation.

SDL background and objectives. For many years, the International Telecommunication Union (ITU) is responsible for all standardization activities concerning SDL, and the results of this work are published as a set of ITU-T Z-series Recommendations[3]. The ITU-T Recommendations Z.100 – Z.107 define the grammar of SDL, whereby the semantics is specified in natural language and the (concrete and abstract) syntax is defined by employing a particular EBNF that is compliant to Z.111 [9]. In addition, a formal specification for SDL is provided as an annex to Z.100 [10], where a first-order predicate logic is used to define the static semantics, and SDL's dynamic semantics is formalized by employing the Abstract State Machine (ASM) formalism. Furthermore, a manually created UML profile for SDL is specified in Z.109 [11].

In order to enable a model-based language development of SDL in the future, our first objective is to provide a (semi-)automatically generated metamodel for SDL which also captures SDL's static semantics. Secondly, and based on this foundation, we also provide an automatically derived UML profile for SDL.

The metamodel. As input for the profile derivation, we generated a metamodel MM_{Domain} based on 180 abstract syntax rules from SDL and 43 'abstract concept' metaclasses MC_{AC} from MM_{UML} (approx. 17 percent of all UML metaclasses). Due to similar language concepts in SDL and UML, we could reuse this high number of metaclasses from MM_{UML} so that we did not have to manually model these concepts for our derived MM_{Domain}. Owing to an automatic optimization during the generation, only 106 metaclasses ($MC_{St} + MC_{AMC}$) are derived for the 180 syntax rules. Thus, MM_{Domain} contains 71 MC_{St}, 35 MC_{AMC} and 43 MC_{AC} metaclasses.

Furthermore, we created 204 OCL *'Constraints'* based on SDL's formal specification in order to capture the static semantics of SDL. Because of the different objectives of the *'Constraints'*, their complexity varies from simple to highly complex. Approximately 50% of the constraints are employed to ensure the syntactical well-formedness, so they have a low or medium complexity. The remaining constraints, e.g., are used to check the compatibility of SDL type definitions. Because this part of the static semantics of SDL is rather complex, also the corresponding OCL *'Constraints'* are highly complex.

---

[3] Homepage of the ITU-T Z-series Recommendations:
http://www.itu.int/itu-t/recommendations/index.aspx?ser=Z.

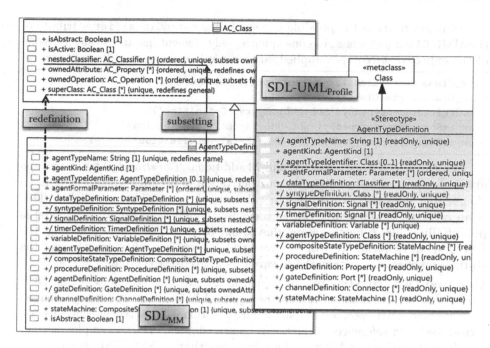

Fig. 6. The `AgentTypeDefinition` MC_{St} metaclass and its derived stereotype.

The derived 'Profile'. All 71 MC_{St} metaclasses of MM_{Domain} are mapped by our approach to an equal number of 'Stereotypes'. Furthermore, 43 'additional' metaclasses that extend UML's `ValueSpecification` metaclass are derived automatically to represent SDL expressions. Even though stereotypes could be used for this purpose, the same approach as applied in Z.109 [11] is employed here so as to ensure the comparability of a manual and an automatic UML profile creation. Since agent type definitions are the most important language concept of SDL, we use the `AgentTypeDefinition` MC_{St} and its derived 'Stereotype' shown in Fig. 6 to discuss the results of our approach.

According to our approach, all attributes of the MC_{St} that redefine/subset attributes of `AC_Class` are mapped to derived and read-only attributes of the «AgentTypeDefinition» stereotype. In addition, an OCL expression is generated for each attribute to enable a value computation at runtime; for example, the OCL expression introduced for the `dataTypeDefinition` attribute computes the value based on the `nestedClassifier` attribute of `Class`:

```
self.base_Class.nestedClassifier->select(isStrictStereotypedBy(
    'SDL-UML::DataTypeDefinition')).oclAsType(uml::Classifier)->asSet()
```

Since UML metaclass attributes are employed to compute the attribute values of stereotypes at runtime, we introduce an additional OCL 'Constraint' for each of these metaclass attributes; otherwise, the static semantics of a derived UML profile, as defined by MM_{Domain}, cannot be preserved. The example constraint shown below restricts the possible values of the `nestedClassifier` attribute of the UML `Class` metaclass. In consequence, only element instances that have one of the expected stereotypes applied, are valid values for `nestedClassifier`.

```
base_Class.nestedClassifier->notEmpty() implies
base_Class.nestedClassifier->forAll(
  isStrictStereotypedBy('SDL-UML::SyntypeDefinition')
  or isStrictStereotypedBy('SDL-UML::AgentTypeDefinition')
  or isStrictStereotypedBy('SDL-UML::DataTypeDefinition') ... )
```

In total, 139 OCL expressions (and 73 additional *'Constraints'*) for stereotype attributes were introduced during our derivation of a UML profile for SDL, so that a user does not have to assign values to these attributes explicitly. This is an advantage over related works, because the effort for creating a model is potentially reduced. Furthermore, due to our particular attribute mapping, the DSL's syntactic structure will be preserved. This is key when transferring the static semantics of a metamodel towards its derived UML profile.

Updated OCL constructs. As argued in the previous section, existing OCL constructs of a metamodel have to be updated before they can be transferred to a derived UML profile. In particular, additional property navigations are introduced, and references to metaclasses are adapted. As an example consider the *'Constraint'* given below, which specifies that a 'SYSTEM' `AgentType-Definition` shall not be owned by any other `AgentTypeDefinition`. The updated *'Constraint'* has an additional navigation to the extended metaclass of the «AgentTypeDefinition» stereotype, and a check whether the owner has the expected stereotype applied.

```
self.agentKind = AgentKind::SYSTEM implies not
  self.owner.oclIsTypeOf(AgentTypeDefinition) -- Metamodel
self.agentKind = SDLUML::AgentKind::SYSTEM implies not self.base_Class
  .owner.isStrictStereotypedBy('SDLUML::AgentTypeDefinition') -- Profile
```

Based on the SDL metamodel, we could successfully evaluate the automatic update and transfer of all 204 OCL *'Constraints'* defined for MM_{Domain} of SDL. Hence, the advantage of our automatic update is that no manual rework for OCL constructs of a derived UML profile is required, in contrast to the approaches discussed in [5, 6, 26].

Discussion. Although we could automatically derive a UML profile based on a metamodel for SDL via our approach, a limitation exists concerning the number of subsetted/redefined attributes that can be processed. According to the MOF, a metaclass attribute cannot only redefine/subset a single attribute but also a set of other attributes. Currently, our approach can only process metaclass attributes that redefine/subset at most one other attribute, because this is sufficient for our derived UML profile for SDL. However, this limitation can be remedied by introducing OCL expressions that calculate attribute values based on more than one metaclass attribute.

As another drawback of our approach, one may argue that it is more appropriate to directly create a UML profile for a DSL of interest instead of specifying a metamodel in a first step. Provided that a metamodel is not of interest, the direct creation of a UML profile might be an option for a new DSL with low complexity. But if someone is faced with the creation of a metamodel and a corresponding UML profile for a DSL with higher complexity such as SDL, then the initial creation of a metamodel should be preferred. In our point of view, especially the specification of OCL *'Constraints'* in the context of a UML profile is more error-prone rather than in the context of a metamodel. This is because, in the first case, one has to also take UML's syntax and semantics into account.

5   Conclusions and Future Work

We proposed a novel approach for the automatic derivation of a UML profile from a metamodel of an existing computer language or DSL. Although other works can be employed to derive UML profiles, our approach supports the processing of MOF-based metamodels, which make use of all modelling concepts provided by the MOF; particularly noteworthy is our support of 'subsetted' and 'redefined' metaclass attributes. Consequently, a generated *'Profile'* does not only contain *'Stereotypes'* but also additional OCL *'Constraints'* that are used to preserve the static semantics. A further novelty of our approach is the automatic update and transfer of OCL constructs contained in a metamodel towards a derived UML profile.

The applicability of our approach was evaluated by deriving a metamodel and a UML profile for SDL [10]. This large case study clearly demonstrated the approach's benefits: whereas we spent months to generate previous generations of SDL's UML profile by hand [11], our new and highly automated approach required only some weeks to do the same. Due to space constraints we could not present the full SDL case study here, but the interested reader can download all necessary components to re-do the case study from [25].

Regarding future work we wish to use our SDL metamodel and UML profile for implementing a new version of our SDL-UML Modeling and Validation (SU-MoVal) framework [12]. In addition, we plan to apply our approach to further DSLs, with the aim of proving its applicability on a larger scale.

Acknowledgments. We thank Gerald Lüttgen of the Software Technologies Research Group at the University of Bamberg, Germany, for his many valuable remarks on this paper. Furthermore, we also thank Richard Paige of the Department of Computer Science at the University of York, U.K., for several discussions on the paper's topic.

References

1. Homepage of the M2T transformation tool Acceleo. http://www.eclipse.org/acceleo/. Accessed 24 Feb 2017
2. Bergmayr, A., Wimmer, M.: Generating metamodels from grammars by chaining translational and by-example techniques. In: Proceedings of the 1st International Workshop on Model-driven Engineering by Example, CEUR Workshop, vol. 1104, pp. 22–31. CEUR-WS.org (2013)

3. Efftinge, S., Völter, M.: oAW xText: a framework for textual DSLs. In: Modeling Symposium at Eclipse Summit, vol. 32, pp. 118–121. eclipsecon.org (2006)
4. Fischer, J., Piefel, M., Scheidgen, M.: A metamodel for SDL-2000 in the context of metamodelling ULF. In: Amyot, D., Williams, A.W. (eds.) SAM 2004. LNCS, vol. 3319, pp. 208–223. Springer, Heidelberg (2005). doi:10.1007/978-3-540-31810-1_14
5. Giachetti, G., Marín, B., Pastor, O.: Integration of domain-specific modelling languages and UML through UML profile extension mechanism. Int. J. Comput. Sci. Applicat. 6(5), 145–174 (2009)
6. Giachetti, G., Marín, B., Pastor, O.: Using UML as a domain-specific modeling language: a proposal for automatic generation of UML profiles. In: Eck, P., Gordijn, J., Wieringa, R. (eds.) CAiSE 2009. LNCS, vol. 5565, pp. 110–124. Springer, Heidelberg (2009). doi:10.1007/978-3-642-02144-2_13
7. Goldschmidt, T., Becker, S., Uhl, A.: Classification of concrete textual syntax mapping approaches. In: Schieferdecker, I., Hartman, A. (eds.) ECMDA-FA 2008. LNCS, vol. 5095, pp. 169–184. Springer, Heidelberg (2008). doi:10.1007/978-3-540-69100-6_12
8. Heidenreich, F., Johannes, J., Karol, S., Seifert, M., Wende, C.: Model-based language engineering with EMFText. In: Lämmel, R., Saraiva, J., Visser, J. (eds.) GTTSE 2011. LNCS, vol. 7680, pp. 322–345. Springer, Heidelberg (2013). doi:10.1007/978-3-642-35992-7_9
9. ITU-T: Recommendation Z.111: Notations and guidelines for the definition of ITU-T languages. International Telecommunication Union (2008)
10. ITU-T: Recommendation Z.100: Specification and Description Language - Overview of SDL-2010. International Telecommunication Union (2011)
11. ITU-T: Recommendation Z.109: Specification and Description Language - Unified Modeling Language profile for SDL-2010. International Telecommunication Union (2011)
12. Kraas, A.: Towards an extensible modeling and validation framework for SDL-UML. In: Amyot, D., Fonseca i Casas, P., Mussbacher, G. (eds.) SAM 2014. LNCS, vol. 8769, pp. 255–270. Springer, Cham (2014). doi:10.1007/978-3-319-11743-0_18
13. Malavolta, I., Muccini, H., Sebastiani, M.: Automatically bridging UML profiles to MOF metamodels. In: Proceedings of the 41st Euromicro Conference on Software Engineering and Advanced Applications, pp. 259–266. IEEE (2015)
14. Noyrit, F., Gérard, S., Selic, B.: FacadeMetamodel: masking UML. In: France, R.B., Kazmeier, J., Breu, R., Atkinson, C. (eds.) MODELS 2012. LNCS, vol. 7590, pp. 20–35. Springer, Heidelberg (2012). doi:10.1007/978-3-642-33666-9_3
15. OMG: MOF Model to Text Transformation Language - Version 1.0. Object Management Group (2008)
16. OMG: Meta Object Facility (MOF) 2.0 Query/View/Transformation Specification - Version 1.1. Object Management Group (2011)
17. OMG: OMG Meta Object Facility (MOF) Core Specification - Version 2.5. Object Management Group (2011)
18. OMG: OMG Unified Modeling Language (OMG UML), Infrastructure, Version 2.4.1. Object Management Group (2011)
19. OMG: OMG Unified Modeling Language (OMG UML), Superstructure, Version 2.4.1. Object Management Group (2011)
20. OMG: UML Profile for MARTE: Modeling and Analysis of Real-Time Embedded Systems, Version 1.1. Object Management Group (2011)
21. OMG: Object Constraint Language - Version 2.4. Object Management Group (2014)

22. Pastor, O., Giachetti, G., Marín, B., Valverde, F.: Automating the interoperability of conceptual models in specific development domains. In: Reinhartz-Berger, I., et al. (eds.) Domain Engineering: Product Lines, Languages, and Conceptual Models, pp. 349–373. Springer, Heidelberg (2013)
23. Scheidgen, M.: Description of languages based on object-oriented meta-modelling. Ph.D. thesis, Math.-Natural Sci. Dept. II, Humboldt-University, Berlin, Germany (2009)
24. Steinberg, D., Budinsky, F., Merks, E., Paternostro, M.: EMF: Eclipse Modeling Framework. Pearson Education, London (2008)
25. SDL-UML Modeling and Validation (SU-MoVal) framework homepage. http://www.su-moval.org/. Accessed 24 Feb 2017
26. Wimmer, M.: A semi-automatic approach for bridging DSMLs with UML. Int. J. Web Inform. Sys. 5(3), 372–404 (2009)

Towards Seamless Hybrid Graphical–Textual Modelling for UML and Profiles

Lorenzo Addazi[1], Federico Ciccozzi[1(✉)] (iD), Philip Langer[2], and Ernesto Posse[3]

[1] School of Innovation, Design and Engineering,
Mälardalen University, Västerås, Sweden
{lorenzo.addazi,federico.ciccozzi}@mdh.se
[2] EclipsSource, Wien, Austria
planger@eclipsesource.com
[3] Zeligsoft, Ottawa, Canada
eposse@zeligsoft.com

Abstract. Domain-specific modelling languages, in particular those described in terms of UML profiles, use graphical notations to maximise human understanding and facilitate communication among stakeholders. Nevertheless, textual notations are preferred for specific purposes, due to the nature of a specific domain, or for personal preference. The mutually exclusive use of graphical or textual modelling is not sufficient for the development of complex systems developed by large heterogeneous teams. We envision a modern modelling framework supporting seamless hybrid graphical and textual modelling. Such a framework would provide several benefits, among which: flexible separation of concerns, multi-view modelling based on multiple notations, convenient text-based editing operations, and text-based model editing outside the modelling environment, and faster modelling activities.

In this paper we describe our work towards such a framework for UML and profiles. The uniqueness is that both graphical and textual modelling are done on a common persistent model resource, thus dramatically reducing the need for synchronisation among the two notations.

Keywords: Hybrid graphical–textual modelling · Multi-view modelling · UML · Profiles · MARTE · Xtext · Papyrus

1 Introduction

Model-Driven Engineering (MDE) has been largely adopted in industry as a powerful means to effectively tame complexity of software and systems and their development, as shown by empirical research [8]. Domain-Specific Modelling Languages (DSMLs) allow domain experts, who may or may not be software experts, to develop complex functions in a more human-centric way than if using traditional programming languages. The Unified Modeling Language (UML) is the de-facto standard in industry [8], the most widely used architectural description language [11], and an ISO/IEC (19505-1:2012) standard. UML is general-purpose, but it provides powerful profiling mechanisms to constrain and extend

© Springer International Publishing AG 2017
A. Anjorin and H. Espinoza (Eds.): ECMFA 2017, LNCS 10376, pp. 20–33, 2017.
DOI: 10.1007/978-3-319-61482-3_2

the language to achieve UML-based DSMLs (hereafter simply 'UML profiles'); in this paper we focus on them. Domain-specific modelling demands high level of customisation of MDE tools, typically involving combinations and extensions of DSMLs as well as customisations of the modelling tools for their respective development domains and contexts. In addition, tools are expected to provide multiple modelling means, e.g. textual and graphical, to satisfy the requirements set by development phases, different stakeholder roles, and application domains.

Nevertheless, support for graphical and textual modelling, two *complementary* modelling notations, is mostly provided in a mutual exclusive manner. Most off-the-shelf UML modeling tools, such as IBM Rational Software Architect [18] or SparxSystems Enterprise Architect [4], focus on graphical editing features and do not allow for seamless graphical–textual editing. This mutual exclusion suffices the needs of developing small scale applications with only few stakeholder types. For larger systems, with heterogeneous components and entailing different domain-specific aspects and different types of stakeholders, mutual exclusion is too restrictive and void many of the MDE benefits. When adopting MDE in large-scale industrial projects, efficient team support is crucial. Therefore, modelling tools need to enable different stakeholders to work on overlapping parts of the models using different modelling notations (i.e., graphical and textual).

Establishing a seamless modelling environment, which allows stakeholders to freely choose and switch between graphical and textual notations, can greatly contribute to increase productivity as well as decrease costs and time to market. Consequently, such an environment is expected to support both graphical and textual modelling in parallel as well as properly manage synchronisation to ensure consistency among the two. The possibility to leverage on different perspectives of the same information always in sync can also boost communication among different stakeholders, who can freely select their preferred visualisation means. A hybrid modelling environment for seamless graphical and textual modelling would disclose the following benefits.

Flexible separation of concerns with multi-view modelling based on multiple notations. The possibility to provide graphical and textual modelling editors for different aspects and sub-parts (even overlapping) of a DSML enables the definition of concern-specific views characterised by either graphical or textual modelling (or both). These views can interact with each other and are tailored to the needs of their intended stakeholders.

Faster modelling tasks. The seamless combination of graphical and textual modelling is expected to reduce modelling time and effort thanks to two factors.

(1) The single developer can choose the notation that better fits her needs, personal preference, or the purpose of her current modelling task. While structural model details can be faster to describe using graph-based entities, complex algorithmic model behaviours are usually easier and faster to describe using text (e.g., Java-like action languages).

(2) Text-based editing operations on graphical models, such as copy&paste and regex search&replace, syntax highlighting, code completion, quick fixes,

cross referencing, recovery of corrupted artefacts, text-based differencing and merging for versioning and configuration, are just few of the features offered by modern textual editors. These would correspond to very complex operations if performed through graphical editors; thereby, most of them are currently not available for graphics. Seamless hybrid modelling would enable the use of these features on graphical models through their textual view. These would dramatically simplify complex model changes; an example could be restructuring of a hierarchical state-machine by moving the insides of a hierarchical state. This is a demanding re-modelling task in terms of time and effort if done at graphical level, but it becomes a matter of a few clicks (copy&paste) if done at textual level.

Decoupling of modelling activities and modelling environment. Models can be edited using any text editor even outside the modelling environment.

In this paper we describe our work on providing a framework able to provide seamless hybrid graphical–textual modelling for UML profiles. The uniqueness of our framework resides in the fact that, differently from current practices, both graphical and textual editors operate on a common underlying model resource, rather than on separate resources, thus heavily reducing the need for synchronisation between the two. Our solutions are built upon open-source platforms and with open-source technologies.

The remainder of the paper is organised as follows. Section 2 provides a snapshot of the states of the art and practice related to hybrid modelling. In Sect. 3 we outline our framework, the intended benefits, and the differences with current practices. Details on the actual solution and exemplifications on a UML profile are provided in Sect. 4. The paper is concluded with evaluation results, in Sect. 5, and an outlook on current and future work, in Sect. 6.

2   States of the Art and Practice

mbeddr [14] is an open-source tool which supports extensions of the C language tailored for the embedded domain. The tool focuses on enabling higher-level domain-specific abstractions to be seamlessly integrated into C through modular language extensions. While mbeddr tackles the very relevant issue of bridging abstraction gaps between modelling and target languages, it does not address the seamless integration of different concrete syntaxes exploiting the same level of abstraction. Umple [22] merges the concepts of programming and modelling by adding modelling abstractions directly into programming languages and provides features for actively performing model edits on both textual and graphical concrete syntaxes. The support for synchronisation is limited, thus prohibiting certain kinds of modification at graphical level.

A plethora of other open-source tools such as FXDiagram [7], LightUML [10], TextUML [21], MetaUML [15], PlantUML [17] focus on textual concrete syntax for actively editing the modelling artefacts, while providing a graphical notation for visualisation purposes only. FXDiagram is based on JavaFX 2 and provides on the fly graphical visualisation of actions done through the textual concrete syntax including change propagation; the focus is on EMF models. LightUML focuses more on reverse engineering by generating a class diagram representation of existing Java classes and packages. TextUML is similar to FXDiagram in the sense that it allows modellers to leverage a textual notation for defining models, in this case UML, and providing textual comparison, live graphical visualisation of the model in terms of class diagrams, syntax highlighting, and instant validation. MetaUML is a MetaPost library for creating UML diagrams through a textual concrete syntax and it supports a number of read-only diagrams, such as class, package, activity, state machine, use case, and component. Similarly, PlantUML allows the modelling of UML diagrams by using a textual notation; graphical visualisations are read-only and exportable in various graphical formats. None of these tools provides means for synchronised editing in both textual and graphical notations nor the possibility to allow customisation of the related concrete syntaxes. Besides FXDiagram, which is DSML independent, the others focus on specific DSMLs, hence providing fixed textual and graphical concrete syntaxes for the considered DSML.

Several research efforts have been directed to mixing textual and graphical modelling. In [1], the authors provide an approach for defining combined textual and graphical DSMLs based on the AToM3 tool. Starting from a metamodel definition, different diagram types can be assigned to different parts of the metamodel. A graphical concrete syntax is assigned by default, while a textual one can be given by providing triple graph grammar rules to map it to the specific metamodel portion. The aim of this approach is similar to ours, but it targets specific DSMLs defined through AToM3 and is not applicable to UML profiles. Charfi et al. [3] explore the possibilities to define a single concrete syntax supporting both graphical and textual notations. Their work is very specific to the modelling of UML actions and has a much narrower scope than our work. In [19], the authors provide the needed steps for embedding generated EMF-based textual model editors into graphical editors defined in terms of GMF. That approach provides pop-up boxes to textually edit elements of graphical models rather than allowing seamless editing of the entire model using a chosen syntax. The focus of that paper is on the integration of editors based on EMF, while ours is to provide seamless textual and graphical modelling for UML profiles. Moreover, the change propagation mechanisms proposed by the authors are on-demand triggered by modeller's commit, while we focus on on-the-fly change propagation across the modelling views. Related to the switching between graphical and textual syntaxes, the approaches in [6,23] propose two attempts at integrating Grammarware and Modelware. Grammarware is a tool by which a mixed model is exported as text. Modelware is a tool by which a model containing graphical and textual content is transformed into a fully graphical model. Transformation from mixed models to either text or graphics is on-demand.

Projective editing is another way to enable different editing views for the same models, as provided by mbeddr and MelanEE [2]. Concrete syntaxes are not stored, only the abstract syntax is persistent. Thereby, the modeller edits the abstract syntax directly, and then selects specific concrete syntax projections of it. The main benefit is the possibility to project the model in various concrete syntaxes depending on the modeller. On the other hand, it complicates modelling activities, since it requires to act directly on the abstract syntax of the model through editors that are much more complex than parser-based text editors. Jetbrains MPS [9], on which mbeddr is based, provides a projective approach similar to MelanEE. Similarly to our approach, Jetbrains MPS uses a single abstract syntax, but it does not entail "real" text editors, rather providing text-like form-based editors, which hinders the use of traditional text-based tool features (e.g. for regex search&replace, diff/merge for versioning).

To summarise, current solutions for mixed textual and graphical modelling present at least one of the following limitations:

- one of the notations is read-only, intended as a mere visualisation means;
- one of the two notations is enforced for a specific, self-contained portion of a DSML only;
- concrete syntaxes are predefined and not customisable;
- synchronisation among different concrete syntaxes is not automated and on-the-fly but rather manual or on-demand.

3   A Hybrid Modelling Framework Based on Xtext and Papyrus

The goal of our work was to provide a hybrid modelling framework for UML and profiles based on de-facto standard open-source tools, i.e. Eclipse Modeling Framework [5] (EMF) as platform, Papyrus [16] for UML (graphical) modelling, and Xtext [24] for textual modelling. In Fig. 1, we depict the differences between existing solutions for hybrid modelling and our framework.

Existing approaches, notably the one by Maro et al. [12], tackle the provision of hybridness by keeping graphical and textual modelling fully detached. Graphical and textual modelling are performed on two separate models, which are separately persistent in two physical resources. Given a UML profile, a corresponding Ecore-based DSML representing the profile is automatically generated

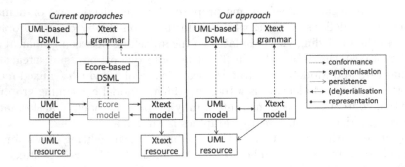

Fig. 1. Current approaches compared to our approach

or manually provided. EMF provides automation for this task, but the resulting Ecore model needs often manual tuning in order to be made usable. Graphical modelling is performed using the UML editors and the model persists as UML model resource. On the other hand, textual modelling is performed using generated Xtext editors and the textual representation persists as an Xtext resource. Moreover, Xtext works internally with an Ecore model resource, which is kept in sync with the textual resource by Xtext itself.

In order to keep graphical and textual models in sync, semi-automated mechanisms in the form of synchronisation model transformations are provided. These model transformations are in fact also generated, thanks to higher-order model transformations (HOTs), this provides a certain degree of flexibility in terms of evolution of the UML profile and automatic co-evolution of the synchronisation mechanisms. Nevertheless, HOTs would not work in case the generated Xtext grammar is customised. This practice is very often needed in order to make the grammar (and related editors) fit the developer's needs.

As a concrete example of the need to customize a DSML grammar, consider the UML-RT language [20]. UML-RT has two core concepts: *capsules* and *protocols*. Capsules are active classes and have a well-defined interface consisting of *ports* typed by protocols. Capsules may have an internal structure consisting of *parts* that hold capsule instances linked by connectors bound to the corresponding capsule ports. All interaction between capsule instances takes place by message-passing through connected ports.

UML-RT has a UML profile. If we start from the UML-RT profile, we obtain an Xtext grammar that contains rules like these:

```
1   Capsule returns Capsule:
2       'Capsule'
3       '{'
4           'base_Class' base_Class=[uml::Class|EString]
5       '}';
6
7   Class returns uml::Class:
8       Class_Impl | Activity | Stereotype | ProtocolStateMachine | StateMachine_Impl
9           | FunctionBehavior | OpaqueBehavior_Impl | Device | Node_Impl
10          | ExecutionEnvironment | Interaction | AssociationClass | Component;
11
12  Class_Impl returns uml::Class:
13      'Class'
14      '{'
15          ('name' name=String0)?
16          ('visibility' visibility=VisibilityKind)?
17          'isLeaf' isLeaf=Boolean
18      ...
19          ('useCase' '(' useCase+=[uml::UseCase|EString]
20              ( "," useCase+=[uml::UseCase|EString])* ')' )?
21      ...
22          ('ownedAttribute' '{' ownedAttribute+=Property
23              ( "," ownedAttribute+=Property)* '}' )?
24          ('ownedConnector' '{' ownedConnector+=Connector
25              ( "," ownedConnector+=Connector)* '}' )?
26      ...
27      '}';
```

This clearly entails a great amount of information related to UML but not relevant to UML-RT. In fact, the rule for **Class_Impl** includes clauses for each and every feature of the UML Class metaclass, many of which we removed for

the sake of space. Of these clauses, many, such as useCase, are irrelevant to
the DSML, and only a few, such as ownedAttribute and ownedConnector, are
relevant, but they do not reflect the concepts of UML-RT, and even the concrete
syntax may not be desirable. For UML-RT, we would like to obtain a grammar
with rules that reflect the DSML's concepts directly and hides away any additional UML structure that may be used to represent the concept. For example,
instead of having a single clause ownedAttribute, we would like to have clauses
for ports and parts, in a rule like this:

```
1    Capsule returns Capsule:
2         'capsule' name=EString
3         '{'
4              (ports+=RTPort)*
5              (parts+=CapsulePart)*
6              (connectors+=Connector)*
7              StructuredTypeCommonCoreFragment
8              BehaviourFragment
9         '}';
```

Xtext is designed for being used with EMF-based modeling languages. The
UML implementation in Eclipse is EMF-based and thus Xtext can be used to
implement textual concrete syntaxes for UML. However, Xtext is not designed
to work with UML profiles. This raises the need for explicit complex synchronisation between the two, both at abstract and concrete syntax level. We provide
a different approach to make Xtext work with UML profiles (right-hand side of
Fig. 1), by exploiting a single underlying abstract syntax (UML-based DSML),
two concrete syntaxes (graphical given by UML and textual given by Xtext),
one single persistent resource (UML resource), and thereby reducing the need for
ad-hoc heavyweight synchronisation mechanisms. Synchronisation is instead performed by Xtext in terms of serialisation and de-serialisation operations between
the UML model and the Xtext model, in the same way as Xtext naturally does
between the Ecore model and the Xtext model. Our solution provides the following improvements to the current state of the practice:

– **Grammar customisability.** The Xtext grammar can be customised and
  refactored to fit the developer's needs. This does not jeopardise the (de-)se-
  rialisation mechanisms as long as it does not break the conformance of models
  to the UML profile specification (i.e., metamodel).
– **Cross-profile hybridness.** Virtually, any UML profile can be leveraged
  without the provision of ad-hoc complex synchronisation transformations. In
  practice, for complex profiles, (de-)serialisation might need additional input
  from the hybrid DSML developer (e.g., stereotypes application transformation
  described in Sect. 4.2).
– **On-the-fly changes propagation.** Model changes done in one view (e.g.,
  UML graphical) are seamlessly reflected and visible on-the-fly in the other view
  (e.g., Xtext textual); existing synchronisation mechanisms propagate changes
  on-demand following a specific request from the developer.
– **Cross-notation multi-view modelling.** Different Xtext grammars and editors representing different sub-sets (even partially overlapping) of the UML
  profile (or several profiles) can seamlessly work on the same UML resource,

along with UML editors. Also in this case, the precondition is that the Xtext grammars enforce model conformance to the entailed profiles.

Other indirect benefits stem from the aforementioned ones. An example is the fact that code generators can reuse a single, shared abstract syntax for both graphical and textual representations of a model, without relying on additional transformations which result in added maintenance costs. Another example is that different stakeholders can view and edit model parts of their collaborators in their preferred syntax (or in a syntax that is optimised for them). In this way, potential inconsistencies can be identified very early already during the modeling process and communication among different stakeholders is greatly improved.

In the next section we describe our hybrid modelling solution from a technical perspective, providing concrete exemplifications of the aforementioned benefits.

4 Technical Solution

Our hybrid graphical–textual UML modelling framework is achieved by combining Papyrus for UML and Xtext. Existing approaches combining UML modelling and Xtext, mentioned in Sect. 2, rely on two completely separated sets of abstract syntax, concrete syntax, and persistent resources. This results in separate graphical and textual modelling, where partial hybridness is achieved by explicit synchronisation between the two concrete syntaxes. Synchronisation is complicated by the fact that graphical and textual abstract syntaxes are separated. Complex exogenous DSML-specific model transformations are needed to realise it. In our solution we provide a more flexible hybrid solution, based on one single abstract syntax (UML-based DSML only, instead of UML-based DSML for graphical and Ecore-based DSML for textual, in Fig. 1), two separated concrete syntaxes (UML model and Xtext model in Fig. 1, needed to overcome limitations of projective approaches), and one single persistent resource.

One major challenge of providing such a solution is that the resource management in Xtext entails the creation and maintenance of a separated Xtext-specific resource. We provide a solution for making Xtext work on the same UML resource as Papyrus, by acting on how the content of the Xtext textual editor is retrieved from and pushed to its underlying resource. Since we are interested in UML profiles, another major challenge is represented by expressing UML stereotypes and their applications in Xtext grammars since there is no concept in Xtext that corresponds to profiling. We solved this challenge by providing a way to define alternative rules, following a superclass/subclass relationship pattern, which enables editing of both stereotype-specific and base UML element properties.

In the next sections we describe in detail how we tackled the two challenges.

4.1 Extending Xtext Resource Management

Xtext does not provide out of the box support for the direct manipulation, including persistence, of UML resources. Xtext models are in fact stored as Xtext resources as plain textual artefacts and managed by the so called `XtextResource`, which is an Xtext-specific implementation of the EMF `resource`. Serialisation and de-serialisation of textual models to and from in-memory Ecore models are managed by dedicated serialiser and parser, which are automatically generated from the related Xtext grammar. Defining an Xtext-based textual language for UML (or any UML profile) causes Xtext to change the default resource associated to the ".uml" file extension from `UMLResource` to `XtextResource`. Intuitively, this change affects all editors in the modelling environment working on UML resources, such as those provided by Papyrus. As soon as an Xtext textual editor is created for files with extension ".uml", UML models would be stored as plain text, hence not manageable by Papyrus model editors.

In order to solve this issue, we reversed the dependency relationship imposed on other editors by Xtext. More specifically, we enhanced the Xtext textual editor content management so to enable its interaction with UML resources too. In practice, the Xtext textual editor relies on a dedicated provider class to access the resource underlying a model, i.e. `DocumentProvider`. When a UML model is opened using an Xtext textual editor, the enhanced `DocumentProvider` retrieves the content of the associated UML resource, serialises it, and populates the textual editor with it. Analogously, each time a textual model is saved in the Xtext textual editor, the enhanced `DocumentProvider` propagates the applied changes to the underlying UML resource by first parsing the editor's content and then building or modifying the UML model to be stored.

4.2   Modelling UML Stereotypes Application in Xtext

Xtext does not provide out of the box support for UML profiles. In order to enable Xtext-based textual languages and related editors to feature UML profiles and stereotypes application, we operated on the way Xtext creates and maintains grammars and parsed models.

Given a grammar specification, Xtext creates a corresponding metamodel defined in Ecore, which we call "grammar metamodel", describing the structure of the grammar's abstract syntax tree. This metamodel can be imported in case the grammar relates to an existing grammar metamodel. Parsing of textual models conforming to an Xtext grammar is stored in-memory in terms of the so called grammar model, which conforms to the grammar metamodel.

Let us walk through the steps to provide support for UML profiles and stereotypes application in Xtext-based textual languages. Below, we depict an excerpt of the Xtext grammar providing a textual language, *MarText*, for the UML profile for MARTE [13].

```
1   import "http://www.eclipse.org/uml2/5.0.0/UML" as uml
2   generate marText "http://www.eclipse.org/papyrus/uml/marte/MarText"
3
4   Model returns uml::Model :
5       'model' {uml::Model} name=ID ('{'
6               packagedElement+=Component*
7       '}')? ';'
8
9   Component returns uml::Component :
10      HwProcessor | HwCache |
11      'component' {uml::Component} name=ID ('{'
12              packagedElement+=Component*
13      '}')? ';'
14
15  HwProcessor returns HwProcessor :
16      'processor' {HwProcessor} name=ID ('{'
17              ('cores:' nbCores=INT ';')? &
18              ('caches:' '{'
19                      packagedElement+=HwCache*
20              '};')?
21      '}')? ';'
22
23  HwCache returns HwCache :
24      'cache' {HwCache} name=ID ('{'
25              'level:' level=INT ';'
26      '}')? ';'
```

First, we import the UML metamodel as baseline for the Xtext grammar to access UML metaclasses during the definition of the grammar rules (line 1 of the MarText grammar). For each stereotype in the profile, we define a dedicated grammar rule for enabling the textual editing of stereotype properties (e.g., HwProcessor stereotype rule at line 15 of the MarText grammar).

While enabling the editing of stereotype properties, we still need to offer the possibility to edit the properties of the base UML element to which the stereotype can be applied. To do so, we first looked at how multiple alternatives for a given grammar rule are represented in the grammar metamodel[1]. Given a rule A, with rules B and C as alternatives, Xtext defines three corresponding metaclasses such that A is a superclass of B and C. We leverage this superclass/subclass relationship pattern by defining a stereotype-specific rule as alternative to the rule for the base UML element to which the stereotype can be applied (e.g., Component is superclass of HwProcessor and HwCache, in lines 9–10 of the MarText grammar). The developer can thereby access both stereotype-specific and base UML element properties as with Papyrus UML model editors.

In order to propagate stereotypes application among the two notations, we acted on how DocumentProvider retrieves and stores contents of the UML resource. We defined an endogenous in-place model transformation, which maps the application of stereotypes to UML base elements by following the superclass/subclass relationship pattern mentioned above and based on the MARTE profile metamodel definition. Going from textual to graphical, the transformation navigates the Xtext model and sets stereotypes to base UML elements in the UML resource accordingly. An example depicted in Fig. 2 is represented by processor processorA in the textual model, which leads to the application of the

---

[1] The interested reader can refer to the Xtext specification [24] for further details about the overall inference process.

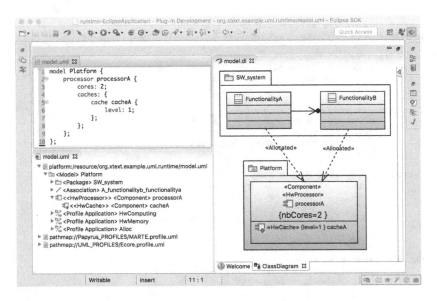

Fig. 2. MarText (top-left), Papyrus tree-based (bottom-left), and Papyrus graphical (right) editors in Eclipse.

stereotypes «Component»«HwProcessor» to processorA in the graphical model. Going from graphical to textual, the transformation navigates the UML resource and reproduces the stereotyped element, without explicitly reporting base UML element info, in the textual format. An example depicted in Fig. 2 is represented by «Component»«HwProcessor» processorA in the graphical model, which leads to the definition of processorA as `processor` in the textual model.

5   Evaluation and Discussion

In Sect. 3, we listed a set of four improvements to current practices brought by our framework. We provided them as follows.

Grammar customisability and cross-profile hybridness. The framework works on a manually edited and customised Xtext grammar for MARTE. Moreover, the solution does not entail complex profile-specific synchronisation transformations between textual and graphical notations. The only transformation needed, for propagating stereotypes application across the notations, is generalisable since based on the superclass/subclass relationship pattern between base UML elements and applicable stereotypes. That is to say, the mechanism itself is cross-profile, while a profile-specific instance of it, as the one we used for MarText, can be generated by a specific profile metamodel definition, in some cases with the help of the hybrid DSML developer.

On-the-fly changes propagation. Model changes done in one view are seamlessly reflected and visible in the other views (graphical, textual and tree-based views in Fig. 2). To appreciate how changes are propagated on-the-fly, the reader can refer to the movie at http://www.mrtc.mdh.se/HybridModelling/demo_ movie.zip.

Cross-notation multi-view modelling. We showed how an Xtext-based textual language (MarText), with related grammar and editor, representing only a sub-set of the HwLogical package of MARTE can seamlessly work on a UML resource containing other UML and MARTE concepts (e.g., UML elements in SW_system package and MARTE «allocated» relations in Fig. 2). For instance, MarText would be suitable for a platform modeller, who might not need or want to view functional details. This is possible thanks to our enhanced Xtext resource management, which, instead of overwriting the in-memory model with plain text, propagates changes directly to the UML resource.

Additionally, we made an experiment to compare modelling times using the different notations in four scenarios: *Create 1*, *Modify 1*, *Create 2*, and *Modify 2*. *Create 1* and *Modify 1* are run on the platform package depicted in Fig. 2. In *Create 1* we model the platform package, and in *Modify 1* we add an additional HwCache cacheB element to the model and assigned to processorA. *Create 2* and *Modify 2* are represented by modelling and modifying (renaming all states from 'state_x' to 'x') a UML state-machine composed of 6 states (1 initial, 1 final, 1 join, 3 normal states) and 5 transitions among the states. The modelling tasks were performed individually by a set of developers, with similar experience in UML modelling with Papyrus and Xtext-based textual languages. All developers got a 2-hours preparation time to study the Xtext languages for MarText and UML state-machines[2]. Table 1 shows the experiment results. We provide the arithmetic mean of the individual sets of values.

Table 1. Mean times for performing the tasks in minutes

Notation	Modelling task				
	Create 1	*Modify 1*	*Create 2*	*Modify 2*	Total
Graphical	1.06	0.27	**0.52**	0.18	2.03
Tree-based	0.46	0.23	2.15	0.22	3.06
Textual	**0.24**	**0.08**	1.42	**0.09**	1.83
Hybrid	(0.24)	(0.08)	(0.52)	(0.09)	**0.93**

Textual editing results faster when creating stereotyped elements and setting their properties (*Create 1*). This is due to the possibility to customise Xtext grammars to only require a minimum amount of information to be entered by the modeller (while the underlying base UML elements are created by our stereotypes application transformation). The same goes for the modification of an existing model by inserting a new model element (*Modify 1*).

---

[2] The Xtext language for state-machines is not in the scope of this paper and was created for experimental purposes only.

The creation of state-machines resulted to be faster with the graphical notation (*Create 2*). This is mainly due to a swifter creation of transitions between states using the graphical view. Transition modelling is also the reason why the tree-based notation resulted way worse than the other two in this scenario (a much higher amount of "clicks" is needed for creating transitions). The textual notation resulted to be faster than the others when renaming model elements, as expected. This is due to textual regex search&replace; while for a bigger model the times for renaming elements would linearly increase if done through tree-based or graphical notations, for the textual notation this is not the case, since regex search&replace would not be affected in the same way by a higher number of hits. Looking at the total modelling times, we can see how combining graphical and textual notations (column 'Total' row 'Hybrid' in Table 1) allows to get the most out of them, resulting faster than all the others.

6   Outlook

In this paper we outlined the initial steps towards a hybrid seamless graphical–textual modelling framework for UML profiles based on Papyrus and Xtext. The uniqueness of our framework is that both graphical and textual modelling act on a single common persistent model resource, thus requiring lower synchronisation effort than current approaches. By seamlessly combining graphical and textual modelling, the framework can mitigate the drawbacks of both as well as emphasise and combine their benefits. We showed several of them, such as flexible separation of concerns, multi-view modelling based on multiple notations, convenient text-based editing operations, and faster modelling activities.

We are currently working on a façade-based approach for improving the encapsulation and reusability of the support for profiles. The idea is to provide means for defining profile-specific custom implementations of complex stereotype elements (as in the case shown in the paper regarding UML-RT), which create and maintain the UML "boilerplate elements" behind them. In the presented solution we only provide limited support for this. Moreover, we are working on a parametric automated generation of Xtext grammars from UML profiles in order to support the creation of hybrid DSMLs.

Acknowledgements. We would like to thank Simon Redding, Francis Bordeleau, and Matthias Tichy for the fruitful discussions and support. This work is partially supported by the Papyrus Industry Consortium(https://wiki.polarsys.org/Papyrus_IC), the EUREKA network Hybrid Modeling project(http://www.eurekanetwork.org/project/id/10700), and the KK-foundation MOMENTUM project(http://www.es.mdh.se/projects/458-MOMENTUM).

References

1. Pérez Andrés, F., De Lara, J., Guerra, E.: Domain specific languages with graphical and textual views. In: Schürr, A., Nagl, M., Zündorf, A. (eds.) AGTIVE 2007. LNCS, vol. 5088, pp. 82–97. Springer, Heidelberg (2008). doi:10.1007/978-3-540-89020-1_7

2. Atkinson, C., Gerbig, R.: Harmonizing textual and graphical visualizations of domain specific models. In: Proceedings of the Second Workshop on Graphical Modeling Language Development, pp. 32–41. ACM (2013)
3. Charfi, A., Schmidt, A., Spriestersbach, A.: A hybrid graphical and textual notation and editor for UML actions. In: Paige, R.F., Hartman, A., Rensink, A. (eds.) ECMDA-FA 2009. LNCS, vol. 5562, pp. 237–252. Springer, Heidelberg (2009). doi:10.1007/978-3-642-02674-4_17
4. SparxSystems Enterprise Architect. http://www.sparxsystems.eu/enterprise architect/. Accessed 17 Feb 2017
5. Eclipse Modeling Framework. https://www.eclipse.org/modeling/emf/. Accessed 17 Feb 2017
6. Engelen, L., van den Brand, M.: Integrating textual and graphical modelling languages. Electron. Notes Theor. Comput. Sci. **253**(7), 105–120 (2010)
7. FXDiagram. http://jankoehnlein.github.io/FXDiagram/. Accessed 17 Feb 2017
8. Hutchinson, J., Whittle, J., Rouncefield, M., Kristoffersen, S.: Empirical assessment of MDE in industry. In: 2011 33rd International Conference on Software Engineering (ICSE), pp. 471–480. IEEE (2011)
9. Jetbrains MPS. https://www.jetbrains.com/mps/. Accessed 17 Feb 2017
10. LightUML. http://lightuml.sourceforge.net/. Accessed 17 Feb 2017
11. Malavolta, I., Lago, P., Muccini, H., Pelliccione, P., Tang, A.: What industry needs from architectural languages: a survey. IEEE Trans. Softw. Eng. **39**(6), 869–891 (2013)
12. Maro, S., Steghöfer, J.P., Anjorin, A., Tichy, M., Gelin, L.: On integrating graphical and textual editors for a UML profile based domain specific language: an industrial experience. In: Proceedings of the 2015 ACM SIGPLAN International Conference on Software Language Engineering, SLE 2015, pp. 1–12. ACM, New York (2015). http://doi.acm.org/10.1145/2814251.2814253
13. UML profile for MARTE. http://www.omg.org/spec/MARTE/. Accessed 17 Feb 2017
14. mbeddr. http://mbeddr.com/. Accessed 17 Feb 2017
15. MetaUML. https://github.com/ogheorghies/MetaUML. Accessed 17 Feb 2017
16. Papyrus. https://eclipse.org/papyrus/. Accessed 17 Feb 2017
17. PlantUML. http://plantuml.com/. Accessed 17 Feb 2017
18. IBM Rational Software Architect. http://www-03.ibm.com/software/products/en/ratsadesigner/. Accessed 17 Feb 2017
19. Scheidgen, M.: Textual modelling embedded into graphical modelling. In: Schieferdecker, I., Hartman, A. (eds.) ECMDA-FA 2008. LNCS, vol. 5095, pp. 153–168. Springer, Heidelberg (2008). doi:10.1007/978-3-540-69100-6_11
20. Selic, B., Gullekson, G., Ward, P.T.: Real-Time Object Oriented Modeling. Wiley & Sons, Chichester (1994)
21. TextUML. http://abstratt.github.io/textuml/. Accessed 17 Feb 2017
22. Umple. http://cruise.eecs.uottawa.ca/umple/. Accessed 17 Feb 2017
23. Wimmer, M., Kramler, G.: Bridging grammarware and modelware. In: Bruel, J.-M. (ed.) MODELS 2005. LNCS, vol. 3844, pp. 159–168. Springer, Heidelberg (2006). doi:10.1007/11663430_17
24. Xtext. http://www.eclipse.org/Xtext/. Accessed 17 Feb 2017

Modeling Architectures
of Cyber-Physical Systems

Evgeny Kusmenko[1], Alexander Roth[1], Bernhard Rumpe[1,2],
and Michael von Wenckstern[1(✉)]

[1] Software Engineering, RWTH Aachen, Aachen, Germany
{kusmenko,roth,rumpe,vonwenckstern}@se-rwth.de
[2] Fraunhofer FIT, Aachen, Germany
http://www.se-rwth.de
http://www.fit.fraunhofer.de

Abstract. Cyber-physical systems (CPS) in automotive or robotics industry comprise many different specific features, e.g., trajectory planning, lane correction, battery management or engine control, requiring a steady interaction with their environment over sensors and actuators. Assembling all these different features is one of the key challenges in the development of such complex systems. Component and connector (C&C) models are widely used for the design and development of CPS to represent features and their logical interaction. An advantage of C&C models is that complex features can be hierarchically decomposed into subfeatures, developed and managed by different domain experts. In this paper, we present the textual modeling family MontiCAR, **Mo**deling and **T**esting of **C**yber-Physical **Ar**chitectures. It is based on the C&C paradigm and increases development efficiency of CPS by incorporating (i) **component and connector arrays**, (ii) **name and index based autoconnections**, (iii) a **strict type system** with **unit** and **accuracy support**, as well as (iv) an advanced **Math language** supporting **BLAS operations** and **matrix classifications**. Arrays and their autoconnection modes allow an efficient way of modeling redundant components such as front and rear park sensors or an LED matrix system containing hundreds of single dimmable lights. The strict type system and matrix classification provide means for integrated static verification of C&C architectures at compile time minimizing bug-fixing related costs. The capabilities and benefits of the proposed language family are demonstrated by a running example of a parking assistance system.

1 Introduction

Development of Cyber-Physical Systems (CPSs) rises domain specific challenges that are rarely present in other software engineering disciplines such as enterprise applications and web development. These challenges mainly originate from steady interactions of such systems with the real world through imperfect sensors and actors while being exposed to complex environments and physical laws.

© Springer International Publishing AG 2017
A. Anjorin and H. Espinoza (Eds.): ECMFA 2017, LNCS 10376, pp. 34–50, 2017.
DOI: 10.1007/978-3-319-61482-3_3

Germany's industrial de facto standard to address these challenges is the exida®/BMW SMArDT[1] approach, which consists of four layers: *object of reflection* (textual requirements and use cases), *logical layer* (functionality modeled by abstract C&C models and underspecified activity diagrams), *concrete technical concept* (deterministic C&C models and C code), and *realization* (e.g., ECUs, CAN-BUS, Flexray, and timing). C&C modeling strengths on the logical layer comprise the ability to describe architectures by components executing computations and information flows modeled via connectors between their interfaces. The paradigm focuses on software features and their logical communication. Due to hierarchal component decomposition, large and complex systems can be developed by different stakeholders in a divide and conquer manner. Prominent examples of C&C languages - used in both academia and industry - are Simulink [28] and LabView [20].

A C&C modeling approach should be easy to use and let the developer focus on the functionality of the system likewise it should reduce the error-proneness in the design phase. To fulfill these demands, we derived a set of requirements for a language to model the logical layer of CPS from a series of automotive, embedded and CPS projects. Today, these requirements are addressed by the intersected features of currently existing C&C modeling approaches rather than by one unified solution. Hence, this paper presents the MontiCAR language family, a textual modeling DSL based on the C&C paradigm. MontiCAR incorporates a strict type system with an integrated unit support allowing developers to work with physical quantities in a type-safe manner and liberating them from unit checks and conversion. MontiCAR types have a value range and a resolution to account for limited operating areas and accuracies of the system components.

Since many CPS tasks can be solved by mathematical models, an advanced math language is an integral part of the MontiCAR language family. Additionally, to guarantee system properties and to increase the performance of the generated code, we introduce a matrix type system that tracks matrix size, matrix elements' type, and algebraic properties. It is used at compile-time to infer variable properties of the computation results for simulation purposes and to choose the best internal data representation (e.g., full or sparse matrix storage).

The main contributions of this paper are: (C1) **a comprehensive comparison of different C&C concepts needed for modeling embedded software**, (C2) **high-Level modeling of dataflows including its semantics**, and (C3) **new concepts for component reuse based on arrays and efficient connector descriptions**.

This paper is structured as follows. First, a running example is described in Sect. 2, which is used to motivate the requirements explained in Sect. 3. Existing C&C modeling approaches are evaluated with respect to these requirements in Sect. 4. Based on these requirements, the following sections present the MontiCAR language family (Sect. 5) with a focus on EmbeddedMontiArc (Sect. 6) and MontiMath (Sect. 7).

---

[1] http://www.exida.pl/EnterTheDOOR/help/soley-generation.htm.

2   Running Example

A running example of a lightweight but incomplete driver assistance software system providing automated emergency braking and visual user feedback is depicted as a simplified C&C architecture in Fig. 1. Since this is a logical model, it does not exhibit any technical details such as assignments of components to concrete ECUs or transmission protocols. The `ParkingAssistant` component interface is defined by its in and out ports: In ports on the left hand side receive signals needed for component computations including the GPS position, speed, steering angle of the vehicle, as well as a port array for complex radar signals containing in-phases and quadrature components for object movement detection. In contrast, out ports on the right hand side represent the calculated results, i.e., user feedback for the dashboard and a `brakeForce` array controlling the car's four brakes.

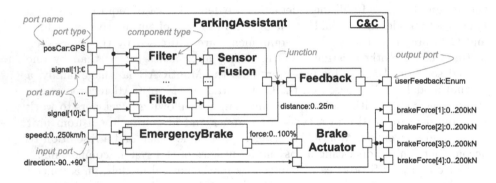

Fig. 1. C&C architecture of an Park Assistant component in automated vehicle.

The behavior of the `ParkingAssistant` (i.e., its concrete computation) is decomposed into several subcomponents each handling one specific task: filtering signals (`Filter`), fusioning sensor data (`SensorFusion`), calculating overall emergency brake effort (`EmergencyBrake`) depending on the distance, assigning concrete brake forces to each wheel (`BrakeActuator`) relative to the car's direction, and creating user feedback. The connectors, depicted by solid arrow lines, represent directed data flows between subcomponents.

A major concern in embedded systems is that most components only guarantee correct behavior for certain working conditions, e.g., radars are only able to detect obstacles within a certain area due to their physical nature. Models need to be enriched with such details to ensure verifiability and to enforce correctness at runtime. For example, `EmergencyBrake` uses radar measurements to execute its task, where it needs an obstacle detection within a predefined range having no blind spots between the sensors' beams. However, it is capable of processing input values outside this area, say all positive distances. The component might not have been designed to cope with unusual inputs such as negative distances.

Hence, it is essential to make supported ranges, operational areas, and accuracies of used types explicit in models so that they can be validated for system integrity and compatibility; e.g., it can be ensured that OEMs only use radars fulfilling the accuracy requirement of `EmergencyBrake` instead of choosing the cheapest one. Furthermore, explicit declarations of the ports' units are essential to make interconnections between ports describing different physical quantities, e.g., lengths and speeds, impossible and to provide automatic conversion between ports working with different unit prefixes such as meters and kilometers, or different systems of units, e.g., metric and imperial. Such static checks are usually not provided by existing C&C languages (cf. Sect. 4).

3 Requirements

From industry cooperations using CPS modeling, we derived the following requirements to solve the challenges introduced in Sect. 1:

- (R1) **Unit support.** In- and output ports should support (R1.1) *metric*, (R1.2) *imperial*, and (R1.3) *customized* units, such as pixel-per-inch.
- (R2) **Unit conversion.** Units should be automatically converted to SI units and prefixes should be resolved (R2.1) for port connections and (R2.2) in mathematical expressions.
- (R3) **Array support.** Redundancy in models should be avoided by supporting (R3.1) *port arrays* and (R3.2) *component arrays*. (R3.3) A convenient mechanism to interconnect and access ports and components should be supported.
- (R4) **Domain and Accuracy.** There is a need for concepts to model the domain, i.e., (R4.1) minimum, (R4.2) maximum, and (R4.3) resolution, of the values exchanged between components, and (R4.4) accuracies for sensor and actuator components. In addition, (R4.5) multiple domains with separate accuracies should be supported, e.g., high accuracy of a distance sensor is essential if the object is near but less important if the object is far away.
- (R5) **Static Analysis.** Theoretical concepts and tools to support *static analysis*, i.e., (R5.1) over- and (R5.2) underflow checks, (R5.3) division by zero, and (R5.4) detection of components in dead paths.
- (R6) **Reuse concepts.** (R6.1) A library concept for components and (R6.2) ports configurable over parameters is needed. Advanced reuse concepts such as (R6.3) *configuration parameters* and (R6.4) *generics* are required to allow modifications of component interfaces and behavior.
- (R7) **Matrix supports.** Discrete control systems are often described by matrix-vector expressions. To reduce error-proneness a type system should support (R7.1) static matrix dimension, (R7.2) units, and (R7.3) detection of domain incompatibilities, e.g., multiplying two 3×3 matrices having the domain $[0,1]^{3 \times 3}$ must result in a $[0,3]^{3 \times 3}$ matrix .
- (R8) **Differential equations.** Physical systems are often modeled by differential equations. A native support can facilitate the system design.

- (R9) **Acausal Modeling support.** Acausal modeling is needed to model systems where the behavior of each system's component depends on the global system architecture rather than having casual data flows with static component behavior. An example is a non-ideal voltage source whose output depends on the load connected.
- (R10) **Operational area.** It should be possible to define the operational area of a system, i.e., the constraints regarding sensor values in which the system is fully operational. For example, if multiple distance sensors are used, the operational area can be defined by at least two sensors detecting the obstacle.

4 Existing C&C Modeling Languages

This section compares the most important C&C modeling languages, listed in Table 1, according to the requirements in Sect. 3.

Most C&C modeling languages do not support units. In SystemC, unit support can be added by defining unit types as C++ preprocessor templates [23, p. 299]. In Simulink, units are used for documentation purposes only, e.g., in the bus editor. Partial unit support is available in xADL extending the meta-schema, Verilog AMS and VHDL AMS. The AMS extensions provides the **nature** concepts for defining a collection of attributes with own unit types [36, 3.6.1]. The unit annotation is passed to the simulator to check compatibility using *Units Value Rule*. Modelica, SysML, LabView, AutoSAR fully support SI units according to ISO 31-1992. Metric, imperial and customized units can be expressed as unit dimensions. Developers might need to provide transformations to SI units for own defined ones. MontiCAR uses the same unit meta model as defined in SysML 1.4 specification Sect. 8.6.4 to support units.

All languages having full SI unit support also allow unit conversions. Simple conversion (R2.1) is possible in AMS languages (Verilog AMS, VHDL AMS), since prefixes such as Pico, Micro are part of the number, e.g., 3 pA still has Ampere as unit. Even though AMS languages support conversion of flow to potential and vice versa (using `disciplines`), they do not support more complex conversions such as kilometer per hour to miles per hour.

Support for port and/or component arrays (R3) is not present in Simulink, SysML, Marte, AutoFocus3, xADL, AutoSAR, LabView, MontiArc, Rapide, SADL, Scade, and TECS. Partial support for arrays is given in Modelica by using a class as a component. Classes can be instantiated as an array. This concept has been reused in MontiCar to support component arrays. Ptolemy supports arrays by using the Java array syntax and semantics, allowing only to define the number of array dimensions but not their concrete array size. Verilog supports one and two dimensional arrays using a similar syntax as Ptolemy. VHDL supports ranged and unconstrained arrays of defined types. SystemC allows to declare array sizes of ports and signals using a C-like syntax. UniCon supports fixed length arrays of simple types. WRIGHT supports multiple instances of pipes, which can be seen as arrays of the same connector.

Table 1. Comparison of C&C tools and standards (*), √: yes, P: partially, -: no

Architectural description language	Unit support (R1)	Unit conversion (R2)	Component/Port arrays (R3)	Domain (R4.1), (4.2)	Resolution (R4.3)	Static analysis (R5)	Configuration parameters (R6.3)	Generics (R6.4)	Matrix Support (R7)	Differential Equation (R8)	Acausal Modeling support (R9)	Operation Area (R10)
Simulink [28]	-	-	-	√	-	p	√	-	√	-	-	-
Modelica*[4,16]	√	√	P	√	√	P	√	√	√	√	√	-
SysML*[31]	√	√	-	P	P	-	√	√	-	-	-	-
Marte*[30]	√	√	-	P	P	-	√	√	√	√	-	-
AutoFocus3 [2]	-	-	-	√	-	√	√	-	-	-	-	-
xADL [11]	P	-	-	P	-	P	P	-	-	-	-	-
AutoSAR*[5,6]	√	√	-	√	√	P	√	-	-	-	-	-
LabView [20]	√	√	-	√	√	√	√	-	√	P	-	-
MontiArc [17]	-	-	-	√	√	P	√	√	-			
MontiCar (this paper)	√	√	√	√	√	√	√	√	√	-	-	√
Ptolemy [14]	-	-	√	-	-	√	√	√	-	-	-	-
Verilog (AMS) [36]	√	P	√	√	√	√	√	√	-	P	√	-
VHDL (AMS) [3,15]	√	P	√	√	√	√	√	√	-	P	-	-
Rapide [25]	-	-	-	-	-	√	√	-	-	-	-	-
SADL [18]	-	-	-	-	-	√	√	-	-	-	-	-
Scade [13]	-	-	-	-	-	√	-	-	-	-	-	-
SystemC [34]	-	-	√	-	-	√	√	√	-	-	-	-
TECS [7]	-	-	-	-	-	√	√	-	-	-	-	-
UniCon [35]	√	-	√	√	√	√	√	-	-	-	-	-
WRIGHT [1]	-	-	√	-	-	√	√	-	-	-	-	-

Multiple languages provide support to specify the domain together with its resolution of a variable as required by (R4). Simulink allows to specify the minimum and maximum values for a signal and a resolution for fixed data types using the data type parameters slope and bias. LabView supports creation of custom scales, which can be linear, polynomial or table based. This facilitates flexibility for the creation of custom resolutions, ranges. However, for types with multiple domains, only table scale is applicable. Modelica allows to specify attributes with a variable declaration. Both, reals and integers support a minimum and a maximum value. A `nominal` attribute can be used for automatic model scaling. AUTOSAR requires all of its integer types to have a constraint subnode to specify a scaling with minimum and maximum values.

SysML allows to create value types that are classifiers having the stereotype «data type» and the corresponding attributes, e.g., `min` and `max`. Using this data type allows setting minimum and maximum values for variables using it, e.g., in an object diagram. Alternatively, OCL constraints can be used to specify ranges and resolutions. Verilog-AMS natures concept supports type parameters such as `abstol`, and `max` absolute tolerance to define tolerances and allowed value ranges primarily for the VLSI domain. VHDL-AMS provides a similar approach but uses tolerances to specify the preciseness of approximations provided by numerical algorithms.

SysML, Marte have no concepts to detect over-, underflows, division by zero or unused components (R5). The Simulink Design Verifier detects division by zero. Over- and underflow checks are done at runtime. However, no compile-time verification is possible. Autofocus 3 uses model checkers (NuSMV/nuXmv [9]) to check variable ranges and find unreachable states. Since xADL is a modeling language without any semantic definition (it also has no denotational semantics introduced by a code generator), it only checks that connectors of models are correct. LabView programs are verified by translating their models to ACL2 solver expressions and formulate theorems that should be proved [21]. Finding duplicates (even semantical ones) in MontiArc is done using MontiMatcher [33]. MontiCAR uses the MontiMatcher framework and extends it with support for checking over-, underflow and divisions by zero by using the MontiMatcher's intermediate controlflow graph for backward compatibility checks. Structural crosscutting specification, C&C views, verification [26] as well as static consistency checks for extra-functional properties [27] are also available in MontiCAR. Ptomely is a Java-based event extension for modeling architectures. Therefore, static analysis tools (e.g., Cibai [24]) for Java programs can be used. Verilog models are checked by translating them to BLIF-MV [10] to perform symbolic verification[2]. In SystemC, type checking, control flow graph analysis, and verifying C pointers or static analysis in general can be done with SCOOT [8].

Enabling component reuse, e.g. of general library ones, can be decomposed into supporting configuration parameters and generics (R6). Simulink supports configuration parameters (`set_param` command), which can be defined arbitrarily. However, Simulink does not support general generics for modifying component interfaces. It only can be done partially, e.g. `Logical Operator` block allows to define the number of input ports. Modelica supports generic components and configuration parameters provided by the Modelica generic block (MBLOCK). SysML does not provide explicit language constructs to model variants but provides a profile mechanism to extend SysML with a concept for variant modeling, i.e., stereotypes. Stereotypes are also used in MARTE to define parameters and

---

[2] http://vlsi.colorado.edu/~vis/whatis.html.

generics. AutoFocus 3 supports parameters that can be used for configuration purposes but lacks support for generic components. By default xADL does not support configuration parameters and generics. However, because it uses XML as the base structure, the tooling supports partial configuration parameters by direct manipulation of the XML schema. In AutoSAR, parameters can also be used to configure components. However, it does not support generics for components. Similar holds for LabView. MontiArc supports concepts for configuration parameters and generic components, which are used in the MontiCAR language family. Being an extension of Java, Ptolemy supports configuration parameters and generics. Verilog, VHDL, Rapide, TECS, UniCon, WRIGHT, and SADL only support configuration parameters but no generics. Scade supports configuration parameters nor generics. Since SystemC is an extension of C++, it supports configuration parameters and adds support for generics.

Several languages implement native matrix support including MAT-LAB/Simulink as one of the most prominent examples, thereby, partially fulfilling (R7). However, MATLAB/Simulink neither provides a strict type system allowing for static checks required by (R7.1), and (R7.3), nor does it allow to specify units for the entries of a matrix. A far more elaborated matrix type system is provided by Modellica [16], which not only allows to define the element types and its dimensions but also units of the matrix elements allowing far more rigorous static checks. Other languages providing matrix support comprise MARTE [30] and LabView. The latter does not allow for the restriction of a matrix to a specified size and, hence, does not provide static checks. Instead, similarly to MATLAB/Simulink, matrices can grow dynamically and checks are only performed at runtime. In contrast, MontiCAR provides full matrix support with a strict type system and unit support with compile-time checks used in system verification. Furthermore, to our knowledge, MontiCAR is the only language using a matrix taxonomy to derive matrix properties for static checks.

Native support for differential equations (R8) is provided by Modelica and MARTE. With support for ordinary differential equations only, LabView partially fulfills this requirement. The same holds for Verilog and VHDL [29]. All other languages do not fulfill requirement (R8).

In Modelica, acausal modeling (R9) is done using flow ports and declarative equations[3]. In Verilog-AMS, acausal modeling (e.g.y Kirchhoff's Flow Law and Potential Law [36, Figs. 1–3]) is done using signal-flow systems. Since MontiCAR is designed for modeling on the logical layer of the SMArDT methodology, there is no need for modeling flow properties, e.g., current or voltage flows. Therefore, Modelica's acausal modeling concept has not been integrated to keep the language syntax slim.

From the overview in Table 1, it can be derived that none of the analyzed modeling languages support definition of an (R10) operational area, e.g., to guarantee a correct behavior for a limited set of environmental conditions. In MontiCAR, we integrated OCL/P to allow for the definition of such constraints.

---

[3] https://www.openmodelica.org/images/docs/Modelica-and-OpenModelica-overview-Peter-Fritzson-120328.pdf.

5   MontiCAR Modeling Family

As was shown in Sect. 4, existing modeling languages fail to provide all necessary means for type-safe and verifiable modeling of cyber-physical systems. Therefore, we present MontiCAR, a modeling language family developed against real industrial requirements gathered in Sect. 3. The structure of the complete MontiCAR modeling family is shown in Fig. 2. In this section we give a short description for each family member.

The base language used by all the other language members is NumberUnit. It contains rules to parse complex numbers, e.g., 2 - 4i or rational numbers with and without units, e.g., -3/7 m/s^2, 0.35, 1N. OCL/P [32] is a Java-based OCL derivative to formulate constraints such as brakePedalPressed implies vehicleAcceleration < 0 m/s^2, i.e., the acceleration should be negative if the brake pedal is pressed. The syntax of MontiMath is very similar to the one of MATLAB except that it forces all its variables to be typed. This language will be introduced in more depth in Sect. 7. The Type language allows the definition of enumerations and C-like structures. An example is provided in Fig. 3. Lines 1–2 define a struct type for GPS coordinates aggregating the scalars latitude and longitude. Pay attention to the type of the two primitive

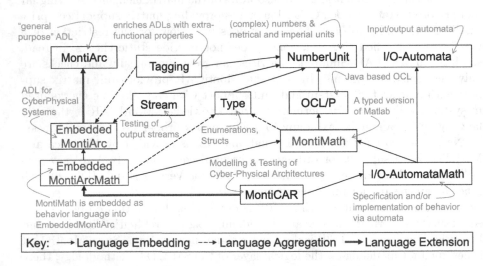

Fig. 2. MontiCAR modeling family.

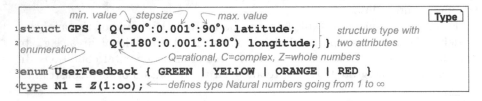

Fig. 3. Define new port types

struct members. We are not interested in the concrete realization of the scalars such as int or float on our level of abstraction. Instead, we specify, that each of the two members is a rational number, denoted by the letter Q according to the set of rational numbers Q. The latitude coordinate can only take values from $-90°$ to $+90°$ whereas a valid longitude must lie between $0°$ and $180°$. We incorporate this range specification in brackets thereby declaring a new type. Moreover, GPS sensors only have a limited resolution. This is declared through the resolution parameter, here taking a value of $0.001°$. An accuracy can also be added to ranges; e.g. Q(-90°:0.001°:90°) $\pm$ 0.02° says that values between $-90°$ to $+90°$ have an accuracy, normally distributed noise, of $0.02°$. Making such constraints explicit will later help us identifying incompatible components, e.g., sensors not providing the required signal resolution. The concrete type implementation is delegetated to the compiler allowing the system designer to focus on the functionality. In line 3 we use enumerations to declare a type in MontiCAR. It can take one of the four possible color values the feedback LED of a driver assistance system can emit. The core language of our family is EmbeddedMontiArc which extends the general purpose Architecture Description Language (ADL) MontiArc [17] used for modeling web and cloud services in a C&C like manner. EmbeddedMontiArc, explained in detail in the next section, supports in contrast to its base language MontiArc additionally port and component arrays, and it overwrites the type system of MontiArc in order to provide unit support and integrate the Type language. The Tagging language [27] enables the developer to enrich EmbeddedMontiArc models with extra-functional properties allowing for semantic consistency checks on C&C architectures. The EmbeddedMontiArcMath language enriches EmbeddedMontiArc models with the possibility to specify the behavior for atomic components by embedding MontiMath syntax which will be demonstrated in Sect. 7. Stream models, based on the stream theory of Broy and Rumpe [22], allow the definition of ordered sequences of input values for C&C input ports and the expected output sequences for all output ports to faciliate unit and integration testing of C&C models. Note that due to language aggregation Stream models have knowledge about the EmbeddedMontiArcMath models, but not vice versa. This allows deploying productive C&C models later-on without their respective test models. I/O-Automata is a language for describing behavior by finite automata. It provides internal variables, states and transitions pointing from a source to a target state. On activation, the automaton goes into the first start states for which the guard conditions are satisfied by the variables provided at the input ports. Moreover, transitions produce output values according to their defined output-port-assignment expressions and activate the automaton's target state. I/O-AutomataMath embeds the MontiMath language for describing guard conditions and output assignments using the Math syntax into the I/O-Automata language. MontiCAR extends EmbeddedMontiArcMath language allowing both Math and I/O-Automata behavior descriptions.

Since presenting the entire MontiCAR modeling family is out of the scope of this paper, the next sections will focus on the two most interesting family members: `EmbeddedMontiArc` for describing CPS features and their interaction as C&C models and the `MontiMath` language for defining the features' behavior.

6   EmbeddedMontiArc

Based on our example introduced in Sect. 2 this section shows how the architecture of embedded and cyber-physical systems can be modeled with Embedded-MontiArc language belonging to the MontiCAR language family.

The EmbeddedMontiArc model for the running example is given in Fig. 4. Line 1 defines the main component, having the `ParkAssistant` type and the derived instance name `parkAssistant`. Similar to Java's convention, all component types start with a capital letter and all component instances with a small one. Lines 2–5 define `ParkAssistant`'s in- and ll.6–7 out ports. An advantage of EmbeddedMontiArc's port arrays, `Z brakekForce[4]`, over MontiArc's solution with one port having a data type array, `Integer[] brakeForce`, is that each port in the port array can be wired-up individually. A port definition has the following structure: *direction*, can be `in` or `out` indicating incoming or outgoing data flow, *port type*, see paragraph **Type** in Sect. 5, *port name*, a small letter Java variable name, and an 1-dimensional *array size* (squared brackets). If the direction is missing such as in l.3, then the one of the previous port definition, here in l.2, is taken. The default value for missing array size is one.

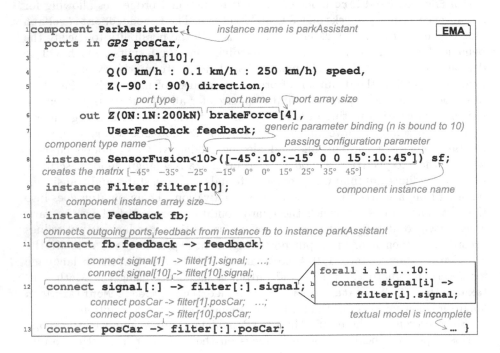

Fig. 4. Textual EmbeddedMontiArc model of `ParkAssistant`

All `ParkAssistant`'s subcomponent instances are listed in ll.8–10, each starts with the `instance` keyword, followed by a component type, instance name, an optional one dimensional array specifier. Note that in MontiArc which is the base language of EmbeddedMontiArc, the keyword `instance` is also `component`. But this ambiguity, `component` for component definitions and component instances, lead to confusion. `ParkAssistant` is decomposed into one `sf` of type `SensorFusion` (l.8), ten `filter` (l.9), one `fb` of type `Feedback` (l.10) instances. The singletons of type `EmbergencyBrake` and `BrakeActuator` in Fig. 1 are skipped in Fig. 4 for presentational reasons. `SensorFusion` component type has a generic parameter binding (in guillemot brackets) specifying the number of input signals needed for fusion, and a configuration parameter passing (in round brackets), specifying sensors' tilt angles. This configuration parameter is a 1×10 vector defined in a MATLAB-like syntax. The difference between a generic and a configuration parameter is that the primer changes the component's interface (has any impact on ports), whereas the latter has no influence on the interface and is only needed for the component behavior.

Lines 11–13 demonstrate the concrete syntax for interconnecting ports of subcomponent instances. While l.11 connects two ports using standard MontiArc syntax, in l.12 we have an EmbeddedMontiArc style interconnection of a port array with an array of components. Thereby, the colon notation, a short-form of `1:end`, selects all entities of the array and connects each entity to a corresponding entity on the right hand side separated by the `->` operator. Instead of the colon syntax, the `forall` syntax shown inside the box in ll.a–c can be used.

7 MontiMath Language

MontiMath is a mathematical matrix based behavior modeling language for MontiCAR. It is mainly inspired by MathJS[4], which supports matrices, units and rational numbers allowing one to solve linear equations exactly. MontiMath is based on MATLAB syntax. Since CPS in automotive and robotic domain mostly describe safety critical systems, MontiMath has - in contrast to existing matrix based languages, such as Modelica, Maple, MATLAB and MathJS - a very strict type system to minimize runtime errors. This type system includes **unit**, **dimension**, and **element ranges** information. Furthermore, it keeps track of **algebraic matrix properties** based on [19].

For variable assignments and matrix expressions MontiMath detects the following errors at compile-time: **Matrix Property Errors** occuring when a matrix violates the defined properties, e.g., diagonal, positive (semi)definite, lower/upper triangular, invertible, symmetric, or hermitian. For example, `diag inv Q^{3,3} A = diag([0km 1 Km 2cm])` declares a rational 3×3 *diag*onal and *inv*ertible matrix variable A, being initialized with a diagonal matrix having values 0 km, 1 km and 2 cm on the main diagonal. This assignment results in a compiler error due to having a value of 0km on the main diagonal and thereby violating the *inv*ertible property. **Dimension Errors**

---

[4] http://mathjs.org.

occur during matrix assignments, e.g., Q^{1,3} = [1 2] and matrix infix operations, e.g., (element-wise) power, (element-wise) multiplication, summation and
equation solving. **Unit Errors** occur when units of matrices are not compatible, e.g., in summation [10cm 7cm] + [7kg 9kg] and assignments. **Out-of-
Bounds Erros** occuring by direct indexing of a non-existing matrix position.
Range Errors occuring when an element in the matrix is not inside the allowed
range or if a rational number is given but only integers are allowed.

Lines 6–11 in Fig. 5 show how MontiMath is applied in the EmbeddedMontiArc SensorFusion component to specify its behavior. Lines 7* and 8* are
not part of the model but are displayed to show how the in and out ports of
EmbeddedMontiArc are adapted to MontiMath matrix variable declarations.
Line 9 defines a rational $n \times n$ matrix allowing values between 0 and 1. The *
operator in cos*(tilt) denotes that the cosine function is applied element-wise
on tilt, returning the vector [cos(tilt(1,1)), ..., cos(tilt(1,n))]. The
diag function creates a diagonal matrix with the elements of tilt on its main
diagonal; the result is assigned to facMatrix. Line 11 multiplies the distance
vector with this facMatrix resulting in a $1 \times n$ column vector with its minimum value assigned to the output port mergedDistance. Assume, in a previous software evolution step l.10 was sin*(diag(tilt)) and now needs to be
replaced by cos* due to a change in the sensors' relative coordinate system.
Since sin(0°) = 0 the element-wise sine of a diagonal matrix is again a diagonal matrix; replacing the sine with a cosine however results in a MontiMath
compiler error due to cos(0°) ≠ 0 making the result non-diagonal. Without the

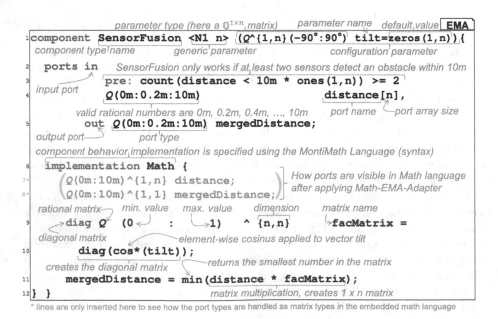

Fig. 5. SensorFusion component with its behavior defined in MontiMath

strong type system and meaningful error messages such a bug may be detected later during tests or at runtime thereby increasing development costs.

Line 2 in Fig. 6 shows the OCL/P pre-/post condition used by Monti-Math's type checker to find out that `cos(0°)=1` and therefore not zero, and ll.5–7 defines the `diag` matrix property in OCL/P requiring all off-diagonal values to be zero which is violated by the expression `cos*(diag(tilt))`. Using the `implies` keyword in l.5 we require that the `diag` property guarantees the `lowerTriangular` and `upperTriangular` properties to be true. This correctness of this specification is then proven by the Z3 [12] solver. Furthermore, already existing matrix properties can be reused via (multiple) inheritance, i.e., the `diag` property could have been defined by `matrix-property<N1 n> diag Q^{n,n} y extends upperTriangular & lowerTriangular`, thereby saving l.7. Lines 8–13 show two other important concepts of MontiMath: Operator overloading based on matrix properties, and function overloading based on matrix dimensions. The first one is used to define more efficient algorithms for special matrix types, as it is done for adding two diagonal matrices in ll.9–11 where only the diagonal elements of the two matrices are added reducing the computational complexity for matrix addition from $\mathcal{O}(n^2)$ to $\mathcal{O}(n)$ for diagonal matrices. Calling the function defined in l.12, `diag(a)` in l.10 returns a vector containing the matrices' diagonal elements; while the outer `diag` having a row vector as its argument creates a diagonal matrix by invoking the function defined in l.13. The decision which function to invoke is based on

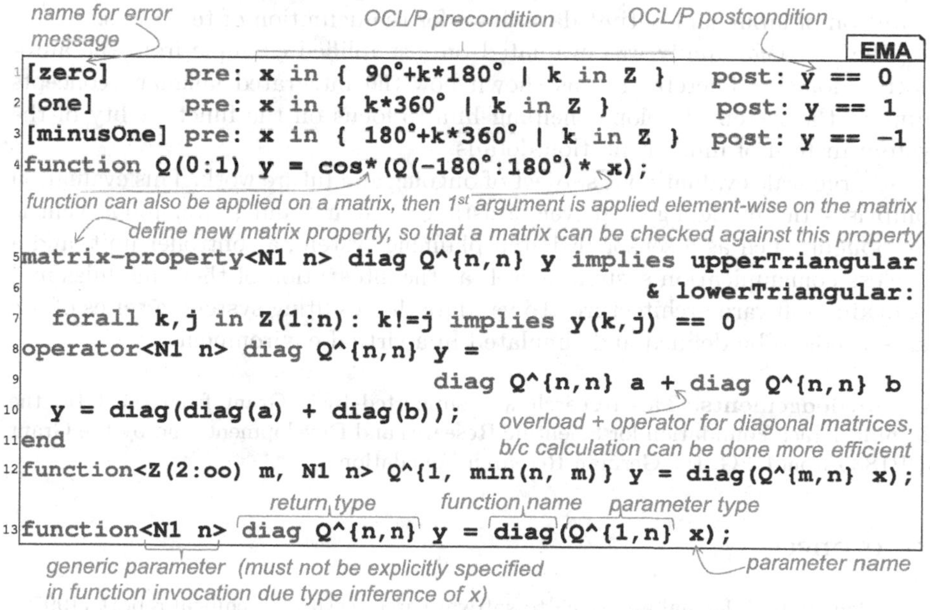

Fig. 6. Function definition in math language (`";"` after function definition is here used to omit the body implementation of the function.)

the matrix dimensions. For this reason the type of the first generic parameter in l.12 cannot be N1, and therefore it is Z(2:oo). Otherwise the compiler cannot infer which overloading of the diag function (ll.12–13) should be invoked in case of a row vector.

The concept of overloading functions based on matrix dimensions is taken from MATLAB. In contrast, our approach makes the overloading with two functions having different generic types explicit. Moreover, in l.13 in Fig. 6, the return type has the return type name y, since MontiMath supports, similar to MAT-LAB, multiple return values and therefore each return value has always a name to differ between multiple return values.

8   Conclusion

We presented the modeling language family MontiCAR for the design of cyber physical system encorporating requirements we derived in multiple case studies. The core of the language family is the architecture description language EmbeddedMontiArc. This core language was extended by a stricter typing than is usually known from modern languages. It includes a unit system, value domain and resolution support. Furthermore, the math language MontiMath is an integral part of the language family which allows for efficient component behavior descriptions. The simple Type language facilitates the aggregation and reuse of data packages without overwhelming the user with unnecessary features such as pointers and inheritance. Finally, a stream language allows a straightforward definition of input and output data flows for the definition of test cases.

The language family was evaluated on a simplified example from the automotive domain. Thereby, it was shown how the integrated language concepts support the system developer helping him to focus on the functionality of the system instead of implementation details.

A large scale evaluation is subject of ongoing and future work. This evaluation comprises the modeling of driver assistance systems and autonomous vehicle components such as a sensor fusion, a planning system, a controller unit, and a wireless communication system as well as the integration of these modules into a working software architecture. To validate the resulting system, a series of use cases needs to be defined and simulated in a virtual environment.

Acknowledgements. This research was supported by a Grant from the GIF, the German-Israeli Foundation for Scientific Research and Development, and by the Grant SPP1835 from DFG, the German Research Foundation.

References

1. Allen, R.J.: A formal approach to software architecture. Technical report (1997)
2. Aravantinos, V., Voss, S., Teufl, S., Hölzl, F., Schätz, B.: AutoFOCUS 3: tooling concepts for seamless, model-based development of embedded systems. In: ACES-MB (2015)

3. Ashenden, P.J.: The Designer's Guide to VHDL, vol. 3. Morgan Kaufmann, San Francisco (2010)
4. Association, M., et al.: Modelica Language Specification. Linköping, Sweden (2005)
5. AUTOSAR: layered software architecture. Technical report 053 (4.3.0), AUTOSAR (2016)
6. AUTOSAR: modeling guidelines of basic software EA UML model. Technical report 117 (4.3.0), AUTOSAR (2016)
7. Azumi, T., Yamamoto, M., Kominami, Y., Takagi, N., Oyama, H., Takada, H.: A new specification of software components for embedded systems. In: ISORC (2007)
8. Blanc, N., Kroening, D., Sharygina, N.: SCOOT: a tool for the analysis of SystemC models. In: Ramakrishnan, C.R., Rehof, J. (eds.) TACAS 2008. LNCS, vol. 4963, pp. 467–470. Springer, Heidelberg (2008). doi:10.1007/978-3-540-78800-3_36
9. Cavada, R., Cimatti, A., Dorigatti, M., Griggio, A., Mariotti, A., Micheli, A., Mover, S., Roveri, M., Tonetta, S.: The NUXMV symbolic model checker. In: Biere, A., Bloem, R. (eds.) CAV 2014. LNCS, vol. 8559, pp. 334–342. Springer, Cham (2014). doi:10.1007/978-3-319-08867-9_22
10. Cheng, S.T., York, G., Brayton, R.K.: Vl2mv: A compiler from verilog to blif-mv. HSIS Distribution (1993)
11. Dashofy, E.M., van der Hoek, A., Taylor, R.N.: A highly-extensible, xml-based architecture description language. In: Conference on Software Architecture (2001)
12. Moura, L., Bjørner, N.: Z3: an efficient SMT solver. In: Ramakrishnan, C.R., Rehof, J. (eds.) TACAS 2008. LNCS, vol. 4963, pp. 337–340. Springer, Heidelberg (2008). doi:10.1007/978-3-540-78800-3_24
13. Dormoy, F.X.: Scade 6: a model based solution for safety critical software development. In: ERTS 2008, pp. 1–9 (2008)
14. Eker, J., Janneck, J.W., Lee, E.A., Liu, J., Liu, X., Ludvig, J., Neuendorffer, S., Sachs, S., Xiong, Y.: Taming heterogeneity-the Ptolemy approach. Proc. IEEE 91(1), 127–144 (2003)
15. Texas Instruments of Electrical and Electronic Engineers: Standard VHDL language reference manual. IEEE Std (1988)
16. Elmqvist, H., Mattsson, S.E., Otter, M.: Modelica-a language for physical system modeling, visualization and interaction. In: Proceedings of the 1999 IEEE International Symposium on Computer Aided Control System Design, pp. 630–639. IEEE (1999)
17. Haber, A.: MontiArc - Architectural Modeling and Simulation of Interactive Distributed Systems. Shaker Verlag (2016)
18. Herbert, J., Dutertre, B., Riemenschneider, R., Stavridou, V.: A formalization of software architecture. In: FM (1999)
19. Horn, R.A., Johnson, C.R.: Matrix Analysis. Cambridge University Press, Cambridge (2012)
20. Instruments, N.: BridgeView and LabView: G Programming Reference Manual. Technical report 321296B–01, National Instruments (1998)
21. Kaufmann, M., Kornerup, J., Reitblatt, M.: Formal verification of LabVIEW programs using the ACL2 theorem prover. In: ACL2 (2009)
22. Klein, C., Rumpe, B., Broy, M.: A stream-based mathematical model for distributed information processing systems-the SysLab system model. In: Formal Methods for Open Object-based Distributed Systems (1997)
23. Lemke, J.: C++-Metaprogrammierung: Eine Einführung in die Präprozessor-und Template-Metaprogrammierung (2016)

24. Logozzo, F.: Cibai: an abstract interpretation-based static analyzer for modular analysis and verification of Java classes. In: Cook, B., Podelski, A. (eds.) VMCAI 2007. LNCS, vol. 4349, pp. 283–298. Springer, Heidelberg (2007). doi:10.1007/978-3-540-69738-1_21
25. Luckham, D.C., Vera, J.: An event-based architecture definition language. IEEE Trans. Softw. Eng. **21**(9), 717–734 (1995)
26. Maoz, S., Ringert, J.O., Rumpe, B.: Verifying component and connector models against crosscutting structural views. In: ICSE (2014)
27. Maoz, S., Ringert, J.O., Rumpe, B., von Wenckstern, M.: Consistent extra-functional properties tagging for component and connector models. In: ModComp (2016)
28. Mathworks: simulink user's guide. Technical report R2016b, MATLAB & SIMULINK (2016)
29. Nikitin, P.V., Shi, C., Wan, B.: Modeling partial differential equations in VHDL-AMS (mixed signal systems applications). In: SOC (2003)
30. OMG: UML profile for MARTE: modeling and analysis of real-time embedded systems. Technical report Version 1.1, OMG Group (2011)
31. OMG: OMG systems modeling language (OMG SysML). Technical report. Version 1.4, OMG Group (2015)
32. Rumpe, B.: Modeling with UML: Language, Concepts, Methods. Springer, Heidelberg (2016)
33. Rumpe, B., Schulze, C., von Wenckstern, M., Ringert, J.O., Manhart, P.: Behavioral compatibility of simulink models for product line maintenance and evolution. In: SPLC (2015)
34. IEEE Computer Society: IEEE standard for standard systemc® language reference manual (2012)
35. Chromatography software: UNICORN 5.0 - User Reference Manual. Technical report 03–0014-90 (2004)
36. Accellera Systems Initiative: Verilog-AMS Language Reference Manual. Technical report 2.4.0, Accellera Systems Initiative standards (2014)

Model Evolution and Maintenance

Systematic Language Extension Mechanisms for the MontiArc Architecture Description Language

Arvid Butting[1], Arne Haber[1,2], Lars Hermerschmidt[1,3], Oliver Kautz[1], Bernhard Rumpe[1], and Andreas Wortmann[1(✉)]

[1] Software Engineering, RWTH Aachen University, Aachen, Germany
{Butting,Haber,Hermerschmidt,Kautz,Rumpe,Wortmann}@se-rwth.de
[2] Schier Consult GmbH, Braunschweig, Germany
[3] AXA Konzern AG, Cologne, Germany
http://www.schier-consult.de,
http://www.axa.de

Abstract. Architecture description languages (ADLs) combine the benefits of component-based software engineering and model-driven development. Extending an ADL to domain-specific requirements is a major challenge for its successful application. Most ADLs focus on fixed features and do not consider domain-specific language extension. ADLs focusing on extensibility focus on syntactic augmentation only and neither consider semantics, nor the ADL's tooling. We present a systematic extension method for the MontiArc component and connector ADL that enables extending its syntax and infrastructure. The MontiArc ADL is built on top of the MontiCore workbench for compositional modeling languages and leverages its powerful language integration facilities. Based on these, we conceived systematic extension activities and present their application to customizing MontiArc for three different domains. This application of software language engineering to ADLs reduces effort for their extension and the presented method guides developers in applying it to their domain. This ultimately fosters the application of ADLs to real-world domain-specific challenges.

Keywords: Model-driven engineering · Architectural programming · Action languages · Software language composition

1 Introduction

Component-based software engineering (CBSE) is a software engineering methodology that advocates the vision of composing complex software systems from off-the-shelf components. Through this, the individual components are supposed to be reused more often, better evaluated, and hence more mature. Nonetheless, most approaches to CBSE rely on exchanging binary or source code components, which are noisy [33] solution domain [8] artifacts that are specific

© Springer International Publishing AG 2017
A. Anjorin and H. Espinoza (Eds.): ECMFA 2017, LNCS 10376, pp. 53–70, 2017.
DOI: 10.1007/978-3-319-61482-3_4

to the general programming language (GPL) they are formulated in. This complicates their reuse and comprehension.

Model-driven development (MDD) lifts models to primary development artifacts that are more abstract, closer to the solution domain, less noisy, better comprehensible, and automatically translatable into solution domain artifacts. Architecture description languages (ADL) [23] are modeling languages for the development of complex software systems. They combine the benefits of CBSE and MDD and have been developed for and applied to multiple challenging domains including automotive [3], avionics [6], and robotics [30]. For each of these domains, completely new ADLs with domain-specific syntax and semantics have been developed from scratch. This is expensive, which is why extending ADLs to specific requirements is one of the major challenges to their successful application [21]. However, most ADLs focus on fixed domain-specific challenges and do not support domain-specific extension. Where this is possible (such as with AADL [6] or xADL [25]), the extensions are mainly of syntactic nature. Leveraging software language engineering enables implementing better extensible ADLs. Based on state-of-the-art software language composition mechanisms [4], we have conceived the MontiArc ADL [17] for extensive systematic extension on top of the MontiCore [20] language workbench. The language engineering mechanisms of MontiCore enable to adjust MontiArc's syntax and infrastructure to domain-specific requirements. Core modeling elements of the MontiArc ADL have been introduced in [17] and an earlier variant extension method has been presented in [12]. Furthermore, the behavior language embedding mechanisms of the MontiArc derivative MontiArcAutomaton have been presented in [27]. This paper specifically contributes

- an augmented method for the structured extension of MontiArc with new syntax and semantics beyond behavior language embedding that considers reuse of well-formedness rules and no longer distinguishes between code generation and simulation; and
- three case studies describing applying this method to extending MontiArc for security architectures, robotics, and cloud-based systems.

In the following, Sect. 2 motivates the benefits of ADL extension by example, before Sect. 3 explains necessary preliminaries. Afterwards, Sect. 4 presents the MontiArc extension method and Sect. 5 describes its application to three domains. Subsequently, Sect. 6 highlights related work and discusses the approach, and Sect. 7 concludes.

2 Example

Consider a company developing distributed cloud systems for massive open online courses. For better abstraction and reuse, the company decides to model the structure of the systems using a component and connector (C&C) ADL. However, the company requires that the architecture's components can (a) be composed from other components to define logical hierarchies; (b) explicate service level requirements; and (c) replicate themselves to scale if necessary. Instead of creating a new ADL from scratch, the company decides to extend an ADL already supporting composed components. They analyze the necessary changes in the ADL's syntax and semantics and determine two extension requirements. **R1**: The syntax supports specifying and storing service level information for each component. Its semantics ensures that the service level for each composed component is at least as good as the sum of service levels of its subcomponents. **R2**: The syntax supports specifying and storing replication conditions per component. Its semantics includes this information to control component replication at runtime.

The base ADL that the company's software engineers will extend is domain-agnostic and features only the core concepts depicted in black in Fig. 1: In this metamodel, a component type has a name and an arbitrary number of incoming and outgoing ports, which define the interface of a component. Furthermore, it can declare subcomponents that have a name and a component type. Each port has a data type and a name. Component types define an arbitrary number of connectors to connect their subcomponents.

The base ADL defines its static semantics (well-formedness) by a set of individual rules and translational dynamic semantics (behavior) via code generation. The static semantics include that (a) at least one port of each component type's subcomponents is connected by at least one connector; (b) connected subcomponents (*i.e.*, sources and targets of connectors) are actually declared in the same component type; and (c) that the types of connected ports are compatible. The dynamic semantics of an ADL govern how messages are passed between components. This ADL employs event-driven message passing in which components start to compute whenever at least one message has arrived. The dynamic semantics are realized by translating components to Java classes implementing this behavior.

The extensions to the metamodel are annotated and highlighted in Fig. 1: Relative to this metamodel, **R1** is translated into an extension of the syntax and semantics for component types. The syntactic extension is realized as the new property `serviceLevel` of `ComponentType` and the semantic extension as a

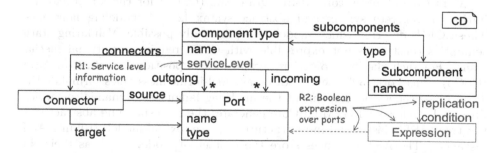

Fig. 1. Metamodel of a C&C ADL with extensions for R1 and R2.

new well-formedness rule. For **R2**, the syntax of subcomponents is extended by a replication expression. The company's engineers reuse a variant of OCL [11] as `Expression` language to enable reasoning over object structures. In conditions, they interpret names as references to ports (*e.g.,* a valid replication condition for a port `users` receiving lists of user data could be "`users.size() > 1`").

To ensure well-formedness of extended models, the engineers add new rules to extend the ADL's static semantics. These include

- service levels are positive numbers;
- the service level of a composed component is at least as high as the sum of service level of its subcomponents;
- the replication conditions respect the types of ports (*i.e.,* it ensures that its equations are type-compatible with the referenced ports); and
- the replication conditions evaluate to Boolean.

Realizing the intended replication behavior requires adding subcomponents at runtime when the conditions are fulfilled. However, in the base ADL's realization of its dynamic semantics, each component type is represented by a Java class yielding a single, fixed attribute for each subcomponent. To achieve flexible replication, the Java classes realizing component types should yield a set of subcomponents for each component type among their subcomponents instead. Moreover, they should feature a new method that checks the replication conditions whenever a message arrives and passes messages to new subcomponents as required. Hence, the company's software engineers extend the ADL's code generator accordingly. This small extension – a few properties, rules, and code generator adjustments – enables the company's engineers to customize the base ADL to their requirements and prevents creating a new ADL from scratch.

3   Preliminaries

MontiArc [17] is a component and connector ADL built on top of the MontiCore language workbench [20]. This enables leveraging MontiCore's powerful software language engineering capabilities, such as language composition and extension [13].

MontiCore employs context-free grammars (CFGs) for the integrated definition of concrete syntax and abstract syntax [20] of modeling languages. These CFGs describe which models are principally possible. Validating static semantics constraints not expressible with CFGs requires additional mechanisms. For such checks, MontiCore features a compositional *context condition* (CoCo) framework [32], where CoCos are well-formedness rules formulated in Java. Code generators implement the modeling languages' dynamic semantics. From a language's CFG, MontiCore generates the corresponding abstract syntax tree (AST) classes and infrastructure to parse textual models [10] into AST instances. The AST instances store the content of models, such as their elements and their relations to each other free from concrete syntax keywords. From each grammar, MontiCore automatically produces a model processing infrastructure that enables to parse models to operate on AST instances, for example, to apply model transformations or CoCo checks. For realization of dynamic semantics, MontiCore further features a template-based model-to-text code generation framework [29], which supports translating AST instances into arbitrary target representations. Moreover, MontiCore supports compositional language integration [1] via inheritance, embedding, and aggregation [13]. Language inheritance allows sublanguages to extend and override productions of its superlanguage. From this, MontiCore produces refined AST classes that inherit from the AST classes of the overridden production. Language embedding is realized by declaring *external* productions in a host grammar, which are abstract in the sense that they cannot be instantiated. To this effect, MontiCore's language configuration models define how productions from other languages are mapped to the external productions of the host grammar. Using this, MontiCore combines the individual parsers accordingly and produces integrated ASTs. Language aggregation enables to relate artifacts of different languages that are specified in separate artifacts.

MontiArc [12,17] is a C&C ADL and modeling infrastructure for the development of distributed systems. It is designed to provide the benefits of a comprehensible core architectural style that can be extended as necessary using the powerful language composition features of MontiCore [14]. Consequently, MontiArc provides a small core of language features that are easy to learn yet powerful enough to model complex software architectures. The language's infrastructure comprises code generators translating models into arbitrary GPL realizations. MontiArc is intentionally designed to be light-weight to keep the language easy to learn and flexibly adaptable. Thus it aims at providing only the most important modeling elements of C&C ADLs and focuses on language and tool chain extensibility. The provided elements are exactly the fundamental elements of architectural descriptions [23]: components, connectors, and configurations. Components are the units of computation in an architectural model and yield well-defined interfaces. Connectors connect the interfaces of components to realize component communication. A configuration is a graph of components and connectors that describes component composition. Following this principle, MontiArc facilitates modeling C&C software architectures with hierarchically structured, interconnected components. The interface of a component is defined

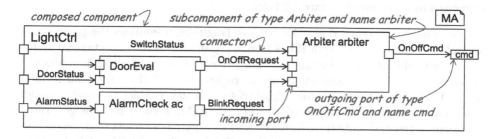

Fig. 2. MontiArc architecture for a light control system with three subcomponents.

by a set of unidirectional, named, and typed ports. Components receive messages via their incoming ports and emit messages via their outgoing ports. Unidirectional connectors connect exactly one source port to one or more target ports. To facilitate component reuse, MontiArc distinguishes between component types and component instances. A component type (denoted "component" in the following) defines the interface of its instances by a set of ports and may comprise component instances ("subcomponents") and connectors defining a configuration. If a component contains subcomponents, it is called composed. Otherwise it is called atomic. Atomic components perform the actual computations of a system. The behavior of a composed component is completely derived from the composition of the behaviors of its subcomponents according to its configuration. The behavior of atomic component has to be implemented by hand, *i.e.*, by providing GPL code implementations. MontiArc provides further language features, such as generic type parameters, configuration parameters, and syntactic sugar for automatically connecting all ports of the same type. A complete description of the MontiArc ADL is available in [12]. Figure 2, for instance, depicts the graphical representation of the component type `LightCtrl`. Listing 1.1 shows its corresponding textual definition. The component consists of four ports (l. 2), three subcomponents (ll. 4–6), and seven connectors (ll. 8–13). Connectors are unidirectional and connect one sending port with one or more receiving ports of compatible data types. The incoming port `switchStatus` of component `LightCtrl`, for instance, is connected to the same-named and same-typed incoming ports of the subcomponents `arbiter` and `doorEval` (l. 9).

```
1  component LightCtrl {
2    port in SwitchStatus, in AlarmStatus, in DoorStatus, out OnOffCmd cmd;   MA
3
4    component AlarmCheck ac;
5    component DoorEval;
6    component Arbiter arbiter;
7
8    connect arbiter.onOffCmd -> cmd;
9    connect switchStatus -> arbiter.switchStatus, doorEval.switchStatus;
10   connect doorStatus -> doorEval.doorStatus;
11   connect alarmStatus -> alarmCheck.alarmStatus;
12   connect alarmCheck.blinkRequest -> arbiter.blinkRequest;
13   connect doorEval.onOffRequest -> arbiter.onOffRequest;
14 }
```

Listing 1.1. Component type `LightControl` with one configuration parameter. It consists of three incoming ports, one outgoing port, three subcomponents among which one is of an inner component type, and seven connectors (*cf.* [12]).

As MontiArc is realized as a MontiCore language, it employs the parsers and AST classes generated by MontiCore from its grammar to translate textual architecture models into AST instances. Using the AST, it applies the handcrafted workflows and model transformations as registered. Based on the transformed ASTs, it creates a symbol table infrastructure, which enables to resolve model (parts) across different models. Ultimately, MontiArc invokes its code generator to translate the (possibly transformed) ASTs into GPL artifacts that depend on classes of a runtime environment (RTE). A RTE consists of GPL artifacts of the same target language as the generated code and supports execution of generated artifacts (for instance, by realizing scheduling or message passing). The RTE's artifacts are independent of the generator's input models and are thus the same for any generated output. We treat the RTE as part of the generated code that remains static, independent of the generator's input models. MontiArc does not provide to define models in graphical syntax, but creating this can be achieved via translation to, e.g., EMF [28].

4   MontiArc Extension Method

Reuse is one of the prime enablers for efficient engineering. The language work-bench MontiCore supports defining reusable languages that can be extended or combined to new languages [14]. We combine its language composition mechanisms with well-defined MontiArc extension points to extend the MontiArc ADL and its infrastructure. This enables customizing the ADL to requirements of specific domains and adding further language processing steps, while most infrastructure parts can be reused with the adjusted language directly. This section presents an integrated method to extend MontiArc that comprises structured activities to extend the ADL, model processing, and code generation. Extending the derived languages follows the same pattern. The method does not support creating a completely different ADL and infrastructure, as the result might not be applicable to the extension method anymore. For example, eliminating the component production by overriding might prevent further customization.

4.1   Extending the Syntax of MontiArc

The first step towards extending MontiArc's syntax is to analyze the intended extension's purpose: If the extension should change structural language elements (*e.g.,* components, ports, connectors), it requires inheriting from MontiArc to enable adding or refining language elements. To add a new component behavior modeling language, it requires embedding that language only. If the changes to MontiArc's syntax should enable adjusted model processing only, MontiArc's many places for stereotypes require even less extension effort. The related activities are illustrated in Fig. 3.

For introducing new modeling elements or refining existing ones, extension by inheritance starts with analyzing which MontiArc productions will be affected. For instance, introducing service level properties to components would require refining the production responsible for components. With MontiCore languages, refinement is realized via grammar inheritance. To make the new language elements accessible for well-formedness checking, language composition, or other processing, the relevant information must be added to the corresponding symbols also. The activities required to extend the symbol table are depicted in Fig. 4. For embedding of modeling languages to describe component behavior, MontiArc relies on MontiCore's language embedding capabilities. This includes that MontiArc provides an external grammar production for the embedding of

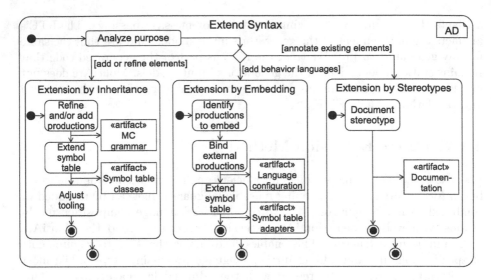

Fig. 3. Extending MontiArc's syntax: new language elements are introduced via inheritance, embedding, or as stereotypes.

grammar productions of embedded languages. First, the productions of the languages to be embedded must be identified. Afterwards, the mapping between the external production and the productions to be embedded is established. The mapping is defined in MontiArc's language configuration. During model processing, MontiCore then combines the parsers generated from the individual languages' grammars according to this mapping. This enables parsing components with embedded behavior models. However, these embedded models are usually unaware of their new operation context: for instance, embedded automata might expect to read inputs from variables. To interpret inputs and outputs of embedded models as references to ports, adapters between their symbols realize proper interpretation. Extension with new stereotypes amounts to providing proper documentation of the new stereotypes and their possible values. Please note that we support stereotypes only for minor and ad-hoc extensions. We advise to use metamodel extension, via inheritance or embedding, instead.

Extending MontiArc's ADL is coupled to extending its symbol table and introducing or refining productions as well as embedding behavior languages might require symbol table extension. After analyzing the cause for symbol table extension, one of the following activities is to be performed.

1. Type language adaptation: MontiArc supports using arbitrary type languages.
2. Reflect behavior language embedding: if the modeling elements of an embedded behavior language are relevant to the symbol table, *e.g.,* for checking inter-language well-formedness, these must be integrated.

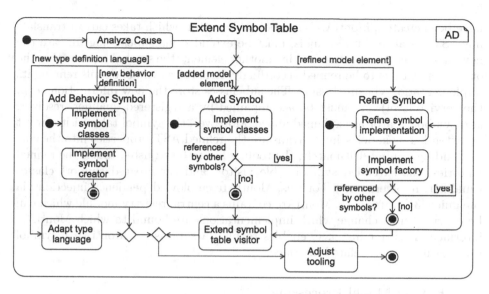

Fig. 4. Activities of extending MontiArc's symbol table.

3. New symbols: if language extension produced completely new modeling elements, such as the replication conditions described in Sect. 2, which require symbols as well, these must be added also.
4. Entry refinement: where modeling elements of MontiArc have been refined, for instance by adding a service level to components, this must be reflected at the corresponding symbols also.
5. Tooling adjustment: depending on the symbol table extension performed, MontiArc's tooling has to be extended accordingly.

Integrating a new type language into MontiArc requires the aggregation of both languages. This enables using the types defined in this language for MontiArc's ports and configuration parameters. Language aggregation is detailed in [32] and comprises the following activities: (1) Adapt symbols of the new type language to MontiArc's type symbol; (2) Create and register *qualifiers* [32] via subclassing. Qualifiers enable relating unqualified names (*e.g.,* `String`) to qualified names (*e.g.,* `java.lang.String`); and (3) Checking type properties requires loading the referenced model. To this end, MontiArc employs MontiCore's symbol resolving [32], which requires creating and registering *resolvers* via subclassing. These resolvers load symbols for qualified names. MontiArc's symbol table yields a dedicated extension point for convenient integration of embedded behavior languages' symbols. This requires creating a proper symbol kind for the behavior language. For example, when embedding automata, such a symbol might comprise information about data sources and data sinks the automaton models operate on. Additionally, qualifiers and resolvers must be provided. Where extension raises the need for integrating completely new symbols, these must be created and registered accordingly. After the entry classes have been created, MontiArc's symbol table visitor, which takes care of translating AST instances into symbols, must be extended via subclassing. In case the new model element is referenced by another element, the symbol representing the other element has to be refined accordingly. Refining a symbol entails refining its implementation via subclassing. The subclasses store the new information (*e.g.,* the service level) and must be accompanied by a registered qualifier, resolver, and symbol creator as explained above. Moreover, the symbol table visitor must be extended by subclassing to translate the refined AST properties into the corresponding symbol. Ultimately, the tooling has to be adjusted to use the refined factories, the extended symbol table visitor, and the created support classes (qualifier, resolver, *etc.*). For this, MontiArc employs dependency injection via the guice [31] framework. MontiArc contains a central registry module which can be overridden to change which implementations are bound to which MontiArc interface. This, for instance, enables to bind a subclass of MontiArc's symbol table visitor to the related interface.

4.2   Extend Model Processing

While extending MontiArc's syntax and symbol table enables introducing new model properties, refining existing ones, and adding stereotypes to models, using these modified elements requires adjusting MontiArc's model processing infrastructure. This may include extension with new workflows, model analyses, or model-to-model transformations as presented in Fig. 5. It does, however, not cover code generator extension, which is described in Sect. 4.3.

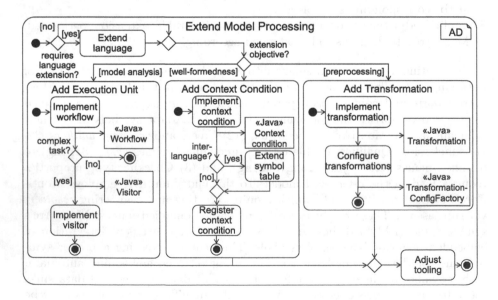

Fig. 5. Activities involved in extending MontiArc's model processing infrastructure.

Every extension of MontiArc's model processing infrastructure may start with extending its ADL as discussed in Sect. 4.1. If MontiArc should be extended with a new model analysis, a new MontiCore execution unit has to be added to its infrastructure. An execution unit is a wrapper for MontiCore workflows and creating a new execution unit requires registering a subclass of MontiCore's DSLWorkflow [19]. These workflows are executable units that perform calculations on the abstract syntax of a model using a visitor pattern variant. The static semantics of MontiArc are realized by a set of context conditions that ensure model well-formedness. If extension requires adding additional conditions, these can be implemented as subclasses of MontiCore's ContextCondition [32]. If the new condition relates models of different languages with another, it might be necessary to add adapters to the symbol table as presented in Sect. 4.1. Ultimately, the new context conditions must be registered by creating and binding a subclass of MontiArc's ContextConditionCreator using guice. If MontiArc is extended with a new model-to-model transformation, an artifact that executes the transformation has to be created. This artifact must implement one of the transformation interfaces for different abstract syntax elements of MontiArc. Configuration requires subclassing TransformationConfigurationFactory and binding it via guice.

4.3 Extend Code Generator

Syntactic extensions often aim at tailoring the language's dynamic semantics, *i.e.,* modified should change the behavior of the model (or generated code). Sometimes, the behavior aimed at can be reproduced by existing modeling elements. In this case, a transformation should be implemented as explained in Sect. 4.2. This section covers the case where semantics preserving transformations are neither possible nor desirable. For MontiArc, this entails adjusting its code generator to alter production of artifacts realizing the modified behavior.

Generally, MontiArc's code generation framework comprises a component-invariant run-time environment (RTE) and templates that produce component-specific artifacts. The RTE specifies properties invariant to individual component models, such as scheduling or message passing. The templates translate the abstract syntax of components to GPL artifacts interfacing the RTE. Hence, MontiArc provides templates for all abstract syntax concerns (*e.g.,* ports, connectors, subcomponents, *etc.*), which are registered at its central generator configuration. Creating a generator configuration consists of binding hook points with FreeMarker templates [29], which should be included (executed) at the hook point's location. By default, a unique start template is used for setting these configuration parameters for components. Figure 6 depicts an overview of the necessary activities for extending the code generator infrastructure after the syntactic extensions, if any, have been performed. If the existing RTE is insufficient for representing the new concepts (*e.g.,* scheduling and message passing remain unaffected), the generated API has to be adjusted, before the template parts can be adjusted.

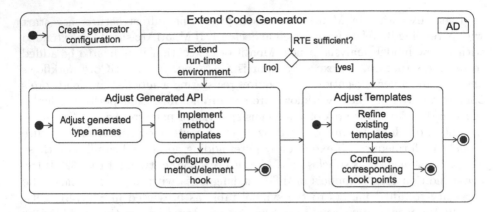

Fig. 6. Code generator extension depends on reusability of the RTE.

Extending the RTE typically consists of (a) subtyping existing classes to refine commonly used method implementations; (b) adding additional methods to interfaces reflecting additional concepts captured by the new syntax; and (c) introducing new interfaces and classes representing new elements that cannot be captured by already existing classes and interfaces of the RTE. Extensions to the RTE entail adjusting the generated API. First, generated type names have to be adjusted with regard to referencing the newly created subclasses instead of the superclasses referenced before. Afterwards, method templates for the new methods added to the interfaces have to be implemented. This typically affects – but is not limited to – the generated code for components.

Ultimately, the generator's hook points have to be configured for new templates created for the new classes and interfaces added to the RTE in step (c) as well as for the new method templates. After incorporating possible RTE extensions, existing generated methods have to be adjusted to reflect the intended meaning of the changes performed on the ADL. To this effect, extension templates have to be implemented first. These templates are used for injecting code into preexisting methods generated by the former templates. Afterwards, the created templates are added to the method hooks in the generator configuration.

Where existing templates must be refined only, for instance to include translating new modeling elements, extension must provide new templates that are registered for hook points of related abstract syntax concerns. The lack of template inheritance in the underlying template engine causes this effort and ongoing work on code generator reuse might alleviate this [9]. However, these new templates can reuse existing templates in a white-box fashion and, thus, contribute new translation as appropriate.

5   Case Studies

MontiArc's extension method has successfully been applied to extend it for different domains. This section presents selected case studies.

```
1  component CashDeskLine {
2    port out PaymentRequest; // to Bank                          MSA
3    component CashDeskUI ui { port out Sale; }
4    component CardReader reader { port out CardHolderData; }
5    component CashDesk cashDesk {
6        port in CardHolderData, in Sale, port out PaymentRequest;
7        trustlevel +1;
8        accesscontrol on;
9    }
10   identity weak ui -> cashDesk;
11   connect ui.sale -> cashDesk.sale;
12   connect encrypted reader.cardHolderData -> cashDesk.cardHolderData;
13   connect encrypted cashDesk.paymentRequest -> paymentRequest;
14 }
```

Listing 1.2. MontiSecArc architecture cash desk line found in supermarkets.

MontiSecArc (MSA) is an extension of MontiArc extended to the description of security architectures that enable the analysis of security flaws [18]. As such, it introduces modeling elements to specify security properties, such as trust levels, encrypted connectors, and identity links. To integrate these elements, which entail changes to abstract syntax, static semantics, and dynamic semantics, the MSA grammar inherits from MontiArc's grammar and introduces rules for the new concepts. It does not introduce new symbols, but refines the symbols for modified modeling elements to reflect the new properties and adds few context conditions related to these properties only. To produce proper Java artifacts, MSE also adjusts existing code generation by incorporating encryption into the RTE's message passing and overrides several templates where necessary. Listing 1.2 illustrates selected MSA features, such as the `trustlevel` (l. 7), which describes that the component provides protection against adversaries. Moreover, the component performs `accesscontrol` for all incoming ports (l. 8). The `weak identity` link from `ui` to `cashDesk` (l. 10) ensures that requests to the `sale` port are authenticated by a user logged in at the `ui` and cannot be spoofed by an adversary. Finally, two connectors are `encrypted` (ll. 12–13) to prevent adversaries from reading and modifying messages on these connections.

```
1  component BumpControl[int min - 1] {
2    port in  Integer distance, in  Timer signal,              MAA
3        out TimerCmd timer,   out Motor right, out Motor left;
4
5    behavior automaton {
6      state idle, drive, back, turn;
7      initial idle                    / {right=Motor.STOP, left=Motor.STOP};
8      idle  -> drive [distance < min] / {right=FWD, left=FWD};
9      drive -> back  [distance < 5*min] / {right=BWD, left=BWD, DOUBLE};
10     // additional transitions
11   }
12 }
```

Listing 1.3. MontiArcAutomaton architecture with embedded behavior model.

MontiArcAutomaton (MAA) is a framework for architecture modeling that extends the MontiArc infrastructure focusing on flexible embedding of component behavior languages and compositional code generation [27]. It extends MontiArc via grammar inheritance and embedding of various component behavior modeling languages. Consequently, it refines symbols of modified modeling elements and adds behavior symbols for the embedded languages. It also reuses all but one context condition of MontiArc and adds several context conditions for the new modeling elements. Moreover, it adds transformations to support various modeling shortcuts. MAA severely extends MontiArc's code generation framework to greatly facilitate behavior language embedding and features code generators producing Java and Python artifacts. As it does not extend MontiArc's scheduling and message passing, its Java generator reuses MontiArc's RTE without modification. For the Python generator, a new, compatible, RTE was devised. For the former, it provides extension templates only, for the latter it replaces all templates. The component `BumpControl` depicted in Listing 1.3 illustrates two of MAA's features: it introduces default parameters to component types (l. 1) and embeds a stand-alone language for I/O$^\omega$ automata to describe component behavior (ll. 5–10). To this effect, it binds the external productions inherited from MontiArc to automata productions for states (ll. 6–7) and transitions (ll. 8–10). To interpret names on transitions as component ports, which the automata are unaware of, MAA adds adapters between MontiArc's port symbols and automaton variable symbols as well as new context conditions (*e.g.,* to respect the direction of ports when reading). MontiArcAutomaton furthermore extends MontiArc's template for atomic components to delegate translation of embedded behavior language models to registered responsible code generators [27].

clArc is an infrastructure focusing on modeling cloud architectures. Its cloud ADL extends MontiArc with replication of ports and subcomponents to support load-balancing, port groups to enable message traceability, and service ports that describe requirements on the environment of the architecture. To introduce these elements clArc also extends MontiArc's grammar via inheritance, refines its symbols, and provides new context conditions on top of MontiArc's context conditions. Code generation produces event-driven Java implementations, hence clArc only refines MontiArc's templates for component hulls, ports, and subcomponent instantiation. Listing 1.4 illustrates clArc's new modeling elements: The port group `UserData` (l. 2), denotes that the following ports belong to a semantic unit for which calculations are performed only if all its ports have received at least one message. Replication, denoted by `[*]` (l. 3), enables instantiating a variable number of component instances at system runtime. The component `UserManagement` also requires a `service` (l. 5) to function properly, which is translated to a dependency to the eponymous Java interface.

```
1 component UserManagement {
2    port group UserData in User usr, in UpdateRequest req;      clarc
3    component UpdateStore store [*];
4    connect usr -> store.user;
5    connect req -> store.request;
6    service required clarc.db.NoSQL;
7 }
```

Listing 1.4. A clArc user management system with replicating subcomponents and port groups.

6   Discussion and Related Work

The systematic extension mechanism of MontiArc enables extending it to cover a great variety of architecture modeling concerns: Besides the variants presented above, it has been extended to support component behavior modeling with a variant of Java/P [16], architecture alignment checking [24], and delta modeling [15]. Following this method enables to reuse great parts of existing tooling, such as transformations, generators, and well-formedness rules. While the present extension mechanism is powerful, it requires MontiCore expertise to understand its language constituents and their interaction. As long as there is no general consensus on the shape of *language components* with interfaces for specific purposes, this remains necessary. Although many language workbenches [5] support extension mechanisms comparable to the mechanism presented here, none provides similar structural guidance to achieve such comprehensive tool chain integration.

Overall, science and industry have produced more than 120 ADLs [21]. These emerged from different domains and consequently focus on different challenges of architecture modeling. Although extensibility is "a key property of modeling notations" [22] most of these ADLs are so-called "first-generation ADLs" [22] that solely focus on technological challenges instead of domain-specific aspects or extensibility. Notable exceptions are the Architecture Analysis and Design Language (AADL) [6], π ADL [26], and xADL [2]: AADL [6] features various modeling elements to describe hardware and software components of embedded systems. Similar to MontiArcAutomaton, AADL can also be extended with behavior modeling languages via sublanguages according to the behavior annex [7]. It does not support structured extension of its syntax or semantics aside from this. The xADL [25] also focuses on architecture extensibility and shares many features with MontiArc (*e.g.,* composed and atomic component types, instantiation, component behavior models). Moreover, it features modeling elements for product lines and variability not supported by MontiArc. Extension in xADL is syntactic and it neither supports non-invasive language aggregation, nor customization of its model processing infrastructure. The π-ADL [26] enables modeling structure and behavior of software architectures based on the π-calculus. It generally also supports to add behavior modeling capabilities as layers on top of its ADL. This ultimately produces a monolithic language composite whose individual languages are difficult to exchange. Moreover, it does not support structured extension of semantics composition of code generators for the individual behavior DSLs.

7   Conclusion

We have presented the MontiArc architecture modeling infrastructure, which leverages the results from software language engineering as realized with the MontiCore language workbench to enable extension of syntax and semantics. At its core, this infrastructure contains a light-weight ADL with extension points for behavior language embedding and integration of type languages. Its infrastructure comprises frameworks to integrate new well-formedness checks, workflows, model-to-model transformations, and code generation capabilities. We have presented an extension method that covers each of these aspects and enables customizing MontiArc to domain-specific requirements. This method alleviates the need for developing a specific ADLs from scratch, which we have illustrated with examples of MontiArc variants for three different domains, and greatly facilitates employing ADLs in different domains. This ultimately fosters their successful application in real-world scenarios.

References

1. Clark, T., Brand, M., Combemale, B., Rumpe, B.: Conceptual model of the globalization for domain-specific languages. In: Cheng, B.H.C., Combemale, B., France, R.B., Jézéquel, J.-M., Rumpe, B. (eds.) Globalizing Domain-Specific Languages. LNCS, vol. 9400, pp. 7–20. Springer, Cham (2015). doi:10.1007/978-3-319-26172-0_2
2. Dashofy, E.M., der Hoek, A.V., Taylor, R.N.: A highly-extensible, xml-based architecture description language. In: WICSA 2001. Proceedings of the Working IEEE/IFIP Conference on Software Architecture, p. 103. IEEE Computer Society, Washington, DC (2001)
3. Debruyne, V., Simonot-Lion, F., Trinquet, Y.: EAST-ADL — an architecture description language. In: Dissaux, P., Filali-Amine, M., Michel, P., Vernadat, F. (eds.) Architecture Description Languages. ITIFIP, vol. 176, pp. 181–195. Springer, Boston, MA (2005). doi:10.1007/0-387-24590-1_12
4. Erdweg, S., Giarrusso, P.G., Rendel, T.: Language composition untangled. In: Proceedings of the Twelfth Workshop on Language Descriptions, Tools, and Applications, LDTA 2012, NY, USA. ACM, New York (2012)
5. Erdweg, S., et al.: The state of the art in language workbenches. In: Erwig, M., Paige, R.F., Wyk, E. (eds.) SLE 2013. LNCS, vol. 8225, pp. 197–217. Springer, Cham (2013). doi:10.1007/978-3-319-02654-1_11
6. Feiler, P.H., Gluch, D.P.: Model-Based Engineering with AADL: An Introduction to the SAE Architecture Analysis & Design Language. Addison-Wesley, Boston (2012)
7. Franca, R.B., Bodeveix, J.P., Filali, M., Rolland, J.F., Chemouil, D., Thomas, D.: The AADL behaviour annex-experiments and roadmap. In: Proceedings of the 12th IEEE International Conference on Engineering Complex Computer Systems, pp. 377–382. IEEE Computer Society, Washington, DC (2007)
8. France, R., Rumpe, B.: Model-driven development of complex software: a research roadmap. In: Future of Software Engineering, FOSE 2007, pp. 37–54 (2007)
9. Greifenberg, T., Müller, K., Roth, A., Rumpe, B., Schulze, C., Wortmann, A.: Modeling variability in template-based code generators for product line engineering. In: Modellierung (2016)
10. Grönniger, H., Krahn, H., Rumpe, B., Schindler, M., Völkel, S.: Textbased modeling. In: 4th International Workshop on Software Language Engineering, Informatik-Bericht, Nashville, vol. 4. Johannes-Gutenberg-Universität Mainz (2007)
11. Group, O.M: OMG Unified Modeling Language (OMG UML), Infrastructure Version 2.3 (10–05-03) (2010)

12. Haber, A.: MontiArc - Architectural Modeling and Simulation of Interactive Distributed Systems. No. 24 in Aachener Informatik-Berichte, Software Engineering, Shaker Verlag (2016)
13. Haber, A., Look, M., Mir Seyed Nazari, P., Navarro Perez, A., Rumpe, B., Voelkel, S., Wortmann, A.: Integration of heterogeneous modeling languages via extensible and composable language components. In: Proceedings of the 3rd International Conference on Model-Driven Engineering and Software Development. Scitepress, Angers, France (2015)
14. Haber, A., Look, M., Mir Seyed Nazari, P., Navarro Perez, A., Rumpe, B., Völkel, S., Wortmann, A.: Composition of heterogeneous modeling languages. In: Desfray, P., Filipe, J., Hammoudi, S., Pires, L.F. (eds.) MODELSWARD 2015. CCIS, vol. 580, pp. 45–66. Springer, Cham (2015). doi:10.1007/978-3-319-27869-8_3
15. Haber, A., Rendel, H., Rumpe, B., Schaefer, I.: Delta modeling for software architectures. In: Tagungsband des Dagstuhl-Workshop MBEES: Modellbasierte Entwicklung eingebetteterSysteme VII, pp. 1–10. fortiss GmbH (2011)
16. Haber, A., Ringert, J.O., Rumpe, B.: Towards architectural programming of embedded systems. In: Tagungsband des Dagstuhl-Workshop MBEES: Modellbasierte Entwicklung eingebetteterSysteme VI. Informatik-Bericht, vol. 2010-01, pp. 13–22. fortiss GmbH, Germany (2010)
17. Haber, A., Ringert, J.O., Rumpe, B.: MontiArc - architectural modeling of interactive distributed and cyber-physical systems. Technical report AIB-2012-03, RWTH Aachen University (2012)
18. Hermerschmidt, L., Hölldobler, K., Rumpe, B., Wortmann, A.: Generating domain-specific transformation languages for component & connector architecture descriptions. In: 2nd International Workshop on Model-Driven Engineering for Component-Based Software Systems (ModComp) (2015)
19. Krahn, H.: MontiCore: Agile Entwicklung von domänenspezifischen Sprachen im Software-Engineering. No. 1 in Aachener Informatik-Berichte, Software Engineering, Shaker Verlag (2010)
20. Krahn, H., Rumpe, B., Völkel, S.: MontiCore: a framework for compositional development of domain specific languages. Int. J. Softw. Tools Technol. Transf. (STTT) 12(5), 353–372 (2010)
21. Malavolta, I., Lago, P., Muccini, H., Pelliccione, P., Tang, A.: What industry needs from architectural languages: a survey. IEEE Trans. Softw. Eng. 39(6), 869–891 (2013)
22. Medvidovic, N., Dashofy, E.M., Taylor, R.N.: Moving architectural description from under the technology lamppost. Inf. Softw. Technol. 49(1), 12–31 (2007)
23. Medvidovic, N., Taylor, R.N.: A classification and comparison framework for software architecture description languages. IEEE Trans. Softw. Eng. 26, 70–93 (2000)
24. Mir Seyed Nazari, P.: Architektur Alignment von Java Systemen. Master's thesis, RWTH Aachen University (2011)
25. Naslavsky, L., Dias, H.Z., Ziv, H., Richardson, D.: Extending xADL with statechart behavioral specification. In: Third Workshop on Architecting Dependable Systems (WADS), Edinburgh, Scotland, pp. 22–26. IET (2004)
26. Oquendo, F.: π-adl: an architecture description language based on the higher-order typed π-calculus for specifying dynamic and mobile software architectures. ACM SIGSOFT Softw. Eng. Notes 29(3), 1–14 (2004)
27. Ringert, J.O., Roth, A., Rumpe, B., Wortmann, A.: Language and code generator composition for model-driven engineering of robotics component & connector systems. J. Softw. Eng. Rob. (JOSER) 6, 33–57 (2015)

28. Ringert, J.O., Rumpe, B., Wortmann, A.: From software architecture structure and behavior modeling to implementations of cyber-physical systems. In: Software Engineering Workshopband (SE 2013). LNI, vol. 215, pp. 155–170 (2013)
29. Schindler, M.: Eine Werkzeuginfrastruktur zur agilen Entwicklung mit der UML/P. No. 11 in Aachener Informatik-Berichte, Software Engineering, Shaker Verlag (2012)
30. Schlegel, C., Steck, A., Lotz, A.: Model-driven software development in robotics: communication patterns as key for a robotics component model. In: Chugo, D., Yokota, S. (eds.) Introduction to Modern Robotics. iConcept Press (2011)
31. Vanbrabant, R.: Google Guice: Agile Lightweight Dependency Injection Framework. Apress, New York (2008)
32. Völkel, S.: Kompositionale Entwicklung domänenspezifischer Sprachen. No. 9 in Aachener Informatik-Berichte, Software Engineering, Shaker Verlag (2011)
33. Wile, D.S.: Supporting the DSL spectrum. Comput. Inf. Technol. 4, 263–287 (2001)

A Feature-Based Approach for Variability Exploration and Resolution in Model Transformation Migration

Davide Di Ruscio[1], Juergen Etzlstorfer[2], Ludovico Iovino[3(✉)],
Alfonso Pierantonio[1], and Wieland Schwinger[2]

[1] University of L'Aquila, L'Aquila, Italy
{davide.diruscio,alfonso.pierantonio}@univaq.it
[2] Johannes Kepler University Linz, Linz, Austria
{juergen.etzlstorfer,wieland.schwinger}@jku.at
[3] Gran Sasso Science Institute, L'Aquila, Italy
ludovico.iovino@gssi.it

Abstract. The key to success with Model-Driven Engineering is the ability to maintain metamodels and their related artifacts consistent over time. Metamodels can evolve under evolutionary pressure that arises when clients and users express the need for enhancements. However, metamodel changes come at the price of compromising metamodel-related artifacts, including model transformations, necessitating their migration to again conform to the evolved metamodel. Restoring conformance of transformations is intrinsically difficult since a multitude of possible migration alternatives exist, which are unfeasible to be inspected manually. In this paper, we present an approach to explore variability in model transformation migration. Employing a feature-based representation of several possible transformation migrations, the approach permits modelers to explore and explicitly discover differences and conflicts among them. Once the desired migration alternatives are selected, the actual migration program is generated and executed by exploiting the EMFMigrate platform.

1 Introduction

As the complexity of software systems escalates, there is an increasing consensus on the need to leverage abstraction. In Model-Driven Engineering [20] (MDE) this is usually accomplished by formalizing domains by means of metamodels that are at the core of this software discipline. As a consequence, complete modeling environments, which consist of a multitude of artifacts including models and model transformations, are formally defined in accordance with their reference metamodels [7]. Similarly to other software artifacts, metamodels can evolve under evolutionary pressure that arises when clients and users express a need for enhancements. Changing a metamodel might break conformance to its dependent artifacts because of the existing dependencies among them [6]: conformance restoring migrations are therefore necessary to re-establish the conformance in

A. Anjorin and H. Espinoza (Eds.): ECMFA 2017, LNCS 10376, pp. 71–89, 2017.
DOI: 10.1007/978-3-319-61482-3_5

the modeling environment. Model transformations are no exception and urge to be *migrated* whenever metamodels they are based on undergo modifications [8].

Analogously to the well-known update view problem in relational databases [1] there are multiple ways of propagating metamodel changes, i.e., there are many alternatives to *migrate* a transformation. The problem is how to choose one i.e., *how is it possible to identify a migration alternative reflecting both the modeler intents and the rationale behind the metamodel refactoring among the viable alternatives?* Existing approaches (e.g., [10, 16]) typically start from a formalization of the metamodel changes to automatically derive *a single* migration. However, these techniques offer a prefixed solution only, which must be used in any context and regardless of the reasons behind the occurred metamodel evolution, entailing the drawback that potential solutions which better fit the modeler intents are left unexplored. However, since multiple solutions are possible, each leading to a differently migrated transformation, it is of utmost importance to identify the one that best fits developers' needs. In particular, small changes in a given metamodel typically correspond to a large number of migration alternatives. Unsupported manual inspection and detection of those is prone to errors, because alternatives might overlap each other, hampering a successful transformation migration.

This paper proposes an approach to represent a set of possible model transformation migration alternatives in response to metamodel evolution to support the user in inspection and detection of migration alternatives. As a result, migration solutions can be better compared as differences and potential conflicts between migration alternatives are denoted by variability points without the necessity of manually inspecting each of them. In this context, the user is supported in choosing the desired migration alternative by means of a feature model [2]. EMFMigrate [23] rules are automatically generated and executed with respect to the selected migration alternative, to migrate the initial transformation to recover its conformance with the evolved metamodel.

Outline. Next section presents a motivating scenario, while Sect. 3 introduces a notation for managing variability in an intensional way and its application on an example. A prototypical implementation is presented in Sect. 4 and related work is discussed in Sect. 5. Finally, Sect. 6 draws conclusions and outlines future work.

2   Motivating Scenario

In this section, we present an explanatory metamodel evolution and its effects on a model transformation. Despite its simplicity, it is able to show the large number of migration alternatives and, thus, the multitude of different migrations a user is confronted with.

Figure 1a shows the *Simple Workplace* metamodel acting as the source metamodel of a transformation, comprising metaclasses for the specification of persons and their corresponding workplaces. According to the metamodel, a `Person` works optionally in an (abstract) `Workplace`, which can be a `Company` or `University`.

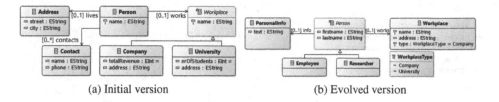

(a) Initial version   (b) Evolved version

Fig. 1. An explanatory Workplace metamodel evolution

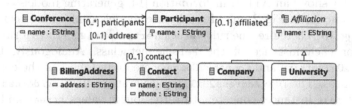

Fig. 2. The conference management metamodel

The specification of `Persons` can include the corresponding `Address` and `Contact` data. `Company` elements consist of the specification of the corresponding `addresses` and `total revenues`. The definition of `University` includes also information about the number of students.

Figure 2 shows the metamodel of a simple conference management system: a `Conference` can have a set of `participants` that can be affiliated with either a `University` or a `Company`. In order to complete the registration to a conference, each participant has to provide the corresponding organizers with a `Billing-Address` and a `Contact`.

```
1  rule Person2Participant {
2    from s: WORKPLACE!Person
3    to t: CONFERENCE!Participant (
4    name <- s.name,
5    affiliated <- s.works,
6    contact <- s.contacts->first(),
7    address <- s.lives
8    )
9  }
10 rule University2University {
11   from s: WORKPLACE!University
12   to t: CONFERENCE!University (
13   name <- s.name
14   )
15 }
16 rule Company2Company {
17   from s: WORKPLACE!Company
18   to t: CONFERENCE!Company (
19   name <- s.name
20   )
21 }
22 rule Address2Billing {
23   from s: WORKPLACE!Address
24   to t: CONFERENCE!BillingAddress
25   (
26   address <- s.street + ',␣' + s.city
27   )
```

```
28 }
29 rule Contact2Contact {
30 from s: WORKPLACE!Contact
31 to t: CONFERENCE!Contact (
32 name <- s.name,
33 phone <- s.phone
34 )
35 }
```

Listing 1.1. Snippet of *SimpleWorkplace2ConferenceManagement*

Listing 1.1 shows an ATL transformation [14] generating models conforming to the metamodel in Fig. 2 out of workplace models conforming to the meta-model in Fig. 1a. Therefore, the rule `Person2Participant` generates a `Participant` instance for each instance of the `Person` metaclass. Analogously, the rules `University2University` and `Company2Company` create instances of the corresponding metaclasses. The rule `Address2Billing` generates a `BillingAddress` instance for each `Address` instance, concatenating the source values `street` and `city` for the target `address` value. The rule `Contact2Contact` generates `Contact` instances.

In order to address unforeseen requirements or to better represent the considered application domain, metamodels can evolve. For instance, the workplace metamodel shown in Fig. 1a is modified to obtain the new version in Fig. 1b by applying the following refactorings:

- *R1. Introduction of subclasses:* the `Employee` and `Researcher` metaclasses are introduced as subtypes of `Person`, which in turn becomes abstract;
- *R2. Split attribute:* the attribute `name` of the metaclass `Person` is split in two attributes with the same type, named `firstname` and `lastname`;
- *R3. Flatten Hierarchy:* the hierarchy between the metaclass `Workplace` and the subclasses `Company` and `University` is reduced to the new version of the `Workplace` metaclass. It contains a new attribute of type `WorkspaceType`, which is a new enumeration representing the pruned subclasses, whose default value is `Company`;
- *R4. and R5. Replace metaclass*: The metaclass `Address` is replaced by the `PersonalInfo` metaclass, and `Contact` is replaced by the `PersonalInfo` metaclass.

Because of these applied metamodel changes, the model transformation in Listing 1.1 has lost its *domain conformance* [13] to the metamodel, and thus, has to be migrated. Migration of model transformations is difficult and can easily give place to inconsistencies and omissions [8]. Moreover, multiple migrations are possible [21], each providing a different solution. Thus, Table 1 shows possible migration alternatives for each applied refactoring. It is worth noting how even simple, *non-breaking changes* [10] induce multiple options of migration according to developer's expertise and goals, which is the case of R1. In particular, if the rule `Person2Participant` (cf. line 1–9 of Listing 1.1) is left unmodified the transformation remains valid, since `Person` instances will be matched by the rule. However, developers might still decide to change the input pattern of the transformation with one of the subclasses, i.e. `Employee` or `Researcher`.

Table 1. Possible migration alternatives for the motivating example

Metamodel change	Possible migration alternatives
R1. Introduce subclasses	*R1a1.* Leave transformation unchanged
	R1a2. Change in-pattern to `Employee`
	R1a3. Change in-pattern to `Researcher`
R2. Split attribute	*R2a1.* Use `firstname`
	R2a2. Use `lastname`
	R2a3. Use concatenation of `firstname` and `lastname`
	R2a4. Delete the affected binding (it is assumed it is not mandatory in the target metamodel)
R3. Flatten hierarchy	*R3a1.* Change input pattern of the affected rule to the remaining class `Workplace` and introduce guards to produce instances of `University` and `Company`
	R3a2. Change input pattern of the affected rule `University2University` to `Workplace` and delete the other rule `Company2Company`
	R3a3. Change input pattern of the rule `Company2Company` to `Workplace` and delete the other rule `University2University`
	R3a4. Delete both rules `Company2Company` and `University2University`
R4. Replace metaclass `Address` with `PersonalInfo`	*R4a1.* Delete rule `Address2Billing`
	R4a2. Change input pattern of the rule `Address2Billing` to the class `PersonalInfo`
	R4a3. Change input pattern of the rule `Address2Billing` to match the class `PersonalInfo`. In addition, add another output pattern to produce also target `Contact` instances
R5. Replace metaclass `Contact` with `PersonalInfo`	*R5a1.* Delete rule `Contact2Contact`
	R5a2. Change input pattern of the rule `Contact2Contact` to be class `PersonalInfo`
	R5a3. Change input pattern of the rule `Contact2Contact` to match the class `PersonalInfo`. In addition, add another output pattern to produce also target `BillingAdress` instances

Refactoring R2 involves the split of the attribute `name` (cf. line 4). The pattern `s.name` in the right hand side of the binding can not be longer queried and thus, needs to be adapted. The corresponding migrations shown in Table 1 are not exhaustive since the use of OCL in ATL transformations increases complexity and gives place to many different solutions. However, possible migration alternatives for the right hand side of the binding can be for instance at least the following expressions: (i) `s.firstname`, (ii) `s.lastname` or (iii) `s.firstname + ' ' + s.lastname`.

Concerning refactoring R3, the rules in lines 10–21 are no longer valid since the types of the input patterns (i.e., `University` and `Company`) have been removed from the initial version of the source metamodel. One possible migration is to change the input patterns of the affected rules by adding conditions based on the new `type` attribute (cf. Fig. 3a), e.g., `s:WORKPLACE!Workplace(s.type=#University)`. Such a "filter" is necessary since in ATL each source model element can match with one rule only [14] and, consequently, the input pattern `Workplace` can not be used in two different rules without any guard. Alternatively, it is possible to drop one of the affected rules and change the input pattern type of the kept rule to `Workplace` (cf. Fig. 3b and c). Another option can be dropping both rules. However, although this would be a syntactically valid option, no instances would be transformed, resulting in a loss of information.

(a) Migration alternative (a)   (b) Migration alternative (b)   (c) Migration alternative (c)

Fig. 3. Possible migration alternatives related to refactoring R3

Among the possible ways to resolve refactoring R4, Table 1 shows three alternatives consisting of dropping the rule `Address2Billing` ($R4a1$), and change the type of its input pattern to `PersonalInfo` ($R4a2$). This would be enough to run the transformation without errors. However, an additional output pattern can be added in order to generate also `Contact` instances ($R4a3$). Similarly to R4, Table 1 shows three alternatives for adapting the sample ATL transformation because of refactoring R5.

When migrating model transformations, which have been compromised by metamodel refactoring actions, developers have to combine different migration alternatives, one for each metamodel refactoring, to obtain a *migration solution*. This represents a major difficulty because alternatives must be combined causing a combinatorial explosion of cases: for instance, the 5 refactorings presented above can give place to

$$3 \times 4 \times 4 \times 3 \times 3 = 432$$

migration alternatives. Although this is an over-approximation since conflicts might occur between migration options as discussed later in the paper, it is highly impractical for the modeler to sort out a myriad of individual alternatives. The problem can be even more complex if the affected transformation has several source and target evolving metamodels[1]. In the remainder of the paper we consider the management of one-to-one model transformations with only the source metamodel evolving, while the target metamodel remains unchanged.

3 Proposed Approach

In this section, we propose an approach to represent, explore, and select migration alternatives for ATL transformations in response to an evolved *source* metamodel. The approach permits to represent all migration alternatives in a single model with variability. Besides having an *intensional* representation of the solution space, i.e., all valid migrations of the transformation, the approach permits the identification of the differences among the alternatives by means of variation points originated from each metamodel refactoring. Moreover, the approach permits to highlight conflicting alternatives, which will be discussed in more detail later.

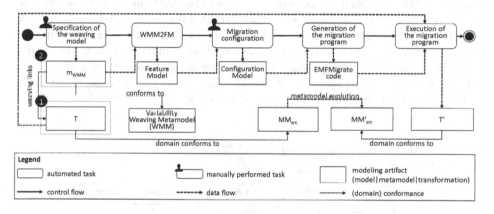

Fig. 4. Overview of the proposed approach

The approach is outlined in Fig. 4, where weaving model m_{WMM} represents possible migration alternatives to be applied on the affected transformation T. The weaving model[2] conforms to the the *Variability Weaving Metamodel* explained in detail in Sects. 3.1 and 3.2. To allow developers exploring the alternatives

---

[1] In order to give more evidence of the difficulties related to the extensional treatment of transformation migrations, which might be required because of metamodel evolutions, our online appendix discusses a list of metamodel changes borrowed from existing catalogues, e.g., [5,12]: http://www.emfmigrate.org/wp-content/uploads/2017/04/appendix.pdf. Such changes are organized with respect to the impact they might have on existing transformations.

[2] Currently, the weaving model m_{WMM} is manually specified even though an automatic creation is feasible as discussed later in the paper. Such a relevant automation step is an important work that we plan to do in the future.

represented in m_{WMM}, the *WMM2FM* transformation automatically generates a feature model, a common mean to represent variability [2] (Sect. 3.3). This is further used to easily determine a valid combination of migration alternatives (Sect. 3.4) and to select a configuration to generate EMFMigrate migration programs, which can be executed to migrate the affected transformations.

3.1 Variability Weaving Metamodel for Representing Different Migration Solutions

The *Variability Weaving Metamodel (WMM)* has been designed in order to be independent from the model transformation language in use. As a result, it can be used without loss of generality for any rule-based transformation language. To this end, a generalization step has been employed to abstract from language dependent concepts in order to define a simplified transformation language very much aligned with the notations given in [11,24], collecting common concepts of model transformation languages (cf. Fig. 5). According to the simplified transformation metamodel, `Module` holds one or more `Rules` that might have `superrules` which are composed of `InPatterns` and `Outpatterns`. An `InPattern` is further composed of `InputElements` and an optional `Guard`. The `OutPattern` is composed of one or more `OutputElements` which have optional `bindings`. It is worth noting that the actual bindings, guards as well as the input and output patterns are expressed as strings in the current version, but are planned to be replaced by including an OCL metamodel, e.g., as done in [18].

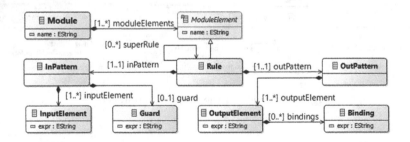

Fig. 5. The Simple Transformation Language (STL) metamodel

As previously said, the variability weaving metamodel relies on the simplified transformation metamodel to deal with all kind of transformation language specificities. Thus, by applying the approach presented in [3], for each metaclass *MC* in the simplified transformation metamodel, corresponding *AddedMC*, *DeletedMC*, and *ChangedMC* metaclasses, e.g., `AddedRule`, are defined in WMM as shown in Fig. 6. WMM permits to represent `Solutions` that are considered as the counterpart for the applied metamodel changes. As shown in Fig. 6, each `Solution` is composed of `Alternatives`, which are disjunct and represent migrations which have to be performed to co-evolve the affected transformation.

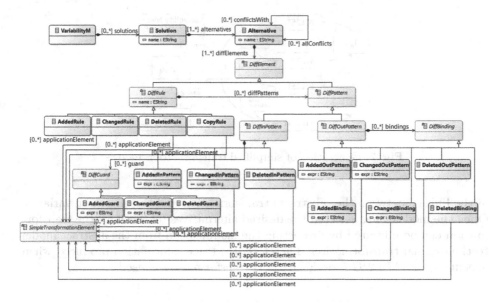

Fig. 6. The Variability Weaving Metamodel (WMM)

Each Alternative consists of DiffElements. A DiffElement can be in turn a DiffRule or a DiffPattern, i.e., the changes that a rule can undergo or that affect a pattern of a rule, respectively. AddedRule, ChangedRule and DeletedRule are provided for added, updated or deleted rules, while CopyRule allows the rule to be copied without actions, which might be a valid choice for some refactorings, e.g., introduction of superclasses. The same concept is replicated for other transformation constructs like patterns that are composed of bindings containing an OCL expression, to be held in the attribute expr. Finally, input patterns can have guards to match only certain input patterns, and also in this case is done using an expression. The references applicationElement from DiffElement link to the abstract class SimpleTransformationElement, which can be specialized for each concept shown in Fig. 5 in order to refer concrete elements of the transformation to be migrated.

An important characteristics of WMM is the specification of *conflicts*, i.e., disjunct choices that must not occur in the same solution. For instance, a migration solution can not contain choices that contribute to the generation of different rules defined on the same input pattern without any guard, thus causing runtime errors due to multiple rules matching the same model element. As another example, a migration solution must not contain choices that refer to an element which has been deleted by another alternative.

As previously mentioned, WMM can be used for managing model transformations specified in different rule-based transformation languages. Thus, a transformation written in a language, such as ATL or ETL [15], can be mapped into its simplified version as shown in Fig. 7. This enables a simpler specification

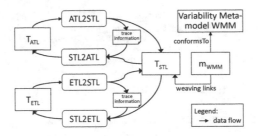

Fig. 7. Generation of simplified transformation models

of the linkage between the (abstract) transformation and the migration variants. Once the modeler has selected the desired alternatives (cf. Sect. 4), the transformation can be migrated by projecting the modification from the abstract model to the original transformation. Therefore, the trace information produced when executing the $ATL2STL$ or $ETL2STL$ transformation is used.

3.2 Specification of Variability Weaving Models

Figure 8 presents a variability model conforming to the WMM and related to the running example. The weavings have been labeled with the same numbers as in Fig. 4, so the left panel is the simplified version of the transformation in Listing 1.1, and the right panel is the associated variability model containing all migration alternatives listed in Table 1.

Please note that the graphical overlay by means of dashed and dotted lines is for presentation purposes only and not visualized in this way in the tool, instead we provide a feature model as graphical decision support which is a common and widely used mean to manage variability in software product lines [2] (cf. Sect. 4). The weaving links have been highlighted as dashed (green) lines, while the link shown as dotted (red) line identifies a conflict in the solutions. The weaving link denoted by the left (green) tooltip maps the `OutPattern` from the simplified transformation model to a `ChangedOutPattern` in the `Alternative R4a1` as part of the `Solution R4`. It comprises a `DeletedBinding` element, which is in turn linked to the affected binding in the simplified transformation model in rule `Person2-Participant`. The corresponding action in Table 1 is denoted by $R4a1$.

Furthermore, a conflict between `Alternative R4a2` and `R5a2` has been identified, using the proposed conflict detection algorithm (cf. Sect. 3.4). In fact, having both alternatives in the solution model would give place to an invalid transformation with two rules matching the same input metaclass, which is forbidden since the input pattern has to be unique. Possible conflicts that can occur when migrating transformations are discussed in Sect. 3.4.

In the following, we show how a feature-based representation of the migration alternatives, as those represented in Fig. 8, can be automatically generated and how it is beneficial in the variability management.

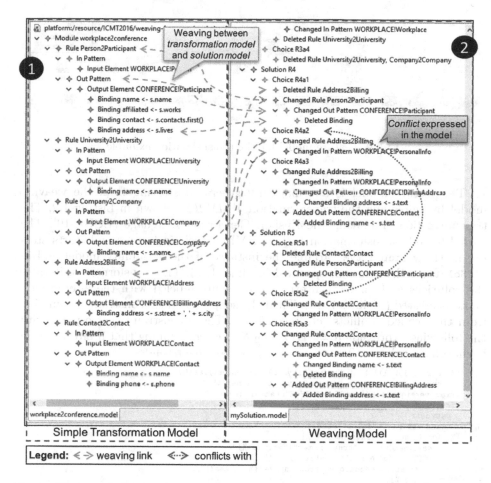

Fig. 8. Excerpt of the variability model for the transformation example (Color figure online)

3.3 Feature Model as Representation for Managing Variability

Figure 9 shows a generated feature model[3] specifying the alternatives for migrating the transformation to cope with the source metamodel evolution. In the context of this paper, the feature model is a compact representation of all migration alternatives and possible conflicts between them, supporting the exploration of the desired migration alternatives.

As shown in Table 1, we consider five refactorings R1–R5 that entail five solutions, each of those has possible alternatives for migration that satisfy the domain conformance relationship. Also, the automatically identified conflict between the alternatives is reflected by means of a constraint in the feature model. Thus, the constraint $R4a2 \Rightarrow \neg R5a2$ defines that if alternative $R4a2$ is chosen, the alternative $R5a2$ is no longer valid and can not be chosen by the modeler.

---

[3] In this work we employed the Eclipse FeatureIDE plugin [22] for specifying feature models.

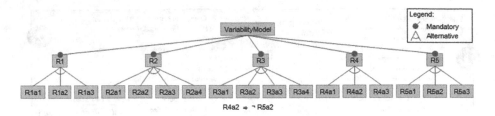

Fig. 9. Feature model for the transformation example

The feature model is automatically generated starting from the weaving model by employing the transformation *WMM2FM* shown in Listing 1.2. The transformation employing the Epsilon Generation Language (EGL) [19]. The model-to-code transformation targets XML as technical space and starts storing in the `variabilityM` variable the instance of the variability model and in `allSolutions` the solutions specified (cf. lines 1, 2). The transformation iterates the solutions and for each alternative a feature labeled with the alternative's name is created (cf. lines 7–13). Then the script generates constraints stemming from the defined conflicts (cf. lines 17–30). Those constraints correspond with the following expression $a \Rightarrow \neg a_1 \wedge \neg a_2 \wedge \ldots \wedge \neg a_n$ defining that if alternative a is chosen, the alternatives $a_1, a_2, \ldots a_n$ are no longer valid.

```
1   [% var variabilityM := VariabilityM.allInstances().at(0);
2       var allSolutions := variabilityM.solutions; %]
3   <?xml version="1.0"encoding="UTF-8"standalone="no"?>
4   <featureModel chosenLayoutAlgorithm="1">
5     <struct>
6     <and abstract="false" mandatory="true" name="VariabilityModel">
7   [% for (s in allSolutions ) { %]
8         <alt mandatory="true" name="[%=s.name%]">
9         [% for (a in s.alternatives) { %]
10         <feature mandatory="true" name="[%=a.name%]"/>
11         [% } %]
12       </alt>
13   [%  }    %]
14     </and>
15    </struct>
16    <constraints>
17   [% for (s in allSolutions) {
18          for (a in s.alternatives) {
19            if (a.allConflicts.size() > 0) { %]
20            <rule>
21            <imp>
22              <var>[%=a.name%]</var>
23              <conj>
24                [% for (conflict in a.allConflicts) { %]
25                  <not><var>[%=conflict.name%]</var></not>
26                [% } %]
27              </conj>
28            </imp>
29            </rule>
30   [%  } } }    %]
31    </constraints>
32    ...
33   </featureModel>
```

Listing 1.2. Fragment of the *WMM2FM* transformation

3.4 Automated Identification of Conflicting Alternatives

In order to further automate the presented approach, we propose an algorithm that automatically identifies conflicts between alternative solutions and sets the corresponding conflict relations in the variability model (cf. Fig. 8). A conflict can be defined as a situation where two different alternatives can not co-exist, since they could raise errors at run-time. The algorithm shown in Algorithm 1 is able to identify the following conflicts, however, the algorithm can be extended or changed if needed, to account for language-specific conflict detections[4]:

(c1) Rules are missing guards avoiding multiple matches for a same model element;

(c2) A rule that has been deleted in one alternative is used in another alternative;

(c3) A binding that has been deleted in one alternative is used in another alternative.

Algorithm 1. Detection of Conflicting Alternatives

```
 1: for all solutions s in model do
 2:     for all alternatives a in s do
 3:         for all rules r in a do
 4:             doubleMatch ← HASDOUBLEMATCH(m, r)
 5:             if doubleMatch <> null then
 6:                 ADDCONFLICT(a, doubleMatch)
 7:             end if
 8:             deletedRule ← ISRULEDELETED(r)
 9:             if deletedRule <> null then
10:                 ADDCONFLICT(a, deletedRule)
11:             end if
12:             for all bindings b in rule r do
13:                 deletedBinding ← ISBINDINGDELETED(b, r)
14:                 if deletedBinding <> null then
15:                     ADDCONFLICT(a, deletedBinding)
16:                 end if
17:             end for
18:         end for
19:     end for
20: end for
```

In particular, all the solutions in the input solution model are queried, and all their alternatives and rules are iterated to check if two rules can potentially match a same model element. Since in ATL this must not occur, it has to be ensured that rules violating such a constraint are marked as conflict. In line 4 of Algorithm 1 it is therefore checked if the current metamodel element is matched by any

---

[4] The auxiliary functions HASDOUBLEMATCH, ISRULEDELETED, ISBINDINGDELETED, and ADDCONFLICT used in Algorithm 1 are reported online: http://www.emfmigrate.org/wp-content/uploads/2017/04/appendix.pdf.

other rule, by calling the auxiliary function HASDOUBLEMATCH. If a double match is detected, then a conflict is added in the model by means of the ADDCONFLICT auxiliary function (cf. line 6). Analogously, in case elements are accessed in one alternative, but deleted in another one a conflict has to be declared. To this end, in line 8 and line 13 the auxiliary functions ISRULEDELETED and ISBINDINGDELETED are executed, respectively and depending on their outcomes the ADDCONFLICT function is executed accordingly.

4   Configuration and Execution of the Feature Model

In order to enable the execution of the migration solution obtained by selecting the alternatives in the considered feature model, we exploit the EMFMigrate migration platform[5]. EMFMigrate provides modelers with languages and tools supporting the coupled evolution of any kind of modeling artifacts. An EMFMigrate specification consists of migration rules as shown in Fig. 10. In particular, a migration program, usually specified by the modeler, is able to migrate artifact A, conforming to the metamodel MM, according to the metamodel differences represented in the model $Delta$, conforming to the difference metamodel proposed in [3] already applied to other co-evolution cases (e.g., [4]).

A migration program consists of a sequence of migration rules mr_i. Each rule is applied on artifact A if the corresponding $guard_i$ evaluated on the difference model $Delta$ holds. The body of a migration rule consists of a sequence of rewriting rules like the following

$$s[guard] \rightarrow t_1[assign_1]; t_2[assign_2]; \ldots t_n[assign_n]$$

where $s, t_1, \ldots, t_n$ refer to metaclasses of MM, and $guard$ is a boolean expression which has to be $true$ in order to rewrite s with t_1, t_2, and t_n. It is possible to specify the values of the target term properties by means of assignment operations (see $assign_i$).

Figure 11a shows the building of migration solution by selecting migration alternatives represented by means of a feature model as discussed in the previous section. The desired options for migration are selected and shown as green crosses. For each selected migration alternative corresponding EMFMigrate migration rules are generated, that can be then executed on the input transformation in order to obtain the migrated one. As one might see, the option $R5a2$ is already grayed out by the tool, since this option is in conflict with the selected one $R4a2$, thus, not available anylonger. Figure 11b shows the generation of the selected migration alternatives and a fragment of the generated EMFMigrate code is shown in Listing 1.3. The shown code is related to the management of the metamodel refactoring $R1$ by means of the selected alternative $R1a2$ (cf. Table 1). Lines 5–17 represent the guard of the rule and thus the

---

[5] A detailed discussion of EMFMigrate is outside the scope of this paper. Interested reader can refer to [6,23] for a detailed presentation of the approach.

migration *migrationName*
include {*library**}
migrate $A : MM$ **with** *Delta* {
  rule mr_1
    [*guard*$_1$] {*rewritingRule** }
  rule mr_2
    [*guard*$_2$] { *rewritingRule** }
  ...

  rule mr_n
    [*guard*$_n$] { *rewritingRule** }
}

Fig. 10. EMFMigrate syntax

metamodel changes that have to match in order to execute the migration specification in line 21. The reported guard corresponds to the metamodel refactoring *R1* involving the metaclasses **Person**, **Employee**, and **Researcher**. The application of the migration in line 21 induces the adaptation of the affected transformation by changing the input patterns typed **Person**, which are all replaced with the class **Employee**.

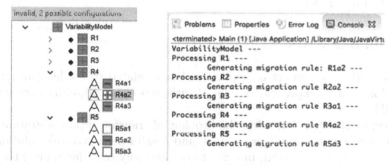

a) Selection of migration alternatives   b) Log of EMFMigrate code generation

Fig. 11. Generation of migration solution code

```
1   migration Workplace2ConferenceManagement-Transformation;
2   migrate SimpleWorkplace2ConferenceManagement.atl : ATL
3     with WorkplaceMMO-WorkPlaceMM2.delta{
4     ...
5     rule migrationR1a2[
6       class person= changeClass(oldperson: class){
7         set abstract=true;
8         ...
9       }
10      class employee=addClass("Employee"){
11        set name="Employee";
12        set eSuperType=person;
13      }
```

```
14        class researcher=addClass("Researcher"){
15          set name="Researcher";
16          set eSuperType=person;
17        }
18      ]
19      {
20        -- input patterns and helper contexts will be assigned to the R1a2 choice
21        o1: OclModelElement where [name = oldperson.name] -> o2: OclModelElement [ name =
              employee.name ]
22      }
23      ...
24      }
```

Listing 1.3. Fragment of the generated EMFMigrate code

With the help of this approach and by taking potential conflicts into account, the number of valid migration alternatives is significantly reduced, resulting in

$$3 \times 4 \times 3 \times 2 \times 2 = 144$$

migration alternatives for the refactoring presented in Table 1, which are significantly less than those that can be obtained without the proposed approach. Furthermore, migration alternatives are reduced even more once some of them are selected, as shown in Fig. 11, thus, helping the user in finding the most appropriate solution. Moreover, the generated EMFMigrate code consists only of those migration rules related to the alternatives that are selected by means of the feature model.

5   Related Work

In this section, we report on work (i) closely related to model transformation migration, and (ii) more widely related with respect to variability in co-evolution in MDE.

Recent approaches tackling the problem of transformation migration mostly aim at providing a unique, predefined, and possible over-writable solution, thus, variability is not supported, but has to be manually considered after the migration, entailing the drawback that generated solutions have to be modified by hand, regardless if the solution has been generated by means of a higher-order transformation [10], predefined migration actions [12,16], or mapping operators [25]. In [9] the authors propose the usage of transformation chains, which are chosen by the user, thus, different solutions can be generated, but having the drawback that the modeler has to be familiar with transformation chains. In [17] a comprehensive set of metamodel changes is proposed, each accompanied with a migration action for models and transformations. Since for the same metamodel evolution, different semantic changes entailing different migration solutions are proposed, variability is slightly considered in the sense, that the evolution designer can incorporate the intention of the evolution when applying the changes. However, support for exploration of different options for migration is not provided, i.e., an intensional representation is not provided.

As a more widely related work, in [21] an approach for the generation of multiple, ranked solutions for model migration (in contrast to transformation migration as proposed in this paper) is presented. Based on the formalization of the conformance relationship, the authors employ logic programming to generate a set of ranked solutions for model migration. However, to the best of our knowledge, an approach supporting variability in the context of transformation migration has not been proposed yet. As a result, one may see that the presented approach is unique in the respect that alternative solutions can be explored and selected by having a suitable representation in terms of a feature model easing the burden of exploring and selecting the ultimately desired solution.

6 Conclusion and Future Work

In this paper, we proposed an approach for exploring and resolving variability during model transformation migration, which is inevitable as a response to metamodel evolution. The approach builds upon an *intensional* representation to explore variability by representing each migration alternative as a dedicated element in a weaving model. Furthermore, potentially arising conflicts between solutions that are not compatible to each other can be explicitly highlighted. In order to support the user not only in exploring but also in resolving variability, a suitable representation in terms of a feature model has been proposed, which is automatically generated from the weaving model. Additionally, EMFMigrate migration actions have been attached to the migration alternatives, which allow for a (semi-)automatic co-evolution of transformations. Besides the possibility of representing alternatives in a compact way, the method provides means for detecting variations among the different solutions. Detection that otherwise should be performed by manually comparing models, which are greatly overlapping one with another.

There are several lines of future work. As already mentioned, we plan on automating the generation of the weaving model, starting form our previous work on generating multiple solutions for model co-evolution [21] in order to create the intensional representation of multiple migration alternatives. Furthermore, we plan on an evaluation in terms of a user study to identify and highlight the major benefits and possible drawbacks of the proposed approach especially from a usability point of view.

Acknowledgment. This work has been partly funded by the Austrian Science Fund (FWF) under grant P 28519-N31 and the OeAD under grant WTZ AR18/2013 and WTZ AR10/2015.

References

1. Bancilhon, F., Spyratos, N.: Update semantics of relational views. ACM Trans. Database Syst. (TODS) **6**(4), 557–575 (1981)
2. Beuche, D., Papajewski, H., Schröder-Preikschat, W.: Variability management with feature models. Sci. Comput. Program. **53**(3), 333–352 (2004)

3. Cicchetti, A., Di Ruscio, D., Pierantonio, A.: A metamodel independent approach to difference representation. J. Object Technol. **6**(9), 165–185 (2007)
4. Cicchetti, A., Ruscio, D., Pierantonio, A.: Managing model conflicts in distributed development. In: Czarnecki, K., Ober, I., Bruel, J.-M., Uhl, A., Völter, M. (eds.) MODELS 2008. LNCS, vol. 5301, pp. 311–325. Springer, Heidelberg (2008). doi:10. 1007/978-3-540-87875-9_23
5. Cicchetti, A., Ruscio, D.D., Eramo, R., Pierantonio, A.: Automating co-evolution in model-driven engineering. In: Proceedings of EDOC, pp. 222–231. IEEE (2008)
6. Di Ruscio, D., Iovino, L., Pierantonio, A.: Coupled evolution in model-driven engineering. IEEE Softw. **29**(6), 78–84 (2012)
7. Di Ruscio, D., Iovino, L., Pierantonio, A.: Evolutionary togetherness: how to manage coupled evolution in metamodeling ecosystems. In: Ehrig, H., Engels, G., Kreowski, H.-J., Rozenberg, G. (eds.) ICGT 2012. LNCS, vol. 7562, pp. 20–37. Springer, Heidelberg (2012). doi:10.1007/978-3-642-33654-6_2
8. Di Ruscio, D., Iovino, L., Pierantonio, A.: A methodological approach for the coupled evolution of metamodels and ATL transformations. In: Duddy, K., Kappel, G. (eds.) ICMT 2013. LNCS, vol. 7909, pp. 60–75. Springer, Heidelberg (2013). doi:10.1007/978-3-642-38883-5_9
9. Garcés, K., Vara, J.M., Jouault, F., Marcos, E.: Adapting transformations to metamodel changes via external transformation composition. Softw. Syst. Model. **13**, 789–806 (2013)
10. García, J., Diaz, O., Azanza, M.: Model transformation co-evolution: a semiautomatic approach. In: Czarnecki, K., Hedin, G. (eds.) SLE 2012. LNCS, vol. 7745, pp. 144–163. Springer, Heidelberg (2013). doi:10.1007/978-3-642-36089-3_9
11. Guerra, E., de Lara, J., Kolovos, D.S., Paige, R.F., dos Santos, O.M.: Engineering model transformations with transml. Softw. Syst. Model. **12**(3), 555–577 (2013)
12. Herrmannsdoerfer, M., Benz, S., Juergens, E.: COPE - automating coupled evolution of metamodels and models. In: Drossopoulou, S. (ed.) ECOOP 2009. LNCS, vol. 5653, pp. 52–76. Springer, Heidelberg (2009). doi:10.1007/978-3-642-03013-0_4
13. Iovino, L., Pierantonio, A., Malavolta, I.: On the impact significance of metamodel evolution in MDE. JOT **11**(3), 3:1–3:33 (2012)
14. Jouault, F., Allilaire, F., Bézivin, J., Kurtev, I.: ATL: a model transformation tool. Sci. Comput. Program. **72**(1–2), 31–39 (2008)
15. Kolovos, D.S., Paige, R.F., Polack, F.A.C.: The epsilon transformation language. In: Vallecillo, A., Gray, J., Pierantonio, A. (eds.) ICMT 2008. LNCS, vol. 5063, pp. 46–60. Springer, Heidelberg (2008). doi:10.1007/978-3-540-69927-9_4
16. Kruse, S.: On the use of operators for the co-evolution of metamodels and transformations. In: International Workshop on Models and Evolution 2011 (2011)
17. Kusel, A., Etzlstorfer, J., Kapsammer, E., Retschitzegger, W., Schwinger, W., Schönböck, J.: Consistent co-evolution of models and transformations. In: MODELS. IEEE, October 2015
18. Richters, M., Gogolla, M.: A metamodel for OCL. In: France, R., Rumpe, B. (eds.) UML 1999. LNCS, vol. 1723, pp. 156–171. Springer, Heidelberg (1999). doi:10. 1007/3-540-46852-8_12
19. Rose, L.M., Paige, R.F., Kolovos, D.S., Polack, F.A.C.: The epsilon generation language. In: Schieferdecker, I., Hartman, A. (eds.) ECMDA-FA 2008. LNCS, vol. 5095, pp. 1–16. Springer, Heidelberg (2008). doi:10.1007/978-3-540-69100-6_1
20. Schmidt, D.C.: Guest editor's introduction: model-driven engineering. Computer **39**(2), 25–31 (2006)

21. Schönböck, J., Kusel, A., Etzlstorfer, J., Kapsammer, E., Schwinger, W., Wimmer, M., Wischenbart, M.: CARE - a constraint-based approach for re-establishing conformance-relationships. In: Proceedings of the APCCM (2014)
22. Thüm, T., Kästner, C., Benduhn, F., Meinicke, J., Saake, G., Leich, T.: FeatureIDE: an extensible framework for feature-oriented software development. Sci. Comput. Program. **79**, 70–85 (2014)
23. Wagelaar, D., Iovino, L., Ruscio, D., Pierantonio, A.: Translational semantics of a co-evolution specific language with the EMF transformation virtual machine. In: Hu, Z., Lara, J. (eds.) ICMT 2012. LNCS, vol. 7307, pp. 192–207. Springer, Heidelberg (2012). doi:10.1007/978-3-642-30476-7_13
24. Wimmer, M., Kappel, G., Kusel, A., Retschitzegger, W., Schönböck, J., Schwinger, W., Kolovos, D., Paige, R., Lauder, M., Schürr, A., Wagelaar, D.: Surveying rule inheritance in model-to-model transformation languages. JOT **11**(2), 3:1–3:46 (2012)
25. Wimmer, M., Kappel, G., Kusel, A., Retschitzegger, W., Schoenboeck, J., Schwinger, W.: Surviving the heterogeneity jungle with composite mapping operators. In: Tratt, L., Gogolla, M. (eds.) ICMT 2010. LNCS, vol. 6142, pp. 260–275. Springer, Heidelberg (2010). doi:10.1007/978-3-642-13688-7_18

On the Influence of Models at Run-Time Traces in Dynamic Feature Location

Lorena Arcega[1,2(✉)], Jaime Font[1,2], Øystein Haugen[3], and Carlos Cetina[1]

[1] SVIT Research Group, Universidad San Jorge, Zaragoza, Spain
{larcega,jfont,ccetina}@usj.es
[2] Department of Informatics, University of Oslo, Oslo, Norway
[3] Department of Information Technology, Østfold University College,
Halden, Norway
oystein.haugen@hiof.no

Abstract. Feature Location is one of the most important and common activities performed by developers during software maintenance and evolution. In prior work, we show that Dynamic Feature Location obtains better results working with models rather than source code. In this work, we analyze how the criteria to create the model traces influence the Dynamic Feature Location results. We distinguish between two different criteria: configuration and architecture. Our Dynamic Feature Location approach is composed of dynamic analysis, information retrieval at the model trace level, and information retrieval at the model level. The evaluation in a Smart Hotel tests whether the traces created following the two criteria modify the results of the Feature Location by measuring recall, precision, and the combination of both (F-measure). The results reveal that in 75% of the cases the traces that follow the architecture criterion outperform the traces that follow the configuration criterion.

Keywords: Models at run-time · Feature location · Reverse engineering

1 Introduction

Software maintenance often involves tedious, time-consuming activities. Lehman et al. [15] pointed out that up to 80% of the lifetime of a system is spent on maintenance and evolution activities. Software maintainers spend from 50% to almost 90% of their time trying to understand a program to make changes correctly. To understand the underlying intents of an unfamiliar system, maintainers look for clues in both the code and the documentation [2].

Feature Location is one of the most important and common activities performed by developers during software maintenance and evolution [8]. Currently, research efforts in Feature Location are concerned with identifying software artifacts that are associated with a program functionality (a feature). In Feature Location approaches, it is common to focus on analyzing source code.

In prior work [3] we show that, for systems based on models at run-time, better results were obtained in Dynamic Feature Location if we analyzed the

© Springer International Publishing AG 2017
A. Anjorin and H. Espinoza (Eds.): ECMFA 2017, LNCS 10376, pp. 90–105, 2017.
DOI: 10.1007/978-3-319-61482-3_6

run-time model instead of the source code. Through this work, our goal is to analyze how the criteria to form the model trace influence the Dynamic Feature Location results. We are interested in two criteria to decide when a snapshot of the run-time model should be added to the trace: (1) configuration criterion, that adds a snapshot of the run-time model to the trace when the model corresponds to a target configuration of the system in a reconfiguration, and (2) architecture criterion that adds a snapshot of the run-time model to the trace each time a change in the run-time model is performed.

Our Dynamic Feature Location approach is composed of dynamic analysis, information retrieval at the model trace level, and information retrieval at the model level. As a result, our approach generates a ranking with the most relevant model elements for the feature to be located. We implemented the second and third steps using a method named Latent Semantic Indexing (LSI), the method that provides better results [16,20,21]. LSI allows software engineers to write queries that are relevant to the feature they want to locate. As a result, the software engineers obtain a ranked list of model elements from the model, which are intended to identify the parts of the model that are significant for the target feature.

We have applied our approach to a Smart Hotel to assess its performance. The case study presents 476 model elements in the architecture model. The evaluation tests how the traces created following the two criteria influence the results of the Feature Location by measuring recall, precision, and the combination of both (F-measure). These are the most common measures for the experiments with information retrieval methods [17,23]. The recall, precision, and F-measure values reveal that the traces that follow the architecture criterion obtain better results than the traces that follow the configuration criterion in 75% of the cases.

The remainder of the paper is structured as follows. In Sect. 2, we present the Smart Hotel and the model traces. In Sect. 3, we describe our approach for Dynamic Feature Location with models. In Sect. 4, we evaluate our approach in the Smart Hotel and we discuss the results. In Sect. 5, we examine the related work of the area. Finally, we present our conclusions in Sect. 6.

2 Background

The running example and the evaluation of this paper are performed through a Smart Hotel [7]. In this section we present the reconfigurations of the Smart Hotel that are performed in response to changes in the context. For instance, a change in the context could be determined by assessing if there is a client in the room or not, or focusing on what activities the client may be performing (sleeping, watching TV, etc.). In addition, this section shows the model traces in which our approach records the execution information.

2.1 Behavior of the Smart Hotel at Run-Time

The Smart Hotel reconfiguration engine determines how the system should be reconfigured in response to a context change, and then it modifies the architecture model accordingly. In models at run-time, a causal connection between the system and the run-time model is defined (there is a bidirectional relation between the source code and the run-time model). This connection allows the models (usually the architecture model) to reflect the software state. This connection can be achieved in different ways, however, the most used implementation is the MAPE-K loop [6,13]. For more details about the reconfiguration engine of the Smart Hotel see [7].

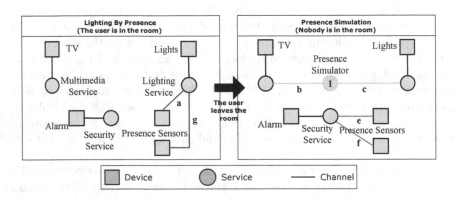

Fig. 1. Smart hotel model reconfigurations

Figure 1 shows two Smart Hotel configurations according to the concrete syntax of the architecture model of PervML [19]. Figure 1 (left) shows a *User in the room* configuration, while Fig. 1 (right) shows a *Nobody in the room* configuration. It can be observed that movement sensors are used for different purposes: lighting (left), and providing information to the security service (right). In addition, the Occupancy simulation service is activated in the *Nobody in the room* configuration, and the connections that are required for this service to communicate with multimedia, lighting, and security services are established.

2.2   Model Execution Traces

In our approach, the execution information is recorded by a model trace of snapshots at run-time. Each execution trace is related to a set of snapshots of the run-time model. In this paper we are interested in two criteria to decide when a snapshot of the run-time model should be added to the trace: (1) configuration criterion, and (2) architecture criterion.

In the configuration criterion, the snapshots are added to the trace when the run-time model corresponds to a target configuration of the system in a reconfiguration. That is, a snapshot is added when the system completes the changes from one configuration to another. In the architecture criterion, the snapshots are added to the trace when a change in the run-time model is performed. That is, a snapshot is added each time a component of the run-time model is deleted

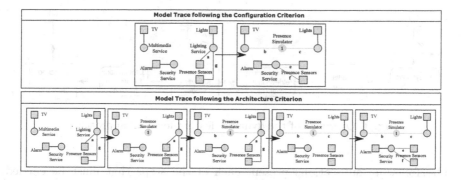

Fig. 2. Different model traces following the different criterion

or created even if the model does not correspond to a target configuration of the system.

Figure 2 shows two different traces for the same reconfiguration (the reconfiguration showed in Fig. 1). The upper part shows a trace composed by the configuration criterion. The first snapshot shows the system when there is a user in the room, and the second snapshot shows the system when the user leaves the room and the corresponding reconfiguration is completed. The bottom part shows a trace composed by the architecture criterion. The first snapshot and the last one are the same, as in the upper part of the figure. However, the rest of the snapshots give more detail on what actions were carried out in the reconfiguration from the first snapshot to the fifth one. For instance, in the second snapshot, the *Presence Simulator* appears; in the third snapshot, the channels that connect the *Presence Simulator* with the *Multimedia Service* and the *Lighting Service* emerge; in the fourth snapshot, the channels that connect the *Lighting Service* with the *Presence Sensors* are deleted; and, finally, in the fifth snapshot, the channels that connect the *Security Service* with the *Presence Sensors* come into sight.

3 Model Based Dynamic Feature Location Approach

Figure 3 shows an overview of our model based Dynamic Feature Location approach. It is composed of three steps: dynamic analysis, information retrieval in the model trace, and information retrieval in a model from the model trace. In the first step, the software engineer executes a scenario, which involves the desired feature to be located. The execution information is recorded by a model trace of snapshots at run-time. Then, the model trace is used as input for the second step of our Dynamic Feature Location. Using information retrieval, the most relevant model for the desired feature is selected from the model trace. This model is used as input for the third step of our approach, which performs information retrieval at the model element level. As a result, the software engineers obtain a ranked list of model elements from the model, intended to identify the parts of the model that are significant for the target feature.

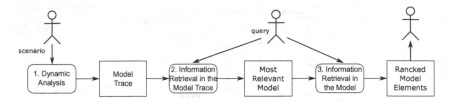

Fig. 3. Overview of the dynamic feature location approach

The following subsections present each of the steps that must be carried out in order to perform the Feature Location at the model level, following our approach. We use the Smart Hotel presented in Sect. 2 throughout the different subsections to illustrate the details with a running example.

3.1 Dynamic Analysis

Execution information is gathered via dynamic analysis, which is commonly used in program comprehension and involves executing a software system under specific conditions. Executing the target feature during run-time generates a feature-specific execution trace. In other words, the input for the execution is a scenario that runs the target feature.

The model trace generated in this step only includes the models that have been executed in the feature-specific scenario. This model trace is the main artifact that our approach uses to locate the target feature.

As an example, we depict a scenario where we want to fix a bug in the gradual light of the Smart Hotel. We follow the information from the bug report to define the scenario that executes the target feature. In this case, a simplified version (due to space constraints) of the scenario is as follows:

'*The software engineer simulates an empty Smart Hotel room. The lights are off. The software engineer simulates that a client enters the room. The lights gradually turn on. The software engineer simulates that the client leaves the room, and then the lights gradually turn off.*'

Our approach implies that the software engineer input is needed and of course, results are sensitive to that input. The software engineer has to decide on a scenario that will run the desired feature.

3.2 Information Retrieval in the Model Trace

In this step we use the model trace extracted in the previous step. In addition, the software engineer has to formulate a query related to the feature that must be located. The model trace and the query can be leveraged to locate the most relevant model for the feature through the use of Information Retrieval (IR). IR works by comparing a set of artifacts to a query, and ranking these artifacts by their relevance to the query.

Typically, the query can come from textual documentation of the products, comments in the code, bug reports or oral descriptions from the engineers. Therefore, the query will include some domain specific terms similar to those used when specifying the models. The knowledge of the engineers about the domain and the models will be useful to select the query from the available sources.

There are many IR techniques that have been applied for feature location tasks. Most of the feature location research efforts show better results when applying Latent Semantic Indexing (LSI) [16,21]. In addition, combining LSI with dynamic analysis improves its effectiveness [20].

In our previous work [3] we adapted LSI, which was traditionally used in code, in order to apply it to models. Summarizing, the text from the models is extracted and a text corpus is created, where each document corresponds to a model or to a subset of model elements of the model. The text corpus is used to create a term-by-document co-occurrence matrix. As LSI does not use a predefined grammar or vocabulary it is very robust regarding outlandish identifier names and stop words. Users can produce queries in natural language and the system returns a list of all the documents in the system, ranked by their semantic similarity to the query.

Models

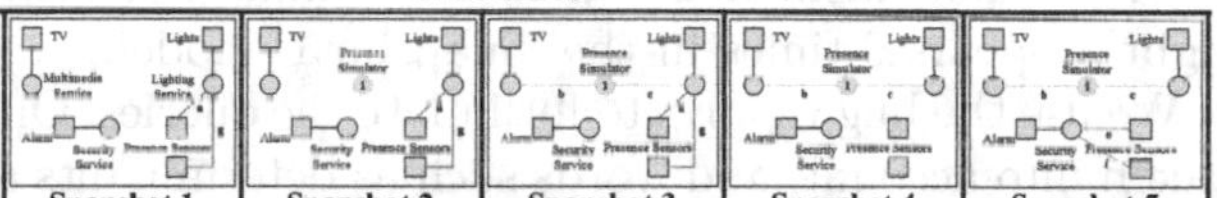

	Snapshot 1	Snapshot 2	Snapshot 3	Snapshot 4	Snapshot 5	Query
room	1	2	0	1	2	1
automated	2	1	0	0	4	0
light	6	5	7	0	0	2
presence	4	2	0	0	1	6
intensity	0	2	1	1	0	1
...	...	...	...	...	...	...
security	1	0	0	1	4	0

Terms

Fig. 4. Information retrieval via latent semantic indexing (LSI)

We adapt each step of the LSI technique to work with the model trace. The adaptation is performed as follows:

- **Creating a corpus:** Each document corresponds to a model of the model trace extracted in the dynamic analysis. Each document (model) includes text from the names of the model elements and the names of the attributes and methods of the model elements that compose that model.

- **Preprocessing:** The type of the attributes and the type of the parameters in the methods are removed. Then, all the identifiers are split. For example, 'IlluminationService' becomes 'illumination' and 'service'. To do this, we apply Natural Language Processing (NLP) techniques, such as tokenizing, Parts-of-Speech (POS) tagging techniques, and stemming techniques [1,12], however, the details of the application of these techniques are out of the scope of this paper.
- **Indexing:** In the term-by-document co-occurrence matrix, the terms (rows) correspond to the names of the model elements and the names of the attributes or methods of the model, and the documents (columns) correspond to the models that have appeared in the model trace. Figure 4 shows the term-by-document co-occurrence matrix, with the values associated to our running example.

  Each row in the matrix stands for each one of the unique words (terms) extracted from our models. Figure 4 shows a set of representative keywords in the domain such as 'room', 'light', or 'presence' as the terms of each row.

  Each column in the matrix stands for the models of the model trace. Figure 4 shows the models of the trace in each column, such as 'Snapshot1', which represents the first model of the model trace.

  Each cell in the matrix contains the frequency with which the keyword of its row appears in the document denoted by its column. For instance, in Fig. 4, the term 'light' appears 6 times in the 'Snapshot1' model.
- **Querying:** We use the bug reports to formulate the queries. Only the relevant terms are taken into account, and words such as determinants and connectors from the language are omitted.

  In Fig. 4, the query column represents the words that appear in the bug report. Each cell contains the frequency with which the keyword of its row appears in the query. For instance, the term 'presence' appears 6 times in the query.
- **Generating results:** In our approach, each document and the query are translated into vectors. The cosine of the angle between the query vector and a document vector is used as a measure of the similarity of the document to the query. The closer the cosine is to one, the more similar the document is to the query. A cosine similarity value is calculated between the query and each document, and then the documents are sorted according to their similarity values. The user inspects the ranked list to decide which of the documents are relevant to the feature.

  We obtain vector representations of the *documents* and the *query* by normalizing and decomposing the *term-by-document co-occurrence matrix* using a matrix factorization technique called *Singular Value Decomposition* (SVD) [14]. SVD is a form of factor analysis, or, more properly, the mathematical generalization of which factor analysis is a special case. In SVD, a rectangular matrix is decomposed into the product of three other matrices. One component matrix describes the original row entities as vectors of derived orthogonal factor values, another describes the original column entities in the same way, and the third is a diagonal matrix containing scaling values such that when the three components are matrix-multiplied, the original matrix is reconstructed.

In this step of our approach, we only take into account the model that presents the best similarity measure. We consider it as the most relevant model for the feature to be located, and as such, it is used as input for the next step.

3.3 Information Retrieval in the Model

In this step we apply LSI at the model element level, considering that each model element is a document. We apply it to the model obtained in the previous step. This model is the most relevant model for the desired feature. However, we want to locate the most relevant model elements for the desired feature. The result of this step is a ranked list of model elements of the model, which are intended to identify the parts of the model that are significant for the target feature.

To that extent, we adapted LSI to work with a model. The main differences from the previous adaptation are the following:

– The input is one model. As such, the terms are extracted taking into account only one model.
– The granularity of the corpus changes. In the corpus creation, each document corresponds to a model element of the most relevant model extracted before.

For generating the results, we apply the same technique as in the previous step (SVD). However, the result in which we are interested is different. In this step of our approach, of all the model elements, only those model elements that have a similarity measure greater than x must be taken into account to measure the quality of the results. A good heuristic that is widely used is $x = 0.7$. This value corresponds to a $45°$ angle between the corresponding vectors. This threshold has yielded good results in other similar works [17,22]. Determining a more generally usable heuristic for the selection of the appropriate threshold is an issue under study, over which further research is needed.

The goal of our approach is to rank the relevant model elements within the top positions. The ranking of model elements is ordered by the values of the cosines.

4 Evaluation: Feature Location in the Smart Hotel

We evaluate how the architecture changes recorded with the snapshots in the model trace influence the results of Feature Location. In other words, we want to evaluate whether all the changes produced in the architecture model when a system reconfiguration is necessary are relevant for feature location. In order to do this, we compare the presented model based Dynamic Feature Location approach using traces following the architecture criterion (DFL-AT), against the same approach using traces following the configuration criterion (DFL-CT).

The quality of the results of Information Retrieval techniques is measured by their recall and precision. These are two of the most common measures for experiments with information retrieval methods [17,23]. For a given query, recall is the percentage of retrieved documents that are relevant to the total number of relevant documents, while precision is the percentage of the retrieved documents that are relevant to the total number of retrieved documents. A measure that combines both recall and precision is the harmonic mean of precision and recall, called the F-measure.

We defined the experimental design of our study using the Goal-Question-Metric method (GQM) [4]. We used the template presented in [5]. The GQM method was defined as a mechanism for defining and interpreting a set of operation goals using measurements. In this evaluation, the object is our Smart Hotel, the purpose is evaluation, the issues are the recall and precision of our Dynamic Feature Location approach, and the context is Feature Location using model traces. We focused on answering this research question: Do the criteria used to form the model trace influence the results of Dynamic Feature Location?

Basili in [4] and Travassos in [24] describe four kinds of studies: in-vivo, in-vitro, in-virtuo, and in-silico. In our case, we chose to carry out in-virtuo experiments, where the real world is described through computer models. This experiment involves the interaction among participants and a computerized model of reality. The simulated environment offers major advantages regarding cost and feasibility against replicating a real-world configuration. In addition, some scenarios such as fires or floods that cannot be replicated in the real world can be described and analyzed in a simulated environment.

In order to evaluate the results of our experiments, we have collected the existing documentation about the bugs in the Smart Hotel. Each bug can be mapped to a subset of model elements of a model, specified with the model fragment formalization capacities of the Common Variability Language (CVL). In other words, for each bug, we know beforehand which is the associated subset of model elements that are involved in the bug. We use the existing knowledge as an oracle to evaluate the results provided by DFL-AT and DFL-CT.

Figure 5 shows the entire process that we followed to evaluate our approach. For the evaluation, we used the Smart Hotel system (Fig. 5(A)). The Smart Hotel

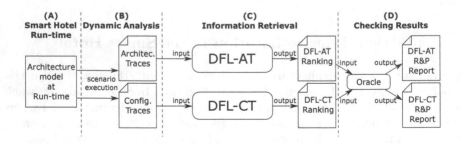

Fig. 5. Overview of the evaluation process

presents 476 model elements in the architecture model. In the evaluation set-up, a simulated environment was used to represent the Smart Hotel.

After running the scenario that executes the feature to be located, our approach generated the model traces (Fig. 5(B)). Then, we run two different Feature Location scenarios, using different traces as input. DFL-AT used the model trace that follows the architecture criterion, and DFL-CT used the model trace that follows the configuration criterion.

DFL-AT produced a ranking of model elements (DFL-AT Ranking), and DFL-CT produced another ranking of model elements (DFL-CT Ranking) for the desired feature (see Fig. 5(D)). The oracle allowed us to know how many of the model elements in the rankings were the ones that realized the desired feature in terms of recall, precision, and F-measure values.

The recall and precision were calculated as follows:

$$Recall = \frac{RankingElements \cap OracleElements}{OracleElements}$$

$$Precision = \frac{RankingElements \cap OracleElements}{RankingElements}$$

The F-measure that combines recall and precision was calculated as follows:

$$F - measure = 2 * \frac{Precision * Recall}{Precision \mid Recall}$$

4.1   Results

We performed this evaluation with thirty bugs extracted from the documentation of the Smart Hotel. We defined the scenarios based on bug reports. On average, the generated traces were as follows: 26 models in the trace following the architecture criterion (DFL-AT) and 9 models in the trace following the configuration criterion (DFL-CT).

Figure 6 shows the recall, precision, and F-measure values for each one of the bugs. On average, DFL-AT obtains a 74.67% recall value while DFL-CT obtains a 64.23% recall value. The values indicate that around the 75% of the model elements that realize the target feature are retrieved. DFL-AT improves the recall result achieved by DFL-CT by around 10%.

Regarding the precision value, on average, DFL-AT obtains a 75.96% while DFL-CT obtains a 65.53%. The values indicate that around the 76% of the model elements retrieved belong to the targeted feature. Once again, DFL-AT improves the precision result achieved by DFL-CT by around 10%.

Consequently, on average, DFL-AT obtains a 74.35% F-measure value, while DFL-CT obtains a 63.02% F-measure value. In 75% of the cases, DFL-AT outperforms the results of DFL-CT.

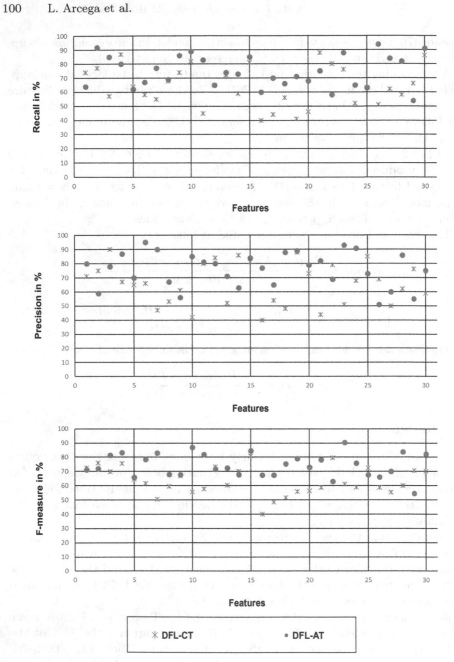

Fig. 6. Recall, precision and F-measure graphs

4.2 Discussion

Our evaluation suggests that Feature Location with model traces following the architecture criterion obtains better results in precision, recall, and F-measure than Feature Location with model traces following the configuration criterion. This is because the manifestation of a bug can occur in a snapshot that does not represent a source or target configuration in a reconfiguration of the system. In other words, a bug can be introduced in the system due to changes made in the architecture model during a reconfiguration.

Analyzing the results, Dynamic Feature Location with model traces following the architecture criterion does not always get the best results. The model traces composed by the architecture criterion have more snapshots that the model traces composed by the configuration criterion (see Sect. 2.2). In addition, two consecutive snapshots of the model trace composed by the architecture criterion are typically more similar that two consecutive snapshots of the model trace composed by the configuration criterion. For instance, in the model trace composed by the architecture criterion, a snapshot may differ from its consecutive one on only a single channel.

The above indicates that, in the step through which we perform information retrieval to extract the most representative model, the search space is larger in the model trace composed by the architecture criterion. In addition, the fact that the models in the trace are similar can imply similarity of terms in the documents of the LSI, therefore causing the technique to not discriminate between some models. However, in 75% of the cases, the Dynamic Feature Location with the model trace composed by the architecture criterion obtains better results than the Dynamic Feature Location with the model trace composed by the configuration criterion.

Finally, when forming the traces in the architecture criterion, only the creation and deletion of model elements are taken into account. In order to obtain better results in Feature Location, further experiments must be performed to analyze if other updates in the model elements should be taken into account.

4.3 Threats to Validity

In this section, we discuss some of the issues that might have affected the results of the evaluation and that may limit the generalizations of the results.

The first issue is regarding whether or not the software system used in the evaluation is representative of those used in practice. Given the scale and complexity of our Smart Hotel, we consider our evaluation to be a good starting point for representing a realistic case. However, this threat can be reduced if we experiment with other software systems of different sizes and domains.

Another issue is the selection of the scenarios to obtain the execution trace. Since we have extracted the information from the bug reports, we can claim that our scenarios are good representatives of features that must be located to solve the most common bugs of the Smart Hotel. In addition, following the information from the bug anyone could define the scenarios. However, depending on the chosen scenarios, the results may differ.

Since the queries formulated to generate the ranked lists depend on the bug reports, the final results are also sensitive to the queries extracted by the software engineers from the bug reports.

5   Related Work

Some approaches related to Feature Location use design-time models to extract variability. Although they do not use models at run-time, their works are based on extracting features using models.

Font et al. [10] show that model fragments extracted mechanically may not be units recognizable by application engineers. They propose identifying model patterns by their human-in-the-loop approach, and conceptualizing them as reusable model fragments. Their approach provides the means to identify and extract those model patterns and further apply them to existing product models. In [11], the work from [10] is extended to handle situations where the domain expert fails to provide accurate information. The authors propose a genetic algorithm for feature location in model-based SPLs. Their comparison with other approach without a genetic algorithm demonstrates that their approach is able to provide solutions upon inaccurate information on the part of the domain expert while the other fails.

Martinez et al. [18] propose an extensible framework that allows a feature to be identified, located and extracted from a family of models. They introduce the principles of this framework and provide insights on how it can be extended for usage in different scenarios. As a result, the initial investment required by the task of adopting a software product line from a family of models is reduced.

All of these works extract model fragments from a given set of models, taking into account their commonalities and variabilities. However, these approaches do not take into account the run-time behavior of systems, and are not focused on Feature Location. Nevertheless, all of them can be used as a base for extracting the model fragments that correspond to the feature to be located.

There are many more research efforts in Dynamic Feature Location techniques based on source-code analysis. Some of these works combine other kinds of analysis (i.e. information retrieval) to obtain more accurate results.

Liu et al. [16] combine information from an execution trace and from the comments and identifiers from the source code. They executed a single scenario which executes the desired feature. All the executed methods are identified based on the collected trace using LSI. The result is a ranked list of executed methods based on their textual similarity to a query.

Revelle et al. [21] apply data fusion for feature location. Their technique combines information from textual, dynamic, and web mining analysis applied to software. Their input is a single scenario that exercises the feature. After running the scenario, they construct a call graph that contains only the methods that were executed. Then, they apply a web-mining algorithm, and the system filters out low-ranked methods. The remaining set of methods is scored using LSI based on their relevance to the input query describing the feature.

Dit et al. [9] present a data fusion model for feature location that is based on the idea that combining data from several sources in the right proportions will be effective at identifying a feature's source code. The data fusion model defines different types of information that can be integrated to perform feature location including textual, execution, and dependence. Textual information is analyzed by IR, execution information is collected by dynamic analysis, and dependencies are analyzed using link analysis algorithms.

Similarly to our technique, all of these feature location techniques use information from different sources. Although they are based on locating features in source code, some of the ideas could be applied to our model based Dynamic Feature Location approach to obtain more accurate results.

In addition, Arcega et al. [3] present a model-based feature location approach. They apply dynamic analysis and information retrieval with run-time models. The evaluation is focused in revealing that model based feature location approaches provide more accurate results. This work extends this approach changing the way the model traces are treated. Through this work, we are focused in finding the information needed in the model traces to obtain more accurate results in Dynamic Feature Location.

6   Conclusion

In the presented work, we analyze how the criteria to create the model traces influence Dynamic Feature Location results. We focus on two different criteria: (1) configuration criterion, that adds a snapshot of the run-time model to the trace when the model corresponds to a target configuration of the system in a reconfiguration, and (2) architecture criterion, that adds a snapshot of the run-time model to the trace each time a change in the run-time model is performed. Our Dynamic Feature Location approach is composed by dynamic analysis, information retrieval at the model trace level, and information retrieval at the model level.

Our evaluation in a Smart Hotel calculates the values of the most common measures for experiments with information retrieval methods (recall, precision, and F-measure). We use these values to compare Dynamic Feature Location with traces created following the architecture criterion against Dynamic Feature Location with traces created following the configuration criterion. The results reveal that in 75% of the cases, Dynamic Feature Location with model traces composed by the architecture criterion obtains better results than Dynamic Feature Location with model traces composed by the configuration criterion.

Our future work involves designing a Feature Location approach that combines model traces and information about the time of the execution. In addition, further experiments are necessary to identify other different criteria to create model traces.

Acknowledgments. This work has been partially supported by the Ministry of Economy and Competitiveness (MINECO) through the Spanish National R+D+i Plan and ERDF funds under the project Model-Driven Variability Extraction for Software Product Line Adoption (TIN2015-64397-R).

References

1. Alves, V., Schwanninger, C., Barbosa, L., Rashid, A., Sawyer, P., Rayson, P., Pohl, C., Rummler. A.: An exploratory study of information retrieval techniques in domain analysis. In: 2008 12th International Software Product Line Conference, pp. 67–76, September 2008
2. Antoniol, G., Gueheneuc, Y.-G.: Feature identification: an epidemiological metaphor. IEEE Trans. Softw. Eng. **32**(9), 627–641 (2006)
3. Arcega, L., Font, J., Haugen, Ø., Cetina, C.: Feature location through the combination of run-time architecture models and information retrieval. In: Grabowski, J., Herbold, S. (eds.) SAM 2016. LNCS, vol. 9959, pp. 180–195. Springer, Cham (2016). doi:10.1007/978-3-319-46613-2_12
4. Basili, V.R.: The role of experimentation in software engineering: past, current, and future. In: Proceedings of the 18th International Conference on Software Engineering, ICSE 1996, pp. 442–449. IEEE Computer Society, Washington, DC (1996)
5. Basili, V.R., Caldiera, G., Rombach, H.D.: The goal question metric approach. In: Encyclopedia of Software Engineering. Wiley (1994)
6. Bencomo, N., Hallsteinsen, S., Santana de Almeida, E.: A view of the dynamic software product line landscape. Computer **45**(10), 36–41 (2012)
7. Cetina, C.: Achieving autonomic computing through the use of variability models at run-time. Ph.D. thesis, Universidad Politécnica de Valencia (2010)
8. Dit, B., Revelle, M., Gethers, M., Poshyvanyk, D.: Feature location in source code: a taxonomy and survey. J. Softw. Maintenance Evol. Res. Pract. **25**(1), 53–95 (2011)
9. Dit, B., Revelle, M., Poshyvanyk, D.: Integrating information retrieval, execution and link analysis algorithms to improve feature location in software. Empirical Softw. Eng. **18**(2), 277–309 (2013)
10. Font, J., Arcega, L., Haugen, Ø., Cetina, C.: Building software product lines from conceptualized model patterns. In: Proceedings of the 2015 19th International Software Product Line Conference, SPLC 2015, Nashville, TN, USA (2015)
11. Font, J., Arcega, L., Haugen, Ø., Cetina, C.: Feature location in model-based software product lines through a genetic algorithm. In: Kapitsaki, G.M., Santana de Almeida, E. (eds.) ICSR 2016. LNCS, vol. 9679, pp. 39–54. Springer, Cham (2016). doi:10.1007/978-3-319-35122-3_3
12. Hulth, A.: Improved automatic keyword extraction given more linguistic knowledge. In: Proceedings of the 2003 Conference on Empirical Methods in Natural Language Processing, EMNLP 2003, Stroudsburg, PA, USA, pp. 216–223. Association for Computational Linguistics (2003)
13. IBM: An architectural blueprint for autonomic computing. Technical report, IBM (2006)
14. Landauer, T.K., Foltz, P.W., Laham, D.: An introduction to latent semantic analysis. Discourse Process. **25**(2–3), 259–284 (1998)
15. Lehman, M.M., Ramil, J., Kahen, G.: A paradigm for the behavioural modelling of software processes using system dynamics. Technical report, Imperial College of Science, Technology and Medicine, Department of Computing, September 2001

16. Liu, D., Marcus, A., Poshyvanyk, D., Rajlich, V.: Feature location via information retrieval based filtering of a single scenario execution trace. In: Proceedings of the Twenty-second IEEE/ACM International Conference on Automated Software Engineering, ASE 2007, New York, NY, USA, pp. 234–243. ACM (2007)
17. Marcus, A., Sergeyev, A., Rajlich, V., Maletic, J.: An information retrieval approach to concept location in source code. In: Proceedings of the 11th Working Conference on Reverse Engineering, pp. 214–223, November 2004
18. Martinez, J., Ziadi, T., Bissyandé, T.F., Le Traon, Y.: Bottom-up adoption of software product lines: a generic and extensible approach. In: Proceedings of the 19th International Software Product Line Conference, SPLC 2015, Nashville, TN, USA (2015)
19. Muñoz, J.: Model driven development of pervasive systems. building a software factory. Ph.D. thesis, Universidad Politécnica de Valencia (2008)
20. Poshyvanyk, D., Gueheneuc, Y.-G., Marcus, A., Antoniol, G., Rajlich, V.: Feature location using probabilistic ranking of methods based on execution scenarios and information retrieval. IEEE Trans. Softw. Eng. **33**(6), 420–432 (2007)
21. Revelle, M., Dit, B., Poshyvanyk, D.: Using data fusion and web mining to support feature location in software. In: IEEE 18th International Conference on Program Comprehension (ICPC), pp. 14–23, June 2010
22. Salman, H.E., Seriai, A., Dony, C.: Feature location in a collection of product variants: combining information retrieval and hierarchical clustering. In: The 26th International Conference on Software Engineering and Knowledge Engineering, Hyatt Regency, Vancouver, BC, Canada, 1–3 July 2013, pp. 426–430 (2014)
23. Salton, G., McGill, M.J.: Introduction to Modern Information Retrieval. McGraw-Hill Inc, New York (1986)
24. Travassos, M.O.B.G.H.: Contributions of in virtuo and in silico experiments for the future of empirical studies in software engineering. In: Proceedings of the Workshop on Empirical Studies in Software Engineering (ESEIW). IEEE Computer Society (2003)

Model-Driven Generative Development

cMoflon: Model-Driven Generation of Embedded C Code for Wireless Sensor Networks

Roland Kluge[1]([⊠]) [iD], Michael Stein[2] [iD], David Giessing[1] [iD], Andy Schürr[1] [iD], and Max Mühlhäuser[2] [iD]

[1] Real-Time Systems Lab, TU Darmstadt, Darmstadt, Germany
{roland.kluge,andy.schuerr}@es.tu-darmstadt.de
[2] Telecooperation Group, TU Darmstadt, Darmstadt, Germany
{stein,max}@tk.tu-darmstadt.de

Abstract. Wireless sensor networks (WSNs) are an indispensable part of the emerging Internet of Things. The topology of a WSN is a graph representing the sensor nodes and their interconnecting links. To reduce the energy consumption of a WSN, a topology control algorithm inactivates inessential links, and the sensor nodes reduce their transmission power while preserving crucial integrity properties (e.g., connectivity). In previous work, we have shown that model-driven engineering allows to prototype topology control algorithms that (i) preserve the specified integrity properties and (ii) can be rapidly evaluated in a network simulator. In this paper, we complement our approach by proposing cMoflon, an open-source tool that generates embedded C code for hardware sensor testbeds. The target platform is the Contiki WSN operating system. To show the applicability of cMoflon, we generate code for three representative topology control algorithms: kTC, l*-kTC, and LMST. A comparison of the generated topology control algorithms with their manually tuned counterparts for TelosB sensor nodes shows that cMoflon generates embedded code that is competitive w.r.t. code memory usage.

Keywords: Code generation · Wireless sensor networks · Model-driven engineering

1 Introduction

Wireless sensor networks (WSNs) are a highly active research area in the emerging Internet of Things [28]. The topology of a WSN is a graph representing the sensor nodes and their (potential) communication links. Sensor nodes are typically battery-powered, which makes reducing the energy consumption of a WSN a key optimization goal. Topology control (TC) [20] tackles this goal: Each node selects a subset of its neighboring nodes and reduces its transmission power to reach its farthest selected neighbor. WSNs are frequently deployed in safety-critical contexts, such as health or wildfire alarm systems [3]. Therefore, developers of TC algorithms must ensure that the output topology of the TC algorithm fulfills important integrity properties (e.g., connectivity).

© Springer International Publishing AG 2017
A. Anjorin and H. Espinoza (Eds.): ECMFA 2017, LNCS 10376, pp. 109–125, 2017.
DOI: 10.1007/978-3-319-61482-3_7

Part of the vision and success story of model-driven engineering (MDE) [26] is to specify systems using formal models to enable analyzing and proving desired and required formal properties. Based on these models, major parts of the specified systems are generated while preserving the proved properties. Several approaches to developing WSN algorithms leverage MDE (e.g., [1,3]). However, despite the importance of TC in the WSN community, we have been, to the best of our knowledge, the first group to propose an MDE approach for developing TC algorithms [10–12]. More precisely, we propose to specify (i) topologies using attributed graphs, (ii) modifications of the topology using graph transformation (GT) [5] and Story-Driven Modeling (SDM) [7], and (iii) integrity properties using graph constraints [9]. This allows us to derive a GT-based TC algorithm specification that is correct-by-construction w.r.t. the specified integrity properties. A tool integration of the MDE tool EMOFLON [13] and the WSN simulation platform SIMONSTRATOR [18] currently allows to rapidly and reproducibly perform a first-order validation of the TC algorithm specification [10,11]. To assess its real-life behavior, a TC algorithm should additionally be evaluated in a hardware testbed environment (e.g., FLOCKLAB [15]). Unfortunately, only few works in the WSN community have dared this step, which may result from the high complexity of and missing tool support for porting a TC algorithm to the target hardware platform [23]. To ease this step, we recently proposed the ToCoCo framework [23] for evaluating TC algorithms based on the CONTIKI [4] WSN operating system. Still, even using ToCoCo, a TC developer has to manually cope with the particularities of embedded C (e.g., memory management).

In this paper, we present CMOFLON[1], a variant of the GT tool EMOFLON that generates embedded C code for the CONTIKI operating system using the ToCoCo framework. The detailed contributions of this paper are as follows:

- We provide an extensible TC metamodel, based on which TC algorithms are specified using SDM (see Sect. 3).
- We provide an extensible code generation process that generates components for the ToCoCo TC evaluation framework for the WSN operating system CONTIKI. Proper memory management of pattern matching results and null-pointer handling is provided by the generated code (see Sect. 4).
- To assess the applicability of CMOFLON, we generate code for the state-of-the-art TC algorithms kTC [22], l*-kTC [23], and LMST [14] and compare the generated TC algorithms with their manually implemented counterparts (see Sect. 5).

The remainder of this paper is structured along the CMOFLON development workflow. In Sect. 2, we introduce the considered TC algorithms. In Sects. 3 and 4, we explain the modeling and code generation support of CMOFLON. In Sect. 5, we evaluate the generated code of the selected TC algorithms. In Sect. 6, we review related work, and, in Sect. 7, we conclude this paper.

---

[1] CMOFLON is open source and available at https://github.com/eMoflon/cmoflon/.

2 A Brief Introduction to Topology Control

In this section, we introduce the required terminology of TC as well as the three TC algorithms that serve as running example.

Topologies: A *topology* is a graph consisting of *(network) nodes* and directed *(communication) links* [20]. Each node can have zero or more *outgoing* and *incoming links*, and each link has one *source* and *target* node. Nodes and links can have *properties*, each having a fixed attribute type. By convention, a link e_{12} has source node n_1 and target node n_2. The *weight* $\mathrm{w}(e_{12})$ of a link e_{12} signifies the cost of using e_{12} for communication (e.g., the distance of its incident nodes). The *state* $\mathrm{s}(e_{12})$ of a link e_{12} captures the processing state of e_{12} during and after the execution of the TC algorithm. The *hop count* $\mathrm{h}_x(n_1)$ *of a node* n_1 *w.r.t. a fixed reference node* n_x equals the minimal number of links that are required to reach n_x from n_1.

Topology control: *Topology control* (TC) [20] identifies links that are inessential w.r.t. the integrity properties of the topology (e.g., connectivity of the topology) and, at the same time, energy-intensive (e.g., due to large weight). A *TC algorithm* accepts an input topology (e.g., consisting of all physically possible links) and returns, as output topology, a classification of the links according to their importance. A TC algorithm is usually executed in parallel on each sensor node, and the input and output topology typically reflect only a local view of the topology (e.g., all nodes and links that are at most two hops away). A link e_{12} can be in one out of three *states*: e_{12} is (i) *active* if it is essential ($\mathrm{s}(e_{12})=$Active, denoted as solid line, e.g., (1)→(2)), (ii) *inactive* if it is inessential and energy-intensive ($\mathrm{s}(e_{12})=$Inactive, denoted as dotted line, e.g., (1)⋯▸(2)), and (iii) *unclassified* if the TC algorithm has not classified e_{12} yet ($\mathrm{s}(e_{12})=$Unclassified, denoted as mixed dotted-solid line, e.g., (1)⋯▸(2)). A TC algorithm changes the state of each link to either Active or Inactive, and the sensor operating system selectively sets links to Unclassified (e.g., when link weights change due to node movement). During operation of TC, we assume that link states are exclusively changed by TC.

In Fig. 1, the input topology is entirely unclassified, indicating that the TC algorithm has not been executed yet. Note that the active links of each output topology form a connected subtopology.

TC algorithms: The following three TC algorithms serve as running examples of this paper. (i) The *kTC algorithm* [22] inactivates the weight-maximal link e_{12} in every directed triangle if the weight of e_{12} is at least k-times larger than the weight of the weight-minimal link in the same triangle. The idea behind kTC is that using two shorter links of low weight requires less energy than using a link with large weight because the required transmission power increases at least quadratically with its weight. (ii) The *l*-kTC algorithm* [23] is a refined variant of kTC that aims to bound the increase in routing path length by a factor a. l*-kTC inactivates a link e_{12} if e_{12} fulfills the kTC condition and if the hop counts $\mathrm{h}_x(n_1)$, $\mathrm{h}_x(n_2)$ of n_1 and n_2 will grow at most by a factor a. (iii) The *local minimum* *spanning tree (LMST) algorithm* [14] determines a minimum spanning tree in its neighborhood and inactivates all links that are not part of this tree. kTC, l*-kTC, and LMST are suitable running examples because they represent a larger class of TC algorithms [10] and manually implemented variants of all algorithms are available for comparison [23]. Many WSN applications (e.g., routing) assume that the output topology is symmetric w.r.t. states. Therefore, an inactive link e_{12} is re-activated after the termination of TC if its reverse link e_{21} is still active.

Figure 1 illustrates the effect of executing kTC, l*-kTC, and LMST with a small input topology. In this example, we use $a = 1.5$ and $k = 2$. In the output topology of kTC, link e_{14} (e_{41}, resp.) is inactive because it is weight-maximal in the triangle consisting of e_{13}, e_{14}, e_{34} (e_{31}, e_{41}, e_{43}, resp.) and its weight is more than 2-times larger than the weight of the weight-minimal link e_{34} (e_{43}, resp.). In the output topology of l*-kTC, the links e_{14} and e_{41} are active because, otherwise, $h_1(n_4)$ would increase by more than $a = 1.5$ from 1 to 2. In the output topology of LMST, all links with a weight of 2 constitute a minimum spanning tree; all other links are inactivated.

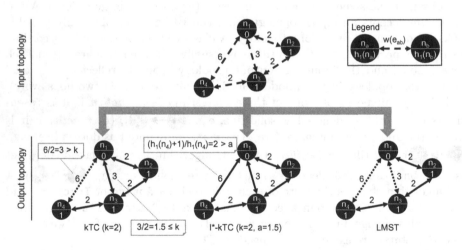

Fig. 1. Applying kTC, l*-kTC, and LMST to the sample input topology (n_1: ref. node)

3   Modeling TC Algorithms with cMoflon

In this section, we illustrate how TC algorithms can be modeled with CMOFLON. We introduce the underlying TC metamodel topology and provide sample specifications for the TC algorithms (l*-)kTC and LMST.

TC metamodel: We assume that the reader is familiar with basic metamodeling concepts [26]. Figure 2 shows the Ecore-based [24] TC metamodel used in this paper. Dashed and dotted frames surround metamodel elements that were introduced to specify (l*-)kTC and LMST, respectively. All other metamodel elements reflect core concepts of TC and form the basic TC metamodel that

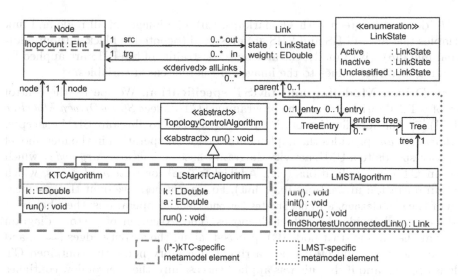

Fig. 2. TC metamodel with additions for kTC, l*-kTC, and LMST

CMOFLON provides to the TC developer. The Node and Link classes represent the nodes and links of a topology. The abstract TopologyControlAlgorithm class serves as superclass for TC algorithms and specifies the abstract run() operation. The enumeration type LinkState represents the three possible link states. The real-valued weight attribute, the state attribute of enumeration type LinkState in class Link, and the integer-valued hopCount attribute in class Node correspond to the link and node properties described earlier. For simplicity, the reference node n_x for $h_x(n)$ is omitted. The src-out and trg-in associations represent that links are directed. The derived allLinks association allows to iterate over all links in the neighborhood of a node. The node association from TopologyControlAlgorithm to Node specifies that a TC algorithm runs on a dedicated node.

Graph transformation: In CMOFLON, TC algorithms are specified using programmed GT. While CMOFLON supports many of the GT features of EMOFLON, we only present concepts required to understand the presented TC specifications. A *graph pattern p* consists of a set of object variables, which are placeholders for model elements [5,19]. A pattern may have *attribute constraints*, which restrict the attribute value of its variables (e.g., using relational operators such as $<$, $>$, or $=$). A *match m of a pattern p in a model M* is an injective mapping from the object variables of p to the elements of M that fulfills all attribute constraints. For a variable v, $m(v)$ is called the *image of v*. A *GT rule R* consists of a left-hand side pattern (LHS) and right-hand side pattern (RHS) [5,19]. A GT rule R is *applicable on a model M* if there is at least one match of LHS in M. An *application of an applicable GT rule R at a match m in a model M* is performed as follows: (i) The images of all variables that appear in LHS but not in RHS are removed from M (denoted in red and with -- markup). (ii) For each variable that appears in RHS but not in LHS, a fresh object of the variable type is added to M (denoted in green with ++ markup). (iii) The images of all node and link variables that are in LHS and RHS are preserved (denoted in black without additional markup). (iv) Finally, the attribute constraints of the RHS are applied by assigning attribute values to the images of the referenced variables.

Story-Driven Modeling and LMST specification: We specify the control flow of a TC algorithm using the programmed GT dialect *Story-Driven Modeling* (SDM) [7]. The specification of LMST in Fig. 3 serves to illustrate SDM concepts. A *story diagram* provides the implementation for an operation in the metamodel and corresponds to a UML activity diagram whose actions are *story nodes*, which contain GT rule applications (e.g., **AddLinkToTree**), or *statement nodes*, which contain operation invocations (e.g., Init). For conciseness, we omit the specification of the init, cleanup, and findShortestUnconnectedLink operations; their behavior is documented inside the note-style boxes. The execution of a story diagram starts at the unique start node (●), proceeds along the activity edges (⟶), and ends at the stop node (◉). Upon arriving at a story node, the contained GT rule is applied, and if the rule was applied successfully, the control flow continues along the activity edge labeled with [Success]. Otherwise, the [Failure] activity edge is taken. Upon arriving at a statement node, the contained operation is invoked. For instance, the execution of the run operation in Fig. 3 starts with the statement node Init, which initializes the auxiliary data structures that store the tentative spanning tree. Using a statement node here allows us to choose how to implement each invoked operation: either using platform-independent SDM or platform-specific code (e.g., for custom memory management). The this object variable is always accessible implicitly. To store the spanning tree, we added the auxiliary classes Tree and TreeEntry to the TC metamodel (see Fig. 2). The story nodes **FindMissingLink**, which binds the object variable link by invoking the findShortestUnconnectedLink operation, and **AddLinkToTree** form a loop that adds links

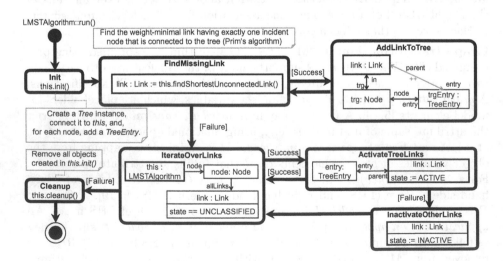

Fig. 3. SDM specification of LMST (Color figure online)

to the spanning tree (sorted by weight) as long as no cycle is created (Prim's algorithm). The story nodes **IterateOverLinks**, **ActivateTreeLinks**, and **Inactiva-teOtherLinks** form the loop that activates (resp. inactivates) all links that are (resp. are not) part of the spanning tree. The operator == (:=, resp.) refers to an equality constraint of the LHS (RHS, resp.) pattern of a rule. Finally, the statement node **Cleanup** frees the tentative spanning tree.

(l*-)kTC specification: Figure 4 shows an SDM specification of l*-kTC consisting of two loops. The first loop (**InactivateLinksInTriangles**) inactivates all links that fulfill the l*-kTC condition, while the second loop (**ActivateRemainingLinks**) activates all remaining links. In contrast to the basic attribute constraints inside variables, the advanced attribute constraints in the framed box state (i) the triangle-condition that is common to kTC and l*-kTC (lines 1 to 5), using cMoflon's built-in attribute constraints, and (ii) the routing-path condition of l*-kTC (line 6), using the custom constraint hopCountOK. For specifying the latter attribute constraint, the TC developer needs to extend the Node class with the hopCount attribute. Note that by removing the latter attribute constraint, we obtain a specification of kTC.

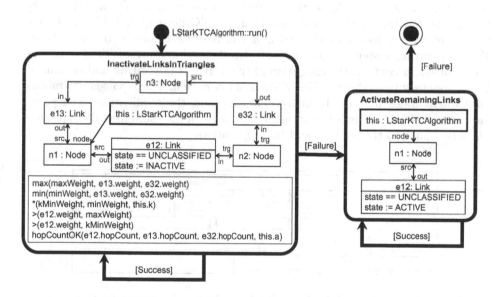

Fig. 4. SDM specification of l*-kTC

Technical modeling aspects: cMoflon is a variant of the EMF-based MDE tool eMoflon [13]. We chose eMoflon because it offers a configurable and automated code generation process. Developing cMoflon, we reused the frontend for metamodeling and SDM, which is an add-in for the modeling tool Enterprise Architect[2]. This reuse ensures full compatibility of cMoflon

---

[2] https://www.sparxsystems.eu/enterprisearchitect.

specifications, e.g., with the tool integration of EMOFLON and the SIMONSTRA-TOR network simulator [10]. CMOFLON supports a subset of Ecore that is, to our experience, relevant for TC developers. Supported metamodeling features comprise EClasses with EOperations (implemented using SDM or platform-specific code) and EAttributes (built-in data types and enumerations), and (single-/multi-valued) EReferences.

4   Generating Code for TC Algorithms with cMoflon

This section describes how CMOFLON generates embedded C code from TC algorithm specifications. We motivate our choice for the ToCoCo evaluation framework as target platform, describe the CMOFLON code generation process, and, most importantly, explain how we tackled the challenges of an extensible model-to-text transformation and memory management in embedded C.

ToCoCo as target platform: The most important decision during the design of CMOFLON was the target platform. As operating system, we chose CONTIKI [4], which is prominent in the WSN community. In [23] we have proposed the ToCoCo framework to ease the implementation of novel TC algorithms by hiding the low-level technical details from the TC developer. While ToCoCo was built with a focus on CONTIKI, it can easily be ported to any C-based WSN operating system. Figure 5 illustrates the architecture of ToCoCo. The *TC component* controls the execution of the active TC algorithm and obtains its input topology from the *neighbor discovery component*. The *topology abstraction component* hides inactive links from routing and the application. The *power control component* adjusts the transmission range of the radio module to provide all active links to the routing and the application.

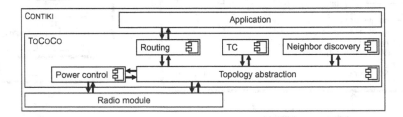

Fig. 5. Architecture of the ToCoCo TC evaluation framework for CONTIKI

Code generation process: Figure 6 shows the three phases of the code generation process of EMOFLON and CMOFLON: import, validation and code generation. The code generation process operates as follows. The EMOFLON frontend persists metamodels and story diagrams in an XMI-based file format. The *import phase* parses these files into an Ecore metamodel with attached story diagrams. The *validation phase* is a model-to-model transformation (M2M) that translates each story diagram into a *control flow model*, which represents a goto-free program in imperative programming languages such as C, C++, or Java. In EMOFLON, the *code generation phase* is a model-to-text transformation (M2T) that uses standard EMF for creating the structural parts of the metamodel, and the DEMOCLES [25] code generator for generating the method bodies based on the control flow models. The developer may provide user-defined code for non-SDM operations. CMOFLON 1.0.0 reuses the import and validation phase of EMOFLON 2.28.0 with minor adjustments (framed gray arrows). Only the code generation module was entirely exchanged (blue arrow: CMOFLON, black arrow: EMOFLON). The reused parts of EMOFLON consist of ca. 358 000 lines of Java and C# code. In contrast, CMOFLON consists of 3 362 lines of Java code (ca. 1% of EMOFLON). This reuse entails a number of benefits. First, CMOFLON profits from the extensively tested code generation process of EMOFLON. No formal verification of the correctness of the code generation process has been carried out so far due to its inherent complexity. However, each version of EMOFLON is tested against a fully automated test suite consisting of real-world projects[3]. Second, CMOFLON profits from improvements in the mainline development of EMOFLON and the underlying code generation engine DEMOCLES.

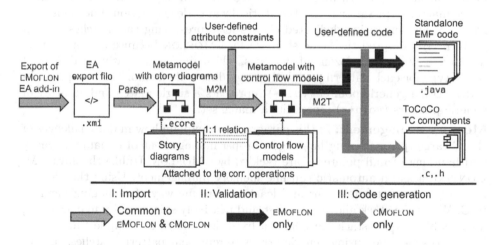

Fig. 6. Build processes of EMOFLON and CMOFLON (EA: Enterprise Architect) (Color figure online)

Basic TC metamodel: Elements from the basic TC metamodel are mapped to internal data structures of the ToCoCo framework for efficiency. The classes Node and Link are mapped to the structural types networkaddr_t and neighbor_t provided by ToCoCo, respectively. The Link::weight attribute is mapped to the existing member of the neighbor_t type. Our implementations for the src-out, trg-in, and allLinks associations build upon CONTIKI's lists data

---

[3] See https://github.com/eMoflon/emoflon-tests/.

type list_t. To efficiently implement Link::state, we introduced a C enumeration LinkState, which mirrors the enumeration LinkState, and added a corresponding attribute to neighbor_t. For compatibility with previous versions of ToCoCo [23], LinkState can be completely removed via a preprocessor directive. When a link is inactivated, the topology abstraction component is notified and hides the inactivated link. When a link is activated or unclassified, its target node is made visible again. Finally, the run() operation of each subclass of TopologyControlAlgorithm results in a dedicated ToCoCo component, represented by a separate CONTIKI process. To enable a rapid prototyping of TC algorithms, (i) the user may switch between the TC components using a single preprocessor directive, and (ii) the generated files (a .c and a .h file per TC component) can be copied without modification into the ToCoCo project structure.

Control flow: For generating the C control flow that steers the GT invocations, we use the modular StringTemplate-based configuration provided by DEMOCLES [25]. Most of the templates for control flow were reused with minor modifications compared to EMOFLON (e.g., if, while-do, do-while). The major challenge of the M2T for story diagrams was the representation and memory management for pattern matches. In EMOFLON, an Object array represents a single match. Type safety is checked statically at code generation time. This approach avoids generating dedicated classes for representing the matches of each pattern. We adopted the same strategy for CMOFLON because a typical specification may contain dozens of patterns, which makes generating a dedicated result type for each pattern prohibitive regarding code memory consumption. In CMOFLON, a generic pointer (void*) represents a single match and an array of generic pointers (void**) represents a match set.

Memory management: In this paragraph, we explain how major challenges of the C target programming language—proper management of dynamic memory and handling of null pointers—are tackled by CMOFLON. Unlike the Java VM, CONTIKI lacks an automatic runtime memory management. Using the *stack* is certainly the most convenient and least error-prone way of managing memory in C. While the stack allows for a fast and relatively safe memory management, all variables on the stack must have a fixed size known at compile time, which is not possible when using generic arrays to represent pattern matches. In contrast, the *heap* allows us to choose the size of allocated memory fragments at runtime. The downside is that memory allocation on the heap is slower, may cause runtime exceptions if memory runs out, and requires a careful manual handling of memory allocations (via malloc) and corresponding deallocations (via free). A third, CONTIKI-specific option is to pre-reserve static memory at compile time. (De-)allocating static memory tends to be faster (due to reduced fragmentation), but the size of the reserved memory must be set at compile time and the reserved memory is no longer available for the heap. To this end, we decided to store handles to matches on the stack (match_t) and to allocate memory on the heap for the actual pattern match contents. CMOFLON cares for the proper pairing of calls to malloc and free. This strategy allows us to switch to a more sophisticated memory management in the future easily (e.g., using smart pointers). For creating and destroying associations and objects, CMOFLON generates appropriate function prototypes, which are implemented by the TC developer. CMOFLON is conservative w.r.t. null pointer checks, i.e., whenever a link variable is traversed during pattern matching, CMOFLON asserts that the result is not null. This behavior could be relaxed by relying on the cardinalities in the metamodel (e.g., that a Link always has exactly one src Node).

User-defined metamodel elements: A major goal of CMOFLON is to generate code lean enough to be used on resource-constrained sensor nodes, and, at the same time, to be extensible enough to support as many current and future TC algorithms as possible. Given the vast number of published TC algorithms (listed in, e.g., [21,27]), we think that it is important to make CMOFLON easily extensible for TC developers rather than trying to cover all TC algorithms upfront. To this end, CMOFLON supports the following types of extensions: adding (E1) custom attributes and associations (e.g., Node::hopCount and entries-tree), (E2) custom attribute constraints (e.g., hopCountOK), and (E3) custom classes (e.g., TreeEntry). In our running example, l*-kTC required (E1) and (E2), and LMST required (E3). Regarding (E1), we generate for each custom attribute and association a function prototype that has to be implemented by the TC developer. To mimic object-orientation, we prepend a synthetic **this** parameter to the parameter list of the generated function, having the type of the surrounding class. Regarding (E2), we follow the same approach to specify advanced attribute constraints as in EMOFLON. We provide code mappings for a set of built-in constraints (e.g., >, <, =, max, min). For custom constraints, the TC developer defines a C code fragment that implements the constraint check and evaluates to **true** or **false**. Regarding (E3), the TC developer provides a mapping to an appropriate C type for each custom metamodel class.

Example: Listing 1 shows part of the generated code for l*-kTC[4]. We simplified the code fragment manually due to space limitations. Line 1 shows the synthetic **this** parameter, having the user-defined type **LSTARKTCALGORITHM_T**. The generated comment on line 2 allows to trace code blocks to their corresponding story diagram element. Line 3 shows how a pattern matching result is returned. Pattern matching results always reside in the heap and are freed after extracting the relevant variables (e.g., in line 6). The memory management is facilitated by the fact that DEMOCLES builds upon hierarchical templates. For instance, lines 1–8 and 10–11 correspond to a single node in the control flow model and are created simultaneously. Possible nested scopes (i.e., while loops or story nodes) are handled recursively.

---

[4] The full source code for all TC algorithms of this paper can be found at https://github.com/eMoflon/cmoflon/releases/tag/cmoflon_1.0.0.

Listing 1 . Excerpt of generated code for (l*-)kTC::run

```
1  void lStarKtcAlgorithm_run(LSTARKTCALGORITHM_T* this){
2    // InactivateLinksInTriangles
3    void** result2_black = pattern_InactivateLinks_black(this);
4    while (result2_black != NULL) {
5      LINK_T* e12 = (LINK_T*) result2_black[5];
6      free(result2_black);
7      void** result3_green = pattern_InactivateLinks_green(e12);
8      free(result3_green);
9      // Possible nested scopes
10     result2_black = pattern_InactivateLinks_black(this);
11   } // End of InactivateLinksInTriangles
12
13   // ActivateRemainingLinks
14   void** result4_black = pattern_ActivateRemainingLinks_black(this);
15   while (result4_black != NULL) {
16     LINK_T* e12 = (LINK_T*) result4_black[1];
17     free(result4_black);
18     void** result5_green = pattern_ActivateRemainingLinks_green(e12);
19     free(result5_green);
20     result4_black = pattern_ActivateRemainingLinks_black(this);
21   } // End of ActivateRemainingLinks
22   return;
23 }
```

5   Evaluation

This section presents and discusses the results of evaluating the generated code for the selected TC algorithms w.r.t. code memory consumption.

Research question: Surprisingly, one of the scarcest resources of a sensor node is its code memory (e.g., 48 kB of code memory for the widely used TelosB sensor node platform [16]). In contrast, the runtime efficiency is of minor importance because a TC algorithm is typically invoked infrequently (e.g., every 10 min). This makes the size of the generated code a key factor for assessing the applicability of CMOFLON. Therefore, we focus on the following research questions.

(RQ1) Is the code generated using CMOFLON small enough (w.r.t. code size) to fit on a typical sensor node?

(RQ2) If yes, how does the code memory consumption change compared to the manually implemented variant of each algorithm?

While being of minor importance in our application scenario, the execution time of the generated TC algorithms should not grow excessively compared to the manual variants, of course.

Setup: We used CMOFLON 1.0.0, ToCoCo 2.0.0, CONTIKI 3.0, and TelosB sensor nodes [16]. This choice allows us to compare our results with the manually implemented algorithms in [23]. The input of this evaluation are seven *sensor images*, which are the ready-to-deploy output binaries of the CONTIKI compiler. Each image contains the CONTIKI operating system, the TOCOCO framework, and a data collection application, which periodically sends a probe message to a fixed node. Images suffixed with "-man" (resp. "-gen") correspond to the manual (resp. generated) variant of each algorithm. The seventh image (named NoTC) results from disabling TC completely and serves as baseline.

Metrics: The metric of this evaluation is the *size* (in byte) of each sensor image, which is the sum of the sizes of the *text segment*, which contains the binary code and constants, and the *data segment*, which contains the initial values of non-constant variables. To measure the image size, we employed the tool `size`[5].

Results: Table 1 summarizes the code size results. The first and second column list the six TC sensor images along with their sizes. The third and forth column show the absolute and relative difference in size of each algorithm compared to NoTC. The fifth and sixth column show the absolute and relative difference in size of the generated compared to the manual variant per algorithm. Δ(NoTC)[%] equals Δ(NoTC)[B] divided by the size of NoTC, and Δ(G-M)[%] equals Δ(G-M)[B] of the generated variant divided by Δ(NoTC)[B] of the manual variant. The code size of the manual variants w.r.t. NoTC increases by 2.2 kB to 3.4 kB, whereas the increase for the generated variants ranges from 4.0 kB to 5.9 kB. The absolute (resp. relative) manual-to-generated increase in size is the smallest for kTC (resp. l*-kTC) with 1.8 kB (resp. +58%), while LMST shows the largest absolute and relative increase in size of 3.4 kB and +137%. When using generated TC algorithms, the relative increase w.r.t. total size increases by 4.8 pp (percentage points) for kTC to 9.2 pp for LMST.

Table 1. Code size of the sensor images (Size of NoTC: 36 917 B)

Algo.	Size [B]	Δ(NoTC)[B]	Δ(NoTC)[%]	Δ(G-M)[B]	Δ(G-M)[%]
kTC-man	39 135	2 218	+6.0		
kTC-gen	40 897	3 980	+10.8	1 762	+79.4
l*-kTC-man	40 293	3 376	+9.1		
l*-kTC-gen	42 247	5 330	+14.4	1 954	+57.9
LMST-man	39 395	2 478	+6.7		
LMST-gen	42 799	5 882	+15.9	3 404	+137.4

Discussion: To our experience, the observed increase in code size is moderate (+79% to +137%) compared to more feature-rich target platforms (e.g., EMF). Notably, CONTIKI, TOCOCO, and the application consume most of the code memory already (ca. 37 kB, i.e., 77% of 48 kB). Even though several MDE approaches generate code for WSNs, we could not find quantitative data comparing the code size of manual and generated variants of the same WSN algorithm.

---

[5] See https://linux.die.net/man/1/size.

We manually inspected the generated code to identify reasons for the differences in code size. First, the generated code contains null checks for each association that is traversed. Future improvements could remove null checks whenever an association is guaranteed to exist (e.g., each link has exactly one source node). Second, each invocation of a story pattern is systematically decomposed into a sequence of several basic pattern invocations that map to the different phases of a GT rule application (as described on page 5). Each pattern invocation results in the creation of an appropriate match (set), which serves as input for subsequent pattern invocations. By refining the control flow analysis, the number of created matches could be reduced (e.g., when none of the results is used further). Third, the generated code contains significantly more functions and function calls. This modularization of the code is important because it helps the TC developer to understand the mapping from the metamodel and SDM elements to the generated code and to customize the M2T (cf. page 11).

We conclude that, regarding RQ1, the generated TC algorithms are definitely small enough to fit on the considered TelosB sensor nodes, and, regarding RQ2, the code memory consumption increases moderately by at most 9.2 pp w.r.t. total image size when applying cMoflon.

Threads to Validity: A major threat to *external validity* is that we focused on three TC algorithms and one type of sensor node. Still, we covered a small, but typical subset of TC algorithms, which work strictly based on limited local knowledge. In previous work, we have shown that many established TC algorithms can be represented in the same way as kTC and l*-kTC [11]. Additionally, the TelosB sensor nodes are comparable w.r.t. code memory to other state-of-the-art sensor nodes[6]. To further mitigate this threat, we will evaluate additional TC algorithms and sensor platforms in our future work. A major threat to *internal validity* is the soundness of the generated code w.r.t. the SDM specification. To mitigate this threat, we deployed all six sensor images in the FLOCKLAB [15] sensor testbed and carefully checked that the output topologies and the application behavior were comparable. The runtime of the generated variant of kTC showed the worst average increase in execution time from 6.3 ms to 17.2 ms, which is acceptable given that TC is executed only once for a 30 min simulation run.

6   Related Work

In this section, we review related approaches for MDE in WSNs and code generation in general. A recent systematic mapping study summarizes 21 MDE approaches for WSNs: 15 approaches allow generating code for C/C++ or NesC and 11 approaches support topologies, but none allows to explicitly specify TC algorithms [6]. Most MDE approaches focus on architectures for WSNs. The AGILLA [3] framework is an agent-based MDE platform for WSNs. The SCATTERCLIPSE [1] framework is an Eclipse-based toolkit for generating and testing WSN applications. The SAMSON framework [17] provides an architecture

---

[6] See also https://en.wikipedia.org/wiki/List_of_wireless_sensor_nodes.

description language of a WSN and allows to generate code for CONTIKI. All of these approaches (would) represent TC as software component, concealing the concrete TC implementation. This makes our approach complementary to many existing MDE middleware approaches: In this context, TC can be seen as a service component that should be configured according to the demands of the active application (e.g., concerning robustness, path lengths). To the best of our knowledge, no other MDE approaches for generating code of TC algorithms exist in the literature. In [2], a C code generator for the Graph Programming Language 2 (GP2) is presented. Similar to the DEMOCLES pattern matching engine, the backend of EMOFLON, GP2 transforms the graph patterns into a depth-first search plan with matching operations. Similar to CMOFLON, each operation corresponds to a particular (hierarchical) code template and the pattern matching is rooted. In contrast to GP2, CMOFLON uses story diagrams for specifying the control flow. Story diagrams support the invocation of arbitrary user-defined operations, and the search plan generation can be easily configured using modules for search plan weights and strategies [25]. While EMF has emerged as de-facto target language for MDE tools, a number of tools support other target platforms (e.g., GrGen.NET [8]). EMF4CPP⁷ aimed to provide full support for creating C++ code from EMF models, but appears to be discontinued. To sum up, we know neither of a tool for generating embedded C code from programmed GT nor of an MDE methodology that constructively integrates integrity properties into the development of TC algorithms and targets the evaluation of the resulting TC algorithms in simulation and testbed environments.

7 Conclusion

Each novel TC algorithm should be evaluated using a WSN testbed to investigate real-world effects and to increase confidence in its applicability. In this paper, we present CMOFLON, an MDE tool for generating embedded C code from a programmed GT specification of TC algorithms for the WSN operating system CONTIKI. The evaluation results indicate that CMOFLON is applicable for the desired purpose. Together with our previous results in [10–12], a developer may now design a GT-based, correct-by-construction TC algorithm and evaluate it rapidly in a simulation *and* testbed environment. In future work, we will evaluate and improve the code memory consumption and the execution time for additional TC algorithms and sensor node types to further strengthen our confidence in the applicability of CMOFLON. A user study may help to investigate how using CMOFLON reduces the development effort and increases reliability of the developed TC algorithms compared to the traditional manual approach.

Acknowledgment. This work has been funded by the German Research Foundation (DFG) as part of project A1 within the Collaborative Research Center (CRC) 1053 – MAKI.

---

⁷ https://github.com/catedrasaes-umu/emf4cpp.

References

1. Al Saad, M., Fehr, E., Kamenzky, N., Schiller, J.: ScatterClipse: a model-driven tool-chain for developing, testing, and prototyping wireless sensor networks. In: Proceedings of the International Symposium on Parallel and Distributed Processing with Applications (ISPA), pp. 871–885 (2008). https://dx.doi.org/10.1109/ISPA.2008.22
2. Bak, C., Plump, D.: Compiling graph programs to C. In: Echahed, R., Minas, M. (eds.) ICGT 2016. LNCS, vol. 9761, pp. 102–117. Springer, Cham (2016). doi:10.1007/978-3-319-40530-8_7
3. Berardinelli, L., Di Marco, A., Pace, S., Pomante, L., Tiberti, W.: Energy consumption analysis and design of energy-aware WSN agents in fUML. In: Taentzer, G., Bordeleau, F. (eds.) ECMFA 2015. LNCS, vol. 9153, pp. 1–17. Springer, Cham (2015). doi:10.1007/978-3-319-21151-0_1
4. Dunkels, A., Gronvall, B., Voigt, T.: Contiki - a lightweight and flexible operating system for tiny networked sensors. In: Proceedings of the International Conference on Local Computer Networks (LCN), pp. 455–462 (2004). https://dx.doi.org/10.1109/LCN.2004.38
5. Ehrig, H., Ehrig, K., Prange, U., Taentzer, G.: Fundamentals of Algebraic Graph Transformation. Springer, Heidelberg (2006). https://dx.doi.org/10.1007/3-540-31188-2
6. Essaadi, F., Ben Maissa, Y., Dahchour, M.: MDE-based languages for wireless sensor networks modeling: a systematic mapping study. In: El-Azouzi, R., Menasché, D.S., Sabir, E., Pellegrini, F.D., Benjillali, M. (eds.) Advances in Ubiquitous Networking 2. LNEE, vol. 397, pp. 331–346. Springer, Singapore (2017). doi:10.1007/978-981-10-1627-1_26
7. Fischer, T., Niere, J., Torunski, L., Zündorf, A.: Story diagrams: a new graph rewrite language based on the unified modeling language and java. In: Ehrig, H., Engels, G., Kreowski, H.-J., Rozenberg, G. (eds.) TAGT 1998. LNCS, vol. 1764, pp. 296–309. Springer, Heidelberg (2000). doi:10.1007/978-3-540-46464-8_21
8. Geiß, R., Batz, G.V., Grund, D., Hack, S., Szalkowski, A.: GrGen: a fast SPO-based graph rewriting tool. In: Corradini, A., Ehrig, H., Montanari, U., Ribeiro, L., Rozenberg, G. (eds.) ICGT 2006. LNCS, vol. 4178, pp. 383–397. Springer, Heidelberg (2006). doi:10.1007/11841883_27
9. Heckel, R., Wagner, A.: Ensuring consistency of conditional graph rewriting - a constructive approach. In: Proceedings of the Joint COMPUGRAPH/SEMAGRAPH Workshop. ENTCS, vol. 2, pp. 118–126. Elsevier (1995). https://dx.doi.org/10.1016/S1571-0661(05)80188-4
10. Kluge, R., Stein, M., Varró, G., Schürr, A., Hollick, M., Mühlhäuser, M.: A systematic approach to constructing incremental topology control algorithms using graph transformation. J. Vis. Lang. Comput. (JVLC) 38, 47–83 (2016). http://dx.doi.org/10.1016/j.jvlc.2016.10.003
11. Kluge, R., Stein, M., Varró, G., Schürr, A., Hollick, M., Mühlhäuser, M.: A systematic approach to constructing families of incremental topology control algorithms using graph transformation. J. Softw. Syst. Model. (SoSyM), 1–41 (2017). https://dx.doi.org/10.1007/s10270-017-0587-8
12. Kluge, R., Varró, G., Schürr, A.: A methodology for designing dynamic topology control algorithms via graph transformation. In: Kolovos, D., Wimmer, M. (eds.) ICMT 2015. LNCS, vol. 9152, pp. 199–213. Springer, Cham (2015). doi:10.1007/978-3-319-21155-8_15

13. Leblebici, E., Anjorin, A., Schürr, A.: Developing eMoflon with eMoflon. In: Ruscio, D., Varró, D. (eds.) ICMT 2014. LNCS, vol. 8568, pp. 138–145. Springer, Cham (2014). doi:10.1007/978-3-319-08789-4_10

14. Li, N., Hou, J.C., Sha, L.: Design and analysis of an MST-based topology control algorithm. IEEE Trans. Wirel. Commun. **4**(3), 1195–1206 (2005)

15. Lim, R., Ferrari, F., Zimmerling, M., Walser, C., Sommer, P., Beutel, J.: FlockLab: a testbed for distributed, synchronized tracing and profiling of wireless embedded systems. In: Proceedings of the ACM/IEEE Conference on Information Processing in Sensor Networks (IPSN), pp. 153–165 (2013). https://doi.org/10.1145/2461381.2461402

16. Polastre, J., Szewczyk, R., Culler, D.: Telos: enabling ultra-low power wireless research. In: International Symposium on Information Processing in Sensor Networks (IPSN), pp. 364–369 (2005). https://dx.doi.org/10.1109/IPSN.2005.1440950

17. Portocarrero, J.M.T., Delicato, F.C., Pires, P.F., Rodrigues, T.C., Batista, T.V.: SAMSON: Self-adaptive Middleware for Wireless Sensor Networks. In: Proceedings of the ACM Symposium on Applied Computing (SAC), pp. 1315–1322. ACM, New York (2016). https://dx.doi.org/10.1145/2851613.2851766

18. Richerzhagen, B., Stingl, D., Rückert, J., Steinmetz, R.: Simonstrator: simulation and prototyping platform for distributed mobile applications. In: Proceedings of the International Conference on Simulation Tools and Techniques (SIMUTools), pp. 99–108. ICST (2015). https://dx.doi.org/10.4108/eai.24-8-2015.2261064

19. Rozenberg, G. (ed.): Handbook of Graph Grammars and Computing by Graph Transformation. Foundations, vol. 1. World Scientific (1997). https://dx.doi.org/10.1142/3303

20. Santi, P.: Topology Control in Wireless Ad Hoc and Sensor Networks, 1st edn. Wiley, Chichester (2005)

21. Santi, P.: Topology control in wireless ad hoc and sensor networks. ACM Comput. Surv. (CSUR) **37**(2), 164–194 (2005). https://dx.doi.org/10.1145/1089733.1089736

22. Schweizer, I., Wagner, M., Bradler, D., Mühlhäuser, M., Strufe, T.: kTC - robust and adaptive wireless ad-hoc topology control. In: Proceedings of the International Conference on Computer Communications and Networks (ICCCN), pp. 1–9 (2012). https://dx.doi.org/10.1109/ICCCN.2012.6289318

23. Stein, M., Petry, T., Schweizer, I., Bachmann, M., Mühlhäuser, M.: Topology control in wireless sensor networks: what blocks the breakthrough? In: Proceedings of the International Conference on Local Computer Networks (LCN), pp. 389–397 (2016). https://doi.org/10.1109/LCN.2016.67

24. Steinberg, D., Budinsky, F., Merks, E., Paternostro, M.: EMF: Eclipse Modeling Framework. Addison Wesley Professional, Boston (2008). http://catalogue.pearsoned.co.uk/educator/product/EMF-Eclipse-Modeling-Framework/9780321331885

25. Varró, G., Anjorin, A., Schürr, A.: Unification of compiled and interpreter-based pattern matching techniques. In: Vallecillo, A., Tolvanen, J.P., Kindler, E., Störrle, H., Kolovos, D. (eds.) ECMFA 2012. LNCS, vol. 7349, pp. 368–383. Springer, Heidelberg (2012). doi:10.1007/978-3-642-31491-9_28

26. Völter, M., Stahl, T., Bettin, J., Haase, A., Helsen, S.: Model-Driven Software Development: Technology, Engineering, Management. John Wiley & Sons (2013)

27. Wang, Y.: Topology control for wireless sensor networks. In: Li, Y., Thai, M.T., Wu, W. (eds.) Wireless Sensor Networks and Applications. Signals and Communication Technology, pp. 113–147. Springer, US (2008). doi:10.1007/978-0-387-49592-7_5

28. Whitmore, A., Agarwal, A., Da Xu, L.: The internet of things-a survey of topics and trends. Inf. Syst. Front. **17**(2), 261–274 (2015). https://dx.doi.org/10.1007/s10796-014-9489-2

Self-adaptive UIs: Integrated Model-Driven Development of UIs and Their Adaptations

Enes Yigitbas$^{(\boxtimes)}$, Hagen Stahl, Stefan Sauer, and Gregor Engels

s-lab - Software Quality Lab, Paderborn University,
Zukunftsmeile 1, 33102 Paderborn, Germany
{enes.yigitbas,hagen.stahl,sauer,engels}@upb.de

Abstract. Self-adaptive UIs have been promoted as a solution for context variability due to their ability to automatically adapt to the context-of-use at runtime. In classical model-driven UI development (MDUID) approaches, self-adaptivity and context management introduce additional complexity since self-adaptation features are distributed in a cross-cutting manner at various locations in the models. This results in a tightly interwoven model landscape that is hard to understand and maintain. In this paper, we present an integrated model-driven development method where a classical model-driven development of UIs is coupled with a separate model-driven development of UI adaptation rules and context-of-use. We base our approach on the core UI modeling language IFML, and focus on a new modeling language for adaptation rules, called AdaptUI. We show how generated UI code is coupled with adaptation services generated from AdaptUI adaptation rules and integrated in an overall UI framework. This allows runtime UI adaptation realized by an automatic reaction to context-of-use changes. The benefit of our approach is demonstrated by a case study, showing the development of self-adaptive UIs for a university library application, utilizing the Angular 2 JavaScript framework.

Keywords: Model-Driven UI Development · UI Adaptation Rules · Self-adaptive UIs · Context-Awareness

1 Introduction

The user interface (UI) is a key component of any interactive software application and is crucial for the acceptance of the application as a whole. However, a UI is not independent from its context-of-use, which is defined in terms of the user, platform and environment [1]. As today's user interfaces of interactive systems become increasingly complex since many heterogeneous contexts of use have to be supported, it is no longer sufficient to provide a single "one-size-fits-all" user interface. Building multiple UIs for the same functionality due to context variability is also difficult since context changes can lead to the combinatorial explosion of the number of possible adaptations and there is a high cost incurred by manually developing multiple versions of the UI [2].

© Springer International Publishing AG 2017
A. Anjorin and H. Espinoza (Eds.): ECMFA 2017, LNCS 10376, pp. 126–141, 2017.
DOI: 10.1007/978-3-319-61482-3_8

In the past, model-driven user interface development (MDUID) approaches were proposed to support the efficient development of UIs. Widely studied approaches are UsiXML [3], MARIA [4], and IFML [5] that support the abstract modeling of user interfaces and their transformation to final user interfaces. However, in classical MDUID approaches, the modeling of self-adaptivity and context management aspects introduce additional complexity since self-adaptation features are distributed in a cross-cutting manner at various locations in the models. This results in a tightly interwoven model landscape that is hard to understand and maintain. Therefore, an integrated model-driven development method is needed where a classical model-driven development of UIs is coupled with a separate model-driven development of UI adaptation rules and context-of-use. In detail, the following challenges have to be addressed to integrate adaptation aspects into MDUID and support the development of self-adaptive UIs in a systematic way:

- *C1: Specification of UI Adaptation Rules*: A language conform to the core UI modeling language IFML, standardized by the Object Management Group (OMG), is required for specifying UI adaptation rules in an abstract manner. With the help of this language, UI designers should be able to separately specify various UI adaptation rules which can adapt the UI at runtime (separation of concerns, abstraction level, extensibility, maintainability).
- *C2: Generation of UI Adaptation Logic*: Based on the specified abstract UI adaptation rules, the adaptation logic needs to be generated for supporting UI adaptation capabilities at runtime.
- *C3: Execution of UI Adaptation at Runtime*: For supporting runtime UI adaptation enabling automatic reaction to dynamic context-of-use changes, the generated adaptation logic needs to be coupled with generated UI code as well as integrated in an overall UI framework.

To address the above described challenges, the contributions of this paper include our vision on enhancing UIs with self-adaptation capabilities in a systematic and model-driven way. Therefore, our contribution covers the following aspects: Firstly, a domain specific language, called AdaptUI, will be presented which supports the specification of abstract UI adaptation rules that cover various adaptation dimensions (e.g. layout, navigation, or task-feature set). Additionally, our approach supports the generation of UI adaptation logic by transforming the abstract UI adaptation rules into an executable representation of the target UI framework. Finally, a rule-based execution engine is integrated in our UI framework for executing the UI adaptations at runtime.

The remaining sections of this paper are organized as follows: Section 2 presents the conceptual solution of our work. In Sect. 3, we present the modeling and integration of UI adaptation concerns in MDUID. Section 4 deals with the implementation of our approach. Section 5 shows the benefit and usefulness of our approach based on a case-study from the domain of university library management. Related work is presented in Sect. 6 and finally Sect. 7 concludes the paper and gives an outlook on future work.

2   Conceptual Solution

Model-driven User Interface Development (MDUID) is a promising candidate for mastering the complex development task of self-adaptive UIs in a systematic, precise and appropriately formal way. Our model-driven solution architecture for self-adaptive UIs is depicted in Fig. 1 and consists of three development paths.

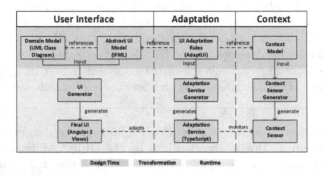

Fig. 1. Model-driven architecture for self-adaptive UIs

The first development path (left side of Fig. 1) addresses the model-driven development of UIs. This development path makes use of an *Abstract UI Model* and a *Domain Model* which are then transformed by a code generator (*UI Generator*) into a *Final UI*. This development path has been subject of extensive research [6] and we already presented the realization and application of an MDUID approach for different target platforms [7,8] (including smartphone, desktop and self-service systems) based on the OMG standard IFML. The first development path supports efficient development of heterogeneous UIs for different target platforms. However, this development path on its own is not enough to support UI self-adaptation capabilities. Therefore, we extended our existing MDUID solution architecture with parallel development paths which support model-driven development of UI adaptation rules and context-of-use. This way, the model-driven UI development path is complemented by an analog development path which is responsible for the UI adaptation concerns. As the UI adaptation path is also based on the paradigm of model-driven development, the solution preserves various advantages of model-driven software development like Separation of Concerns, Extensibility or Maintainability. In general, the main idea of the model-driven adaptation path (in the middle of Fig. 1) is to support the specification of abstract *UI Adaptation Rules* in alignment to the standardized abstract UI modeling language IFML. The specified *UI Adaptation Rules* serve as an input for the *Adaptation Service Generator* which transforms them into an *Adaptation Service*. The *Adaptation Service* is responsible for adapting the generated *Final UI* at runtime. The third development path (right side of Fig. 1) is responsible for characterizing the dynamically changing context-of-use parameters. A *Context Model* that is referenced by the *UI Adaptation Rules*, supports the abstract specification of heterogeneous context-of-use situations. Based on the *Context Model*, the *Context Sensor Generator* allows the generation of various *Context Sensors* like accelerometer, GPS, brightness or noise level. The *Context Sensors* provide context information data that are monitored by the generated *Adaptation Service* to decide on how to adapt the UI at runtime.

In this paper, we are especially focusing on the adaptation path and its integration in the MDUID approach. For illustrating the interplay between the generated final user interface, the *Angular2 Views*, and the *Adaptation Service* as well as to present the effect of specified UI adaptation rules on the final user interface, we elaborate on the adaptation approach. Figure 2 shows a detailed overview of the UI adaptation approach containing the main layers and components for realizing self-adaptive UIs that are able to automatically react to changes in their context-of-use.

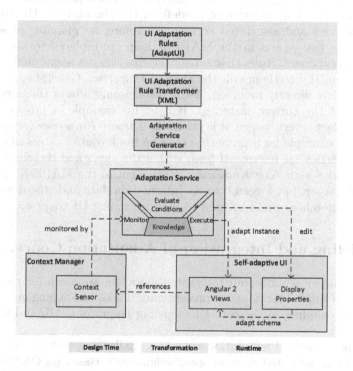

Fig. 2. Model-driven specification and adaptation of UIs

The first layer starts with the specification of *UI Adaptation Rules* at design time. The specification language is AdaptUI, a domain-specific language developed in this work which is explained in more detail in the next section. In the second layer, the abstract adaptation rules are transformed into an XML format by the *UI Adaptation Rule Transformer*. The goal of this transformation is to store the adaptation rules in a universal, common file format, that is easily traversable for further transformation processes. The next step in the generation process, is the transformation to an executable *Adaptation Service*. This transformation is done by the *Adaptation Service Generator*. The output of the generator is the *Adaptation Service* which characterizes a runtime component in the third layer. The *Adaptation Service* implements an adaptation loop similar to IBM's MAPE-K loop [11]. Main runtime components besides the *Adaptation Service* are the *Context Manager* and the *Self-adaptive UI*. The *Context Manager* provides the generated context information through *Context Sensors* which are specified in the *Context Model*. The *Self-adaptive UI* consists of two subcomponents: The *Angular 2 Views* which are responsible for representing the UI and *Display Properties* which are affected by the adaptation rules and contain the adaptable schema and type information of the UI. Context information which are generated by *Context Sensors* are monitored by the *Adaptation Service*. Unlike the MAPE-K loop with its analysis and plan phases, the *Adaptation Service* relies on the application of predefined (by the abstract UI Adaptation Rules) conditions and associated actions. Therefore, no planning of actions is necessary. The two phases in the MAPE-K loop are replaced by the *Evaluate Conditions* component. Rules that satisfy the conditions are executed. The rules can modify the UI directly or edit the *Display Properties*. General approach here is that the UI is directly modified, if the change only affects the current view (adaptation of the current instance). If it is, for example, a property change that would affect several pages, it is set in the *Display Properties* (adaptation of schemas). An example for a property could be the layout of tables in the whole UI. The properties are referenced from within the views and thereby can adapt the layout and design. The *Knowledge* component of the MAPE-K loop is not focus of this paper, but logged context information data and stored adaptation states and preferences could be used to infer upcoming UI adaptations.

3   Modeling and Integration of Adaptation Concerns

In this section, we describe our integrated modeling approach for representing UI adaptation rules. Therefore, we present our UI adaptation language AdaptUI and show its coupling to the core UI modeling language IFML and to context modeling.

Specifying sound UI adaptation rules is a challenging task which should be supported by a dedicated domain specific language. Based on OMG's core UI modeling language IFML, we developed a new modeling language for UI adaptation rules, the language AdaptUI. AdaptUI allows domain experts, for example web designers, to model adaptation concerns by specifying the conditions and actions for UI adaptations. To support various adaptation techniques for devising self-adaptive model-driven UIs, AdaptUI enables specification of different UI adaptation rules. The following main categories of UI adaptation types are supported by AdaptUI: task-feature-set, navigation, and layout adaptation. Task-feature-set adaptation supports UI adaptation by flexibly showing and hiding UI

interaction elements like tables, buttons, text-fields etc. Navigation adaptation
means that the navigation flow of the UI can be flexibly adapted based on the
contextual parameters by adding, deleting or redirecting links between user interface flows. Finally, layout adaptation deals with adaptation rules that support
layout optimization like changing font size, colors or splitting screens to divide
a complex UI view into multiple views so that for example small screen sizes are
satisfied. Figure 3 shows a modeling example of UI adaptation rules based on our
language AdaptUI. On the left side of this figure, small excerpts of the core UI
models are depicted. There is an abstract UI model based on IFML which shows
the representation of two UI view containers *booksView* and *bookDetailsView*
which are connected by a navigation edge *showDetails*. To enable the specification of data bindings in IFML, the corresponding classes from the domain model
are referenced, in our case the class *Book*. To support the separate specification of
UI adaptation rules in addition to the IFML model in a comfortable way, AdaptUI allows to specify and bind different adaptation rules to the IFML modeling
elements. In the center of Fig. 3, an example specification of an AdaptUI navigation adaptation rule is shown, which is called "'Navigate to BookDetails"'.
This AdaptUI rule defines that the specific view *bookDetailsView* can be only
reached, if a specific user context is satisfied. For defining this rule, AdaptUI
rules are referencing a context model where relevant contextual parameters are
described. In the case of our example, the user role student has to be satisfied
so that the *bookDetailsView* can be reached. In a similar way, various other UI
adaptation rules like adapt brightness or set table layout (see Fig. 3) can be
specified to react to potential context-of-use changes.

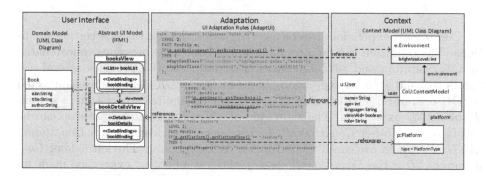

Fig. 3. Specification of AdaptUI adaptation rules

An overview of the general structure of the AdaptUI language is shown in
Fig. 4. The root element of all elements in AdaptUI is the *AdaptUI-Model*. It
contains the definition of a *Flow* (chosen to be conform to the terminology of used
rule engine Nools[1]) containing arbitrary number of *AdaptationRule* elements.
An *AdaptationRule* consists of the *RuleName*, *FactDefinition*, a *PriorityLevel*,

---

[1] https://github.com/C2FO/nools.

Conditions and *Actions*. The *FactDefinition* is given as the class name in the final Angular 2 application and an identifier by which it is referred to within the rule. To decide in which order rules are executed if more than one satisfies all conditions, the *PriorityLevel* is used as indicator for priority. Higher level means that the rule is executed before rules with lower level.

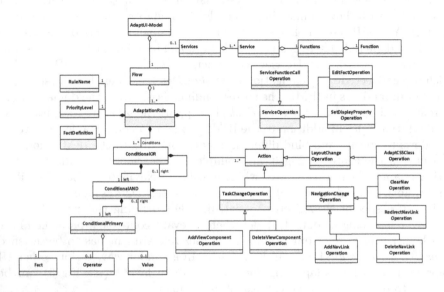

Fig. 4. Structure of AdaptUI-DSL

Conditional expressions can be used to check if the fact satisfies certain conditions. The condition can be a combination of boolean expressions concatenated by OR-operators and AND-operators. For this, AdaptUI provides several elements to build such an expression. The *ConditionalOR* elements are connected by OR-operators. The left side of such a *ConditionalOR* expression is a *ConditionalAND* expression. The right side of a *ConditionalOR* expression can be empty or be another *ConditionalOR* expression. The elements in a *ConditionalAND* expression are concatenated by an AND-Operator. The left side of *ConditionalAND* is the *ConditionalPrimary*, which is a boolean expression made up of just a fact or a combination of fact, operator and value. The right side of a *ConditionalAND* can be either another *ConditionalAND* or be empty.

The *Actions*, which were introduced in the beginning of this paragraph, are executed if the conditions are satisfied. The supported *Actions* of the AdaptUI language are based on the action categories defined in our previous work [8] and cover the adaptation operations *TaskChangeOperation*, *NavigationChangeOperation* and *LayoutChangeOperation*. A fourth type proposed in our prior previous work is a *ComposedAction* which combines multiple actions of the first three categories. In AdaptUI, the *ComposedAction* type is implicitly modelled by the composition relation between *AdaptationRule* and *Action*.

Beside a *Flow* an *AdaptUI-Model* can also contain *Services* in the target language of the UI. This means, the services referenced here are existing Angular 2 services that are used within the web application. The definition of these services enables the user of the language to use them later on in the rule specification. A *Service* is defined by its name and relative location to the *Services* folder of the Angular 2 implementation. A *Service* can contain interfaces to *Functions* which also have a *Function* with its name attribute. Both, *Functions* and *Services* are referred to by their respective ID. To allow editing facts or call Angular 2 services through an *AdaptationRule*, an additional category, *ServiceOperation*, is included in the Actions.

4 Implementation

We implemented an *IFML2NG2* generator to support the utilization of our modeling and development approach for devising self-adaptive UIs. The realized generator automatically creates Angular 2 views, based on the IFML model and domain model, and the adaptation service, based on the AdaptUI rule specification. In the following, we focus on and briefly describe the implementation of *AdaptUI*, the *Adaptation Service Generator* and the *Runtime Components* to support UI adaptation at runtime (see Fig. 2).

4.1 AdaptUI

For specifying abstract UI adaptation rules, the described UI adaptation language *AdaptUI* is used. Foundation of *AdaptUI* is the open-source framework Xtext[2] for development of programming languages and domain-specific languages. The defined language also comes with support of an infrastructure integrated in the Eclipse IDE. Features include syntax highlighting and code completion as useful tools for the user of *AdaptUI*.

4.2 Adaptation Service Generator

The goal of the *Adaptation Service Generator* is the automated creation of an Angular 2 service that allows the adaptation of the UI at runtime. The adaptations to the UI are expressed in a rule-based form in an XML format. Based on this input file, the *Adaptation Service Generator* generates an Angular 2 service containing the JavaScript rules engine Nools. Nools is an efficient RETE-based rule engine written in JavaScript and provides an API for specifying fact and rules. The *Adaptation Service Generator* is implemented with Xtend[3] and receives the UI adaptation rules in an XML format as input. Structurally, it consists of the components *NoolsServiceGenerator*, *NoolsRuleGenerator*, *NoolsConditionGenerator* and *NoolsActionGenerator* (see Fig. 5). These components are responsible for creating an injectable Angular 2 service for monitoring the context model and executing adaptation operations.

---

[2] http://www.eclipse.org/Xtext.
[3] http://www.eclipse.org/xtend.

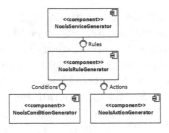

Fig. 5. Structure of the adaptation service generator

The base structure of the Angular 2 service, generated by the *NoolsService-Generator*, consists of the required Angular 2 imports, the class declaration of the service and the implementation of the Nools flow. The flow is composed of all the rules defined in the abstract UI adaptation rules. For each rule it is defined under which conditions the rule actions are executed. The generation of the individual rules is delegated to the *NoolsRuleGenerator*. For each adaptation rule the name is the name of the abstract UI adaptation rule. The salience of the rule is the priority level of the rule and corresponds to the level defined in the *AdaptUI* rule specification. In addition to that, the rule fact is defined by the factType and factName attributes. The generation of the conditions and adaptation operations of the rule is delegated to the *NoolsConditionGenerator* and the *NoolsActionGenerator* respectively.

The *NoolsConditionGenerator* is responsible for creating the rule conditions. All child elements of the conditions element are combined with the OR-operator. If there is a conditionGroup element, all child elements of the conditionGroup are combined with the AND-operator. The result is a string of concatenated conditions with operators. Likewise, to generate the actions that the rule should execute when the conditions are satisfied, the *NoolsActionGenerator* is called with the actions element as parameter and, additionally, the mapping of services and functions defined in the abstract UI adaptation rule specification. However, there is a defined set of actions. If the action element is unknown, there is no code created. This means, that if there are new possible actions added to the schema definition, they also need to be implemented in the *NoolsActionGenerator*.

4.3   Runtime Components: Adaptation Service, Self-adaptive UI and Context Manager

At runtime, we have the components *Adaptation Service, Self-adaptive UI* and *Context Manager*. The *Self-adaptive UI* is generated by our *IFML2NG2* generator. Its Angular 2 views consist of an HTML template, which is used to render the UI in the browser, and an Angular 2 component, which is implemented in TypeScript and manages the view. Likewise, the *Adaptation Service* is generated as Angular 2 service and is also implemented in TypeScript. As described in the earlier section, the *Adaptation Service* uses Nools, a JavaScript based rule engine, for monitoring the context information provided by the *Context*

Manager. In our current implementation, the *Context Manager* and the *Display Properties* (see Fig. 2) are implemented manually and independently from the generation pipeline in TypeScript. However, to ensure the integration of the adaptation loop, they are referenced within the *AdaptUI* specification. The facts of the *AdaptUI* rule specification reference the different context-of-use information stored in the context model of the *Context Manager.* Furthermore, it is possible to define UI adaptation operations that should change the schema used by the view elements of the UI.

At runtime, the *Adaptation Service* monitors the context information and executes the adaptation rules whose conditions are satisfied. To adapt the UI view elements on instance level, JQuery is used to directly manipulate the DOM tree of the view. Changes only affect the current UI view element and do not persist on other UI views. When changing the schema for a group of view elements in the *Display Properties*, the adaptation affects the properties of all view elements of this type. This also includes instances of this view element type on subsequently visited views. This is done by binding the layout class of the view elements of this type, represented by CSS classes, to the properties stored within the *Display Properties.*

5 Case Study

The case study setting is based on an example scenario which is derived from the university library management domain (see Fig. 6). The scenario setting is a library web application for universities which is called "LibSoft". LibSoft provides core library management functionality like searching, reserving and lending books. LibSoft's UI can be accessed by heterogeneous users and user roles (like student or staff member) through a broad range of networked interaction devices (e.g. smartphones, tablets, terminals etc.) which are used in various environmental contexts (e.g. brightness, loudness, while moving etc.). Depending on the situation, users are able to access their library services where, when and how it suits them best. For example, if the user wants to pursue a self-determined cross-channel book lending process, she can begin an interaction using one channel (search and reserve a book with her laptop at home), modify the transaction on her way using a mobile channel, and finalize the book lending process at the university library via self-check-out terminal or at the staff desk. In the example scenario described above, each channel has its own special context-of-use and eventually the contextual parameters regarding user, platform and environment can dynamically change. Figure 7 shows such a context-of-use (CoU) change from CoU2 to CoU4 (compare Fig. 6). The depicted context-of-use object model excerpts in Fig. 7 illustrate how different contextual parameters regarding user, platform and environment can change. Therefore, it is important to continuously monitor the context-of-use parameters and react to possible changes by automatically adapting the UI for the new context-of-use situation.

Already a small set of contextual parameters can highly influence the UI since lots of context situations can occur if the context-of-use parameters dynamically

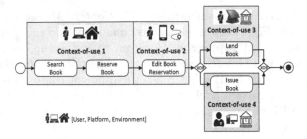

Fig. 6. Example scenario: UIs in dynamically changing context-of-use situations.

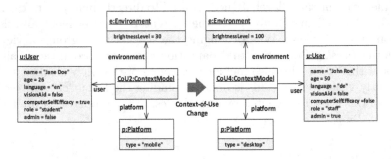

Fig. 7. Context-of-use object model excerpts

change. Based on the different context dimensions, various adaptations to the UI can be specified and integrated in the web application. The integration happens, as explained within the earlier sections, by specifying the adaptation rules with the help of AdaptUI and using the specification as input for the generator. For utilizing our approach in the case study setting, an IFML model, representing the views and navigational flows of the UI, a domain model and a set of UI adaptation rules were created as described in Sect. 3. The specified models were transformed into final user interfaces using our *IFML2NG2* generator.

Screenshots of the resulting self-adaptive UI are depicted in Fig. 8. According to the monitored context information for CoU2, the layout for the UI is optimized for a mobile device used in a darker environment, because the user Jane is editing her book reservation while travelling to the library and it is already quite dark outside (see left side of Fig. 8). Also, the UI is adapted to the user properties by enabling access to the functions and navigation available to students. The UI language is set to English as it is preferred by the user Jane. Since Jane is recognized as a self-efficacious user with the application, she gets extended functionalities, like a more complex search and filter mechanism for the list view of the books. When the context changes from CoU2 to CoU4, the generated self-adaptive UI adapts itself automatically to the new contextual parameters. In this case, the staff members view on a desktop device with a wider and brighter layout is shown, displaying the list of reserved books, because in CoU4 a staff member, John Roe, uses his desktop computer to issue the book to Jane. Additionally,

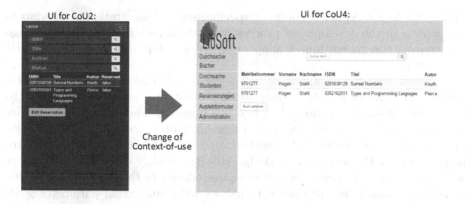

Fig. 8. UI adaptation according to different contexts-of-use

to the functionalities and functions available to staff members, John is provided with a link to the administration interface, because he is granted access to the administration interface. The UI Language is set to German and the search and filter mechanisms of the list are simplified, because he just started using LibSoft and is, therefore, not yet self-efficacious. Since the location is a well-lit library, the brightness of the environment is high.

The case study demonstrates the benefit of our approach for supporting the development of self-adaptive UIs and showcases our solution approach for addressing the introduced challenges C1–C3. Through the separate specification of abstract AdaptUI rules the modeling of adaptation concerns is supported in a comfortable way. The case study also shows how generated UI code is coupled with adaptation services generated from AdaptUI adaptation rules and integrated in an overall UI framework. As shown in the example scenario, this allows runtime UI adaptation realized by an automatic reaction to context-of-use changes.

6 Related Work

Recent research provides various approaches that support the model-based and model-driven development of UIs and their adaptations.

Model-based and model-driven development methods have been discussed in the past for various individual aspects of a software system and for different application domains. This applies to the development of the data management layer, the application layer or the user interface layer. The CAMELEON Reference Framework (CRF) [1] provides a unified framework for model-based and model-driven development of UIs. UIs are represented in CRF on the following levels of abstraction: Tasks and Domain Models, Abstract User Interface (AUI) Model, Concrete User Interface (CUI) Model and Final User Interface (FUI). UsiXML [3], MARIA [4] and IFML [5] are widely studied approaches for model-driven UI development which were applied in various domains. However, these approaches do not explicitly cover the specification and integration of UI adaptation aspects in the development process by providing a UI adaptation language that enables the generation of adaptation services for supporting runtime UI adaptation.

In recent research, adaptive or self-adaptive UIs have been promoted as a solution for context variability due to their ability to automatically adapt to the context-of-use at runtime [2]. A key goal behind self-adaptive UIs is plasticity denoting a UI's ability to preserve its usability despite dynamically changing context-of-use parameters [9]. In practice, especially in the context of web design, the paradigm of Responsive Web Design (RWB) is widely used to adapt the layout of a web page in response to the characteristics of the used device. While RWB adaptation rules are mainly focusing on the contextual parameter *Platform*, considering device characteristics like screen size or resolution, our approach also focuses on the contextual parameters *User* and *Environment* allowing the specification of advanced adaptation rules and automatic adaptation to complex context-of-use situations.

In [10] the authors present a hierarchy of adaptability properties for software systems, referred to as self-* properties. Based on this work, the authors present in [2] how some of these properties are applicable to the domain of self-adaptive UIs. Similar to the idea that self-* properties of self-adaptive software systems can be applied to self-adaptive UIs, it is possible that general reference architectures for self-adaptive systems can be also applied to self-adaptive UIs. We will give a brief overview of these architectures. The MAPE-K loop, which was used in our approach, was created by IBM as a reference model for autonomic computing [11]. MAPE-K considers software systems as a set of managed resources that is adapted by an adaptation manager which consists of the components Monitor, Analyze, Plan, Execute, and Knowledge. Similar reference architectures for self-adaptive systems are Rainbow [12] and the Three Layer Architecture [13]. Beside these general architectures for self-adaptive systems, there are also specific reference architectures for adaptive UIs like CAMELEON-RT [14], CEDAR [15] or FAME [16]. Furthermore, different approaches like Supple [18], MASP [19], MyUI [20] or RBUIS [21] present methods, techniques and tools for supporting the development of adaptive UIs. However, these approaches do not focus on the generation of UI adaptation logic in the means of adaptation services.

On the intersection of MDUID and UI adaptation, several transformation-based approaches like [22] or [23] were proposed that make use of adaptation rules based on a context model to adapt UIs. There are also other approaches using different techniques to adapt UIs, like [24] which uses machine learning or [17] where a genetic algorithm is used to calculate a well suited UI adaptation. Compared to these approaches, our model-driven approach for developing self-adaptive UIs, provides a dedicated rule-based UI adaptation language and supports the generation of adaptation services allowing runtime UI adaptation.

7 Conclusion and Outlook

In this paper, we present an integrated model-driven development approach for self-adaptive UIs where a classical model-driven development of UIs is enhanced and coupled with a separate model-driven development of UI adaptation rules and context-of-use. Based on OMG's core UI modeling language IFML, we propose a new modeling language for UI adaptation rules, the language AdaptUI. We present how generated UI code is coupled with adaptation services generated from AdaptUI adaptation rules and integrated in an overall UI framework. This allows runtime UI adaptation realized by an automatic reaction to dynamically changing context-of-use parameters like user profile, platform, and usage environment. We demonstrate the benefit of our approach by a case study, showing the development of self-adaptive UIs for a university library application, utilizing the Angular 2 framework.

In ongoing research, we investigate the acceptance and user-friendliness of self-adaptive UIs by conducting usability studies with potential end-users. In addition to that, we analyze how additional context information properties can be automatically monitored and generated by context sensors to be used for further UI adaptation. Further research will also cover the application of quality assurance techniques to our presented model-driven UI adaptation approach, which enable the provisioning of hard guarantees concerning self-adaptivity characteristics such as adaptation rule set stability and deadlock freedom. Furthermore, we plan to enhance our proposed UI self-adaptation loop through the implementation of a knowledge component. In this context, it is conceivable to apply learning algorithms based on the user's assessment of executed adaptation operations to further improve UI adaptations.

Acknowledgement. This work is based on "KoMoS", a project of the "it's OWL" Leading-Edge Cluster, partially funded by the German Federal Ministry of Education and Research (BMBF).

References

1. Calvary, G., Coutaz, J., Thevenin, D., Limbourg, Q., Bouillon, L., Vanderdonckt, J.: A unifying reference framework for multi-target user interfaces. Interact. Comput. **15**, 289–308 (2003)
2. Akiki, P.A., Bandara, A.K., Yu, Y.: Adaptive model-driven user interface development systems. ACM Comput. Surv. **47**(1), 64:1–64:33 (2014)
3. Limbourg, Q., Vanderdonckt, J.: USIXML: a user interface description language supporting multiple levels of independence. In: Engineering Advanced Web Applications: Proceedings of Workshops in Connection with the 4th International Conference on Web Engineering. Rinton Press, pp. 325–338 (2004)
4. Paternò, F., Santoro, C., Spano, L.D.: MARIA: a universal, declarative, multiple abstraction-level language for service-oriented applications in ubiquitous environments. ACM Trans. Comput. Hum. Interact. **16**(4), 1–19 (2009)
5. Brambilla, M., Fraternali, P.: Interaction Flow Modeling Language - Model-Driven UI Engineering of Web and Mobile Apps with IFML. The MK/OMG Press, New York (2014)

6. Paternò, F., Santoro, C.: A logical framework for multi-device user interfaces. In: Proceedings of the 4th ACM SIGCHI Symposium on Engineering Interactive Computing Systems (EICS 2012), pp. 45–50. ACM, New York (2012)

7. Yigitbas, E., Kern, T., Urban, P., Sauer, S.: Multi-device UI development for task-continuous cross-channel web applications. In: Casteleyn, S., Dolog, P., Pautasso, C. (eds.) ICWE 2016. LNCS, vol. 9881, pp. 114–127. Springer, Cham (2016). doi:10.1007/978-3-319-46963-8_10

8. Yigitbas, E., Sauer, S.: Engineering context-adaptive UIs for task-continuous cross-channel applications. In: Bogdan, C., Gulliksen, J., Sauer, S., Forbrig, P., Winckler, M., Johnson, C., Palanque, P., Bernhaupt, R., Kis, F. (eds.) HCSE/HESSD -2016. LNCS, vol. 9856, pp. 281–300. Springer, Cham (2016). doi:10.1007/978-3-319-44902-9_18

9. Coutaz, J.: User interface plasticity: model driven engineering to the limit! In: Proceedings of the 2nd ACM SIGCHI Symposium on Engineering Interactive Computing Systems. ACM, pp. 1–8 (2010)

10. Salehie, M., Tahvildari, L.: Self-adaptive software: landscape and research challenges. ACM Trans. Auton. Adapt. Syst. 4, 1–42 (2009)

11. IBM. An Architectural Blueprint for Autonomic Computing (2006)

12. Garlan, D., Cheng, S.-W., Huang, A.-C., Schmerl, B., Steenkiste, P.: Rainbow: architecture-based self-adaptation with reusable infrastructure. Computer 37(10), 46–54 (2004)

13. Kramer, J., Magee, J.: Self-managed systems: an architectural challenge. In: Proceedings of the Workshop on the Future of Software Engineering. International Conference on Software Engineering. IEEE, pp. 259–268 (2007)

14. Balme, L., Demeure, A., Barralon, N., Coutaz, J., Calvary, G.: Cameleon-RT: a software architecture reference model for distributed, migratable, and plastic user interfaces. In: Markopoulos, P., Eggen, B., Aarts, E., Crowley, J.L. (eds.) EUSAI 2004. LNCS, vol. 3295, pp. 291–302. Springer, Heidelberg (2004). doi:10.1007/978-3-540-30473-9_28

15. Akiki, P.A., Bandara, A.K., Yu, Y.: Using interpreted runtime models for devising adaptive user interfaces of enterprise applications. In: Proceedings of the 14th International Conference on Enterprise Information Systems. SciTePress, pp. 72–77 (2012)

16. Duarte, C., Carric, L.: A conceptual framework for developing adaptive multimodal applications. In: Proceedings of the 11th International Conference on Intelligent User Interfaces. ACM, pp. 132–139 (2006)

17. Blouin, A., Morin, B., Beaudoux, O., Nain, G., Albers, P., Jézéquel, J.-M.: Combining aspect-oriented modeling with property-based reasoning to improve user interface adaptation. In: Proceedings of the 3rd ACM SIGCHI symposium on Engineering interactive computing systems (EICS 2011). ACM, 85–94 (2011)

18. Gajos, K.Z., Weld, D.S., Wobbrock, J.O.: Automatically generating personalized user interfaces with supple. Artif. Intell. 174(12–13), 910–950 (2010)

19. Feuerstack, S., Blumendorf, M., Albayrak, S.: Bridging the gap between model and design of user interfaces. In: Christian Hochberger, R.L. (ed.) Lecture Notes in Informatics, pp. 131–137 (2006)

20. Peissner, M., Haebe, D., Janssen, D., Sellner, T.: MyUI: generating accessible user interfaces from multimodal design patterns. In: Proceedings of the 4th ACM SIGCHI Symposium on Engineering Interactive Computing Systems (EICS 2012). ACM, pp. 81–90 (2012)

21. Akiki, P.A., Bandara, A.K., Yu, Y.: Engineering adaptive model-driven user interfaces. IEEE Trans. Softw. Eng. 42(12), 1118–1147 (2016)

22. López-Jaquero, V., Montero, F., González, P.: T:XML: a tool supporting user interface model transformation. In: Hussmann, H., Meixner, G., Zuehlke, D. (eds.) Model-Driven Development of Advanced User Interfaces, pp. 241–256. Springer, Heidelberg (2011)
23. Sottet, J.-S., Ganneau, V., Calvary, G., Coutaz, J., Demeure, A., Favre, J.-M., Demumieux, R.: Model-driven adaptation for plastic user interfaces. In: Baranauskas, C., Palanque, P., Abascal, J., Barbosa, S.D.J. (eds.) INTERACT 2007. LNCS, vol. 4662, pp. 397–410. Springer, Heidelberg (2007). doi:10.1007/978-3-540-74796-3_38
24. Hariri, A., Tabary, D., Lepreux, S., Kolski, C.: Context aware business adaptation toward user interface adaptation. Commun. SIWN 3, 46–52 (2008). Springer-Verlag

Iterative Model-Driven Development of Software Extensions for Web Content Management Systems

Dennis Priefer[1,2]([✉]), Peter Kneisel[2], and Daniel Strüber[3]

[1] Philipps-Universität Marburg, Marburg, Germany
[2] Institute for Information Science, Technische Hochschule Mittelhessen,
Gießen, Germany
{dennis.priefer,peter.kneisel}@mni.thm.de
[3] Institute for Computer Science, University of Koblenz and Landau,
Koblenz, Germany
strueber@uni-koblenz.de

Abstract. Dynamic web applications powered by Web Content Management Systems (WCMSs) such as Joomla, WordPress, or Drupal dominate today's web. A main advantage of WCMSs is their functional extensibility by standardized WCMS extensions. However, the development and evolution of these extensions are challenging tasks. Due to dependencies to the core platform and other WCMS extensions, the code structure of an extension includes a large defect potential. Mistakes usually lead to website crashes and are hard to find, especially for inexperienced developers.

In this work, we define a model-driven development (MDD) process and apply it during the development of software extensions for the WCMS Joomla. To address two separate scenarios, involving the development of independent and dependent WCMS extensions, we use an MDD infrastructure, comprising a domain-specific language, a code editor, and reverse engineering facilities. In addition, we provide evidence indicating that our model-driven approach is useful to generate extensions with consistent interdependencies, demonstrating that the main issues of extension development in the WCMS domain can be addressed using a model-driven approach. By applying the MDD infrastructure on actual projects, we additionally present the lessons learned.

Keywords: Model-driven development · Web content management systems · Joomla

1 Introduction

In today's web engineering practice, the creation of functionally rich web applications from scratch is an outdated process. Instead, web developers use a variety of *Web Content Management Systems* (WCMSs) [16] providing the main functionality of typical web applications, such as management of users, content, menus, media and templates, as well as multi-language support.

© Springer International Publishing AG 2017
A. Anjorin and H. Espinoza (Eds.): ECMFA 2017, LNCS 10376, pp. 142–157, 2017.
DOI: 10.1007/978-3-319-61482-3_9

If the functional needs of WCMS administrators exceed the core functionality of a WCMS, it needs to be functionally augmented. Examples for additional functionality include web shops, file repositories, image galleries, or the management of domain-specific data, such as conference information. When using an open source WCMS, developers can change the code basis in order to add additional features to the WCMS. A less intrusive mechanism is based on *software extensions* that can be deployed to a running WCMS instance by an administrator without changing the platform (see Fig. 1). This approach can ensure a consistent system even if the WCMS platform undergoes a version update.

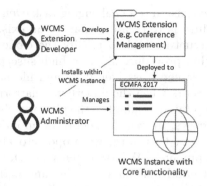

Fig. 1. Functional extension of a WCMS instance

The most popular WCMSs are *WordPress* [5], *Joomla* [2], and *Drupal* [1]. WordPress holds the largest market share by far (58,8% of all CMSs and 27,6% of all web pages [4]) followed by Joomla (7,1% of all CMSs and 3,3% of all web pages), and Drupal (4,7% of all CMSs and 2,2% of all web pages). For other well-known CMSs like *Magento* [3] and *Typo3* [6], the market share is significantly lower compared to these top three WCMSs. All of these systems provide extensibility in the form of installable software extensions. Norrie et al. [17] explain the success of WordPress as a result of its user-friendliness and extensibility. In particular, end-users without advanced technical skills benefit from its capability to create and publish a web site in a few minutes. Extensibility in the form of a plug-in mechanism empowers users with a technical background to customize a WordPress instance according to their needs. Yet this plug-in mechanism is relatively simple, based on the exposure of an interface by the platform core used to augment the core with additional code. Support for more complex extensions, such as domain-specific data management and presentation or event-triggered extensions, is lacking. If such extensions are developed using hand-written code, significant challenges to maintainability arise.

A more sophisticated extension mechanism is offered by Joomla. In contrast to most other WCMSs such as WordPress or Drupal, Joomla supports a variety of extension types to facilitate the development of feature-rich extensions. For instance, **components** are an extension type that provides full data management capabilities, whereas **modules** offer presentation utilities for the data managed by some component. This allows the development of new extensions using data of existing ones, e.g. a module presenting data of a 3rd party component. The extension mechanism provided by Joomla is based on an API as well as naming conventions: For a consistent deployment to the core platform, an extension must conform to an elaborate standard file and code structure.

Even though the extension mechanism of Joomla is powerful, extension developers face several issues during development and evolution. Developing a new extension is a challenging task even for experienced developers. A typical procedure is to create a clone of an existing extension complying with the standard structure and to modify the clone to satisfy the new requirements. However, this procedure shows a high susceptibility to errors. For instance, mismatches between class identifiers and file names might go unnoticed. Another problem occurs when the underlying platform evolves and existing extensions have to be updated to adapt to the platform changes. If the amount of extensions to migrate grows, the required effort for updating the extensions can increase tremendously.

In this work, we propose to apply a model-driven approach to the development of WCMS extensions. Our approach is based on the observation that a good amount of the file and code structure of popular WCMSs is made up of generic and schematically recurring fragments. The use of a domain-specific language and code generator is a promising means to reduce the development effort for WCMS extensions. In particular, we consider the two typical scenarios during WCMS extension development: The development of completely independent extensions as well as of extensions depending on existing extensions. We show how a model-driven approach is suitable to support developers during these tasks.

We exemplify our approach by illustrating its application to Joomla, a mainstream WCMS with a particularly sophisticated extension mechanism. In particular, we propose **JooMDD**, an infrastructure for the model-driven development of Joomla extensions. JooMDD comprises a DSL and model editor, a code generator, and a model extraction tool.

This work is the first to address the distinct challenge of developing interdependent WCMS extensions, an issue that does not occur in the simpler case of regular web application development. However, the model-driven development of WCMSs has been addressed in earlier works. In particular, the approaches presented in [19,21,24] address the model-driven development of concrete WCMS instances, but do not take their extensibility into account.

We introduce the technical background and common use-cases of developing Joomla extensions in Sect. 2 and present our MDD tools, including support for reverse engineering, in Sect. 3. Section 4 describes our process to address the typical development scenarios faced by Joomla extensions developers. We give example applications of our approach in Sect. 5 and share the lessons learned in Sect. 6.

2   Extension of Joomla Instances

This section describes the technical background of Joomla extensions and introduces typical use-cases for their development. The use-cases concern the differences in the extensions interdependencies between each other. So, we can clarify the different variants during our process definition in Sect. 4.

The Joomla platform provides a custom API for the functional expansion of its core functionality through installable extensions. Extensions come in different types of varying complexity, spanning the full range from complex extension types with their own dedicated data management to simple function libraries.

The most complex extension type is called **component**. Components usually have their own data management. To this end, the Joomla core database is extended with additional tables. To work together with the Joomla core, components must exhibit a file and code structure that follows a specific scheme. Figure 2 shows an example of this scheme.

On file and code level, the scheme implements the Model-View-Controller

	Name of the Component	MVC Type	Name of the View
▼ 🗀 com_users			
▼ 🗀 controllers			
📄 group.php	class	Users	Controller	Group
📄 groups.php	class	UsersControllerGroups	
▼ 🗀 models			
📄 group.php	class	Users	Model	Group
📄 groups.php	class	UsersModelGroups	
▼ 🗀 views			
▶ 🗀 group	class	Users	View	Group
▶ 🗀 groups	class	UsersViewGroups	

Fig. 2. File and code structure of a Joomla component (Extract)

(MVC) pattern [13]: views use models for data access; controllers can perform data updates using the models and can also process view requests. While components typically use their own custom data, a common practice is to use data of other components within the view. The MVC classes must comply with the illustrated scheme. Otherwise, the Joomla instance containing the component may produce errors.

Another wide-spread extension type are **modules**, which can be used to place any content within pre-defined module positions on a page of a Joomla instance. Common module types are menus, search fields, breadcrumbs, or login sections. Modules often use the data of an available component. Typically, modules display a data entry from an underlying database of a component.

Developing Joomla extensions features two use-cases. First, developing independent extensions such as components which have their own data management and, second, dependent extensions, which use artefacts of existing extensions such as modules, that in turn use the database of a component.

2.1   Use Case 1: Creating Independent Extensions

The first use-case is the development of independent extensions which can be used within a running Joomla instance. The advantage of independent extensions occurs during their evolution. If a developer changes the extension, no side-effects due to dependencies occur. However, it is important to comply with the development guidelines to ensure a correct interplay between the extension and the running core system where it is installed. Even subtle errors can lead to unexpected crashes that are not discovered until runtime.

2.2   Use Case 2: Creating Dependent Extensions

Components and modules stand out for their interplay with other extensions. It is common practice to use artefacts of existing extensions within a component or module to increase the functionality of a Joomla system without developing software fragments anew. Components may reuse models or view templates by other components, while modules use the database of existing components, since they usually provide no own data management. This allows developers to augment existing extensions (e.g. 3rd-party extensions) without changing their code base.

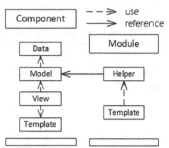

(a) Module referencing to an existing component model for data access

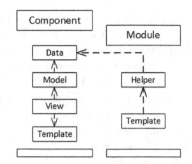

(b) Module uses the database of a component directly

```
class ConferenceHelper
{
    public static function &getList($params = null)
    {
        JModelLegacy::addIncludePath(
            JPATH_ROOT .
            '/components/com_conference/models',
            "Conference"
        );
        $model = JModelLegacy::getInstance(
            'Talks',
            "ConferenceModel",
            array('ignore_request' => true)
        );
        $items = $model->getItems();
        return $items;
    }
}
```

(c) Module referencing to an existing component model for data access (code)

```
class ConferenceHelper
{
    public static function &getList($params = null)
    {
        $db     = JFactory::getDbo();
        $query  = $db->getQuery(true);
        $query->select($db->quoteName(
            array('id', 'title', 'speaker')));
        $query->from($db->quoteName(
            '#__conference_talks'));
        $db->setQuery($query);
        $items = $db->loadResults();
        return $items;
    }
}
```

(d) Module uses the database of a component directly (code)

Fig. 3. Usual dependencies between modules and components

Figure 3 illustrates common dependencies between modules and components on the example of an existing conference component, which is augmented by a dependant module for the representation of conference talks. Figures 3a and b illustrate the dependency variants in an abstract manner, whereas Figs. 3c and d show the minimal amount of required code to establish these dependencies. The code shows the corresponding variants of both dependencies as part of a helper file within a module. This file represents the model of a module. The first variant of dependency features the use of a component model within a module via **reference**, using inclusion methods of Joomla's singleton implementation (JModelLegacy), whereas the second variant illustrates the **direct use** of a component's database by using SQL statements.

In this work we focus on the model-driven development of components and models, with support for both use-cases. While we addressed the less complicated use-case 1 in our earlier work [18], our extended infrastructure and process address both use-cases.

3   JooMDD - MDD Infrastructure for Joomla Extensions Including Reverse Engineering Support

This section presents JooMDD, our infrastructure for the model-driven development of Joomla extensions[1].

JooMDD supports Joomla extension developers with a set of MDD tools: A DSL and editor for the creation of extension models, a code generator for Joomla extensions, and a tool to extract extension models from legacy extension code.

We used Xtext [12] and Xtend [11] to develop the infrastructure. Xtext allows the definition of a DSL in the form of annotated EBNF grammar. Based on this definition, it supports the generation of infrastructure components, such as a text-based instance editor, an EMF domain model, and an API for the DSL which can be used independently within a Java-based application. Xtend is a Java-based programming language with dedicated support for the definition of code generator templates. By using these tools, the rapid development and implementation of a high quality MDD infrastructure is enabled.

3.1   Domain-Specific Language for Joomla Extensions

We created **eJSL**, a DSL for the description of Joomla-based software extensions. The language consists of three parts: a part to model the data management of Joomla extensions (**entities**), a part for the definition of a page flow of extension views (**pages**), and a part for the description of an extension structure (**extensions**).

The *entities* and *pages* parts are platform-independent, that is, not bound to either Joomla or to WCMSs in general. The design of these parts has been influenced by the Simple Web Application Language (SWAL) presented in [9], which describes the data and the page flow of a web application.

The purpose of the *extension* part is the specification of particular Joomla extensions, rendering it the platform-specific part of eJSL. Extensions can be mapped to existing pages and entities. In particular, components and modules are extension types which mainly consist of views to illustrate any kind of data. Therefore the language allows optional references between these extension types and pages. By adding

Fig. 4. Page reference within an extension (eJSL model)

additional information to such a page reference, it is possible to describe dependencies between extensions in an abstract way. Figure 4 illustrates the definition of a page reference within an extension definition in an eJSL model. It is possible to define a use reference to the model of a component (frontend or backend),

---

[1] JooMDD can be downloaded from GitHub https://github.com/icampus/JooMDD.

the database of a conference or an existing webservice, which can also be part of a component. Hereby it does not matter, if the page reference is made within a component, or a module description. If no such reference is specified by the user, this knowledge must be provided in the generator instead.

To use the DSL we provide plugins for the most commonly used development environments in the WCMS domain which are *IntelliJ IDEA*, *PhpStorm*, and *Eclipse*. The editor plugin of JooMDD is customized for integration with each of these environments. The plugin provides a textual editor with syntax highlighting, error messages, dependency checks, and auto completion support for keywords and references between model elements.

3.2   Generator for Joomla Extensions

We have implemented our generator using Xtend templates. The main decomposition of the generated code follows the division of the DSL into entities, extensions, and pages, supporting traceability between models and the generated code. The generator supports the two use-cases we described earlier in Sects. 2.1 and 2.2. If a new and independent extension is to be developed, the generator creates the full extension code. In the case of using a an existing extension as reference within another extension, it is possible to describe the augmentation within the model (e.g. as part of a page reference as described in Sect. 3.1). So, the generator is able to only generate the depending extension, but not the existing extension anew. Both cases will be examined further within Sects. 4 and 5.

3.3   Tool Support for the Reverse Engineering of Existing Joomla Extensions

JooMDD supports developers during the creation or *forward engineering* of a new Joomla extension and the reengineering or migration of a legacy extension.

We developed the prototype **jext2eJSL** to support the reverse engineering of Joomla extensions by a model extraction from the code of existing Joomla 3.x extensions (PHP, HTML, JavaScript, and SQL files) as input. The tool creates an extension model based on the eJSL language with the main model elements as entities, pages and extensions. In particular, it supports the common Joomla extension types. Our specialized use-case for the tool is described in Sect. 2.2: The creation of a new extension with dependencies to an existing one. Usually the existing extension must be modelled as well to allow references on the model level. This step can completely be dropped by using the model extraction tool. The extracted model contains all information needed to model (and generate) new extensions based on the existing one. jext2eJSL matches the Joomla standard file and code schemes. Therefore, the input extensions must follow these schemes and implement the required patterns such as MVC for components to ensure that the extracted models are as complete as possible.

4   Iterative Process for Extension Development

In this section, we describe an iterative process to reduce development effort and error-proneness during the development of independent Joomla extensions. In addition we take the interdependencies between extensions into account to allow the development of new extensions that use artefacts of existing extensions as well. Each of these use-cases can be addressed during one iteration of our process. In fact, the second use-case requires an iteration of the process every time the existing extension evolves, to avoid side effects due to inconsistencies.

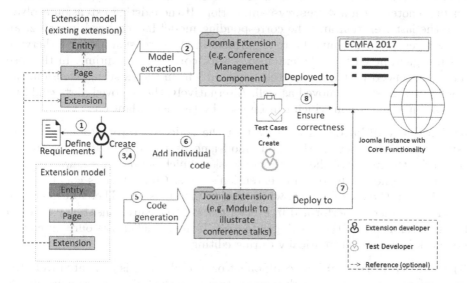

Fig. 5. One iteration during the iterative development of Joomla extensions

The process, outlined in Fig. 5, is made up of eight steps. In this illustration we focus on the development of components and modules, whereas our infrastructure provides support to adapt the process to all available extension types. One iteration consists of the following steps:

(1) Collect Requirements: Requirements for the extensions are collected in a suitable form, such as an analysis model in the form of a class diagram. In particular, these requirements may comprise managed data, views, relationships between views and data, and the extension structure. In this phase the decision to use artefacts of an existing extension within a new one can be made. This decision effects the subsequent steps of our process.

(2) Model Extraction (optional): In the case that a model of existing extensions, usually a component, is required, the *jext2eJSL* tool is used to extract such models automatically. Though, every evolution on existing extensions requires a new run of the process with this step as a main requirement to ensure the correct interplay between existing and dependant extensions. If an independent extension is to be developed, this step is skipped.

(3) Model Engineering: The identified requirements are used to create or update an extension model. In the initial development case, the modeller creates a new model with entities, pages, and the desired extension structure with regard to the requirements. If the extension should use artefacts of an existing extension, such as a module using the model of an existing component, a corresponding model of the existing extension must exist (created in step 2). References between extensions will be addressed during the subsequent code generation. To distinguish existing from new extensions, existing model artefacts can be denoted with a @preserve annotation. If the existing extension evolved since the last iteration and the corresponding model has changed in step 2, all affected dependencies must be re-engineered in the extension model. Otherwise it is not guaranteed that the extensions work correctly at runtime. In the case that a referenced part is completely removed within the existing extension, the dependency must be removed as well. Alternatively, the removed parts could be part of a new extension which can be used by the dependant one.

(4) Model Validation: To ensure that the code generator produces a valid result, the consistency of the input model needs to be validated upfront. In particular, the model of the existing extension which is used by a new extension must correspond to the existing extension's code. Code changes could lead to side effects in the Joomla page, which uses both extensions. Therefore, step 2 of the process must be performed in every iteration to ensure consistency between the model and code of the existing extension. If the modeller uses our text editor, the check happens automatically during editing.

(5) Code Generation: The component or module code is generated from the extension model. In each case the generator creates the full code for an installable extension. Thereby code is generated for all model elements that do not carry an @preserved annotation. In the case of creating an dependent extension, the specified references are incorporated within the generated code.

(6) Add Individual Code (optional): To support extensions with an elaborate application logic, the user may add individual code fragments to the generated code. A dedicated mechanism is required to guard such individual fragments for later runs of the code generator.

(7) Deployment to Joomla instance (optional): The generated extension can be installed within a running Joomla instance. In the case of a depending extension it must be provided, that all required extensions are installed as well. In addition they must be consistent to their corresponding models to ensure a flawless interaction between the new and the existing extensions.

(8) Test Creation: The correctness of the generated extension is ensured by tests. By performing integration tests, the correct interplay between the new and already installed extensions. Currently, these tests are required to be written by a human developer. Since the extensions under test are schematically redundant, the test cases usually present a large extent of schematic duplication as well, offering an opportunity for further automation. However, the automation of this step is left to future work.

The process is supported by our MDD infrastructure as follows: We provide jext2eJSL as model extractor for step 2, a DSL and corresponding editors for step 3 and 4, and a code generator for step 5. We do not provide dedicated support of the handling of individual fragments in the generated code, as required for the optional step 6, but an off-the-shelf solution can be used for this purpose.

5   Application of the Approach

In this section, we describe our experiences of applying the previously described process for both use-cases, creating a component and expanding an existing one by a depending module.

5.1   Creating a New Component

We devised a simple conference management component as an extension to the Joomla core. During the requirements step, we identified the analysis model shown in Fig. 6 to support the management of a conference with its participants, talks, agenda, and rooms. In our case it was sufficient to display these data in the standard Joomla CRUD views for the management of component-related data.

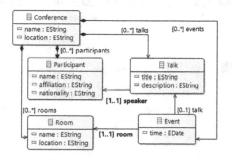

Fig. 6. Analysis model for conference management

Specifically, each entity should be displayable in a custom list and details view, such as those shown in Fig. 7.

The image shows these views from the perspective of a Joomla administrator who can make the same views visible to site visitors using a menu entry. Based on these requirements, we designed an extension model[2] which can be used as input for our code generator. The generator then creates a full installable conference component that can be used to manage the required entities; no manual addition of individual source code is required.

5.2   Creating a Module Using an Existing Component

We applied our approach to the *users* component, a core component which is pre-installed on each Joomla instance. The component manages the users and user groups of a Joomla instance as Fig. 8a illustrates. However, there is no

---

[2] An excerpt of the extension model can be found in [18].

Fig. 7. List and details view within a Joomla instance (Backend)

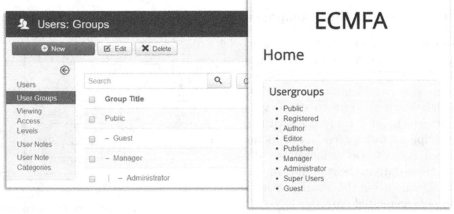

(a) Users Component
(Management of User Groups
in the Backend)

(b) New Usergroups Module using Data of the Users Component
(Frontend)

Fig. 8. User groups management within existing component and new module

way of illustrating the existing user groups within the frontend of a Joomla site. Therefore, we explore the case of adding a new module to the existing component using its model as DAO, to provide a new representation of user groups.

The users component is developed by core developers of the Joomla community. It was suitable for the exploration of our approach due to its high level of compliance with the Joomla standard, a general requirement for step 2 above and of our reverse engineering tool jext2eJSL. To this end, we first use jext2eJSL to extract an extension model from the given component. The resulting model provides entities, pages, and the extension specification which can be referred by new extensions. To avoid the generation of code for these existing elements, they are annotated with a @preserve tag.

```
eJSLModel "Users_augmented" {
    eJSL part: CMS Extension {
        extensions {
            Module Usergroups {
                Manifestation {...}
                *Page : users.groups
                from : users.users
                data backendDAO
}}}}
```

```
public static function &getList($params = null)
{
    JModelLegacy::addIncludePath(
        JPATH_ROOT .
        '/administrator/components/' .
        'com_users/models',
        "Users");
    $model = JModelLegacy::getInstance(
        'groups',
        "UsersModel",
        array('ignore_request' => true));
    $items = $model->getItems();
    return $items;
}
```

(a) New Usergroups Module (eJSL Model)

(b) References within the DAO of the new Module

Fig. 9. New usergroups module

To implement the new module, we create a new eJSL model and add a module specification as Fig. 9a illustrates. Using the model as input, the code generator creates the module with the dependency to the existing component as shown in Fig. 9b. Since the generated file and code structure is fully compliant with the Joomla standard, the module can be deployed directly to an existing Joomla website. Once installed, it works together with the already installed organizer component by using its model as DAO for the data which has to be shown - in our case the user groups which are managed by the component (see Fig. 8b).

To explore the usefulness of our process for other components, we successfully applied it to the conference component of the first case and a component for resource management [7] we developed by hand over the course of six years.

6   Lessons Learned

In this section we address the lessons learned of our process based on its application. We discuss the strengths and weaknesses of the approach and point out the limitations of this work.

We investigated the usefulness of our approach by applying it in the domain of the Joomla WCMS, a particularly critical example domain due to its sophisticated extension mechanism that leads to many code and structure duplications. Due to these duplications the biggest strength of our approach reveals. During both application scenarios, development speed increased since most of the code was generated. In addition, the defect potential of the new extensions was tremendously decreased, because all generated fragments adhere to the given coding guidelines of Joomla. In both cases the extensions were installable and applicable without adding a line of code by hand.

Within the application of the second use case a requirement for creating a dependency from a new extension to an existing one was the creation of a model using our model extraction tool. After the extraction, the existing extension is depicted in an abstract manner. So, it could be used for being referenced by new extensions. A nice effect is the capability of using the model of the existing extension as a means of documentation, or a first version of the same extension, which may be developed in a model-driven manner. If an existing extension evolves, the model must be extracted anew. This could lead to inconsistencies between models of the existing and new extension. However a re-engineering on the model level allows a more rapid adjustment in contrast to a manual change of the dependencies in the extensions' code - especially if the dependencies concern different code fragments but are specified in same part of the model.

Beside the described strengths of the approach we discovered some weaknesses during the application. The main weakness is the management of individual code. If an extension which is developed using our approach evolves, individual fragments are not considered within the extension model. This could lead to problems at runtime, since the individual parts could depend on generic fragments, which have been changed or removed. To detect and fix error-prone fragments, an adequate test suite is required. Otherwise they wont be detected.

During the case of developing a new dependant extension, the problem of individual code occurs in an earlier stage. During the model extraction of an existing extension, only the parts which adhere strictly to the Joomla standard can be found and abstracted. Individual parts remain unnoticed and can only be reused by a new extension if the dependencies are added to the generated code by hand. However, this procedure impairs the benefit of our approach.

Even though our approach can be successfully applied, our work includes some threats to validity with regard to the applied development scenarios. In our application, we create a new independent component and a module, which uses artefacts of an existing component. These use-cases are common in the domain, but not the only ones existing. This is a threat to the conclusion validity, since our process is intended to develop extensions in general independent of their type. Especially, the second case should be further examined in future work. This includes the collection of possible dependencies between different extension types and their incorporation into our process. The main threat to external validity is that we only instantiated out approach for the Joomla WCMS. It yet has to be studied if it is also suitable for other WCMSs, since the infrastructure parts must be rewritten to the specific needs of the given WCMS. More extensive studies of the generalizability of our results are left to future work. However, the successful approach which is illustrated in this paper, allows an optimistic expectation for other WCMSs.

7 Related Work

Several related works deal with applying model-driven engineering to application development in the WCMS domain. Most of these works propose platform-independent meta-models for the development of specific WCMS instances [15, 21,24]. The approach by Saraiva et al. is the first to also investigate code generation for concrete WCMS instances [19]. However, none of these works addresses the extensibility of WCMSs through standardized extension types taking their interdependencies into account. As we have argued in this work, the creation of such WCMS extensions is a tedious and error-prone process of significant practical relevance. Dependencies between newly developed and existing extensions are not provided in any of these works. Our work is the first to tackle this challenge by providing suitable abstractions and automation facilities.

Model-driven principles have been applied to address augmentation issues in the WCMS domain. Trias et al. [22] introduce a reengineering method and a reverse engineering tool for the migration of complete WCMSs, for instance, from a web page to WordPress. Even though this approach can potentially improve the model extraction step in our process, it is currently tailored to WordPress, a WCMS with limited extensibility features. The usefulness for other WCMSs has yet to be investigated. Vermolen et al. [23] present an approach for the evolution of data models. As this approach provides a well-defined strategy to deal with changes to existing data entities, incorporating it into our work will help us to improve the flexibility during the augmentation of existing extensions.

Apart from these works, there is little recent research on the development practices for WCMSs, an observation that is confirmed by Norrie et al. [17].

General MDD approaches for the web domain such as the ones in [8,10,14,20] can be used to create complete websites in a model-driven manner, but are not suitable for our considered problem since they do not address WCMSs and the model-driven development of their extensions.

8 Conclusion

Instances of Web Content Management Systems are commonly used as dynamic web applications in today's web. Using an open source WCMS, developers can add additional features by the use of software extensions, which can be installed into a running WCMS instance. However developing these extensions can be a time-consuming and complex task, even for experienced extension developers. Especially, the interdependencies between different extensions can lead to unwanted errors if they are not sufficiently considered during development. In this work, we introduce an iterative process using a set of tools to develop Joomla extensions in a model-driven way. In addition, we introduce a domain-specific language for the creation of abstract extension models and a code generator which derives a platform-specific implementation for the Joomla platform. This allows the rapid development of Joomla 3.x extensions adhering to both the platform-specific development guidelines and interdependencies between different extensions. To ensure the usefulness of our approach, we applied it to two development scenarios - the development of a new and independent conference component and of a new user groups module, which illustrates the data of an existing Joomla core component.

Our future plans span over two research directions. First, we plan to improve the existing DSL and tools, in particular to provide support for other WCMSs, such as WordPress and Drupal. Second, based on anecdotal evidence from our communication with Joomla representatives, there is interest in using JooMDD for the development of extensions within the Joomla community [18]. This situation allows us to provide our infrastructure directly to a large group of developers for a field study in vivo. Using this exposure opportunity, we intend to infer the usefulness of our approach empirically.

References

1. Drupal.org. https://www.drupal.org
2. Joomla!.org. https://www.joomla.org
3. Magento - eCommerce Software & eCommerce Platform Solutions. https://magento.com/
4. Usage Statistics, Market Share of Content Management Systems for Websites. http://w3techs.com/technologies/overview/content_management/all
5. WordPress.org. https://wordpress.org
6. TYPO3 - The Enterprise Open Source CMS. https://typo3.org/
7. Antrim, J.: Technische Hochschule Mittelhessen - THM Organizer. https://www.thm.de/organizer/
8. Brambilla, M.: Interaction flow modeling language: Model-driven UI engineering of web and mobile apps with IFML. Morgan Kaufmann, Waltham (2015)
9. Brambilla, M., Cabot, J., Wimmer, M.: Model-Driven Software Engineering in Practice. Morgan & Claypool, San Rafael (2012)
10. Ceri, S., Fraternali, P., Bongio, A.: Web Modeling Language (WebML): a modeling language for designing web sites. Comput. Netw. **33**(1–6), 137–157 (2000)
11. Efftinge, S., Spoenemann, M.: Xtend - Modernized Java, 02 December 2015. http://www.eclipse.org/xtend/
12. Efftinge, S., Spoenemann, M.: Xtext - Language Engineering Made Easy! 11 February 2016. https://eclipse.org/Xtext/
13. Gamma, E., Helm, R., Johnson, R., Vlissides, J.: Design Patterns: Elements of Reusable Object-oriented Software. Addison-Wesley Longman Publishing Co., Inc., Boston (1995)
14. Kraus, A., Knapp, A., Koch, N.: Model-Driven Generation of Web Applications in UWE. Ludwig-Maximilians-Universität München, München (2008)
15. Martínez, S., Garcia-Alfaro, J., Cuppens, F., Cuppens-Boulahia, N., Cabot, J.: Towards an access-control metamodel for web content management systems. In: Sheng, Q.Z., Kjeldskov, J. (eds.) ICWE 2013. LNCS, vol. 8295, pp. 148–155. Springer, Cham (2013). doi:10.1007/978-3-319-04244-2_14
16. McKeever, S.: Understanding web content management systems: evolution, lifecycle and market. Ind. Manage. Data Syst. **103**(9), 686–692 (2003)
17. Norrie, M.C., Geronimo, L., Murolo, A., Nebeling, M.: The forgotten many? a survey of modern web development practices. In: Casteleyn, S., Rossi, G., Winckler, M. (eds.) ICWE 2014. LNCS, vol. 8541, pp. 290–307. Springer, Cham (2014). doi:10.1007/978-3-319-08245-5_17

18. Priefer, D., Kneisel, P., Taentzer, G.: JooMDD: a model-driven development environment for web content management system extensions - demonstration paper. In: Proceedings of the International Conference on Software Engineering and Companion, ICSE Companion 2016. ACM, New York (2016)

19. de Sousa Saraiva, J.: Development of CMS-based Web Applications with a Multi-Language Model-Driven Approach. Dissertation, Universidade Técinica de Lisboa, Lisbon, Portugal (2012)

20. Svansson, V., Lopez-Herrejon, R.E.: A web specific language for content management systems. In: Proceedings of the OOPSLA Workshop on Domain-Specific Modeling, Montréal, Canada (2007)

21. Trias, F.: Building CMS-based web applications using a model-driven approach. In: 2012 Sixth International Conference on Research Challenges in Information Science (RCIS), pp. 1–6

22. Trias, F., de Castro, V., López-Sanz, M., Marcos, E.: RE-CMS: a reverse engineering toolkit for the migration to CMS-based web applications. In: Proceedings of the Annual ACM Symposium on Applied Computing, SAC 2015, pp. 810–812. ACM, New York (2015)

23. Vermolen, S.D., Wachsmuth, G., Visser, E.: Generating database migrations for evolving web applications. In: Proceedings of the ACM International Conference on Generative Programming and Component Engineering, GPCE 2011, pp. 83–92

24. Vlaanderen, K., Valverde, F., Pastor, O.: Model-driven web engineering in the CMS domain: a preliminary research applying SME. In: Filipe, J., Cordeiro, J. (eds.) ICEIS 2008. LNBIP, vol. 19, pp. 226–237. Springer, Heidelberg (2009). doi:10.1007/978 3 642 00670 8_17

Model Consistency Management

Efficient Consistency Checking
of Interrelated Models

Harald König[1]([☒]) and Zinovy Diskin[2]

[1] University of Applied Sciences FHDW Hannover, Hanover, Germany
`harald.koenig@fhdw.de`
[2] McMaster University, Hamilton, Canada
`diskinz@mcmaster.ca`

Abstract. Software design normally requires a collection of interdependent models conforming to different metamodels. These *multi-models* present different views of interest and may be consistent only if they simultaneously satisfy a set of inter-model constraints. A straightforward approach to inter-model consistency checking is to run constraint validations on the model union (merge). If, in model repairing scenarios, single constraints are (re-)checked, these validations are carried out on a small view (localization) of a big model merge. This "merge-prior-to-localization"-approach is not efficient, because of considerable matching and merging workload. We propose to perform *early localization* in order to reduce the data space being subject to commonality search. The algorithm is based on a new method to formally specify the inter-relation of an arbitrary number of heterogeneously typed models.

1 Introduction

System design is based on different conceptual views of the required solution. These views are represented by models, which differ in their business content and in the language they are expressed in, such that comparing or merging of models, i.e. integration of heterogeneous artefacts, becomes an obstacle. Moreover, the merge of consistent instances of the models can result in an artefact violating *inter-model constraints*, i.e. constraints that spread over all or at least some of the involved models. Hence, when the data is integrated, (re-)checking inter-model and intra-model consistencies becomes a challenge.

A comprehensive view of the set of involved models must consider them as a single artefact—a *multi-model*, i.e., an integral collection of heterogeneous models each one conforming to its own metamodel. We call these individual models *components* of the multi-model. The following example shows that the merge of legal artefacts can result in an artefact violating inter-model constraints. Consider two car insurance models M_1 and M_2. In the former, class 'Contract' has an attribute 'insuranceLevel' (with values 'standard', 'extended'), while in M_2, class 'Policy' has a property 'traffic telematics enabled'. Suppose that despite their different names, 'Contract' and 'Policy' denote the same business concept. Then the domain may be subject to the constraint that extended contracts

A. Anjorin and H. Espinoza (Eds.): ECMFA 2017, LNCS 10376, pp. 161–178, 2017.
DOI: 10.1007/978-3-319-61482-3_10

must be controlled via traffic telematics. This inter-model constraint cannot be declared in either of the models: M_1 knows nothing about telematics, and M_2 does not know about insurance levels. Suppose we have two legal instances A_i of their respective models M_i, $i = 1, 2$. Considering them together as a single *multi-instance* needs checking validity of the inter-model constraint, for which we must also relate instances of Contract to instances of Policy. Thus, a multi-instance is actually a triple (A_1, A_2, A_0) where A_0 is a mapping/relation between Contract and Policy instances specifying that, e.g., a contract instance c in A_1 equals a policy p in A_2.[1] It is clear that depending on mapping A_0, the inter-model constraint above can be violated even though component instances A_i are perfectly legal.

Global consistency checking of interrelated software artefacts requires understanding and formalizing the interplay of the following operations on instances and multi-instances:

- **Matching** takes a multi-instance with unrelated components as its input, and outputs all detected sameness relationships/overlaps (in our example, $(c\colon Contract, p\colon Policy) \in A_0$, where we write $i\colon T$ to denote an instance i of type T). We call the multi-instance augmented with overlaps (i.e., the triple (A_1, A_2, A_0) in the example) a *matched* multi-instance.
- **Merge** takes this matched multi-instance and outputs a single instance A, namely the amalgamation of the components of the multi-instance modulo the sameness declarations. The output is called a *merged* instance.
- **Localization** takes a (possibly merged) instance A and a constraint declaration c on its model M as its input, and outputs only those elements of A that are typed over those elements of M that are affected by the constraint declaration.

Whereas merge and localization can be carried out automatically, matching is often only semi-automatic and needs manual support to be correct.

To check consistency of a multi-instance $\mathcal{A} = (A_1, \ldots, A_n)$ against an inter-model constraint (e.g. 'extended contracts must be controlled via traffic telematics'), a straightforward approach is to use the matching operation to define sameness relations between components, and then check the merged instance against the constraint. The latter checking uses localization, and hence the entire approach can be encoded as MML (Match→Merge→Localize). However, using this approach as an algorithm for consistency checking would be impractical, because of the necessity to build big and unfeasible model merges, especially with matching being a very expensive operation.

A more efficient approach is *early localization*, LMM, proposed in our previous paper [14]. Localization is moved at the very beginning of inter-model consistency checking, so that matching and merging are only performed for those small parts of instances that localization found to be responsible for the validity of the

---

[1] This may happen, if an insurance company and one of its insurance intermediaries both store the contracts that this intermediary has sold, but if they store them w.r.t. different database schemas.

constraint. Not only does this significantly reduce matching and merging work-load, it also enables better tailored and stepwise model repairing, e.g., in model co-evolution scenarios, or in incremental consistency checking [3]. However, our previous paper [14] only covers the case of two model components, i.e. multi-instances $\mathcal{A} = (A_1, A_2)$, such that common concepts can always be maintained by tracking *pairs* of matched entities as in our example above.

In the present paper, we generalize the LMM-approach for the case of an arbitrary number of models. For this, we needed to address two challenging issues. *Issue 1*: Instead of complicated handling of binary, ternary, and maybe higher-order overlap relations, a unified and manageable specification of complex inter-relations of $n \geq 3$ models is required. *Issue 2*: Costly matching activities should be properly distributed between consecutive automatic localization and merging in order to minimize the corresponding workload. To address Issue 1, we elaborated an advanced formalism for specifying interrelation of n models, which is based on partial mappings. To address Issue 2, we use several results from category theory [2] and prove the MML-LMM-equivalence (which is mathematically non-trivial).

The paper is structured into three main parts. Section 2 introduces our running example, Sect. 3 explains the three major operations mentioned above, and Sect. 4 explains why LMM is more efficient than MML, yet yields the same results.

2   Running Example

We consider an example which will illustrate all constructions we will perform and facts we will declare. Suppose that certain authorities are interested in social clustering of inhabitants of a city or a country, or even how people around the

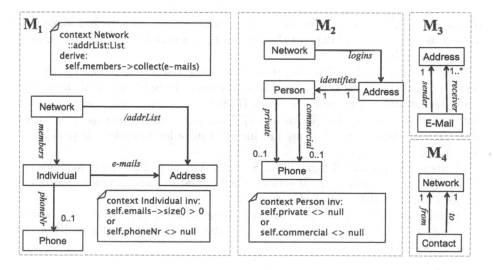

Fig. 1. Several domain models

globe flock together. Social networks provide the chance to observe, measure and monitor this clustering. Figure 1 presents two different UML models of social networks, M_1 and M_2. Some of the social networks maintain their data according to M_1, others according to M_2.

Model M_1 shows that a network has a set of members, each having a set of emails and, optionally, a phone number (the default multiplicity is 0..*). The lower OCL constraint states that a member must have either e-mail or a phone. The model also shows a derived attribute/addrList, giving the set of all member addresses (note the upper OCL constraint). Model M_2 specifies maintenance of email addresses that serve as logins, and every Address identifies one and only one Person. The latter have to provide a private or a commercial phone number (or both).

Model M_4 describes data that an intelligence agency keeps to monitor e-mail communications between social networks. M_3 also monitors communication by recording some of the e-mail metadata. In order to collaborate, the two agencies decide to consolidate their knowledge. Hence, they have to find out whether their collective data is consistent in, at least, the following sense specified by an inter-model constraint *consistentEmailContact* further abbreviated *consEC*: *For any two networks* $n_1 : Network@M_1$, $n_2 : Network@M_2$ *instantiating the respective classes in model* M_1 *and* M_2 *the number of contacts in the set*

$$Contact(n_1, n_2) = \{c : Contact \mid c.from = n_1 \;\; and \;\; c.to = n_2\},$$
and the number of emails in the set

$$Email(n_1, n_2) = \{e : E\text{-}Mail \mid e.sender \in n_1.addrList \;\; and \;\; e.receiver \cap n_2.logins \neq \emptyset\},$$ *are equal.* Note that this inter-model constraint involves all four models.

3   Background and Definitions

In this section, we present necessary background knowledge. We introduce new notations (Sect. 3.1) and explain the three main operations *Localization, Matching*, and *Merging*.

Localization (Sect. 3.2) means to focus to those parts of a model, on which a certain constraint is declared, (see the forthcoming Definition 1) and simultaneously retype affected instance portions (Definition 2), such that constraint validation logic can be reused (Definition 3). Notations and definitions of Sects. 3.1 and 3.2 are taken from [4]. They are included in order to make our paper self-contained.

Matching is presented formally in Sect. 3.3. We extend former definitions [9], which enable to consider a collection of individual models as one big artefact, i.e. as a multi-model (Definitions 4 and 5).

Finally, in Sect. 3.4, we pick up and adapt ideas of [22] to formally define merging of multi-models (Definition 6), i.e. the interpretation of a multi-model as a single model.

3.1   Notations and Terminology

We encode models and their instances by directed graphs This is common in many research disciplines, e.g. Graph Transformations, Model-Driven Engineering [8,16,18], or the Diagrammatic Predicate Framework (DPF) [4,21]. Especially, UML artefacts such as object diagrams and class diagrams but also sequence diagrams, state-charts, or activity diagrams, can adequately be encoded with graphs. Figure 2 shows how UML class diagram M_1 from Fig. 1 can be represented as a graph: Classes become vertices (ellipses in Fig. 2) and associations become directed edges. In addition, constraints are translated to constraint declaration nodes equipped with dashed lines to show their scope. These elements (red with a color display) actually encode a mapping between graphs as we will explain in Sect. 3.2. As constraints are formally diagram predicates, a graph with constraint declarations is called a *DP-graph*. Similarly, objects in a UML object diagram become vertices, and links between them become edges. E.g. in graph A in Fig. 3, there is one *Network*-object with three login addresses that in turn identify three persons. Person b declares a private phone number, which also is the commercial number of person c.

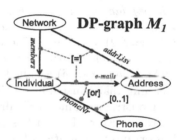

Fig. 2. DP-graph representing model M_1 from Fig. 1 (Color figure online)

As in Fig. 3 elements in a graph come equipped with typing information, i.e., there is a mapping τ from elements in graph A to elements in the model graph M (here, $M = M_2$ from Sect. 2), which maps a vertex or an edge $x : T$ in A to vertex or edge T in M, resp. This mapping must preserve the incidence between vertices and edges, and is called a *graph morphism* (see Fig. 3 for an illustration). Any graph morphism f between graphs G and G' is written as $f : G \to G'$. Thus, our major construct below will be pairs (A, τ) with A a graph and $\tau : A \to M$ a graph morphism.

The graph-based view also has the advantage that $\tau' : A' \to M'$ can be data A' typed over model M', or $\tau'' : A'' \to M''$ can be a model A'' that conforms to a metamodel M''. We adhere to this abstraction by using the following terminology and notations:

- Any artefact A with typing information is called an **instance** of its **model** M.
- The assignment $\tau : A \to M$ is called **typing mapping** or **typing morphism**.
- Instead of writing (A, τ) for the above mentioned pair, we write $\tau : A \to M$. Since A is encoded in τ as its domain, we do not loose information, if we just write τ. The assignment τ (together with its domain A) is called a **typed graph**.

3.2 Localization

A key feature of constraints used in MDE is their *diagrammatic* nature: the set of elements over which a constraint is declared is actually a diagram of some shape specific for the constraint. E.g., the shape of any multiplicity constraint is a single arrow, and the shapes of constraint [or] and [=] used in Fig. 1 are, respectively, a span of two arrows and an arrow triangle.

Table 1. Sample constraints

Name, c	Shape, S^c
[0..1]	$(1) \xrightarrow{12} (2)$
[or]	$(1) \xleftarrow{01} (0) \xrightarrow{02} (2)$
[=]	$(0) \xrightarrow{01} (1) \xrightarrow{12} (2)$, $\xrightarrow{02}$

To declare a constraint named c over a model graph M, we recognize the constraint shape in the graph and label the respective configuration by the constraint name. Formally, we first declare a *signature* of constraints, i.e., a set of constraint names/labels, each one assigned with its *(arity) shape* denoted, for a constraint c, by S^c. For example, Table 1 specifies a simple signature consisting of three constraints, which were used in Fig. 1. Now, to declare a constraint c over a graph M, we need to specify a graph morphism $\delta: S^c \rightarrow M$ called *(shape) binding*. E.g. in Fig. 3, constraint $c = [or]$ is declared via binding δ with $\delta(01) = priv$, $\delta(02) = comm$, which automatically implies $\delta(0) = Person$, $\delta(1) = \delta(2) = Phone$. The elements in M, the shape is mapped to, are the *image* or *range* or, else, the *scope* of the binding, the respective graph is denoted $\mathrm{rg}(\delta)$. The pair (c, δ) is called *constraint declaration*. In the sequel, we write $c@\delta$, meaning that constraint c is imposed on model M at the range of binding δ.

Constraint name "or" already suggests its semantic interpretation in this context: "Every Person has either a private *or* a commercial phone, or both". Importantly, *semantics* of a constraint is, in general, defined irrespective to the binding by defining a *validating* function $\mathrm{VALIDATE}_c(\tau^* : C_X \rightarrow S^c)$: BOOLEAN

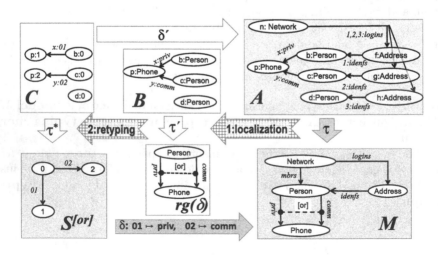

Fig. 3. Localization and further Retyping of Typed Graph τ

which inputs a typed graph τ^*: $C_X \to S^c$, i.e., an instance C_X typed over c's shape, and outputs Boolean truth iff the instance is considered to be satisfying the constraint. (We have subscripted the elements with X to emphasize that we take an arbitrary graph typed over S^c.) For constraint [or], typed graph τ^* is defined to satisfy the constraint iff every vertex v in graph C_X with $\tau^*(v) = 0$ either has at least one outgoing edge e_1 with type $\tau^*(e_1) = 01$, or at least one outgoing edge e_2 with type $\tau^*(e_2) = 02$ (or both).

To check whether a typed graph τ: $A \to M$ satisfies a constraint $c@\delta$, we need properly select a respective small (local) part of τ and check wrt. c's semantics described above. For this, we need the following operation.

Definition 1 (Localization). *The input for the operation consists of two graph morphisms δ: $S^c \to M$ and τ : $A \to M$ with common target M. The output is a mapping τ' : $B \to \mathsf{rg}(\delta)$, where B is the subgraph of A consisting of all elements x, for which $\tau(x) \in \mathsf{rg}(\delta)$, and $\tau'(x) = \tau(x)$ for all elements $x \in B$. We write $\tau' = \mathbf{localize}(\delta, \tau)$.*

For example, Fig. 3 shows how localization works for a constraint declaration [or]. Given graphs and graph mappings are shaded, computed ones are blank. Notched arrows with grid-filled bodies show applications of the respective operations (Definitions 1 and 2). The range of binding map δ is the graph in the middle of the lower part. Then we compute the part B of graph A, consisting of elements whose τ-types belong to $\mathsf{rg}(\delta)$. This gives us a typed graph τ' typed in model $\mathsf{rg}(\delta)$—the result of localization. The next step is to retype graph B to model S^c by inverting mapping δ—the result is shown in the figure as typed graph τ^*: $C \to S^{[or]}$, and is formally defined as follows.

Definition 2 (Retyping). *Let τ' : $B \to \mathsf{rg}(\delta)$ be a localized typed graph according to Definition 1. Then we construct graph C as follows: It has vertices v:t for all vertex pairs $(v$:$T, t)$ in $B \times S^c$ for which $\delta(t) = \tau'(v$:$T)$, and edges e:t for all edge pairs $(e$:$T, t) \in B \times S^c$ for which $\delta(t) = \tau'(e$:$T)$. This yields morphisms τ^* : $C \to S$ defined by $\tau^*(x$:$t) = t$ and δ' : $C \to A$ defined by $\delta'(x$:$t) = x$ for all $(x$:$t) \in C$. We write $\tau^* = retype_\delta(\tau')$.*

Now we can apply function VALIDATE$_c$ to typed graph τ^*.

Definition 3 (Consistency Checking). *Typed graph τ : $A \to M$ satisfies constraint declaration $c@\delta$, if and only if*

$$validate_c(retype_\delta(localize(\delta, \tau))) = true.$$

Note also mapping δ': $C \to A$ which plays an important role in instance repairing: if a constraint violation is detected in graph C (e.g. if some vertex v with $\tau^*(v) = 0$ has no outgoing edges), it can immediately be highlighted in A by using traceability δ'.

3.3   Matching

Modelling a complex system usually results in a *multi-model*, i.e., a set $M_1, \ldots, M_n$ of model components for some $n \geq 1$. For example, Fig. 1 shows a multimodel consisting of four models to be considered as a collective arte-fact, e.g., in order to investigate the mentioned inter-model constraint *consEC*. Consequently, heterogeneously typed graphs $\tau_j : A_j \rightarrow M_j$ must be analysed altogether. For this, one has to consider *overlaps* in models $M_1, \ldots, M_4$, i.e. the definitions of common terminology in different models. Whereas concept *Address* occurs in three of the above-mentioned models, it also happens that names of common concepts differ: *Individual* in M_1 and *Person* in M_2 are dif-ferently named, yet both domains speak of the same concept.

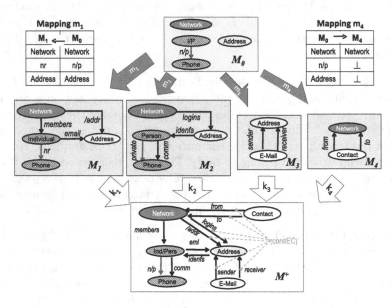

Fig. 4. Matching of concepts in models $M_1, \ldots, M_4$ and resulting merged graph M^+ (Color figure online)

It is our goal to *formally* match common concepts: It is well-known, that in the case of two models M_1 and M_2 this can be achieved with a (binary) span of two graph morphisms $M_1 \xleftarrow{m_1} M_0 \xrightarrow{m_2} M_2$, where auxiliary graph M_0 speci-fies the corresponding binary relation: Any two elements $x_1 \in M_1$ and $x_2 \in M_2$ (vertices or edges) are declared to be the same, if there is $x \in M_0$ such that $m_1(x) = x_1$ and $m_2(x) = x_2$. But this is no longer helpful, if there are $n \geq 3$ models: If we would work with many spans, transitivity constraints have to be guaranteed, cf. the approach in [20]. If we work with n-ary spans $m_i : M_0 \rightarrow M_i$ ($1 \leq i \leq n$), we only obtain n-tupels of same concepts. This, however, is unfea-sible, because we must simultaneously maintain pairs (e.g. *Individual/Person*) and triples (*Address*) of common concepts, although $n = 4$ in the example.

The solution of this problem are *partial* morphisms $M_0 \xrightarrow{m_i} M_i$ as shown in the upper half of Fig. 4, where two mappings, total m_1 and partial m_4, are specified by tables near them; mappings m_2 and m_3 can be easily understood analogously (note also similar shading of mapped nodes). A *partial* morphism $G \xrightarrow{f} G'$ preserves the edge-vertex incidence in the same way as total morphisms, but may only partially be defined on G, e.g., m_4 is not defined on elements n/p and Address of model M_0. However, if it is defined for an edge e, it must be defined on e's source and target as well; e.g., the source and target of arrow $n/p@M_0$ are mapped by m_1 to the respective source and target of arrow $nr@M_1$. The incomplete arrow $\rightharpoonup$ shall remind of the incomplete definition of the morphism. In general, model M_0 specifies overlap of models $M_1 \ldots, M_n$ as follows: If $x_{i_1} \in M_{i_1}, x_{i_2} \in M_{i_2}, \ldots, x_{i_k} \in M_{i_k}$ $(k \geq 2)$ shall be declared to be identical, M_0 must contain some x_0, for which $m_{i_j}(x_0)$ is defined for all $j \in \{1, \ldots, k\}$ and $m_{i_j}(x_0) = x_{i_j}$, resp. Moreover all other m_l $(l \notin \{i_1, \ldots i_k\})$ are undefined at x_0. We call x_0 a *sameness witness* for sticking together $x_{i_1} \in M_{i_1}, x_{i_2} \in M_{i_2}, \ldots, x_{i_k} \in M_{i_k}$, and M_0 is called the *gluing graph*. E.g., in Fig. 4, graph morphisms $m_1, \ldots, m_4$, of which m_1, m_2 are total and m_3, m_4 are proper partial, specify the following commonalities:

1. *Phone* in M_1 and M_2, but also *Individual* and *Person* despite their different names;
2. Attributes *phoneNr* and *private* in M_1 and M_2, too;
3. Also *Address* in M_1, M_2, and M_3 as expected;
4. Finally, classes *Network* in models M_1, M_2, M_4.

Note that declaration 2 infers declaration 1 because a matched association yields matching of its source and target, too.

Definition 4 (Multi-model). *The configuration of models $M_1, \ldots, M_n$, gluing graph M_0, and partial morphisms $(M_0 \xrightarrow{m_j} M_j)_{1 \leq j \leq n}$ is called a* multi-model $\mathcal{M}$. *It is completely determined by the involved partial morphisms (their domain and codomain specifying all participating graphs), such that we often write $\mathcal{M} = (m_j)_{1 \leq j \leq n}$.*

We now define *matching* of instances typed over multi-model $\mathcal{M} = (M_0 \xrightarrow{m_j} M_j)_{1 \leq j \leq n}$.

Definition 5 (Multi-instance and Matching).

– *A discrete (or unrelated) multi-instance over $\mathcal{M}$ is a collection*

$$\mathcal{T} = (\tau_j : A_j \to M_j)_{1 \leq j \leq n}$$

of typed graphs.
– *A matched multi-instance over $\mathcal{M}$ is a collection $(\tau_i : A_i \to M_i)_{0 \leq i \leq n}$ (note that a new typed graph $\tau_0 : A_0 \to M_0$ is added to $\mathcal{T}$) together with type*

compatible partial graph morphisms $A_0 \xrightarrow{a_j} A_j$ $(1 \leq j \leq n)$. A matched multi-instance over $\mathcal{M}$ is denoted

$$\mathcal{J}^m = ((\tau_i : A_i \rightarrow M_i)_{0 \leq i \leq n}, (A_0 \xrightarrow{a_j} A_j)_{1 \leq j \leq n})$$

with the corresponding short notation $\mathcal{J}^m = ((\tau_i)_{0 \leq i \leq n}, (a_j)_{1 \leq j \leq n})$.

- **Matching** of a discrete multi-instance $\mathcal{J}$ is the process of finding a matched multi-instance $\mathcal{J}^m$. We write $\mathcal{J}^m = match(\mathcal{J})$.

In this context, partial morphisms a_j play the same role as morphisms m_j: While the m_j's control type matching, a_j declare sameness of elements in the instance graphs (instance matching). Type compatiblity means that gluing of elements in instance graphs is only possible, if their respective types are glued, as well. Thus matching is an enhancement of $\tau_1, \dots, \tau_n$ with $\dots$

1. $\dots$ morphism $\tau_0 : A_0 \rightarrow M_0$ specifying typing of sameness witnesses of A_0 and $\dots$
2. $\dots$ overlap specification of instances $A_1, \dots, A_n$ via gluing graph A_0 and partial morphisms $A_0 \xrightarrow{a_j} A_j$ in the same way as for multi-models (cf. Definition 4).

This is illustrated in the upper part of Fig. 5: Mapping of the morphisms is again according to shadings. The matching is based on the model matches in Fig. 4, but, due to lack of space, limited to the match of only two typed graphs τ_1 and τ_2. Gluing graph A_0 specifies that Individual 1 in A_1 and Person 1 in A_2 are the same person, and that the phone number in A_1 coincides with the private number in A_2. Type compatibility holds, because A_0 specifies gluing only of elements, whose respective types are also glued.

3.4   Merging

The merge operation is shown in the lower half of Fig. 4: Models M_j are unified modulo their overlaps, which yields graph M^+, in which $Ind/Pers$ represents $Individual$ from M_1 and $Person$ from M_2, which are declared the same, because $m_1(I/P) = Individual$ and $m_2(I/P) = Person$. Similarly, the other commonalities 1 to 4 on page 8 are specified. Note that e.g. vertex $Contact \in M_4$ is not reached by m_4 and thus not identified with any other concept. The same is true for $E\text{-}mail$ and also for all edges except nr and $priv$. Note also that we follow our shading discipline: as matching needs, in general, a user's input, it is not entirely automatic and hence elements produced by matching are shaded; in contrast, merge is an entirely automatic operation and its results are blank.

   A precise definition of the merge operation is given in [13], where we also explain how graph morphisms $k_1, \dots, k_4$ in Fig. 4 arise in general: k_j maps each element x in M_j to the element in M^+, which represents x in the merge. Each k_j is called the *recognition* of M_j in M^+. For example, the equality $k_1(Individual) = Ind/Pers = k_2(Person)$ represents the fact that these concepts coincide. This merging can be extended to instances:

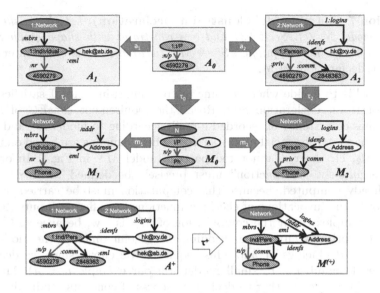

Fig. 5. Matching of Multi-instances (τ_1, τ_2) and resulting merged typed graph τ^+

Definition 6 (Merge of Multi-instance). *Let*

$$\mathcal{J}^m = ((\tau_i : A_i \to M_i)_{0 \leq i \leq n}, (A_0 \xrightarrow{a_j} A_j)_{1 \leq j \leq n})$$

be a matched multi-instance. Then in the same way as for models the instance
merge A^+ *of graphs* $A_1, \ldots, A_n$ *modulo their matched overlap* $(a_j)_{1 \leq j \leq n}$ *together
with recognition morphisms* $l_i : A_i \to A^+$ $(0 \leq i \leq n)$ *is constructed. It can be
shown [1] that this uniquely yields a typed graph* $\tau^+ : A^+ \to M^+$, *which is
compatible with recognitions*[2]. *We write* $\tau^+ = merge(\mathcal{J}^m)$.

An example is shown in Fig. 5: A^+ contains the identified person according to
gluing specification A_0. She is a member of both social networks, her login is the
e-mail-address from network 2. E-mail-address from network 1 and commercial
phone number are added. $\tau^+ : A^+ \to M^{(+)}$ is shown in the lower part. We wrote
$M^{(+)}$, because the model merge only covers two of the four models.

4   Inter-model Constraint Checking

In this chapter, an algorithm is introduced which efficiently verifies consistency
of a collection of typed graphs, i.e. a discrete multi-instance $\mathcal{J} := (\tau_j : A_j \to M_j)_{1 \leq j \leq n}$ over multi-model $\mathcal{M} = (M_0 \xrightarrow{m_j} M_j)_{1 \leq j \leq n}$, against a single inter-
model constraint declaration $c@\delta$.

---

[2] The type of the recognitions must be equal to the recognition of the types [13].

Definition 7 (Inter-model Constraint Declaration). *Let M^+ be the merge of multi-model $\mathcal{M}$ (cf. Sect. 3.4) and c a constraint with shape graph S^c (cf. Sect. 3.1). A binding mapping $\delta : S^c \rightarrow M^+$ (written $c@\delta$) is called* inter-model constraint declaration *on $\mathcal{M}$.*

Our goal is to decide whether some discrete multi-instance $\mathcal{T}$ satisfies inter-model constraint declaration $c@\delta$. Recall the requirement $consEC$ of Sect. 2, which claims consistency of recorded e-mails according to model M_3 and stored contacts due to M_4 for social networks $n_{1/2}$, whose domains are based on models M_1 and M_2, cf. the red annotated part in model M^+ in Fig. 4. In order to do this accurately, "satisfaction" must precisely be defined. We assume M^+ to be already computed, because this computation must be carried out only once prior to the invocations of checking functions for different inputs $(\mathcal{T}, c@\delta)$. Moreover, complexity for the computation of M^+ is low, because M^+ can be computed algorithmically by partitioning the disjoint union of the models due to the specified glueings in M_0. This requires little effort, since we deal with a manageable number n of small models (in our example $n = 4$). Matching effort (e.g. to decide whether to declare sameness of concepts "Individual" and "Person") is acceptable.

Match→Merge→Localize (MML): A natural definition for a discrete multi-instance $\mathcal{T}$ to satisfy an inter-model constraint declaration $c@\delta$ on $\mathcal{M}$, written $\mathcal{T} \models_{\mathsf{MML}} c@\delta$, is given in terms of the operations of Sect. 3, cf. also [22]:

$$\mathcal{T} \models_{\mathsf{MML}} c@\delta \iff \mathcal{T} \overset{\boldsymbol{match}}{\rightarrow} \mathcal{T}^m \overset{merge}{\rightarrow} \tau^+ \overset{localize(\delta,\tau^+)}{\rightarrow} (\tau^+)'$$
$$\overset{retype_\delta}{\rightarrow} (\tau^+)^* \overset{validate_c}{\rightarrow} true/false$$

I.e. the discrete multi-instance $\mathcal{T}$ is matched (Definition 5), merged (Definition 6), and localized (Definition 1). The subsequent three steps are exactly the applications for checking a single instance as described in Definition 3. Because of the order of the operation's application, we call this approach "Match→Merge→Localize" (MML).

The only non-automatic and hence costly step is matching (highlighted by the bold face type), i.e. the search for commonalities, because, in general, there is manual or at least semi-automatic activity to be performed. This can easily be seen when investigating properties of persons: An algorithm can not decide whether a person with name "Dustin Hoffman" and an individual with name "Dustin Hoffmann" are in fact identical (the difference in their last name may be due to a typing error). Thus, an algorithm can increase efficiency, if matching workload is reduced.

Since matching is the first step in the MML-approach, it must be carried out on the *total* collection of data. This is the most serious disadvantage of the MML-approach, as we can demonstrate in our running example: Although constraint declaration $c@\delta = consEC$ does not affect individuals/persons in M^+ (see Fig. 4), MML demands to deal with *all* personal data during computation of τ^+: One has to find all matches of individuals (typed in M_1) with persons (typed in M_2). Experience, however, shows that data of the same person stored in different databases may differ due to typing errors (see above) or inconsistent updates. Eliminating these contradictions in large databases (with probably thousands of redundantly captured data records) is a very costly manual activity and hopeless in many cases. Hence, using this approach as an algorithm for consistency checking would be impractical.

Localize→Match→Merge(LMM): To check satisfaction of a single constraint declaration more efficiently, we propose to perform *early localization separately per component* of the multi-instance: Let S^c be the shape of the given constraint c. The shape for $c = consEC$ is shown in the upper half of Fig. 6. In Fig. 4, it is bound to M^+ according to the shading and the letters $: C \mapsto Contact, N \mapsto Network, f \mapsto from$, etc. In order to determine the constraint affected part *separately* for each component, we define for each $j \in \{1, \ldots, n\}$ the shape S_j^c. It is the reduction of the constraint shape of c, which affects component M_j.

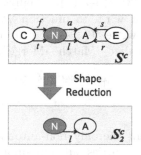

Fig. 6. Shape reduction w.r.t. model M_2

This is shown for the declaration's affected part in M_2 in Fig. 6: The reduced shape S_2^c consists of vertices N and A and edge l. Let $\delta_j : S_j^c \to M_j$ be the corresponding restricted binding mapping. In the case of M_2 it assigns N to $Network$, A to $Address$, and l to $logins$. Figure 7 shows δ_2 in the lower part. In M_2 the remaining affected part is marked with a dashed line from the constraint name. For $j = 2$, Fig. 7 illustrates the steps that now follow. Early localization (step 1): All typed graphs τ_j are localized along the restricted bindings (cf. Definition 1) yielding τ_j'.

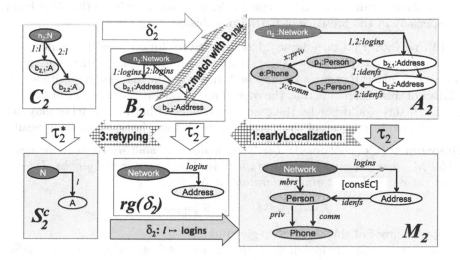

Fig. 7. Early Component Localization for typed graph τ_2

Then the reduced data spaces are subject for matching specifications (commonality search, Definition 5). I.e. we traverse data $B_1, \ldots, B_n$ and declare samenesses of instance elements, step 2. This is illustrated in Fig. 7 with an arrow out of B_2 ("match with $B_{1/3/4}$"). After that these reduced typed graphs together with their gluing specification are retyped (Definition 2) w.r.t. δ_j in step 3 ($\tau_j' \mapsto \tau_j^*$). Finally, these instances are merged (Definition 6) and validated w.r.t. to function VALIDATE$_c$ (cf. Sect. 3.2, this is not shown in Fig. 7). We write $\mathcal{T} \models_{\mathsf{LMM}} c@\delta$ for this approach due to the operation sequence "Localize→Match→Merge". This can be summarized: $\mathcal{T} \models_{\mathsf{LMM}} c@\delta \iff$

$$\mathcal{T} \stackrel{\forall j: localize(\delta_j, \tau_j)}{\rightarrow} \mathcal{T}' = (\tau_1', \ldots, \tau_n') \stackrel{match}{\rightarrow} (\mathcal{T}^m)' \stackrel{\forall j: retype_{\delta_j}}{\rightarrow} (\mathcal{T}^m)^*$$

$$\stackrel{merge}{\rightarrow} \tau'' \stackrel{validate_c}{\rightarrow} true/false.$$

Again the only non-automatic step (matching) is highlighted. However, while MML carries out matching on the entire data space, LMM matches on already localized (i.e. reduced) data. In our example this means that we avoid matching of persons and phone numbers, because they are not affected by the constraint declaration. From the remarks in the end of the previous section, it is now clear that this yields considerable progress.

It is now important to state equivalence of MML and LMM, i.e., prove that they yield the same result for all inputs. This is not obvious for two reasons:

1. It has to be checked that the output of a previous operation in LMM conforms to the demanded input of the next operation, e.g. we have to show that the output of operation *merge* is a graph typed over the shape graph of constraint c (only in this case is function VALIDATE applicable).
2. It is not immediately clear how to formally compare multiple separated localization and retyping *before* merging in the LMM-approach on the one hand and single localization and retyping *after* merging in MML on the other hand, especially in the presence of partial morphisms.

In [13], we show that once issue 2 has a positive solution, then 1 automatically follows. And we explain, how an abstract version of the law of distributivity in category theory [11] ensures validity of 2. However, the main prerequisite for the validity of this theorem is that the overall metamodel is the category of directed graphs. If this would not be the case, equivalence of both approaches may fail, as we showed in an example in [14]. We state all these facts as our main result:

Theorem 1 (Correctness). *Let $\mathcal{T}$ be a discrete multi-instance over multi-model $\mathcal{M}$ where all models and instances are based on directed graphs. Let $c@\delta$ be an inter-model constraint declaration on $\mathcal{M}$, then*

$$\mathcal{T} \models_{\mathsf{MML}} c@\delta \iff \mathcal{T} \models_{\mathsf{LMM}} c@\delta.$$

A detailed proof of this theorem is given in [13].

We illustrate the algorithm along the example of Sect. 2 where $c@\delta = consEC$: Suppose that social networks n_1 and n_2 have several members with their respective e-mail-addresses and phone numbers. Early localization reduces the data space, such that it only contains network objects n_1 and n_2 and some e-mail-addresses as shown in the left two columns of Table 2 (B_1 and B_2) together with sender and receiver information ($b_{3,1}$, $b_{3,2}$) of one e-mail-object e in B_3 and one recorded contact con from n_1 to n_2 in B_4. For B_2 see also Fig. 7. We do not list edges of the instance graphs in Table 2, because they are not subject to matching. From the coinciding e-mail-address strings, the algorithm now generates auxiliary graph $B_0 = \{ang\colon A, bar\colon A, n_1\colon N, n_2\colon N\}$ (a graph only with vertices and no edges) and appropriate partial mappings $a_j : B_0 \to B_j$ ($j \in \{1, \ldots, 4\}$) where $a_1 : B_0 \to B_1$ maps as follows: $ang \mapsto b_{1,2}$, $bar \mapsto b_{1,1}$, $n_1 \mapsto n_1$. In the same way $a_2 : B_0 \to B_2$ maps: $ang \mapsto b_{2,1}$, $bar \mapsto b_{2,2}$, $n_2 \mapsto n_2$. a_3 only maps $ang \mapsto b_{3,1}$, a_4 is $n_1 \mapsto n_1$, $n_2 \mapsto n_2$. Hence the system proposes samenesses $b_{1,1} = b_{2,2}$, $b_{1,2} = b_{2,1} = b_{3,1}$, which the user may confirm.

Table 2. Instance matching

B_1	B_2	B_3	B_4
n_1: Network	n_2: Network	e: E-mail	con: Contact
$b_{1,1} =$:barack@us.gov	$b_{2,1} =$:angela@bt.de	$b_{3,1} =$:angela@bt.de(sender)	n_1(from)
$b_{1,2} =$:angela@bt.de	$b_{2,2} =$:barack@us.gov	$b_{3,2} =$:justin@ottawa.ca(receiver)	n_2(to)

Subsequent retyping and validation (automatic by the algorithm) yields an inter-model but localized picture: Although one intelligence agency recorded a contact from n_1 to n_2 in B_4, there is no e-mail sent with sender a member of n_1 and receiver from n_2 because $b_{3,2}$ does not occur in B_2. This violation can still be highlighted with the help of maps δ'_j. In our example this would be δ'_4, which highlights the contact from n_1 to n_2 in A_4, since it has no counterpart in A_3.

5 Related Work

Operations *matching*, *merging*, and *consistency checking* have been discussed in a wide variety of approaches. There is an enormous literature on model matching and merging, whose surveying, even brief, would need a separate paper. We will just mention several works that have a direct relation to the present paper and were influential for us.

Matching. In our context, explicit specification of inter-model correspondences is a central issue, and different types of notation and techniques were developed [20]. Besides the usual distinction between manual and (semi-) automatic procedures, e.g., [24], more sophisticated approaches have been elaborated [12]. A distinctive feature of our approach is that the set of correspondences is reified as a special model M_0 endowed with partial correspondence mappings. This is a standard categorical idea, which was repeatedly employed in multi-modeling frameworks based on category theory, the most prominent being [23], where the correspondencies are themselves subject of evolution. More specifically, the idea to formally connect many models with partial mappings has its origin in [9], see also [10]. Spans with partial legs were also used in [5].

Merging and Consistency Checking. There is a major distinction in the way consistency checks are specified. The most direct approach is via monitoring satisfiability of *consistency rules* specified in a special language "understanding" all local models [17]. In contrast to our approach, matching is only allowed when elements have same types *and* same names such that matching can well be automated. A different approach is consistency checking via merging (CCVM). It was discussed for homogeneous structural modeling in [22] and for behavioral modeling in [7] and generalized for the heterogeneous case in [5]. Constraint specifications are imposed upon the merged model. An essential advantage of CCVM approaches over monitoring consistency rules is that complex types of model matching are allowed. However, as checking is based on "late localization", these approaches are practically inefficient; see [14] for a detailed survey.

6   Conclusion and Future Work

We presented a framework and an algorithm for consistency checking of a system of complexly inter-related multiple models, in which the use of the expensive match operation is significantly minimized. The key idea is to do localization—the main ingredient of consistency checking—before model matching and merging, and thus do the latter for as minimal as possible parts of the component models. We prove that LMM and MML algorithms produce the same Boolean value for any given multimodel and inter-model constraint, but LMM is much more effective for big models with big overlaps. Being based on graphs, the algorithm is independent of concrete modelling languages.

We plan the following future work. We are going to evaluate the algorithm in the tooling framework developed at Bergen University College [15]—the idea is to enhance the DPF editor to make it inter-model aware. It has to be analysed whether our approach scales in larger use-cases.

The next natural step is to extend multi-model consistency checking to multi-model-repairing [19] by extending the framework into an update propagation framework. The challenge will be to find an appropriate generalization of the (binary) delta-lens framework [6] for the case of $n \geq 3$ models. Another direction is to incorporate into the framework we developed in this paper the ideas of incremental consistency checking [3].

References

1. Arbib, M., Manes, E.: The Categorical Imperative. Academic Press, New York, San Francisco, London (1975)
2. Barr, M., Wells, C.: Category Theory for Computing Sciences. Prentice Hall, Upper Saddle River (1990)

3. Diskin, Z., König, H.: Incremental consistency checking of heterogeneous multi-models. In: Milazzo, P., Varró, D., Wimmer, M. (eds.) STAF 2016. LNCS, vol. 9946, pp. 274–288. Springer, Cham (2016). doi:10.1007/978-3-319-50230-4_21

4. Diskin, Z., Wolter, U.: A diagrammatic logic for object-oriented visual modeling. Electr. Notes Theor. Comput. Sci. **203**(6), 19–41 (2008). http://dx.doi.org/10.1016/j.entcs.2008.10.041

5. Diskin, Z., Xiong, Y., Czarnecki, K.: Specifying overlaps of heterogeneous models for global consistency checking. In: Dingel, J., Solberg, A. (eds.) MODELS 2010. LNCS, vol. 6627, pp. 165–179. Springer, Heidelberg (2011). doi:10.1007/978-3-642-21210-9_16

6. Diskin, Z., Xiong, Y., Czarnecki, K.: From state- to delta-based bidirectional model transformations: the asymmetric case. J. Object Technol. **10**(6), 1–25 (2011). http://dx.doi.org/10.5381/jot.2011.10.1.a6

7. Easterbrook, S.M., Chechik, M.: A framework for multi-valued reasoning over inconsistent viewpoints. In: Proceedings of the 23rd International Conference on Software Engineering, ICSE 2001, Toronto, Ontario, Canada, 12–19, pp. 411–420 (2001). http://dx.doi.org/10.1109/ICSE.2001.919114

8. Ehrig, H., Ehrig, K., Prange, U., Taentzer, G.: Fundamentals of Algebraic Graph Transformations. Springer, Heidelberg (2006)

9. Fiadeiro, J.L.: Categories for Software Engineering. Springer, Heidelberg (2005)

10. Fiadeiro, J.L., Lopes, A., Maibaum, T.S.E.: Synthesising interconnections. In: Algorithmic Languages and Calculi, IFIP TC2 WG2.1 International Workshop on Algorithmic Languages and Calculi, Alsace, France, 17–22, pp. 240–264, February 1997

11. Goldblatt, R.: Topoi: The Categorial Analysis of Logic. Dover Publications, Mineola (1984)

12. Kessentini, M., Ouni, A., Langer, P., Wimmer, M., Bechikh, S.: Search-based meta-model matching with structural and syntactic measures. J. Syst. Softw. **97**, 1–14 (2014). http://dx.doi.org/10.1016/j.jss.2014.06.040

13. König, H., Diskin, Z.: Consistency checking of interrelated models: long version. Technical report, University of Applied Sciences, FHDW Hannover (2017). http://fhdwdev.ha.bib.de/public/papers/02017-01.pdf

14. König, H., Diskin, Z.: Advanced local checking of global consistency in heterogeneous multimodeling. In: Wąsowski, A., Lönn, H. (eds.) ECMFA 2016. LNCS, vol. 9764, pp. 19–35. Springer, Cham (2016). doi:10.1007/978-3-319-42061-5_2

15. Lamo, Y., Wang, X., Mantz, F., Bech, Ø., Sandven, A., Rutle, A.: DPF workbench: a multi-level language workbench for MDE. Proc. Est. Acad. Sci. **62**, 3–15 (2013). http://www.kirj.ee/public/proceedings_pdf/2013/issue_1/Proc-2013-1-3-15.pdf

16. de Lara, J., Guerra, E.: Formal support for model driven development with graph transformation techniques. In: Actas del Taller sobre Desarrollo Dirigido por Modelos, MDA y Aplicaciones, Granada, España, 13 Septiembre 2005 (2005). http://ceur-ws.org/Vol-157/paper04.pdf

17. Lopez-Herrejon, R.E., Egyed, A.: Detecting inconsistencies in multi-view models with variability. In: Kühne, T., Selic, B., Gervais, M.-P., Terrier, F. (eds.) ECMFA 2010. LNCS, vol. 6138, pp. 217–232. Springer, Heidelberg (2010). doi:10.1007/978-3-642-13595-8_18

18. Mens, T.: On the use of graph transformations for model refactoring. In: Lämmel, R., Saraiva, J., Visser, J. (eds.) GTTSE 2005. LNCS, vol. 4143, pp. 219–257. Springer, Heidelberg (2006). doi:10.1007/11877028_7

19. Rabbi, F., Lamo, Y., Yu, I.C., Kristensen, L.M.: A diagrammatic approach to model completion. In: Proceedings of the 4th Workshop on the Analysis of Model Transformations Co-located with the 18th International Conference on Model Driven Engineering Languages and Systems (MODELS 2015), Ottawa, Canada, 28 September 2015, pp. 56–65 (2015). http://ceur-ws.org/Vol-1500/paper7.pdf

20. Romero, J.R., Jaen, J.I., Vallecillo, A.: Realizing correspondences in multi-viewpoint specifications. In: Proceedings of the 13th IEEE International Enterprise Distributed Object Computing Conference, EDOC 2009, Auckland, New Zealand, 1–4, pp. 163–172 (2009). http://dx.doi.org/10.1109/EDOC.2009.23

21. Rutle, A., Rossini, A., Lamo, Y., Wolter, U.: A formal approach to the specification and transformation of constraints in MDE. J. Log. Algebr. Program. **81**(4), 422–457 (2012). http://dx.doi.org/10.1016/j.jlap.2012.03.006

22. Sabetzadeh, M., Nejati, S., Liaskos, S., Easterbrook, S.M., Chechik, M.: Consistency checking of conceptual models via model merging. In: 15th IEEE International Requirements Engineering Conference, RE 15–19th, 2007, New Delhi, India, pp. 221–230 (2007). http://dx.doi.org/10.1109/RE.2007.18

23. Schürr, A.: Specification of graph translators with triple graph grammars. In: Mayr, E.W., Schmidt, G., Tinhofer, G. (eds.) WG 1994. LNCS, vol. 903, pp. 151–163. Springer, Heidelberg (1995). doi:10.1007/3-540-59071-4_45

24. Sousa, J., Lopes, D., Claro, D.B., Abdelouahab, Z.: A step forward in semi-automatic metamodel matching: algorithms and tool. In: Filipe, J., Cordeiro, J. (eds.) ICEIS 2009. LNBIP, vol. 24, pp. 137–148. Springer, Heidelberg (2009). doi:10.1007/978-3-642-01347-8_12

Finding Achievable Features and Constraint Conflicts for Inconsistent Metamodels

Hao Wu[✉]

Department of Computer Science,
National University of Ireland, Maynooth, Ireland
haowu@cs.nuim.ie

Abstract. Determining the consistency of a metamodel is a task of generating a metamodel instance that not only meets structural constraints but also constraints written in Object Constraint Language (OCL). Those constraints can be conflicting, resulting in inconsistencies. When this happens, the existing techniques and tools have no knowledge about which constraints are achievable and which ones cause the conflicts. In this paper, we present an approach to finding achievable metamodel features and constraint conflicts for inconsistent metamodels. This approach allows users to rank individual metamodel features and works by reducing it to a weighted maximum satisfiability modulo theories (MaxSMT). This reduction allows us to utilise SMT solvers to tackle multiple ranked constraints and at the same time locate conflicts among them. We have prototyped this approach, incorporated it into an existing modelling tool, and evaluated it against a benchmark. The preliminary results show that our approach is promising and scalable.

1 Introduction

The metamodelling approach plays a key role in Model-Driven Engineering (MDE), it paves the way for enabling many other MDE approaches such as model transformation, language engineering and business process modelling [1–3]. A metamodel captures the syntax for a set of *models* and allows users to form a design at a higher level of abstraction. A valid model or an *instance* of a metamodel conforms to all of the constraints imposed by its features. These constraints vary according to the metamodel structural features such as multiplicities for an association to class invariants written in Object Constraint Language (OCL). Then the task for checking consistency of a metamodel becomes finding a valid instance. However, this is a challenging task since an instance needs to meet all kinds of constraints defined over that metamodel. Recent studies have shown that this task can be tackled via well-engineered constraint solvers [4–6].

Many metamodels in practice are not consistent due to the conflicts in a number of constraints imposed by different features such as the multiplicities of an association or class invariants. These conflicts could be caused by user errors or features being over-constrained in the design. When this happens, current modelling tools terminate and report inconsistent metamodels, or are unable

© Springer International Publishing AG 2017
A. Anjorin and H. Espinoza (Eds.): ECMFA 2017, LNCS 10376, pp. 179–196, 2017.
DOI: 10.1007/978-3-319-61482-3_11

to generate a valid instance. However, in many cases users may wish to know how many metamodel features can be fulfilled in their current design and which constraints cause the conflicts, then use this information to further refine their metamodels. For example, a user may be interested in finding the minimum number of features that cause conflicts in a metamodel, and fix them in a new design. In other cases, users could use their domain specific knowledge to rank individual features and look for a model that could fulfill as many as features possible.

In this paper, we present an approach to finding two kinds of information when a metamodel is inconsistent. (1) The set of achievable metamodel features based on their rankings. (2) The set of structural constraints or class invariants that cause conflicts. In our approach, both kinds of information are computed using an SMT solver. The use of an SMT solver has several advantages. First, we can perform *fast* satisfiability checks on not only pure boolean constraints but also complex structures with a number of numeric constraints. Second, it does not introduce a substantial implementation overhead since an SMT solver is treated as a *black-box* engine.

Contributions. The contributions of this paper can be summarised as follows:

1. We present a simple annotation that allows users to rank individual meta-model features (Sect. 3.1), and a reduction to weighted MaxSMT problem so that we can compute the set of achievable metamodel features based on their rankings (Sect. 3.2).
2. Inspired by the work of Liffiton and Sakallah on extracting conflicts [7], we present a novel technique for finding constraint conflicts by solving the set cover problem (Sect. 3.3).
3. We have implemented a prototype tool, tapped it into an existing modelling tool and evaluated it against a benchmark for scalability (Sect. 4).

2   A Running Example

In this section, we provide a small example that will be used throughout this paper to illustrate our approach. This example is shown in Fig. 1, representing a metamodel that models a real world example of students in a university choosing multiple modules to study. This metamodel is enriched with 8 class invariants ($inv1$ to $inv8$). Each invariant is ranked by using an integer value. For example, each student must have a unique id number ($inv4$), and can only choose modules that are in their year ($inv5$). In this example, we use numbers 1 to 6 to distinguish a student's year, and students that are in year 6 are considered as research students. Thus, a university has some non-research and research students ($inv6$).

This metamodel is inconsistent and has a maximum number of 6 achievable invariants. This is due to the two conflicts among the invariants in Fig. 1. The first conflict is obvious and it is caused by the invariants $inv1$ and $inv2$ defined for the *age* attribute. However, the second conflict is not easy to identify. This conflict is caused by the invariants that there must exist some research and non-research students ($inv6$) choosing some modules ($inv7$) in their corresponding year ($inv5$). But there are modules that are only available for non-research students ($inv8$: between year 1 and 5).

However, in the real world each individual invariants may be treated differently based on user's domain specific knowledge. For example, a university may consider a registration procedure that students choosing modules in their corresponding year ($inv5$) is more important than choosing some modules ($inv7$). In this context, a maximum number of 6 invariants is achievable with the preference that $inv5$ is more favourable than $inv7$. Therefore, by allowing more favourable constraints to be achieved first is more suitable for users wishing to distinguish priorities among different invariants.

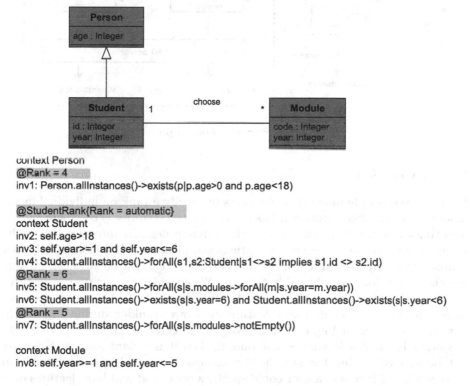

```
context Person
@Rank = 4
inv1: Person.allInstances()->exists(p|p.age>0 and p.age<18)

@StudentRank{Rank = automatic}
context Student
inv2: self.age>18
inv3: self.year>=1 and self.year<=6
inv4: Student.allInstances()->forAll(s1,s2:Student|s1<>s2 implies s1.id <> s2.id)
@Rank = 6
inv5: Student.allInstances()->forAll(s|s.modules->forAll(m|s.year=m.year))
inv6: Student.allInstances()->exists(s|s.year=6) and Student.allInstances()->exists(s|s.year<6)
@Rank = 5
inv7: Student.allInstances()->forAll(s|s.modules->notEmpty())

context Module
inv8: self.year>=1 and self.year<=5
```

Fig. 1. An example of a ranked metamodel describing how a student can choose multiple modules to study. The ranks are highlighted in the shaded area. Our approach concludes that this metamodel has a maximum number of 6 achievable invariants and 2 conflicts: ($inv1, inv2$) and ($inv5, inv6, inv7, inv8$).

3   The Approach

Figure 2 provides an overview workflow of our approach. Briefly, this is viewed as three steps. First, users use a simple annotation to rank individual metamodel features. The approach then determines the consistency of a metamodel. If there is at least one class that cannot be instantiated, then all metamodel features along with OCL constraints will be reduced to a weighted MaxSMT problem and solved by an SMT solver. The returned solution is a set that contains all possible ways of maximising the number of achievable metamodel features based on their rankings. Finally, to find constraint conflicts among all metamodel features, the approach treats all features equally including OCL constraints, formalises them into the set cover problem and solves it by using an SMT solver.

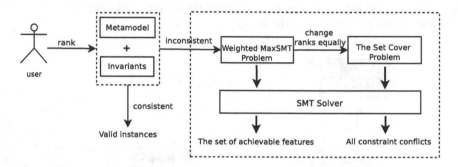

Fig. 2. An overview of our approach.

3.1   Annotation

We provide a simple annotation for users to specify a rank on individual metamodel features. This annotation has the basic form: '$@Rank = c$', where $c \in \mathbb{Z}^+$ denoting a metamodel feature is ranked via an non-negative integer c. Currently, we allow users to rank classes, associations and invariants. If a metamodel has a conflict, then any ranked features cause that conflict might be switched off during the search for the achievable features. We consider all metamodel features ranked with integer c as *soft features*. A soft feature with higher ranking is more favourable to be selected than a feature with lower ranking during the search. For example, $inv5$ in Fig. 1 is more likely to be chosen compared to $inv7$. On the other hand, if a feature is *not* ranked, then it is a *hard feature* that must not be ignored during the search. For example, $inv8$ in Fig. 1 must hold, no matter what. Therefore, a user could specify a set of soft and hard features over a metamodel by using this annotation.

Sometime users wish to use a single ranking criteria to treat a group of class invariants. For example, all invariants defined for a specific class are equally important. In this case, another type annotation: '$@Name\{Rank = c\}$' is introduced, where $Name$ is an identifier for the annotation, and $c \in \mathbb{Z}^+$. For example, in Fig. 1 the annotation '$@StudentRank$' specifies that every invariant defined under the class *Student* is ranked using automatic ranking. However, users may override current ranking criteria by specifying a different rank through '$@Rank = c$'. For example, an automatic ranking is initially specified for $inv5$

and *inv*7 but it is overwritten by the new values of 6 and 5. The remaining invariants are ranked using automatic ranking.

Ranking Criteria. A metamodel feature can be ranked in two ways: (1) Users rank an individual metamodel feature into a soft feature based on their domain specific knowledge[1]. (2) In situations, where users feel they can let the program automatically handle a particular feature for them, an automatic ranking criteria is provided. In default settings, all metamodel features are initially treated as hard features. However, users may override default settings by using the keyword 'automatic'. All features annotated with 'automatic' are assigned a specific value internally and automatically calculated as follows.

Automatic Ranking. The automatic ranking for a class is calculated based on the number of attributes and operations (including those inherited from an abstract class) defined within. This is because a class that contains more attributes and operations typically describes more information about a system than a class with fewer attributes and operations. For an association, it is calculated by adding up the rank defined on each association end[2]. For a class invariant, we calculate the size of its abstract syntax tree (AST). The larger size of an invariant's AST, the more likely a stricter constraint will be imposed on a metamodel[3]. For example, the invariants (except for *inv*2 and *inv*7) defined for *Student* class are automatically assigned with a rank based on the size of their ASTs. In Fig. 3, we can see that *inv*3 is assigned with a value of 9.

Fig. 3. The abstract syntax tree for *inv*3 from Fig. 1 has a total of 9 nodes.

3.2 Reducing to Weighted MaxSMT

Our reduction to SMT is a procedure that traverses a set of soft features defined on a metamodel and automatically generates a set of SMT formulas. Each generated formula consists of two parts.

---

[1] Note that a metamodel could be ranked in 3 different scenarios: (1) Partially ranked (a mixture of soft and hard features). (2) Totally ranked (soft features only). (3) Not ranked (hard features only).

[2] Currently, we assume that each association end is owned by a class.

[3] An invariant could be written in multiple ways. Here, we assume all class invariants were written in a consistent way. For example, using *self* to constrain attributes and *allInstances*() for quantifiers and navigations.

The first part is an SMT encoding of a specific metamodel feature[4]. Currently, the formula in this part is similar to the encoding of metamodel features into first-order logic (FOL) [8]. We support an encoding of a variety of metamodel features such as classes, inheritance, associations, and class invariants. For invariants written in OCL, we also support navigation, nested quantifiers and operations on generic collection data types such as *include*. These encodings are similar to those used in [9]. Currently, we do not support *string* operations.

The second part of the formula is central to our approach. Using the formulas generated for this part, we are able to apply a rank on a specific metamodel feature when the constraint imposed by that feature is achievable.

Given a total k number of soft features, we let F_i be an SMT formula that encodes the *ith* soft feature in a metamodel. We now introduce an integer type auxiliary variable Aux_i whose range is $\{0, 1\}$. We then generate Formula 1. The idea behind this formula is that we associate each F_i with an auxiliary variable so that it is *equisatisfiable* to the original F_i. This is ensured by *part a* and *part b* in Formula 1 since both parts can not be satisfiable simultaneously. Therefore, we can check whether a feature encoded by formula F_i is achievable via testing the satisfiability of Formula 1.

$$\left(\bigwedge_{i=1}^{k} F_i \vee \left(\underbrace{Aux_i = 1}_{part\ a} \right) \right) \wedge \left(\underbrace{\left(\sum_{i=1}^{k} Aux_i \right) = 0}_{part\ b} \right) \tag{1}$$

Now let V^{W_i} be an SMT encoding for a user specified rank W_i of the *ith* soft feature. Note that $V^{W_i} \geq 0$ (no negative value is allowed). We now generate Formula 2. The implication of this formula is built on Formula 1. If Formula 1 is satisfiable, then each $Aux_i = 0$ and F_i must also be satisfiable. This means that the constraint imposed by *ith* soft feature can be achieved. Thus, we must assign an integer constant c to V^{W_i} to indicate that the corresponding rank is achieved. Otherwise, there must exist some F_is that are not satisfiable. In this case, we simply disable the corresponding rank by assigning 0 to V^{W_i}.

$$\bigwedge_{i=1}^{k} \left(\left((Aux_i = 0) \Rightarrow (V^{W_i} = c) \right) \wedge \left((Aux_i = 1) \Rightarrow (V^{W_i} = 0) \right) \right), \text{where } c > 0. \tag{2}$$

Finally, we form a weighted MaxSMT problem by generating Formula 3. We generate this formula only when Formula 1 is not satisfiable. This is because if Formula 1 is satisfiable, then a metamodel is consistent. Intuitively, we know some F_is are not satisfiable, and both *part a* and *part b* from Formula 1 cannot be satisfiable at the same time. Now to make Formula 1 become satisfiable, we remove *part b* (Formula 1) and rewrite it as *part c* (Formula 3). This forces some of the auxiliary variables (Aux_i in Formula 1) to be evaluated to 1. In other

---

[4] Note that for this part a user could still use an existing SMT encoding, no changes are required.

words, we fix some number m and if there are some features that cannot be met, then the associated auxiliary variables (Aux_i) must be evaluated to 1 in order to be satisfiable. Thus, in this way we can work out m number of constraints imposed by metamodel features that cannot be fulfilled. In the meantime, we also check whether it is possible to achieve a total of rank of c based on the remaining number of metamodel features (*part d* in Formula 3). If c is the maximum number we can find to make Formula 3 satisfiable, then c is a solution to our weighted MaxSMT problem.

$$\underbrace{\left(\left(\sum_{i=1}^{k} Aux_i \right) = m \right)}_{part\ c} \wedge \underbrace{\left(\left(\sum_{i=1}^{k} V^{W_i} \right) = c \right)}_{part\ d}, \text{where } 1 \leq m \leq k, 1 \leq c \leq \sum_{i=1}^{k} W_i.$$

(3)

Now that we have formed weighted MaxSMT problem from ranked metamodel, the goal here is to find a maximum total rank from all ranked metamodel features, namely weighted MaxSMT solution. To reduce the number of satisfiability checks, we employ a binary-search based algorithm to search for this maximum total rank. This algorithm iteratively asks an SMT solver to solve Formula 3 and look for an integer that could maximise the rank. If the maximum rank is found, the algorithm then enumerates all possible ways of achieving this value by blocking all previous successful assignments until no more weighted MaxSMT solutions can be found. Note that if a metamodel contains hard features only, then the algorithm returns a maximum number of achievable metamodel features.

3.3 Finding Constraint Conflicts

In [7], the authors reveal that the set of conflicts among SAT formulas can be captured by the set cover problem[5]. Inspired by their work, we directly use this information to find constraint conflicts of metamodel features by further solving the set cover problem using an SMT solver. A conflict among a set of metamodel features essentially is a *minimal unsat core*. This core is a set of unsatisfiable SMT formulas and all *proper* subsets of the core are satisfiable. Though only few of the SMT solvers provide unsat core extraction, such extraction is not guaranteed to find *all minimal* unsat cores [10]. For example, the Z3 SMT solver only finds one conflict (*inv1*, *inv2*) for the example in Fig. 1.

Relationship to the Set Cover Problem. Formally, a set cover problem can be defined as: given a finite universe $U = \{S_1, S_2, ..., S_n\}$ and a collection of subsets $I_1, I_2, ..., I_k \subseteq U$, find a sub collection (set) of I_is, $i \subseteq \{1, 2, ..., k\}$ such that $\bigcup I_i = U$. The sub collection is minimum if it uses fewest I_is to cover U and such collection is called *a minimum set*.

To illustrate that the set cover problem captures the conflicts among the set of metamodel features. We use the example from Fig. 1 except that we treat all invariants (*inv1* to *inv8*) *equally* this time and solve them to derive a total of

---

[5] The hitting set problem is an instance of the set cover problem.

MaxSMT Solutions	I_1	I_2	I_3	I_4	I_5	I_6	I_7	I_8
$S_1 = \{I_2, I_5\}$	0	1	0	0	1	0	0	0
$S_2 = \{I_2, I_6\}$	0	1	0	0	0	1	0	0
$S_3 = \{I_2, I_7\}$	0	1	0	0	0	0	1	0
$S_4 = \{I_2, I_8\}$	0	1	0	0	0	0	0	1
$S_5 = \{I_1, I_5\}$	1	0	0	0	1	0	0	0
$S_6 = \{I_1, I_6\}$	1	0	0	0	0	1	0	0
$S_7 = \{I_1, I_7\}$	1	0	0	0	0	0	1	0
$S_8 = \{I_1, I_8\}$	1	0	0	0	0	0	0	1

Fig. 4. An example that illustrates how the set cover problem captures the conflicts among metamodel features. For example, a conflict between $inv1$ (I_1) and $inv2$ (I_2) in Fig. 1 can be identified here, since I_1 covers $\{S_5, S_6, S_7, S_8\}$ and I_2 covers $\{S_1, S_2, S_3, S_4\}$.

8 different solutions ($S_1, S_2, ..., S_8$), as shown in Fig. 4. Each solution describes a way of maximising the number of class invariants in Fig. 1, namely they are MaxSMT solutions. A matrix is then formed with each row describing one solution and each column denoting a class invariant from Fig. 1. For example, in Fig. 4 row $S_1 = \{I_2, I_5\}$ denotes a way of achieving 6 numbers of invariants by deactivating 2 invariants $inv2$ and $inv5$ (in Fig. 1). In the first row, we use a 1 to mark these two invariants that can *not* be achieved, and 0 to mark the remaining invariants that can be achieved.

To find conflicts among these invariants, consider each column $I_i \subseteq \{S_1, ..., S_8\}$ that covers only rows marked with a 1 in that column. We say an S_i is covered if and only if at least one of the elements is covered. For example, column I_1 covers row S_5, S_6, S_7, and S_8, while column I_3 covers no rows. A conflict can now be identified by finding a sub collection (set) of I_is such that the union of I_is covers all rows (S_1 to S_8). Such a set is a minimal unsat core: it is minimal in the sense that the removal of any element from the set results in at least one of the rows becoming uncovered. For example, set $\{I_1, I_2\}$ forms a minimal unsat core and thus $inv1$ and $inv2$ (from Fig. 1) conflict with each other. Another conflict can be identified by forming the set $\{I_5, I_6, I_7, I_8\}$.

Solving the Set Cover Problem. In general, finding one solution to the set cover problem is NP-complete, and finding a minimum set is NP-hard [11]. To tackle this problem, we present a novel technique that allows us to find all metamodel constraint conflicts via SMT solving. This technique first computes a set of achievable metamodel features (MaxSMT solutions) and formulates an $m \times n$ matrix M similar to the one in Fig. 4. Then it automatically generates a set of SMT formulas capturing the set cover problem and uses an SMT solver to find metamodel constraint conflicts.

The core idea of this technique is to formalise the set cover problem into a set of numeric constraints so that we can utilise SMT solvers' well-engineered

$$M = \begin{array}{c} \\ S_1 \\ S_2 \\ S_3 \\ \vdots \\ S_m \end{array} \overset{\displaystyle I_1 \quad I_2 \quad I_3 \quad \cdots \quad I_n}{\begin{bmatrix} a_{11} & a_{12} & a_{13} & \cdots & a_{1n} \\ a_{21} & a_{22} & a_{23} & \cdots & a_{2n} \\ a_{31} & a_{32} & a_{33} & \cdots & a_{3n} \\ \vdots & \vdots & \vdots & \ddots & \vdots \\ a_{m1} & a_{m2} & a_{m3} & \cdots & a_{mn} \end{bmatrix}}$$

Fig. 5. A matrix M representing the set cover problem.

arithmetic reasoning engine to quickly explore the search space. To form such constraints, we first define this $m \times n$ matrix M in Fig. 5:

- each entry $a_{ij} \in \{0, 1\}$ is an element from a set (S_i and I_j), and 1 denotes that $a_{ij} \in S_i \wedge a_{ij} \in I_j$, otherwise the entry is not in both S_i and I_j.
- each S_i denotes a set of metamodel features that can not be achieved.
- each I_j denotes a subset of S_is in the jth column, depending on whether $a_{ij} = 1$.

Let mappings $S_i \mapsto V^{S_i}$, $I_j \mapsto V^{I_j}$ and $a_{ij} \mapsto V^{a_{ij}}$ be SMT encodings of S_i, I_j and each entry a_{ij} of M respectively, where V^{S_i}, V^{I_j} and $V^{a_{ij}}$ are SMT integer variables whose range are $\{0, 1\}$. We now generate a set of SMT formulas which captures the set cover problem. The range value 1 denotes that an element or a set is selected (covered) while 0 indicates that it is unselected.

We first generate Formula 4 stating that S_i is selected (covered) if one of the a_{ij}s in ith row is selected. Otherwise if all a_{ij}s (in ith row) are not chosen, then S_i can not be covered. For example, in Fig. 4, we say S_1 can be covered by either the entry in the 1st row and 2nd column (a_{12}) or another entry in the 1st row and 5th column (a_{15}), as both of them are set to 1 ($S_1 = \{a_{12}, a_{15}\}$).

$$\bigwedge_{i=1}^{m} \left(\left(\left(\bigvee_{\substack{j=1 \\ a_{ij} \in S_i}}^{n} V^{a_{ij}} = 1 \right) \Rightarrow \left(V^{S_i} = 1 \right) \right) \wedge \left(\left(\bigwedge_{\substack{j=1 \\ a_{ij} \in S_i}}^{n} V^{a_{ij}} = 0 \right) \Rightarrow \left(V^{S_i} = 0 \right) \right) \right)$$

(4)

Intuitively, Formula 5 encodes a constraint indicating that if the subset I_j is selected, then all of its elements must be selected as well. Otherwise no elements in I_j can be selected. This formula guarantees that either I_j is chosen or it is not chosen at all. This rules out the possibility of a partial selection of I_j's elements. This is because when a subset is not chosen (used), then none of the elements of it should be selected. This condition is enforced by using a conjunction to connect all elements in I_j to make sure that none of its elements are selected. For example, if subset I_5 in Fig. 4 is not chosen, then its two elements at the $5th$ column, marked as 1 (a_{15} and a_{55}) are also not selected ($I_5 = \{a_{15}, a_{55}\}$).

$$\bigwedge_{j=1}^{n} \left(\left(\left(V^{I_j} = 1 \right) \Rightarrow \left(\bigwedge_{\substack{i=1 \\ a_{ij} \in I_j}}^{m} V^{a_{ij}} = 1 \right) \right) \wedge \left(\left(V^{I_j} = 0 \right) \Rightarrow \left(\bigwedge_{\substack{i=1 \\ a_{ij} \in I_j}}^{m} V^{a_{ij}} = 0 \right) \right) \right)$$

$$(5)$$

Finally, we generate an integer equality shown in Formula 6 describing the restriction that every S_i must be covered (*part a*) by some subsets I_js (*part b*). To find all possible combinations of subsets (I_j) that cover S_is, we use the algorithm in Fig. 6 to iteratively ask an SMT solver to find an answer for *part b*, starting from 1 subset to n subsets. If this equality is satisfiable (line 5), we then have a solution to the set cover problem with k subsets covering all S_is. Otherwise, there is no solution to the set cover problem with k subsets. Finally, we interpret those V^{I_j}s assigned with 1 as the chosen subsets (line 6) and find the next solution by blocking all previous solutions (line 7).

$$\left(\underbrace{\left(\sum_{i=1}^{m} V^{S_i} \right) = m}_{part\ a} \right) \wedge \left(\underbrace{\left(\sum_{j=1}^{n} V^{I_j} \right) = k}_{part\ b} \right), \text{ where } 1 \leq k \leq n. \qquad (6)$$

Input   : A matrix M representing metamodel constraint conflicts as the set cover problem.

Output: A set s containing all solutions to the set cover problem including all minimum sets.

1 $k \leftarrow 1$
2 $s \leftarrow \emptyset$
3 $Solver.add(Formula\ 4 \wedge Formula\ 5 \wedge Formula\ 6[part\ a])$
4 **while** $k \leq n$ **do**
5 $\quad$ **while** $SMTSolve\left(\left(\sum_{j=1}^{n} V^{I_j} \right) = k \right) = $ **SAT do**
6 $\quad\quad$ $s \leftarrow s \cup Interpret(V^{I_j})$
7 $\quad\quad$ $Solver.add(\textbf{BlockingFormula})$
8 $\quad$ **end**
9 $\quad$ $k \leftarrow k + 1$
10 **end**
11 **return** s

Fig. 6. An algorithm that iteratively calls an SMT solver and returns all solutions to the set cover problem. The first set of solutions found by this algorithm must be the set containing all minimum sets since k starts from 1.

4   Implementation and Evaluation

We have prototyped the approach described in Sect. 3 into a tool called MaxUSE[6] and incorporated it into the exisiting USE modelling tool [12]. We choose USE mainly because it is a widely used modelling tool that has its own specification language that we can alter for our requirements. We modified its grammar and abstract syntax trees so that it now reads in a metamodel that is fully or partially ranked. It traverses a metamodel and automatically generates a set of SMT2 formulas [13]. MaxUSE currently uses Z3 as its solving engine [10]. It incrementally solves these formulas and interprets each successful assignment as a solution. Our implementation is approximately 7000 lines of Java code.

4.1   Evaluation

Forming Benchmark. To extensively evaluate MaxUSE's capability, we first collect a group of metamodels (Group A in Table 1) from [14], and use them as candidate metamodels. For each candidate metamodel, we calculate a configuration in terms of its number of classes, associations (different multiplicities), invariants, conflicts, navigations, quantifiers, logic/arithmetic operators, and breadth/depth of inheritance trees. We then develop a generator that can generate USE specifications based on different sized configurations. This generator is approximately 2100 lines of Java code. We use this generator to generate another four groups (Group B, C, D and E in Table 1) of metamodels using the configurations calculated from the metamodels in Group A. Currently, MaxUSE supports OCL constructs used in these metamodels.[7] For each group, we generate 5 metamodels ranging from small to large size. Finally, we randomly inject a number of conflicts into each metamodel and gather them as a benchmark as shown in Table 1. For example, for Group D we use a configuration that allows us to specify the number of diamond shapes and OCL constraints over an inheritance tree. This is because we use the DS metamodel from Group A as a candidate and this metamodel contains an OCL constraint over a diamond shaped inheritance tree. Therefore, every metamodel in Group D also has a number of constraints over this property based on its size.

Performance Evaluation. We evaluate MaxUSE on an Intel(R) Xeon(R) machine with eight 3.2 GHz cores. However, our current implementation uses only one core. Table 1 records MaxUSE's performance against different sized metamodels. For each group in Table 1, we first randomly rank each metamodel including the use of automatic rankings and run MaxUSE to find one solution. We then equally rank each metamodel and ask MaxUSE to find all possible solutions including conflicts. This is because an equally ranked metamodel more likely to have multiple solutions. All the performances are recorded in the 'Single' and 'All' columns in Table 1. We observe that MaxUSE takes less than *one*

---

[6] Available at https://github.com/classicwuhao/maxuse.
[7] MaxUSE cannot handle the OAI metamodel due to recursive structures. Instead, we add the SM metamodel into Group A (similar to Fig. 1 in Sect. 2).

Table 1. The benchmark for evaluating MaxUSE. 'Formulas' denotes the number of SMT2 formulas generated. 'Rank' denotes the achieved maximum rank ('Max') out of a total rank distributed ('Total'). 'Single' and 'All' denote the time (in seconds) spent by MaxUSE on finding a single and all possible solutions respectively. '#/sec' means that the number of solutions and seconds used. '†' indicates that MaxUSE determines that a metamodel is consistent. '*' denotes that MaxUSE cannot find solutions within 9 hours.

		Number of			Rank		Single (sec) Mix Ranked		All (#/sec) Eq Ranked	
		Classes	Assocs	Invs	Formulas	Max	Total	Solution	Conflict	Solution(s)	Conflict(s)
Group A	CS	3	1	6	19	15	15	NA	NA	NA	NA
	WR	2	2	7	33	36	40	4.01	0.16	1/3.53	1/0.5
	DS	4	0	1	16	14	16	0.14	0.19	2/0.14	1/0.89
	OAI†	1	1	7	NA	NA	NA	NA	NA	NA	NA
	SM	3	1	8	31	79	91	0.33	0.08	8/0.44	2/0.15
Group B	B1	13	5	27	169	490	498	3.97	0.43	2/2.22	2/0.44
	B2	24	9	45	285	521	556	15.90	0.16	12/22.53	5/0.83
	B3	33	14	68	420	792	821	31.49	0.58	6/54.89	5/11.92
	B4	46	15	90	539	620	622	67.37	0.22	2/100.87	2/1.42
	B5	57	19	136	729	881	894	560.12	1.45	24/1609.12	6/3.48
Group C	C1	13	5	29	171	237	268	5.59	0.05	12/18.49	7/0.59
	C2	24	11	43	276	470	478	15.76	0.83	4/14.70	2/0.84
	C3	35	17	66	418	570	581	59.46	0.07	1/68.79	2/1.12
	C4	46	15	98	549	605	630	342.98	1.50	4/226.05	4/1.66
	C5	57	15	156	765	1004	1045	2853.65	0.57	72/5467.75	11/5.49
Group D	D1	13	2	22	136	171	189	3.03	0.17	1/4.17	6/0.46
	D2	26	9	47	294	259	329	17.56	0.23	1/23.09	13/0.91
	D3	33	3	61	329	520	596	21.74	0.42	6/34.74	9/0.98
	D4	46	9	101	525	452	651	68.17	0.39	3/90.08	34/1.24
	D5	56	18	166	805	1089	1291	15904.21	2.33	174/29368.16	46/19.22
Group E	E1	10	6	31	162	69	72	6.26	0.07	1/7.38	1/0.32
	E2	15	12	39	224	217	233	83.36	0.08	2/66.48	4/0.55
	E3	30	18	37	312	238	243	392.22	0.729	1/47.75	1/0.71
	E4	18	18	105	511	483	515	405.51	0.68	7/5959.61	20/3.90
	E5*	18	18	167	698	NA	415	NA	NA	NA	NA

second to determine whether a metamodel is consistent or not, and find the maximum weight and conflicts within a reasonable amount of time in most cases. The longest time taken by MaxUSE is approximately 8 hours to get 174 solutions for the D5 metamodel. In general, MaxUSE finds all conflicts much faster than finding all weighted MaxSMT solutions. This is because searching for an optimal solution requires significant computation by Z3. Once all solutions are found, MaxUSE can utilise them to solve the set cover problem much faster. In some cases, MaxUSE could not find solutions. This is mainly due to Z3 spending a significant amount of time on solving a large number of formulas combining nested quantifiers and inequalities. For example, for the E5 metamodel, Z3 was stuck with a particular value and could not progress to next possible optimal value within 9 hours. In general, it is an extremely challenging task for any algorithms to find an optimal value for such a large number of complicated formulas.

This is because the nature of this particular optimisation problem typically has a massive search space.

Quality of Computed Constraint Conflicts. For the conflicts found in these metamodels from the benchmark in Table 1, we compare them against actual injected conflicts to assess how accurate they are. The injected conflicts covers a wide range of different metamodel features including multiplicities on association ends, different type of attributes and inheritance relationships among multiple classes. We classify our comparison results as either "exact", "near" or "miss" and record them into Table 2. Here, "exact" means that MaxUSE finds conflicts that match exactly with injected conflicts. In other words, each one (set) is minimal and removal of any members can make a metamodel become consistent. "near" means that MaxUSE is able to identify all conflicts that are close enough to the injected ones. We consider they are "near" because each reported conflict is a slightly larger set containing those injected ones as a subset. For example, MaxUSE may list the a class containing conflicted invariants as a part of the returned conflicts. Thus, users could easily understand this information and use this in a latter stage for debugging or fixing conflicts. "miss" indicates that MaxUSE returns at least one "conflict" that is not related to any of those injected conflicts. We suspect that this is probably caused by heuristic algorithms used internally in Z3. Despite this inaccuracy, we believe that the results here show the potential of our approach to finding constraint conflicts for inconsistent metamodels.

Table 2. Quality of computed constraint conflicts for metamodels in Table 1.

Group A		Group B		Group C		Group D		Group E	
CS	NA	B1	exact	C1	near	D1	exact	E1	near
WR	exact	B2	near	C2	exact	D2	near	E2	near
DS	exact	B3	exact	C3	near	D3	exact	E3	exact
OAI	NA	B4	near	C4	near	D4	near	E4	miss
SM	exact	B5	exact	C5	near	D5	near	E5	NA

Lessons Learnt. From the evaluation results, we have learned three important lessons:

1. MaxUSE can maximise the number of achievable features and pinpoint conflicting constraints without the need for manual interactions. However, in some cases when Z3 is unable to handle formulas, an interactive mode is necessary. For example, when Z3 could not solve formulas generated for the $E5$ metamodel within a specified time frame, we pause MaxUSE and manually choose a possible optimal value. MaxUSE is then able to resume the search. However, selecting such a value is quite tricky and requires that one has knowledge about how things work inside the solver.

2. In terms of scalability, the number of ranked features is proportional to the solving time of MaxUSE. Additionally, we suggest that one could gain better performance by ranking individual metamodel features into hard features or using a set of relatively smaller ranks. For example, if a metamodel has 100 features one may consider to rank them using a range of integers from 1 to 100 rather than choosing from 101 to 200.

3. Computing all constraint conflicts sometimes can be significantly more expensive than finding one conflict since there could be an exponential number of them. In this case, we find it is necessary to let users decide when to stop MaxUSE for enumerating all constraint conflicts. This is because some constraint conflicts are not independent. Therefore, the dependent conflicts can be used to identify other conflicts without exhaustive enumeration. In the future, we plan to address this issue and enhance our algorithm for finding constraint conflicts.

4.2   Threats to Validity

The major threat to external validity concerns the benchmark we form in Table 1. This benchmark is based on the metamodels collected from [14]. Since these metamodels do not cover the full set of OCL constructs, this introduces a gap between our implementation and full OCL constructs. We acknowledge that the evaluation results of this benchmark only give us a preliminary assessment of MaxUSE. In the future, we plan to cover more OCL constructs including operational constraints and string operators.

The most significant threat to internal validity concerns the performance of MaxUSE which is mainly dependent on the Z3 SMT solver. In some cases, the first run of Z3 fails to find solutions. However, further runs typically resolve this issue. This introduces an additional performance overhead. We surmise that this is caused by the heuristic algorithms used in Z3. In the future, we plan to overcome this by plugging in multiple SMT solvers and allow users to switch among them for the best performance.

5   Related Work

The majority of the research in metamodel/UML class diagram-based reasoning/verification concentrates on answering the question [5,6,9,15-18]: whether a metamodel is consistent or not. We focus on the situation when a metamodel is not consistent, then what information we should give back to users to help them refine their metamodels. We believe that providing the maximum number of achievable features and finding constraint conflicts among them is useful for users to further refine their metamodels. Moreover, this paper also demonstrates the feasibility and scalability of tackling *ranked* metamodel features in an existing modelling environment by introducing SMT solving.

Much research work has sought to formalise metamodels or UML class diagrams into different types of logics [8,9,19–30]. With recent advances in constraint solving, SAT/SMT solvers have been widely adapted to verifying metamodel/UML class diagrams. Among them, Büttner et al. [8] and Clavel et al. [9,28] directly map a metamodel and its OCL constraints into first-order logic that can be handled by SMT solvers. Büttner et al. use the Z3 SMT solver to verify the correctness of the ATL transformation, while Clavel and Dania use Prover 9 and Z3 to check the satisfiability of OCL constraints. We use a similar idea to encode the metamodel and OCL constraints, but differ by solving ranked OCL constraints and the set cover problem. By introducing ranked features to a metamodel and solving the set cover problem, users are able to maximise the number of features based on their domain specific knowledge and find constraint conflicts.

Cabot et al. propose a detailed systematic procedure that uses constraint programming to program UML/OCL class diagrams into a Constraint Satisfaction Problem (CSP) [16,31,32]. The main advantage is that CSP provides a high-level language so that a particular constraint problem is programmable. Their approach can check a variety of correctness properties including weak and strong satisfiability by generating a different number of instances for every class. Instead of presenting an encoding of metamodel and OCL constraints, our work focuses on reducing a set of ranked metamodel features to a weighted MaxSMT problem and finding a maximum number of achievable features and conflicts at the same time. Further, our approach presented in this paper can be easily incorporated into existing SAT/SMT based approaches without tuning original encodings.

Alloy uses first-order relational logic as its specification language to model the problem domain and reduce it to SAT instances [33–35]. It directly supports finding minimal conflicts in the specification [36]. However, this functionality is not guaranteed to find all minimal conflicts. Therefore, approaches using Alloy as a basis for constraint solving engine are also restricted by this functionality. [4,37–40]. Further, Alloy's engine is limited to unranked constraints so users are not able to rank individual constraints, whereas our approach focuses on maximising all ranked features.

6 Conclusion

In this paper, we have presented an approach to finding achievable features and constraint conflicts for inconsistent metamodels. Our approach is unique in the sense that we allow users to rank individual metamodel features and find achievable features and constraint conflicts by using a state-of-the-art SMT solver. Further, our SMT encodings presented in this paper could be used as an add-on to existing SMT based approaches. Thus, this gives us an advantage of avoiding the tuning of existing SMT encodings. To demonstrate feasibility and scalability, we have implemented this approach into a prototype tool and evaluated it against a benchmark. Our evaluation results suggest that the approach is promising and scales reasonably well on a large number of metamodel features. In the future, we plan to extend this approach to metamodel transformation verification and develop a technique that is able to guide users step-by-step in refining/synthesizing transformation rules based on their specified preferences.

References

1. Jouault, F., Kurtev, I.: Transforming models with ATL. In: Bruel, J.-M. (ed.) MODELS 2005. LNCS, vol. 3844, pp. 128–138. Springer, Heidelberg (2006). doi:10. 1007/11663430_14
2. Zschaler, S., Kolovos, D.S., Drivalos, N., Paige, R.F., Rashid, A.: Domain-specific metamodelling languages for software language engineering. In: Brand, M., Gašević, D., Gray, J. (eds.) SLE 2009. LNCS, vol. 5969, pp. 334–353. Springer, Heidelberg (2010). doi:10.1007/978-3-642-12107-4_23
3. Becker, J., Rosemann, M., Uthmann, C.: Guidelines of business process modeling. In: Aalst, W., Desel, J., Oberweis, A. (eds.) Business Process Management. LNCS, vol. 1806, pp. 30–49. Springer, Heidelberg (2000). doi:10.1007/3-540-45594-9_3
4. Kuhlmann, M., Hamann, L., Gogolla, M.: Extensive validation of OCL models by integrating SAT solving into USE. In: Bishop, J., Vallecillo, A. (eds.) TOOLS 2011. LNCS, vol. 6705, pp. 290–306. Springer, Heidelberg (2011). doi:10.1007/ 978-3-642-21952-8_21
5. Wille, R., Soeken, M., Drechsler, R.: Debugging of inconsistent UML/OCL models. In: 2012 DATE, pp. 1078–1083 (2012)
6. Wu, H., Monahan, R., Power, J.F.: Exploiting attributed type graphs to generate metamodel instances using an SMT solver. In: 7th TASE, Birmingham, UK (2013)
7. Liffiton, M.H., Sakallah, K.A.: Algorithms for computing minimal unsatisfiable subsets of constraints. J. Autom. Reason. 40(1), 1–33 (2008)
8. Büttner, F., Egea, M., Cabot, J.: On verifying ATL transformations using 'off-the-shelf' SMT solvers. In: 15th MoDELS, pp. 432–448 (2012)
9. Clavel, M., Egea, M., de Dios, M.A.G.: Checking unsatisfiability for OCL constraints. Electronic Communication of the European Association of Software Science and Technology, vol. 24 (2009)
10. Moura, L., Bjørner, N.: Z3: an efficient SMT solver. In: Ramakrishnan, C.R., Rehof, J. (eds.) TACAS 2008. LNCS, vol. 4963, pp. 337–340. Springer, Heidelberg (2008). doi:10.1007/978-3-540-78800-3_24
11. Karp, R.M.: Reducibility among combinatorial problems. In: Complexity of Computer Computations, pp. 85–103 (1972)
12. Gogolla, M., Büttner, F., Richters, M.: USE: a UML-based specification environment for validating UML and OCL. Sci. Comput. Program. 69(1–3), 27–34 (2007)
13. Barrett, C., Stump, A., Tinelli, C.: The SMT-LIB standard: version 2.0. In: Proceedings of the 8th International Workshop on Satisfiability Modulo Theories, Edinburgh, UK. Elsevier Science (2010)
14. Gogolla, M., Büttner, F., Cabot, J.: Initiating a benchmark for UML and OCL analysis tools. In: Veanes, M., Viganò, L. (eds.) TAP 2013. LNCS, vol. 7942, pp. 115–132. Springer, Heidelberg (2013). doi:10.1007/978-3-642-38916-0_7
15. Soeken, M., Wille, R., Drechsler, R.: Encoding OCL data types for SAT-based verification of UML/OCL models. In: Gogolla, M., Wolff, B. (eds.) TAP 2011. LNCS, vol. 6706, pp. 152–170. Springer, Heidelberg (2011). doi:10.1007/ 978-3-642-21768-5_12

16. Cabot, J., Clarisó, R., Riera, D.: On the verification of UML/OCL class diagrams using constraint programming. J. Syst. Softw. **93**, 1–23 (2014)
17. Balaban, M., Maraee, A.: Finite satisfiability of UML class diagrams with constrained class hierarchy. ACM Trans. Softw. Eng. Methodol. **22**(3), 24:1–24:42 (2013)
18. Wu, H.: Generating metamodel instances satisfying coverage criteria via SMT solving. In: The 4th MODELSWARD, pp. 40–51 (2016)
19. Beckert, B., Keller, U., Schmitt, P.H.: Translating the object constraint language into first-order predicate logic. In: Verify Workshop at FLoC, Copenhagen, Denmark (2002)
20. Maraee, A., Balaban, M.: Efficient reasoning about finite satisfiability of UML class diagrams with constrained generalization sets. In: Akehurst, D.H., Vogel, R., Paige, R.F. (eds.) ECMDA-FA 2007. LNCS, vol. 4530, pp. 17–31. Springer, Heidelberg (2007). doi:10.1007/978-3-540-72901-3_2
21. Brucker, A.D., Wolff, B.: HOL-OCL: a formal proof environment for UML/OCL. In: Fiadeiro, J.L., Inverardi, P. (eds.) FASE 2008. LNCS, vol. 4961, pp. 97–100. Springer, Heidelberg (2008). doi:10.1007/978-3-540-78743-3_8
22. Kyas, M., Fecher, H., de Boer, F.S., Jacob, J., Hooman, J., van der Zwaag, M., Arons, T., Kugler, H.: Formalizing UML models and OCL constraints in PVS. Electron. Notes Theor. Comput. Sci. **115**, 39–47 (2005)
23. Soeken, M., Wille, R., Kuhlmann, M., Gogolla, M., Drechsler, R.: Verifying UML/OCL models using boolean satisfiability. In: DATE, pp. 1341–1344 (2010)
24. Queralt, A., Artale, A., Calvanese, D., Teniente, E.: OCL-Lite: finite reasoning on UML/OCL conceptual schemas. Data Knowl. Eng. **73**, 1–22 (2012)
25. Dania, C., Clavel, M.: OCL2FOL+: Coping with undefinedness. In: OCL@MoDELS (2013)
26. Semeráth, O., Vörös, A., Varró, D.: Iterative and incremental model generation by logic solvers. In: Stevens, P., Wąsowski, A. (eds.) FASE 2016. LNCS, vol. 9633, pp. 87–103. Springer, Heidelberg (2016). doi:10.1007/978-3-662-49665-7_6
27. Przigoda, N., Wille, R., Drechsler, R.: Ground setting properties for an efficient translation of OCL in SMT-based model finding. In: 19th MoDELS, pp. 261–271. ACM (2016)
28. Dania, C., Clavel, M.: OCL2MSFOL: a mapping to many-sorted first-order logic for efficiently checking the satisfiability of OCL constraints. In: 19th MoDELS, pp. 65–75. ACM (2016)
29. Wu, H., Monahan, R., Power, J.F.: Metamodel instance generation: a systematic literature review. CoRR abs/1211.6322 (2012)
30. Wu, H.: An SMT-based approach for generating coverage oriented metamodel instances. Int. J. Inf. Syst. Model. Des. **7**(3), 23–50 (2016)
31. González Pérez, C.A., Buettner, F., Clarisó, R., Cabot, J.: EMFtoCSP: a tool for the lightweight verification of EMF models. In: Formal Methods in Software Engineering: Rigorous and Agile Approaches, Zurich, Suisse (2012)
32. Cabot, J., Clarisó, R., Riera, D.: Verification of UML/OCL class diagrams using constraint programming. In: IEEE ICST V&V Workshop, Berlin, Germany, pp. 73–80. IEEE Computer Society (2008)
33. Jackson, D.: Alloy: a lightweight object modelling notation. ACM Trans. Softw. Eng. Methodologies **11**(2), 256–290 (2002)
34. Torlak, E., Jackson, D.: Kodkod: a relational model finder. In: Grumberg, O., Huth, M. (eds.) TACAS 2007. LNCS, vol. 4424, pp. 632–647. Springer, Heidelberg (2007). doi:10.1007/978-3-540-71209-1_49

35. Milicevic, A., Near, J.P., Kang, E., Jackson, D.: Alloy*: a general-purpose higher-order relational constraint solver. In: 37th ICSE. IEEE Press (2015)
36. Torlak, E., Chang, F.S.-H., Jackson, D.: Finding minimal unsatisfiable cores of declarative specifications. In: Cuellar, J., Maibaum, T., Sere, K. (eds.) FM 2008. LNCS, vol. 5014, pp. 326–341. Springer, Heidelberg (2008). doi:10.1007/978-3-540-68237-0_23
37. Anastasakis, K., Bordbar, B., Georg, G., Ray, I.: UML2Alloy: a challenging model transformation. In: Engels, G., Opdyke, B., Schmidt, D.C., Weil, F. (eds.) MODELS 2007. LNCS, vol. 4735, pp. 436–450. Springer, Heidelberg (2007). doi:10.1007/978-3-540-75209-7_30
38. Maoz, S., Ringert, J.O., Rumpe, B.: CD2Alloy: class diagrams analysis using alloy revisited. In: Whittle, J., Clark, T., Kühne, T. (eds.) MODELS 2011. LNCS, vol. 6981, pp. 592–607. Springer, Heidelberg (2011). doi:10.1007/978-3-642-24485-8_44
39. Garis, A., Cunha, A., Riesco, D.: Translating alloy specifications to UML class diagrams annotated with OCL. In: Barthe, G., Pardo, A., Schneider, G. (eds.) SEFM 2011. LNCS, vol. 7041, pp. 221–236. Springer, Heidelberg (2011). doi:10.1007/978-3-642-24690-6_16
40. Kuhlmann, M., Gogolla, M.: From UML and OCL to relational logic and back. In: France, R.B., Kazmeier, J., Breu, R., Atkinson, C. (eds.) MODELS 2012. LNCS, vol. 7590, pp. 415–431. Springer, Heidelberg (2012). doi:10.1007/978-3-642-33666-9_27

Model Consistency for Distributed Collaborative Modeling

Gerson Sunyé[(✉)]

AtlanMod Group (Inria, IMT Atlantique, and LS2N),
LS2N – University of Nantes, Nantes, France
gerson.sunye@univ-nantes.fr

Abstract. Current collaborative modeling tools use a centralized architecture, based on version control system, where models are updated asynchronously. These tools depend on a single server and are not completely adapted for collaborative modeling, where update reactivity is essential. In this paper, we propose a framework for building collaborative modeling tools which provides synchronous model update. The framework is based on a peer-to-peer architecture and uses a consistency algorithm for model updating.

1 Introduction

As collaborative modeling becomes more and more popular, changing the way that modelers interact with colleagues to design and create documents, there is a growing need for tools and techniques that enable effective collaboration. A first response for this need is the emergence of online web-based modeling tools, e. g., Lucidchart [24] or GenMyModel [9], and of standalone modeling tools coupled with control version systems, as the recent release of MetaEdit+ [31].

In this paper, we propose a model consistency approach for providing the bases of collaborative modeling tools. This approach is inspired from cooperative editing systems, introduced in Sect. 2.1 and is based on the Eclipse Modeling Framework [26], EMF, the *de-facto* standard framework for building modeling tools, which is introduced in Sect. 2.2.

The goal of our approach is to provide the basis for developing modeling tools with following characteristics: (i) *distributed*: collaborative tools can be deployed on distributed nodes, connected by networks with different latency times, and do not require a centralized server for update integration; (ii) *reactive*: the response for integrating remote updates is fast with low latency; (iii) *synchronous*: local updates are broadcast to other nodes right after their execution.

Differently from other approaches that use a generic control-version server, e. g., Git or SVN, or a model-specific one, e. g., EMFStore [12], the approach does not use versions and resolves conflicts automatically aiming at a simple goal, that all model replicas are consistent. The advantages and limits of the approach with respect to other research efforts are discussed in Sect. 5.

To ensure that remote changes are integrated with the same execution order in all nodes, the approach classifies the relations between updates into four

© Springer International Publishing AG 2017
A. Anjorin and H. Espinoza (Eds.): ECMFA 2017, LNCS 10376, pp. 197–212, 2017.
DOI: 10.1007/978-3-319-61482-3_12

distinct types: independent, dependent, equivalent, and conflictual. Independent updates can be executed in any order, while dependent ones must always follow the same order. Equivalent updates produce the same result and thus only one should be executed, and conflictual updates produce different results depending on their execution order. The integration of the latter is more complex and may result in undoing local changes and re-executing them after the integration. Section 3 describes the approach an the integration algorithm, as well as a simple example that illustrates the approach.

To validate the integration algorithm through implementation, we develop a prototype that uses EMF notifications to capture local updates and the publish–subscribe architectural pattern [4] to broadcast them to remote nodes. Section 4 describes the implementation.

2   Background

This section introduces the principles of cooperative editing systems, which inspired our work, and some of the modeling concepts implemented in EMF that help the comprehension of the model consistency approach.

2.1   Cooperative Editing Systems

A real-time cooperative editing system consists of a set of interconnected nodes where locally to each node, users perform changes on a shared document. Each node propagates its local changes to the remote nodes, which integrate them to the local copy of the shared document. The system maintains the consistency among the different copies. A cooperative editing system is said to be consistent if it maintains the following properties [29]:

Convergence. When the same set of operations have been executed at all nodes, all copies of the shared document are identical.

Causality Preservation. For any pair of operations O_a and O_b, if $O_a \rightarrow O_b$, then O_a is executed before O_b at all nodes.

Intention Preservation. For any operation O, the effects of executing O at all sites are the same as the intention of O, and the effect of executing O does not change the effects of independent operations.

A common solution to achieve consistency is to use an operational transformation approach [28], which consists of an integration algorithm and a transformation function. The integration algorithm is responsible for performing, broadcasting, and receiving operations, while the transformation function is responsible for detecting and merging concurrent operations. The transformation function often relies on vector clocks, e. g., GOTO [28] and ABT [18]. A vector clock is an array of logical clocks, one clock per node, associated to each operation and used to determine the causality between operations. The limit of vector clocks is that the size of the exchanged messages grows with the number of nodes, creating a bottleneck that prevents these systems to scale. A scalable alternative to vector clocks is to use semantic causal dependency [16,20], declared with respect to operation preconditions. For instance, consider a Graph on which two operations are performed, $O_1 = createVertex(A)$ and $O_2 = createVertex(B)$. There is no casual dependency between this two operations since their execution order can be interchanged. However, if a third operation $O_3 = createEdge(A, B)$ is considered, then there is a casual dependency: the execution of O_3 requires that vertices A and B exist, i. e., O_3 must be executed after O_1 and O_2.

While cooperative editing systems focus on documents and on casual dependency of operations on characters, we believe that their techniques and algorithms can also be applied to structured data models.

2.2 EMF

The Eclipse Modeling Framework is a set of components that aims at helping developers to create sophisticated modeling tools [26]. Similarly to other modeling frameworks, e. g., MDR [19] and NSUML [22], it proposes a modeling language, Ecore, and code generation facilities to create Java underlying models, specific to each Ecore model. In EMF terms, the Java generated modeling elements are (subclasses of) **EObject** and their meta-types, the elements of an Ecore model, are instances of **EClass**. Unlike the other frameworks, EMF introduces the concept of *Resource*, a container for modeling element instances (**EObject** sub-instances), which is independent from Ecore models. Indeed, a resource can contain a subset of instances from the same underlying model, as well as instances from other models. Resources are mainly used to persist instances on different formats: e. g., XMI, relational databases [25], or NoSQL databases [7,21].

Resources respect the containment relationship: when an instance is attached to a resource, so are all its contents. Conversely, when an instance is detached from a resource, all its contents are also detached. Resources are responsible for assigning identities to instances, needed to serialize and unserialize references to instances that use the Java object identity as identifiers. Identities are unique among instances from the same modeling element (**EObject** subclass). Instances from a resource can reference instances from a different resource, provided that both resources belong to the same *Resource Set*. Each resource has an unique identifier, used as an index in the global *Registry*, another EMF concept introduced along with resources.

Since EMF does not distinguish models by their contents, i. e., another language syntax or real-world concepts, we refer to the contents of a model as *Instances* and to the modeling language elements as *Types*.

3   Model Consistency Approach

We consider a distributed system of interconnected nodes, where each node contains models expressed in different modeling languages. Nodes also contain resources, which are composed of instances from different modeling languages.

In this system, any subset of nodes can share one or more resources: each node contains a replica of a shared resource and performs query and update operations on it. To ensure that all replicas of a shared resource are consistent, we propose the following approach:

1. Each update operation in a shared resource is first executed locally.
2. Thereafter, the operation is broadcast to all nodes containing replicas of the shared resource.
3. These nodes receive and integrate the update operation. The integration may result in undoing a locally executed operation, executing a new operation, and redoing that operation.

Shared resources are basically EMF resources that have replicas spread over a set of nodes and that are defined as follows:

Definition 1 (Shared Resource). *A* Shared Resource *is a tuple* $\mathcal{R} = \langle \text{RID}, N,$ $I, F \rangle$ *where:* RID *is the resource unique identifier, N is a set of nodes sharing the resource, I is a set of instances, and F is a set of features (i. e., instance attribute values and references between instances).*

Locally to each node, Java object identifiers (i. e., memory addresses) are commonly used as identifiers for instances and features. However, in a distributed environment, we must ensure the following propositions concerning the unique identification of resources, instances, types, and features.

Proposition 1. *Every node has an unique identity through the network, denoted by* NID.

The unicity of a NID may be ensured either locally, e. g., using a UUID, or distributively, e. g., using a naming server.

Proposition 2. *Every shared resource has an unique identity across the network, denoted by* RID. *This identity is independent from the node that created the resource and is ensured by a* Global Resource Registry, *which also helps nodes to find available shared resources.*

The registry is a simple associative array that may be implemented by a single node or by a Distributed Hash Table [23,27].

Proposition 3. *Each instance has an unique identity across the network, denoted by* OID, *which depends on its containing resource and is independent from the node where it was created. An instance belonging to a shared resource has the same identity across all resource replicas.*

Proposition 4. *Each type and each feature of a type have unique identities across the network, denoted by* TID *and* FID, *respectively. A pair (* OID,FID *) identifies the value of feature* FID *on instance* OID.

The unicity of a type is usually ensured by its name and the name (or URI) of its modeling language. The unicity of a feature may be ensured by its name or by a natural number.

3.1 Update Operations

We consider only operations that modify the contents of a shared resource, i. e., operations that: add/remove instances to/from a resource, modify the values of instance monovalued features, or modify the valued of instance multivalued features. The specification of these operations is listed below:

- *attach*(RID, OID): adds instance OID to the shared resource RID.
- *detach*(RID, OID): removed an instance from a shared resource.
- *set*(OID, FID, v): sets the value of feature FID to value v.
- *unset*(OID, FID): unsets feature FID.
- *add*(OID, FID, v) adds value v at the end of the multivalued feature FID.
- *remove*(OID, FID, i): removes value of multivalued feature FID at index i.
- *move*(OID, FID, s, t): moves value of multivalued feature FID from source index s to target index t.
- *clear*(OID, FID): clears all values of multivalued feature FID.

Update operations can be formulated using simple mathematics. The following equation expresses the relation between a resource $\mathcal{R}$ and a resource $\mathcal{R}'$ that was modified by operation O.

$$\mathcal{R} = O * \mathcal{R}'$$

The operator "*" denotes the application of an update operation to a resource. Updating a resource means applying n operations O_i to a resource $\mathcal{R}'$ in a stepwise manner:

$$\mathcal{R} = O_1 * O_2 * \ldots * O_{n-1} * O_n * \mathcal{R}'$$

Two operations can be either dependent on, independent of, equivalent to or conflictual with each other. We define independent (or concurrent) operations as follows:

Definition 2 (Independent Operations). *Given any shared resource $\mathcal{R}$ and any two operations O_a and O_b are said to be* independent *of each other if they are commutative, i. e., if an only if $O_a * O_b * \mathcal{R} = O_b * O_a * \mathcal{R}$.*

Conceptually, each operation O is associated to an original context C_O, i. e., the sequence of operations required to bring a resource from its initial state to the state where O can be applied.

Definition 3 (Dependent Operations). *Given any operations O_a and O_b, and C_{O_a}, the original context of operation O_a, O_a is said to be* dependent *on O_b if and only if $O_b \in C_{O_a}$.*

When two operations have the same original context and are not independent, they are said to be conflictual. For instance, operations $set(\text{OID}_a, \text{FID}_1, v_a)$ and $set(\text{OID}_a, \text{FID}_1, v_b)$ are conflictual.

Definition 4 (Conflictual Operations). *Given any shared resource $\mathcal{R}$ and any two operations O_a and O_b and their original contexts C_{O_a} and C_{O_b}, O_a and O_b are said to be* conflictual *if and only if $C_{O_a} = C_{O_b}$ and $O_a * O_b * \mathcal{R} \neq O_b * O_a * \mathcal{R}$.*

In most cases, operations have different contexts and therefore are independent. For instance, the operations *set* and *remove* both concern features, but since features cannot be mono and multivalued at the same time, they are obligatory independent.

Some operations may produce the same result, even when they come from different nodes. For instance, two operations *clear*, or two operations *remove* or *add* of the same value, produce the same results on the same features.

Definition 5 (Equivalent Operations). *Given any shared resource $\mathcal{R}$ and any two operations O_a and O_b and their original contexts C_{O_a} and C_{O_b}, O_a and O_b are said to be* equivalent *if and only if $C_{O_a} = C_{O_b}$ and $O_a * \mathcal{R} = O_b * \mathcal{R}$.*

3.2   Casual Dependencies

The casual dependency relation, denoted by "$\rightarrow$", expresses that one operation happened before another and is commonly based on time [17,29]. In our approach, we adopt a semantic casual dependency [16,20]. The idea is not to establish whether a given operation O_a at node n_1 was generated before operation O_b at node n_2, but whether O_b depends on O_a. For instance, the operation $O_a = attach(\text{RID}_1, \text{OID}_a)$ precedes operation $O_b = set(\text{OID}_a, \text{FID}_1, value)$, $O_a \rightarrow O_b$, since object OID_a must exist before feature FID is set. Conversely, two operations O_a and O_b are said to be independent (or concurrent), if and only if neither $O_a \rightarrow O_b$ nor $O_b \rightarrow O_a$, which is expressed as $O_a \parallel O_b$.

In our approach, we adopt following propositions concerning the semantic casual dependencies between conflictual operations. In these propositions, we assume that the operations have the same original contexts.

Let us denote by $O^{Attach(i)}$ an operation that attaches an instance i to a resource, by $O^{Detach(i)}$ an operation that detaches an instance i from a resource, and by O^{Any} any feature-related operation.

Proposition 5. *For any Instance i, we have the following semantic casual dependency: $O^{Attach(i)} \rightarrow O^{Any(i)} \rightarrow O^{Detach(i)}$.*

Two *attach()* operations cannot be conflictual, since instances attached to different shared resource replicas have different identifications, according to Proposition 3. Two *detach()* operations are equivalent since they produce the same result.

There is no semantic casual dependency between Operations on monovalued features with the same original context, *set* and *unset*. However, it can be established for operations on multivalued features, *add*, *remove*, *clear*, and *move*.

Let us denote by FID a multivalued feature, by $O^{Add(\text{FID})}$ an operation and adds a value to FID, by $O^{Remove(\text{FID})}$ an operation that removes an element from FID, by $O^{Clear(\text{FID})}$ an operation that clears FID, and by $O^{Move(\text{FID})}$ an operation that moves around a value in FID.

Proposition 6. *For any multivalued feature* FID, *we have the following casual dependencies:*

- $O^{Move(\text{FID})} \rightarrow O^{Remove(\text{FID})}, O^{Clear(\text{FID})}$
- $O^{Move(\text{FID})} \parallel O^{Add(\text{FID})}$
- $O^{Clear(\text{FID})} \rightarrow O^{Add(fid)}$
- $O^{Remove(\text{FID})} \rightarrow O^{Clear(\text{FID})}$
- $O^{Add(\text{FID})} \parallel O^{Remove(\text{FID})}$

Differently from the other operations, O^{Move} parameters are indexes, instead of values. Therefore, any operation that changes the position of a value affects the behavior of O^{Move}. In the opposite, O^{Move} operations do not affect operations that use values as parameters. O^{Move} and O^{Add} are independent, since a value is added to the end of the feature and do not affect a move operation. $O^{Clear(fid)}$ precedes $O^{Add(fid)}$ because when the first operation is executed, it is not aware of the value added by the second one. $O^{Remove(\text{FID})}$ precedes $O^{Clear(\text{FID})}$, otherwise the first operation could raise an error (value not found). Finally, $O^{Add(\text{FID})}$ and $O^{Remove(\text{FID})}$ are independent, even if their arguments are the same. Indeed, the first operation adds a value to the end of a feature, while the second one removes the first occurrence of a value.

In complement to the casual dependency between operations from different types, we have the following casual dependencies between operations of the same type:

- Two *add* or two *remove* operations are either independents or equivalents.
- Two *clear* operations are equivalents.
- Two *move* operations are independents if the range of values between the source and the target indices do not overlap.

3.3   Integration Algorithm

To propagate local changes to remote nodes, nodes send an *update messages* for each operation executed locally. We define update messages as follows.

Definition 6. *An* Update Message *is a tuple* $\mathcal{M} = \langle n, \mathcal{R}, O, C \rangle$ *where: n is the source node,* $\mathcal{R}$ *the shared resource, O is the executed operation, and* C_O *is the operation original context.*

The integration requires that each node implements a precedence relation, according to the following proposition:

Proposition 7. *For all nodes sharing a resource, there is a precedence relation denoted by* "$\prec$", $\prec: \mathcal{M} \times \mathcal{M} \rightarrow \mathbb{B}$, *such as for any pair of update messages* (m_a, m_b), $m_a \prec m_b$ *produces the same result in all nodes.*

A simple way to ensure that the precedence operator behaves the same in all nodes is to use properties belonging to the message: e. g., the source node, the operation arguments, a hash function on the arguments, etc.

The integration also requires that each node implements a context-equivalent relation, according to the following proposition:

Proposition 8. *For all nodes sharing a resource, there is a context-equivalent relation denoted by "⊔", ⊔: $\mathcal{M} \times \mathcal{M} \to \mathbb{B}$, such as for any pair of update messages (m_a, m_b), $m_a \sqcup m_b$ if and only if $C_{m_a} = C_{m_b}$.*

Algorithm 1 describes the integration of update messages on nodes. Each node has a local history of integrated remote messages, denoted by $\mathcal{H}$ and receives an update message m. The integration first verifies if an equivalent message exists in $\mathcal{H}$ and stops the integration if it is the case. Then, it searches all messages that are context-equivalent with m and that should precede m, adds these messages to the set *successors* and removes them from $\mathcal{H}$. After the removal, message m is executed and added to $\mathcal{H}$. Lastly, the integration re-executes all *successors* and adds them to $\mathcal{H}$.

Algorithm 1. Update Message Integration

Input: m, an Update Message; $\mathcal{H}$, the local history.
if $\exists h, h \in \mathcal{H} \land h \equiv m$ **then**
  ∟ **return**
$successors \leftarrow \{h \mid h \in \mathcal{H} \land m \prec h \land m \sqcup h\}$;
$\mathcal{H} \leftarrow \mathcal{H} - successors$;
foreach $each \in successors$ **do**
  ∟ $undo(each)$
$execute(m)$;
foreach $each \in successors$ **do**
  ∟ $execute(each)$
$\mathcal{H} \leftarrow H + \{m\} + successors$;

3.4   Example

Figures 1a and b present respectively the Ecore model for a Graph modeling language (GraphML) and a model containing an instance of this language, i. e., a graph. This graph contains 7 instances, each one with an unique identifier:

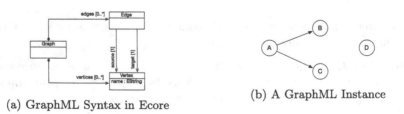

(a) GraphML Syntax in Ecore

(b) A GraphML Instance

Fig. 1. Simple example

- the graph itself, identified by g.
- 4 vertices (and their identifiers): "A" (a), "B" (b), "C" (c), and "D" (d).
- 2 edges, identified by ab and ac.

Let us suppose a collaborative environment, where a shared resource containing this graph is being modified by three different nodes, performing the following modifications:

Node 1 : renames vertex a to "A1".
Node 2 : renames vertex a to "A2" and deletes vertex d.
Node 3 : creates a new vertex e, named "E", and adds it to graph g; creates a new edge ae between a and e and adds it to graph g; and deletes vertex d.

Table 1 presents a summary of the operations generated by these modifications. These operations are first executed locally at each node and then broadcast to the other nodes. We present the integration of operations on each node in the next sections. In this example, the order nodes receive remote operations from remote nodes is arbitrary. Nevertheless, if different orders occurs, the integration result would be the same.

Table 1. Summary of operations at Nodes 1, 2, and 3.

Node 1	Node 2	Node 3
$O_1^1 = set(a, \#name, \text{"A1"})$	$O_1^2 = set(a, \#name, \text{"A2"})$	$O_1^3 = attach(e)$
	$O_2^2 = remove(g, \#vertices, d)$	$O_2^3 = set(e, \#name, \text{"E"})$
	$O_3^2 = detach(d)$	$O_3^3 = add(g, \#vertices, e)$
		$O_4^3 = attach(ad)$
		$O_5^3 = add(g, \#edges, ae)$
		$O_6^3 = set(ad, \#target, e)$
		$O_7^3 = set(ad, \#source, a)$
		$O_8^3 = remove(g, \#vertices, d)$
		$O_9^3 = detach(d)$

3.5 Integration at Node 1

Node 1 receives operations $O_{1..3}^2$ from Node 2 and integrates them sequentially. Operations O_1^1 and O_1^2 conflict: they both modify the value of the same feature and have equivalent contexts. Node 1 uses the precedence relation to determine that $O_1^1 \prec O_1^2$ and executes operation O_1^2. Operations O_2^2 and O_3^2 are not conflictual with the precedent ones and are executed.

Then, Node 1 receives operations $O_{1..9}^3$ from Node 3. Operations O_1^3 and O_2^3 concern a new instance, are independent and are executed. O_3^3 and O_2^2 concern the same feature from the same instance, however, they are independent (Proposition 6) and O_3^3 is executed. $O_{4..7}^3$ are all independent and are executed.

Operation O_8^3 is equivalent to O_2^2 and O_9^3 is equivalent to O_3^2. Both operations are not executed. This results in the following history of operations:

$$\mathcal{H}_1 = \{O_1^1, O_1^2, O_2^2, O_3^2, O_1^3, O_2^3, O_3^3, O_4^3, O_5^3, O_6^3, O_7^3\}.$$

3.6 Integration at Node 2

Node 2 receives operations $O_{1..9}^3$ from Node 3. Similarly to the precedent integration at Node 1, Node 2 executes operations $O_{1..7}^3$, which are independent and does not execute operations O_8^3 and O_9^3, which are equivalent to O_2^2 and O_3^2.

Then, Node 2 receives O_1^1 from Node 1, which conflicts with operation O_1^2. Node 2 uses the same precedence relation as Node 1 to determine that $O_1^1 \prec O_1^2$ and cannot execute operation O_1^1. It first undoes operation O_1^2, executes O_1^1 and re-executes O_1^2. This results in the following history of operations:

$$\mathcal{H}_2 = \{O_2^2, O_3^2, O_1^3, O_2^3, O_3^3, O_4^3, O_5^3, O_6^3, O_7^3, O_1^1, O_1^2\}.$$

3.7 Integration at Node 3

Lastly, Node 3 receives and integrates operations $O_{1..3}^2$ from Node 2, without executing O_2^2 and O_3^2. Then, it receives O_1^1 from Node 1, which conflicts with operation O_1^2, as in the other nodes. The very same precedent relation determines that $O_1^1 \prec O_1^2$ and operation O_1^1 cannot be executed. Thus, Node 3 first undoes operation O_1^2, and then executes O_1^1 and re-executes O_1^2, resulting in the following history of operations:

$$\mathcal{H}_3 = \{O_1^3, O_2^3, O_3^3, O_4^3, O_5^3, O_6^3, O_7^3, O_8^3, O_9^3, O_1^1, O_1^2\}.$$

3.8 Discussion

After integration, all three nodes have equivalent replicas of the same shared resources, all three local histories are equivalent ($\mathcal{H}_1 \equiv \mathcal{H}_2 \equiv \mathcal{H}_3$), ensuring convergence and intention preservation. The integration algorithm ensures that in all nodes, the only pair of conflictual operations, (O_1^1, O_1^2), is executed in the same sequence, i.e., in all nodes $O_1^1 \rightarrow O_1^2$.

If Node 1 is not satisfied with the name of Vertex a and renames it again, creating operation $O_2^1 = set(a, \#name, \text{``A1''})$, this operation is broadcast and executed on the other nodes without conflicts. Indeed, since both operations (O_1^1, O_1^2) belong to the original context of O_2^1, i.e., O_2^1 depends on O_1^1 and on O_1^2 (Definition 3).

4 Prototype Implementation

To validate the integration algorithm, we develop a prototype in Java (v. 1.8), based on EMF (v. 2.12). While the algorithm could be implemented in other languages and other modeling frameworks, we choose EMF to benefit from resource management and the change notification framework. We use the distributed hash table TomP2P DHT [5] to implement the distributed shared resource registry and the HornetQ messaging system [11] to broadcast change messages. The initial validation of the prototype uses PeerUnit [1], a distributed test architecture.

In this section, we present the main design and implementation choices adopted for the prototype. The source code is available on GitHub[1].

4.1   Identities

In EMF, types and features are identified by integer numbers, associated to a package (**EPackage**). A package is a *Façade* [10] for the generated underlying model. It uses a namespace URI, originated from the source Ecore model, as identity. Thus, types (and features) can be identified by a URI and one (or two) integers. Similarly to packages, instances also use a URI as an identity, when no indentity attribute exists.

While using URI as identities ensures their unicity, URI are long strings which are not adapted for network message exchanges. To avoid this problem and use more efficient identities, we introduce a distributed version of the package registry. This class is basically a map that allows retrieving packages from its Id and an Id from the package URI. The shared resource class is also a map that allows retrieving instances from their Id. Figure 2 sketches these two classes.

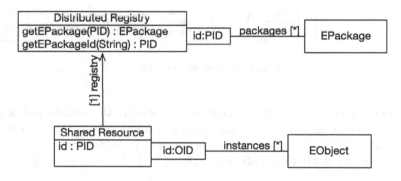

Fig. 2. Distributed registry

To ensure the unicity of an instance Id, we adopt the high-low strategy [2]. The identity of an instance is then the Id of the shared resource it is attached to (high part) and an unique identifier within this resource (low part). This same strategy is used for types and features. Figure 3 sketches these identities and their relationships.

We use EMF adapters to associate an OID to instances when they are attached to a shared resource, avoiding the modification of the different **EObject** implementations.

---

[1] https://github.com/sunye/model-consistency.

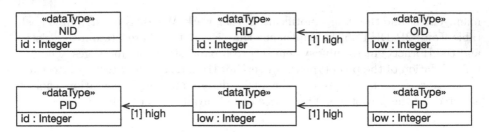

Fig. 3. Identity datatypes

4.2   Update Notification

The EMF change notification framework is an enhanced implementation of the Observer and the Adapter design patterns [10], where the adapter class is also an observer. When any feature of an instance is changed, its adapters receive informations about the change.

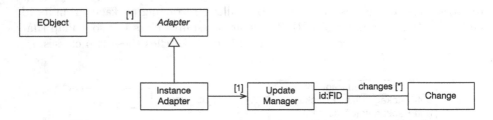

Fig. 4. Update notification

Figure 4 depicts a UML class diagram representing the update notification mechanism. When an instance is changed, the instance adapter receives a notification and forwards it to the update manager. The latter stores the change, which is later broadcast to remote nodes through the Publish-subscribe service.

4.3   Original Context and Precedence

To detect conflicts between operations, each operation is associated to an original context, i. e., the state of the shared resource when the change was done. We adopt two different strategies to establish the original context, both based on the changed feature. For operations on manovalued features, we use the previous value of the feature. According to this rationale, two operations have the same original context if the previous values of the concerned feature are the same.

Multivalued features are more complex, since sending all values of a collection would be too expensive. In this case, hashing the collection values is a more efficient alternative, albeit still expensive. We adopt an alternative strategy, which consists in keeping track of the node that originated the last change and of the of the number of times the feature has been structurally modified (analogously to the **modCount** field in the Java **AbstractList** class).

To determine the precedence relation between two conflictual operations, we adopt a straightforward strategy, we use a hash function to calculate the hash values of the operation values. The operation that has the lower hash value precedes the operation with the greater one. This strategy works for operations on mono and multivalued features, except for the *move* operation, which does not have any associated value. In this case, we first compare the source indices and if they are equal, we compare the target indices. An operation with the lower index precedes the one with the greater index.

5 Related Work

Standard control version systems, e.g., CVS, Subversion, or Git, are not fully adapted for collaborative modeling. Although models can be exported to XMI, a textual format that could be managed by a version system, this approach would not be successful. Indeed, XMI files are generated dynamically and this generation does not ensure neither that the order of XML tags nor that tag identification attributes remain unchanged across different generations. In consequence, the version system may detect several conflicts on two XMI files representing the same model.

To avoid these issues, academic and industrial projects developed control version systems dedicated to models. EMFStore [12] from TU Munich, Model-CVS [14] from TU Vienna, MetaEdit+ [31], and Modelio Constellation [8] from Softeam implement RCS' well-oiled checkout-update-commit pattern for EMF resources. They consider the semantics of modeling languages and thus can correctly support model merging and conflict detection. They differ from our tool by supporting asynchronous cooperative work, while we focus on synchronous cooperative work.

The EMFStore project also proposes a synchronous real-time extension [15], based on the Bonjour peer-to-peer protocol. While their project has the same goal as ours, they adopt a different approach for change integration on nodes, which is based on Git. More precisely, they use hash values to identify change operations (packages) and maintain a reference to the parent operation. When conflicts occur, the tool asks the user to solve them. We believe that our semantic casual dependency is more pertinent for detecting conflicts and that the use of local context information instead of hash numbers consumes less resources.

Koshima et al. propose DiCoMEF [13], a collaborative model-editing framework. Similarly to our approach, this tools detects conflicts at a low granularity level, the update operations. Unlike our approach, operations can be annotated with multimedia information to help users to manually solve conflicts.

Model repositories such a Morsa [21] and Eclipse CDO [25] use a pessimistic locking approach as a support for collaborative modeling. In this centralized approach, users lock the elements they want to edit, preventing others from accessing these elements. Chechik et al. propose the use of a property locking approach for more efficient locking [6]. They use the semantic of the modeling language to avoid users to introduce changes that could generate inconsistencies for other users.

Hawk [3] is a distributed model indexing framework for file-based models. Hawk uses a NoSQL database to store and update continuously metadata information from these models, to provide efficient and scalable model querying.

6 Conclusion and Future Work

The model consistency approach presented in this paper is an initial step towards effective collaborative modeling. However, a large amount of work still remains. Currently, the approach does not ensure the security of the system and does not provide a service to send efficiently large resources through the network. This is an issue when nodes open shared resources with an important initial size.

Additionally, the approach does not consider some syntax rules that are specific to modeling languages. For instance, if two software modelers are editing the same UML diagram and create two classes with same name, this would not be considered as an error, since these classes would have different identities. However, the diagram would not be valid according to the UML wellformed rules.

The approach adopts a data consistency algorithm, where changes are small and conflicts are automatically solved. The approach must be integrated into existing modeling tools to evaluate the impact of these choices on the usability of the tools during collaborative modeling. Furthermore, we want to analyze the impact of these choices when performing a complex sequence of changes, e.g., when performing different refactorings on UML models [30].

As future work, we will integrate the approach to NeoEMF [7] and extend it to provide a distributed repository of models, as well as a service to allow inter-resource references.

References

1. de Almeida, E.C., Sunyé, G., Le Traon, Y., Valduriez, P.: Testing peer-to-peer systems. Empirical Softw. Eng. **15**(4), 346–379 (2010)
2. Ambler, S.W.: The Object Primer: Agile Model-Driven Development with UML 2.0, 3rd edn. Cambridge University Press, Cambridge (2004)
3. Barmpis, K., Kolovos, D.S.: Towards scalable querying of large-scale models. In: Cabot, J., Rubin, J. (eds.) ECMFA 2014. LNCS, vol. 8569, pp. 35–50. Springer, Cham (2014). doi:10.1007/978-3-319-09195-2_3
4. Birman, K., Joseph, T.: Exploiting virtual synchrony in distributed systems. SIGOPS Oper. Syst. Rev. **21**(5), 123–138 (1987). http://doi.acm.org/10.1145/37499.37515
5. Bocek, T.: Tomp2p a p2p-based high performance key-value pair storage library, February 2017. https://tomp2p.net/

6. Chechik, M., Dalpiaz, F., Debreceni, C., Horkoff, J., Ráth, I., Salay, R., Varró, D.: Property-based methods for collaborative model development. In: Joint Proceedings of the 3rd International Workshop on the Globalization Of Modeling Languages and the 9th International Workshop on Multi-Paradigm Modeling co-located with ACM/IEEE 18th International Conference on Model Driven Engineering Languages and Systems, GEMOC+MPM@MoDELS 2015, Ottawa, Canada, pp. 1–7, 28 September 2015. http://ceur-ws.org/Vol-1511/paper-01.pdf

7. Daniel, G., Sunyé, G., Benelallam, A., Tisi, M., Vernageau, Y., Gómez, A., Cabot, J.: Neoemf: a multi-database model persistence framework for very large models. In: Proceedings of the MoDELS 2016 Demo and Poster Sessions co-located with ACM/IEEE 19th International Conference on Model Driven Engineering Languages and Systems (MoDELS 2016), Saint-Malo, France, pp. 1–7, 2–7 October 2016. http://ceur-ws.org/Vol-1725/demo1.pdf

8. Desfray, P.: Model repositories at the enterprises and systems scale: the modelio constellation solution. In: 2015 International Conference on Information Systems Security and Privacy (ICISSP), p. IS-17, February 2015

9. Dirix, M., Muller, A., Aranega, V.: GenMyModel: An Online UML Case Tool. ECOOP (2013). https://hal.archives-ouvertes.fr/hal-01251417, poster

10. Gamma, E., Helm, R., Johnson, R., Vlissides, J.M.: Design Patterns: Elements of Reusable Object-Oriented Software. Addison Wesley Professional, Reading (1995)

11. Giacomelli, P.: Hornetq Messaging Developer's Guide. Packt Publishing Ltd. (2012)

12. Koegel, M., Helming, J.: Emfstore: a model repository for EMF models. In: Proceedings of the 32nd ACM/IEEE International Conference on Software Engineering, ICSE 2010, vol. 2, Cape Town, South Africa, pp. 307–308, 1–8 May 2010. http://doi.acm.org/10.1145/1810295.1810364

13. Koshima, A.A., Englebert, V.: Collaborative editing of emf/ecore meta-models and models: conflict detection, reconciliation, and merging in dicomef. Sci. Comput. Program. **113**, 3–28 (2015). http://dx.doi.org/10.1016/j.scico.2015.07.004

14. Kramler, G., Kappel, G., Reiter, T., Kapsammer, E., Retschitzegger, W., Schwinger, W.: Towards a semantic infrastructure supporting model-based tool integration. In: Proceedings of the 2006 International Workshop on Global Integrated Model Management, GaMMa 2006, pp. 43–46. ACM, New York (2006). http://doi.acm.org/10.1145/1138304.1138314

15. Krusche, S., Brügge, B.: Model-based real-time synchronization. Softwaretechnik-Trends **34**(2) (2014). http://pi.informatik.uni-siegen.de/gi/stt/34_2/index.html

16. Ladin, R., Liskov, B., Shrira, L., Ghemawat, S.: Providing high availability using lazy replication. ACM Trans. Comput. Syst. **10**(4), 360–391 (1992). http://doi.acm.org/10.1145/138873.138877

17. Lamport, L.: Time, clocks, and the ordering of events in a distributed system. Commun. ACM **21**(7), 558–565 (1978). http://doi.acm.org/10.1145/359545.359563

18. Li, R., Li, D.: Commutativity-based concurrency control in groupware. In: Zhang, T. (ed.) Proceedings of the 1st International Conference on Collaborative Computing: Networking, Applications and Worksharing, San Jose, CA, USA. IEEE Computer Society/ICST, 19–21 December 2005. http://dx.doi.org/10.1109/COLCOM.2005.1651251

19. Matula, M.: Netbeans metadata repository. Technical report, Sun Microsystems (2003)

20. Oster, G., Urso, P., Molli, P., Imine, A.: Data consistency for P2P collaborative editing. In: Hinds, P.J., Martin, D. (eds.) Proceedings of the 2006 ACM Conference on Computer Supported Cooperative Work, CSCW 2006, Banff, Alberta, Canada, pp. 259–268. ACM, 4–8 November 2006. http://doi.acm.org/10.1145/1180875.1180916

21. Pagán, J.E., Cuadrado, J.S., Molina, J.G.: Morsa: a scalable approach for persisting and accessing large models. In: Proceedings of the 14th MoDELS Conference, Wellington, New Zealand, pp. 77–92 (2011). http://dl.acm.org/citation.cfm?id=2050655.2050665

22. Plotnikov, C.: Novosoft metadata framework and uml library (2002). http://nsuml.sourceforge.net

23. Ratnasamy, S., Francis, P., Handley, M., Karp, R., Schenker, S.: A scalable content-addressable network. In: SIGCOMM 2001: Proceedings of the 2001 Conference on Applications, Technologies, Architectures, and Protocols for Computer Communications, pp. 161–172. ACM, New York (2001)

24. Lucidchart Software, March 2017. https://www.lucidchart.com

25. Steinberg, D.: Fundamentals of the eclipse modeling framework. Tutorial presented at EclipseCon, March 2008. http://www.eclipsecon.org/2008/index1000.html

26. Steinberg, D., Budinsky, F., Paternostro, M., Merks, E.: EMF - Eclipse Modeling Framework. The Eclipse series, 2nd edn. Pearson Education, London (2008)

27. Stoica, I., Morris, R., Karger, D., Kaashoek, M.F., Balakrishnan, H.: Chord: a scalable peer-to-peer lookup service for internet applications. In: SIGCOMM 2001: Proceedings of the 2001 conference on Applications, Technologies, Architectures, and Protocols for Computer Communications, pp. 149–160. ACM, New York (2001)

28. Sun, C., Ellis, C.A.: Operational transformation in real-time group editors: issues, algorithms, and achievements. In: CSCW 1998, Proceedings of the ACM 1998 Conference on Computer Supported Cooperative Work, Seattle, WA, USA, pp. 59–68, 14–18 November 1998. http://doi.acm.org/10.1145/289444.289469

29. Sun, C., Jia, X., Zhang, Y., Yang, Y., Chen, D.: Achieving convergence, causality preservation, and intention preservation in real-time cooperative editing systems. ACM Trans. Comput. Hum. Interact. 5(1), 63–108 (1998). http://doi.acm.org/10.1145/274444.274447

30. Sunyé, G., Pollet, D., Traon, Y.L., Jézéquel, J.: Refactoring UML models. In: Proceedings of the 4th International Conference on UML 2001 - The Unified Modeling Language, Modeling Languages, Concepts, and Tools, Toronto, Canada, pp. 134–148, 1–5 October 2001. http://dx.doi.org/10.1007/3-540-45441-1_11

31. Tolvanen, J.P.: Metaedit+ for collaborative language engineering and language use (tool demo). In: Proceedings of the 2016 ACM SIGPLAN International Conference on Software Language Engineering, pp. 41–45. ACM (2016)

Model Verification and Analysis

Model-Based Privacy Analysis
in Industrial Ecosystems

Amir Shayan Ahmadian[1]([✉]), Daniel Strüber[1], Volker Riediger[1],
and Jan Jürjens[1,2]

[1] Institute for Software Technology,
University of Koblenz-Landau, Koblenz, Germany
{ahmadian,strueber,riediger}@uni-koblenz.de
[2] Fraunhofer-Institute for Software and Systems Engineering ISST,
Dortmund, Germany
http://jan.jurjens.de

Abstract. Article 25 of Regulation (EU) 2016/679 on the protection of
natural persons with regard to the processing and the free movement of
personal data, refers to data protection by design and by default. Privacy and data protection by design implies that IT systems need to be
adapted or focused to technically support privacy and data protection.
To this end, we need to verify whether security and privacy are supported
by a system, or any change in the design of the system is required. In this
paper, we provide a model-based privacy analysis approach to analyze
IT systems that provide IT services to service customers. An IT service
may rely on different enterprises to process the data that is provided by
service customers. Therefore, our approach is modular in the sense that it
analyzes the system design of each enterprise individually. The approach
is based on the four privacy fundamental elements, namely purpose, visibility, granularity, and retention. We present an implementation of the
approach based on the CARiSMA tool. To evaluate our approach, we
apply it to an industrial case study.

1 Introduction

A main problem for IT service providers is to avoid data breaches and provide
data protection. According to a global survey [1], 88% of people are concerned
about who can access their private data. In Germany, 72% of people expect the
government to keep out of their personal data.

Article 25 of Regulation (EU) 2016/679 refers to data protection by design
and by default [3]. This requires that service providers verify if the required privacy levels are fulfilled according to legal requirements and customers' privacy
preferences. Furthermore, they must implement appropriate technical and organizational measures in an effective manner, and integrate proper safeguards into
the processing to support such requirements.

There exist a range of privacy enhancing technologies (PETs) [6,14–16,23],
which provide strong privacy guarantees in different domains. However, according to Spiekermann [28,29], *privacy and data protection by design and by default*

© Springer International Publishing AG 2017
A. Anjorin and H. Espinoza (Eds.): ECMFA 2017, LNCS 10376, pp. 215–231, 2017.
DOI: 10.1007/978-3-319-61482-3_13

are powerful terms, and include more than the process of uptaking a few PETs. Cavoukian [10], who first introduced the term *privacy by design (PbD)*, defines *PbD* as the idea to integrate privacy and data protection principles in a system's design, and to recognize privacy in an enterprise's management processes.

Based on these considerations, PbD implies the design of a system must be analyzed with regard to privacy preferences and, where necessary, be improved to technically support privacy and data protection. Article 5 of Regulation (EU) 2016/679 stipulates six principles for the processing of personal data: Personal data must be (a) processed lawfully, (b) collected for specified and legitimate *purposes*, (c) adequate and limited to what is necessary regarding the purposes (*granularity*), (d) accurate and kept up to date, (e) kept no longer than necessary (*retention*), and (f) protected against unauthorized processing (*visibility*). These principles correspond to the *key elements of privacy* introduced in Barker et al.'s seminal taxonomy [7]: *purpose, visibility, granularity,* and *retention.*

System-level privacy analysis is particularly challenging in today's digital society, where industrial ecosystems play a key role. Specifically, an enterprise may depend on or cooperate with other enterprises to provide an IT service to a service customer. For instance, an enterprise as a service customer of an insurance enterprise may send personal data of its employees to the insurance enterprise to issue health insurance contracts for them. The insurance enterprise must assess the solvency of the employees before issuing an insurance contract. Therefore, the personal data of each employee will be transmitted to a financial institute for the relevant assessments. Performing a privacy analysis on such a system's design requires analyzing the relevant components of the insurance enterprise, and the financial institute; and the respective interfaces between the components. To support cases where the system design of the relevant enterprises and components are not entirely available, each enterprise must be analyzed individually.

In this paper, we investigate the following research questions: **RQ1:** How can a modular privacy analysis be performed on the system's design of the IT services in industrial ecosystems, where an IT service is the result of cooperation of different service providers? **RQ2:** How can be analyzed if the key elements of privacy are supported by the systems' design of services that process personal data?

To address these questions, we present a model-based approach to support the analysis of the system's design concerning privacy. Using the system models, the privacy requirements are considered from early stages of the system's design and the development process. Our approach is modular in the sense that it analyzes the system design of each enterprise separately. The approach is based on the fundamental taxonomy of the four privacy key elements [7]. We integrated it into the CARiSMA tool [2], which was originally designed to make a security analysis based on the UMLsec profile available to developers [21] and is now extended to address privacy.

The paper is organized as follows. In Sect. 2, the necessary background is provided. In Sect. 3, we describe our approach on model-based privacy analysis. In Sect. 4, we evaluate our approach using a case study. In Sect. 5, we discuss related work. Finally, in Sect. 6, we conclude.

2   Background

Below, we present the necessary background for this paper.

2.1   The Four Key Elements of Privacy

In what follows, we briefly describe the four fundamental privacy elements presented in [7]: purpose, visibility, granularity, and retention.

- **Purpose** is the basic element of data privacy. It indicates the authorized reasons to access data [13]. Service providers must record and track the purposes for which the data is collected and is processed.
- **Visibility** indicates who is allowed to access or use the data provided for an authorized purpose. In other words, visibility controls the number and kind of users who can access the data.
- **Granularity** refers to characteristics of data that could be used to facilitate proper use of the data, where there exists different valid accesses for various purposes. In other words, data granularity specifies how much precision is provided in response a query. This is important when the service customer requires the service provider to provide personal data to a third party [13].
- **Retention** refers to the need to restrict access or remove the data after they have been used for the intended purposes.

2.2   Model-Based Security Analysis Using UMLsec

UMLsec [21] provides a model-based approach to develop and analyze security critical software systems, in which security requirements such as confidentiality, integrity, and availability are expressed within UML diagrams [24]. UMLsec is provided as an UML profile, using the standard UML extension mechanism. In UMLsec, different stereotypes and tags are used to annotate UML diagrams with security properties. The CARiSMA tool [2] performs the corresponding security analysis for security properties such as secure information flow [18] and has been applied to various industrial applications (e.g. [19]). Some of the analysis techniques have also been ported to the code analysis level [12]. UMLsec does not support the analysis of a system concerning privacy.

3   Model-Based Privacy Analysis

The terms that are used in this paper are based on the terms and definitions of Regulation (EU) 2016/679. According to this Regulation, a data controller determines the purposes and the means for the processing of personal data (privacy preferences). In our work, a service customer is a data controller, who provides personal data and specifies the privacy preferences of these data. A data processor processes personal data on behalf of the controller. When we talk of service providers, we mean either a data processor, who directly processes the provided

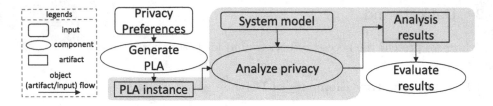

Fig. 1. Model-based privacy analysis by exploiting PLAs.

data, or a data controller, who transfers to other data processors the data and their privacy preferences specified by the service customer.

The work presented in this paper is a part of our ongoing research [5] to provide a method on privacy analysis of IT systems by exploiting privacy level agreements (PLAs). PLAs are appendixes to service level agreements, and offer a structured way to communicate the level of personal data protection provided by a service providers to service customers. PLAs are based on EU personal data protection and privacy legal requirements [11]. Figure 1 presents the overview of this privacy analysis method. In [5], we provided a meta-model formalizing PLAs to specify privacy preferences. In this paper (as it is highlighted in Fig. 1), given privacy preferences (contained in a PLA) and system model, we introduce an approach to model-based privacy analysis based on the four key privacy elements. Following the privacy analysis, the analysis results are evaluated. This evaluation is out of scope of this paper. The results of this evaluation are: (I) Privacy-centric questions, which are used to define privacy questionnaires to collect additional feedback from data controllers on privacy preferences. (II) Privacy measures to protect personal data (adheres to PLA outline, Sect. 4). (III) Conflicts between the system model and privacy preferences.

3.1 The Modular Privacy Analysis

The scenario introduced in Sect. 1 is illustrated in more detail in Fig. 2. Car manufacturing *enterprise A* wants to issue a health insurance for its employees and, therefore, sends personal data of the employees to insurance *enterprise B*. Together with the personal data, *enterprise A* specifies the privacy preferences. For instance, it may specify that *enterprise B* is not authorized to use the credit card number and the birthdate of an employee for marketing purposes, and that it must delete these information five years after the termination of health insurance contracts. Such privacy preferences are specified in *PLA-x*, which is concluded between the car manufacturing enterprise and the insurance enterprise. To issue a health insurance for an employee, the insurance enterprise needs to assess the financial status of the employee and therefore, sends the personal data of the employee to *enterprise C* (a financial institute). *Enterprise A* is not aware of this data transmission. A PLA must be concluded between the insurance enterprise and the financial institute (*PLA-y*), in which the privacy preferences of *enterprise A* are included. Similarly, the financial institute may

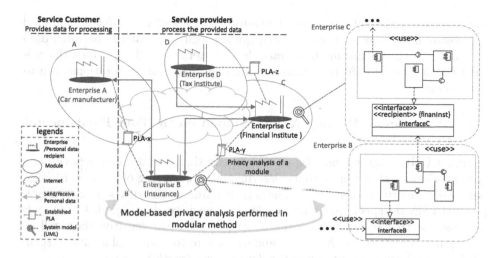

Fig. 2. An illustration of an industrial ecosystem containing four modules.

send the personal data of the employee to a tax institute (*enterprise D*) to collect some information about the employee.

To perform a privacy analysis on such a system design, where several enterprises process personal data, we need to perform a modular analysis, in which each enterprise and its corresponding interfaces are analyzed individually. The reasons to perform modular privacy analysis are: (I) PLAs are needed as input to privacy analysis. Since *PLA-y* might differ from *PLA-x* and contain additional privacy preferences, the financial institute (*enterprise C*) must be analyzed individually. (II) System models of all data processors and data controllers may not be available. In case that the system model for one of the involved enterprises is not available, a privacy analysis is still desirable. In the scenario, if the system model of the financial institute is not available, a privacy analysis on the insurance enterprise is still possible. Since the privacy preferences of *enterprise A* are contained in *PLA-y*, at some point a privacy analysis on the financial institute may be performed (when the system model is available).

Definition 1 (*Module*). *A module is a data processor or a data controller together with its all interfaces to other recipients, where according to Regulation (EU) 2016/679 a recipient is a controller, processor, or data subject (personal data owner), to which personal data are disclosed.*

Per Definition 1, Fig. 2 contains four modules. *Module A* is a data controller, i.e. *module A* acts as a service customer that provides personal data and specifies the privacy preferences. *Modules B, C, and D* are recipients and cooperate in the processing of the data provided by *module A*. Therefore, these three modules are analyzed separately to verify if they support the privacy preferences.

According to Definition 1, this analysis needs to address the interfaces between the involved modules. In the right part of Fig. 2, the structures of *modules B and C* are specified using two UML component diagrams, together with the respective provided interfaces. The interface provided by *module C* and used by *module B* is annotated with ≪recipient≫ specifying that the personal data is transferred from *module B* to *module C*. Later, we will introduce the privacy profile that is used to annotate UML diagrams with annotations such as ≪recipient≫.

3.2 Model-Based Privacy Analysis Based on the Four Fundamental Privacy Elements

Different UML diagrams may be used to specify the structure and behavior of a system. Figure 3 shows an activity describing the processing of credit card number within the insurance scenario. The activity is annotated with ≪dataPrivacy≫ {creditCardNo}, specifying that a piece of sensitive data (creditCardNo) is processed in this activity. According to this activity, the sensitive data will be stored in a database (*storeNumber*), and will be sent to a financial institute (*send-ToBank*) to check the solvency of the data subject (*verifySolvency*).

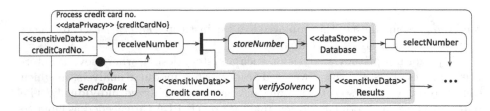

Fig. 3. Design model excerpt (*process credit card no.* Activity) which highlights the need to perform a privacy analysis.

Based on the four privacy elements, we need to analyze the activity to verify if (I) the *creditCardNo* is only processed for the purposes that are mentioned in the privacy preferences, (II) access to the sensitive data is restricted to authorized persons, (III) the granularity level is respected when sensitive data are sent to the bank, and (IV) deletion or restriction mechanisms are in place to ensure that sensitive data stored in a database, such as *creditCardNo*, are eventually deleted or restricted. To this end, we propose four corresponding privacy checks. In what follows, first we give a high-level description of these checks:

- **Purpose-check:** First, this check analyses the system's behavior and structure to identify the system operations that process personal data, and their objectives (purposes). Moreover, it determines if operations that process personal data belong to different systems. Finally, the objectives of the operations are compared with the purposes specified in the privacy preferences by the data controller.
- **Visibility-check:** The check identifies all the data recipients, and it verifies if they are authorized to process personal data. Moreover, concerning one module, this check verifies who is allowed to access personal data. This could be verified by identifying all owners of system operations that process personal data.

- **Granularity-check:** According to [13], granularity is important when personal data are disclosed to other recipients. Based on the interfaces to other recipients, this check verifies if the granularity level is respected by data transmissions.

- **Retention-check:** In the first step, the check verifies if appropriate operations exist to restrict or delete the personal data. Moreover, the check analyzes the system behavior to determine if such an operation will be eventually applied.

The annotations used in Fig. 3 enable these privacy checks. In the following section, we introduce a complete list of these annotations. Since the systems are modeled using UML, we use a UML extension mechanism to specify them.

3.3 UML Privacy Extension

As a basis to implement the privacy checks described in Sect. 3.2, we introduce two UML extensions. First, the *privacy* profile, allowing elements in UML models to be annotated with privacy-specific information. Second, the *rabac* profile, allowing the generation and enforcement of access control policies for such elements, using the *role- and attribute based access control* model (RABAC, [17]). The *rabac* profile is an extension of UMLsec's *rbac* profile [21]. On top of *rbac*'s *role* and *right* tags, *rabac* allows a refined control management using an *attributeFilter* tag. In nutshell, by using attributes, there is no need to increase the number of roles in a system in many cases, and the problem of role explosion will be prevented. We use *rabac* to define the visibility check, introducing it as a separate profile, since it is not specific to privacy. The complete list of stereotypes together with their tags is provided in Fig. 4.

Stereotype	Tags	UML Element	Description
Privacy profile			
«dataPrivacy»	data	Behavior	enfoces privacy analysis
«sensitiveData»		NamedElement	personal data [3]
«recipient»	enterprise	NamedElement	data recipient [3]
«granularity»	level	Parameter	the granularity level
«objective»	purpose	BehavioralFeature	purposes of operations
rabac profile			
«abac»	roles, rights, attributeFilter	Package	enforces role-attribute-based access control
«abacAttribute»	name	Operation	rabac for an attribute
«abacRequire»	accessRight, filter	Operation	rabac for an operation

Fig. 4. Privacy and *rabac* profiles.

Privacy Profile. The terms and names used for the stereotypes and the tags comply with the terms and the definitions of *Regulation (EU) 2016/679* [3].

≪**dataPrivacy**≫: Behavioral specification mechanism may be annotated with this stereotype, specifying the existence of personal data in the behavior which is modeled using the corresponding diagram. Tag *data* specifies a set of personal data.

≪**sensitiveData**≫: A NamedElement may be annotated with this stereotype specifying the element is or contains sensitive data. The definition of sensitive data complies with the definition of personal data provided in Article 4 (1) of Regulation (EU) 2016/679 and particularly adheres to the definition of special categories of personal data provided in Article 9. Additionally, and regarding the controller's preferences, a piece of data that must not be revealed or disclosed could be also annotated with this stereotype.

≪**recipient**≫: A NamedElement may be annotated with this stereotype *recipient* stating that the element is a controller, or a processor, to which the sensitive data are disclosed.

≪**granularity**≫: A Parameter may be annotated with this stereotype together with its tag *level* specifying the level of the precision of data provided in response a query. In other words, granularity is assumed as a new attribute for a parameter, where a parameter [24] is an argument used to pass information into or out of an invocation of a behavior.

≪**objective**≫: A BehavioralFeature such as an Operation may be annotated with this stereotype together with its tag {purpose} specifying the purposes of the operation (BehavioralFeature). Tag {purpose} specifies a set of purposes for an operation.

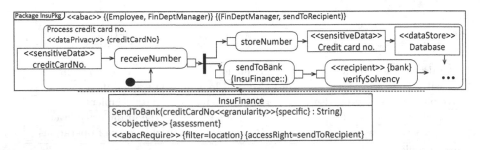

Fig. 5. Design model excerpt annotated with the privacy and *rabac* profiles.

Figure 5 shows an excerpt from the activity provided in Fig. 3, and a class from a class diagram of the insurance system. For space reasons, we only show the relevant actions and classes. The annotation ≪dataPrivacy≫ {creditCardNo} specifies that a piece of personal data (*creditCardNo*) is processed in this activity. ≪recipient≫ {bank} specifies that the *verifySolvency* Action is performed not in the *insurance*, but in the recipient *bank*. Based on the annotation ≪granularity≫ {specific}, the granularity-check must analyze the parameters that are annotated with ≪sensitiveData≫ concerning the granularity level *specific*. The *sendToBank* Action is a CallOperationAction, i.e., it invokes an Operation as specified in the *InsuFinance* Class. This operation is annotated with ≪objective≫ {assessment} specifying *assessment* as the purpose of the operation and, transitively, the purpose of the *sendToBank* Action.

rabac Profile. *rabac* enables the verification of visibility requirements on personal data. For each operation of a system, a set of data subjects with different roles, who are authorized to process personal data, is defined. Throughout the analysis, this information is compared to the provided privacy preferences. In what follows, the stereotypes of *rabac* together with their tags are explained:

≪abac≫: A Package is annotated with this stereotype and its tags, namely *roles*, *rights*, and *attributeFilter* to specify *role-attribute-based access control* is enforced in the system model. The values of *roles* and *rights* are tuples of the following form: (*dataSubject, associatedRole*), and (*associatedRole, accessRight*) respectively. The former one links a role to a data subject, while the later one associate a right to a role (similar to *rbac* [21]). Tag *attributeFilter* specifies a set of attributes (defined in classes). Based on these attributes, it is possible to define access rights.

≪abacAttribute≫: An Operation may be annotated with this stereotype, with tag *name* to specify a specific attribute with a corresponding value to invoke the operation.

≪abacRequire≫: An Operation or a Transition may be annotated with *abacRequire* with tags *filter*, and *accessRight* to specify the respective attribute and the access right to invoke the operation. Tag *accessRight* enables on to identify the associated role and data subject that are authorized to perform the operation.

In Fig. 5, Operation *sendToBank* is annotated as follows: ≪abacRequire≫ {filter = location} {accessRight = sendToRecipient}. This means that the *accessRight* for this operation is *sendToRecipient*. Considering ≪abac≫, the associated role for this *accessRight* is *FinDeptManager*, who is allowed to invoke the *sendToBank* Operation.

In the following section, we explain how theses stereotypes are used to perform a privacy analysis.

3.4   Privacy Checks

Generally, we explain the privacy checks using UML Activities (for detailed information on Activities see [24]). Before we explain the privacy checks, we need to define the privacy preferences to be specified by a data controller who provides the personal data.

Definition 2 (*Privacy Preferences*). *Let P be a partially ordered set of all defined purposes, V be a partially ordered set of all subjects to whom the data is* *visible, G be a set of all possible granularity levels, and R be a set of retentions conditions. The privacy preferences of a piece of personal data pd is defined as a tuple:*

$$PrP_{pd} = (P', V', g, r)$$

where $P' \subseteq P$, $V' \subseteq V$, $g \in G$, and $r \in R$.

According to Definition 2, purpose and data subject sets are defined as partially ordered sets. This enables us to organize these two sets in lattice structures, where each node presents a purpose or a data subject and each edge represents a hierarchical relation between two purposes or data subjects where they subsume each other, i.e. one purpose or data subject is more specific than the other. For instance, concerning visibility, in a lattice which organizes the data subjects, *marketing department* and *sales department* are the descendent (children) of *business department*, and are more specific (for more information, see [13]).

Purpose-check. The upper part of Fig. 6 shows an excerpt from a design model. The lower part demonstrates two lattices, namely a purpose-lattice, and a visibility-lattice (simplified for space reasons). The purpose-lattice presents the set of all possible purposes in the system. The parts shown with dashed lines specify the privacy preferences for *creditCardNo*, which are specified by the data controller (car manufacturing enterprise). For instance, in the purpose-lattice, the *creditCardNo* may be processed for purpose *assessment* and its child purposes.

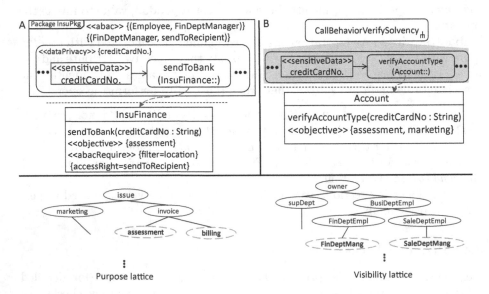

Fig. 6. Design model excerpt and lattices. Purpose, and visibility-checks use the highlighted stereotypes.

Based on the purpose-lattice and the purposes defined in the provided privacy preferences, the purpose-check for each action of the activity processing a piece of personal data (annotated with ≪sensitiveData≫) identifies the objective. According to the specification of Activities [24], two cases may happen:

(I) For a **CallOperationAction** (Fig. 6, part A), the corresponding operation in the class diagram is directly identified. Then the purpose-check compares the objectives of the operation to the privacy preferences (purpose-lattice). For instance, in our example, *assessment* is specified as the purpose for the *sendToBank* Operation. Since *assessment* is included in the privacy preferences (purpose-lattice) as an authorized purpose to process *creditCardNo*, the check is successful.

(II) For a **CallBehaviorAction** (Fig. 6, part B), the activity invoked by the CallBehaviorAction is analyzed. Similar to case (I), if the actions of this activity are CallOperationActions, the objectives of the corresponding operations are identified and compared with the privacy preferences. For instance, in Fig. 6, a mentioned purpose of the *verifyAccountType* Operation is *marketing*, which is not specified as a valid purpose in the privacy preferences. Therefore, the purpose-check is not successful.

Visibility-check. Similar to purpose-check, the visibility-check assumes a lattice such as the one in Fig. 6. The visibility-lattice presents all possible data subjects to whom *creditCardNo* may possibly be disclosed. The dashed parts specify the authorized data subjects according to the privacy preferences. Considering the annotations ≪ abacRequire ≫ {accessRight = sendToRecipient} and ≪ abac ≫ {(FinDeptMang, sendToRecipient)}, the visibility-check identifies that the model specifies *FinDeptMang* (finance department manager) processes *creditCardNo*. Since *FinDeptMang* is authorized to process *creditCardNo* in the privacy preferences, the check is successful.

Granularity-check. The supported granularity levels are *none, existential, partial,* and *specific*. Obviously, *none* means that nothing about a piece of personal data may be revealed in response to a query. *Existential* means that a query may only be answered by specifying if a piece of personal data exists or not. *Partial* means that a piece of data is revealed only partially. For instance, for numeric data, a range of numbers is specified. *Specific* means that a piece of data is precisely provided in response to a query.

Granularity is important when a piece of personal data is transferred to a recipient, that is, another enterprise. In to Fig. 7, the granularity-check first

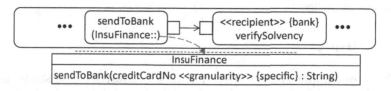

Fig. 7. Design model excerpt. The granularity-check uses the highlighted stereotypes.

identifies if a piece of personal data is transferred to another enterprise for processing, using the ≪sensitiveData≫ and ≪recipient≫ annotations. Afterwards, similar to the purpose-check, the corresponding Operation is identified by verifying the action and the respective class. Using the ≪granularity≫ specified for the parameters, the level of granularity used by the operation will be ascertained. The specified level will be compared to the granularity level given in the privacy preferences. For instance, in Fig. 7, if we assume the granularity level specified by the data controller in the privacy preferences is partial, the check fails.

Retention-check. The retention-check verifies that whenever a piece of personal data is stored in a database, an action exists to eventually restrict access to or delete this data. According to the specification of Activites [24], a node annotated with ≪dataStore≫ acts as a database holding object tokens.

The retention-check verifies if in an activity a piece of personal data (an object annotated with ≪sensitiveData≫) is stored in a node annotated with ≪dataStore≫. Afterwards, the retention-check verifies if a selection on the ≪dataStore≫ node exists, which retrieves the piece of personal data, and subsequently an action with *restrict* or *delete* purpose exists that restricts or deletes the piece of personal data.

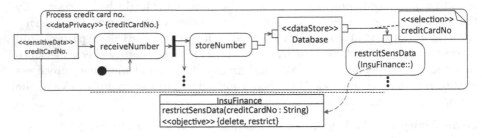

Fig. 8. Design model excerpt. Retention-check can be executed using the highlighted stereotypes.

For instance, in Fig. 8, *creditCardNo* is stored in a database. This implies that a selection shall retrieve *creditCardNo* and an action of purpose *deletes* or *restricts* shall process *creditCardNo* before the activity terminates. If such an action does not exist, then the retention-check is not successful. Similar to the purpose-check, by mapping the action to a respective operation in a class, its purposes are identified.

4   Case Study

To evaluate our approach, we applied it to an industrial case study, namely *birth certificate registration* scenario in Municipality of Athens (MoA). MoA is a public administration (PA) in Athens. This case study is one of the case studies

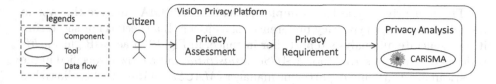

Fig. 9. An excerpt from the architecture of *VisiOn Privacy Platform (VPP)*

of *VisiOn* research project [4]. In this project a privacy platform to evaluate and analyze privacy levels of a PA system, and generate a privacy level agreement between a citizen and a PA to enforce privacy policies, is developed.

In Fig. 9, an excerpt from the architecture of *VisiOn Privacy Platform (VPP)* is presented. Three components of VPP architecture are represented. (I) Privacy assessment, providing a questionnaire to obtain the privacy preferences of a citizen, (II) Privacy requirement, determining privacy requirements based on the preferences of a citizen. (III) Privacy analysis, analyzing the system model of a PA considering privacy requirements. Our model-based privacy analysis approach is implemented and integrated into the privacy analysis component. The implementation of our approach is based on the CARiSMA tool [2]. CARiSMA enables the developers and IT system designers to annotate UML diagrams with security-specific information, using *UMLsec*, and privacy-specific information, using the profiles introduced in this work. The annotated diagrams can be analyzed using privacy and security checks.

MoA is in the process of developing a new system called MACS. MACS shall provide different online services to citizens, such as issuing a birth certificate. To provide such services, MoA requires citizen's personal data such as their *Registry Number of Social Insurance (RNSI)*. Moreover, MoA may cooperate with other public administrations such as central tax institute and financial institutes.

In our case study, we model the *birth certificate registration* using a selection of UML diagrams. Our privacy and *rabac* profiles are used to annotate these diagrams with privacy-specific stereotypes. Figure 10 illustrates the annotation of an operation with the ≪abacRequire≫ stereotype from the *rabac* profile, as facilitated by the Eclipse CARiSMA perspective.

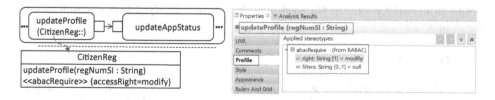

Fig. 10. Excerpts from class diagram and activity diagram of *birth certificate registration* scenario, together with the property view of the CARiSMA perspective in Eclipse.

The four privacy checks, as implemented in CARiSMA, analyze the system model concerning the privacy preferences of a citizen. If a check is not successful, it will generate an analysis report. For instance, in Fig. 10, if accessRight *modify* is defined as an accessRight for *MACSadministrator*, but a citizen specified in the questionnaire that only department manager (*MACSDeptManager*) is allowed to process *RegNumSI*, the visibility-check is not successful, and a report specifying the violation and its reasons is generated. Such reports later will be evaluated and may result in the application of an appropriate privacy-preserving measure, or the generation of privacy-centric questions.

In this case study, all the relevant classes of the MACS system together with corresponding activities to describe the behavior of the system are modeled. Moreover, the interfaces and relevant classes and related activities of a bank, which is responsible for approving an invoice issued by MACS, are modeled.

Results of this case study include that our approach is successfully applied to a software system in industrial ecosystem with complex structure and behavior. More specifically, concerning the research questions investigated in this work, results include the following: **RQ1:** We defined the term module in industrial ecosystems concerning the system's design of IT services, and we introduced modular privacy analysis in such ecosystems, in the sense that enterprises that cooperates with each other to process personal data are analyzed separately. **RQ2:** We introduced a UML privacy extension (the privacy profile, and *rabac* profile) to enable four privacy checks to analyze a system model based on the key four privacy elements.

Since generally, CARiSMA is based on the analysis of the system models that are modeled using UML diagrams, to perform the privacy analysis using the four checks, the MoA system and the cooperating systems must be modeled using UML. Based on these considerations, in this paper the privacy profile is defined for UML elements. However, concerning the description of each stereotype (Sect. 3.3), the privacy concepts may be adapted for other modeling languages. Furthermore, concerning the fact that IT systems may be modeled using different modeling languages, a transformation may be defined to perform the privacy checks on such models. Moreover, by evaluating the results of the case study, we observed that by performing privacy analysis on system models, not all privacy issues of the systems may be handled. However, as we previously mentioned (Sect. 1), the system models enable us to consider key privacy elements from early stages in the system's design, and verify if privacy preferences are supported.

5   Related Work

Generally, model-based privacy analysis has attracted little attention in the scientific literature so far. A possible explanation is the earlier lack of legal incentives driving its adoption process. Our work is motivated particularly by Article 25 of Regulation (EU) 2016/679, which is the current state of European legislation.

In [30], an extension of privacy agreement levels by implementing access purposes for individual personal information in a lattice structure is introduced.

This approach enables service customers to control the use of individual data. However, in this approach no privacy analysis regarding customer preferences is performed.

In [13], a lattice-based privacy-aware access control model is introduced. In their approach, they provide a concrete privacy enhancing technique to control the access to a system concerning the four key privacy elements. However, using this approach, one is not able to perform a privacy analysis to verify if privacy preferences are supported by a system's design, so that the design can be improved when necessary.

UMLsec [20, 21] provides an approach to develop and analyze security critical software, in which security requirements such as integrity, availability, and confidentiality are specified in system models. Moreover, the security analysis techniques have been integrated with the requirements elicitation phase [9, 27]. However, UMLsec analysis does not consider privacy.

In [8], the authors provide a UML profile for privacy-aware applications. This profile enables one to describe a privacy policy that is applied by an application and keep track of which elements are in charge of enforcing it. This profile does not enable one to analyze a system's design.

In [22], the authors propose a method (PriS) for incorporating privacy user requirements into the system design process. PriS provides a methodological framework to analyze the effect of privacy requirements on organizational processes. The authors focus on the integration between high-level organizational needs and IT systems. A privacy analysis is not conducted on a system's design.

In [25, 26], the authors provide a model-based privacy 'best practice', and a variety of guidelines and techniques to assist experts and software engineers to consider privacy when the systems are designed. However, they only focus on top-level security and privacy goals, and they do not perform a privacy analysis.

6 Conclusion

We have introduced a modular model-based privacy analysis approach for industrial ecosystems. The approach is based on four key privacy elements, namely purpose, visibility, granularity and retention. A set of stereotypes are introduced to express key privacy elements within the diagrams in a UML system specification. This annotations enable four privacy checks, which adhere to the four key privacy elements. The approach is integrated into VisiOn project, in which a platform for privacy analysis of public administration systems is provided.

As we mentioned in Sect. 1, privacy by design implies that the system's design of IT services must be analyzed to verify if the required privacy levels are fulfilled, and where necessary appropriate technical and organizational measures must be implemented to support privacy and data protection. In the future, we will investigate how the results from our privacy analysis can be evaluated to identify proper technical and organizational measures.

Acknowledgements. This research was partially supported by the research project Visual Privacy Management in User Centric Open Environments (supported by the EU's Horizon 2020 program, Proposal number: 653642).

References

1. Personal data in the cloud: The importance of trust. Technical report, Fujitso Global Business Group, Tokyo 105-7123, Japan, September 2010
2. CARiSMA (2016). https://rgse.uni-koblenz.de/carisma/
3. The European Parliament and the Council of the European Union, Regulation (EU) 2016/679 on the protection of natural persons with regard to the processing of personal data and on the free movement of such data. Official J. Eur. Union, vol. 199, pp 1–88 (April 2016)
4. VisiOn Project (2016). http://www.visioneuproject.eu/
5. Ahmadian, S., Jürjens, J.: Supporting model-based privacy analysis by exploiting privacy level agreements. In: 8th IEEE International Conference on Cloud Computing Technology and Science (CloudCom 2016) (2016)
6. Antignac, T., Métayer, D.: Privacy by design: from technologies to architectures. In: Preneel, B., Ikonomou, D. (eds.) APF 2014. LNCS, vol. 8450, pp. 1–17. Springer, Cham (2014). doi:10.1007/978-3-319-06749-0_1
7. Barker, K., Askari, M., Banerjee, M., Ghazinour, K., Mackas, B., Majedi, M., Pun, S., Williams, A.: A Data Privacy Taxonomy, pp. 42–54. Springer, Heidelberg (2009)
8. Basso, T., Montecchi, L., Moraes, R., Jino, M., Bondavalli, A.: Towards a UML profile for privacy-aware applications. In: 2015 IEEE International Conference on Computer and Information Technology; Ubiquitous Computing and Communications; Dependable, Autonomic and Secure Computing; Pervasive Intelligence and Computing, pp. 371–378, October 2015
9. Breu, R., Burger, K., Hafner, M., Jürjens, J., Popp, G., Wimmel, G., Lotz, V.: Key issues of a formally based process model for security engineering. In: Sixteenth International Conference "Software & Systems Engineering & Their Applications", Paris (2003)
10. Cavoukian, A., Chibba, M.: Advancing privacy and security in computing, networking and systems innovations through privacy by design. In: Proceedings of the 2009 conference of the Centre for Advanced Studies on Collaborative Research, 2–5 November 2009, Toronto, Ontario, Canada, pp. 358–360 (2009)
11. Cloud Security Alliance: Privacy Level Agreement [V2]: A Compliance Tool for Providing Cloud Services in the European Union (2013)
12. Dupressoir, F., Gordon, A.D., Jürjens, J., Naumann, D.A.: Guiding a general-purpose C verifier to prove cryptographic protocols. J. Comput. Secur. **22**(5), 823–866 (2014). http://dx.doi.org/10.3233/JCS-140508
13. Ghazinour, K., Majedi, M., Barker, K.: A lattice-based privacy aware access control model. In: International Conference on Computational Science and Engineering, CSE 2009, vol. 3, pp. 154–159, August 2009
14. Gürses, S., Gonzalez Troncoso, C., Diaz, C.: Engineering privacy by design. In: Computers, Privacy & Data Protection (2011)
15. Hafiz, M.: A pattern language for developing privacy enhancing technologies. Softw. Pract. Exper. **43**(7), 769–787 (2013)
16. Hoepman, J.H.: Privacy Design Strategies, pp. 446–459. Springer, Heidelberg (2014)

17. Jin, X., Sandhu, R.S., Krishnan, R.: RABAC: role-centric attribute-based access control. In: International Conference on Mathematical Methods, Models and Architectures for Computer Network Security (MMM-ACNS), pp. 84–96 (2012)
18. Jürjens, J.: Secure information flow for concurrent processes. In: Palamidessi, C. (ed.) CONCUR 2000. LNCS, vol. 1877, pp. 395–409. Springer, Heidelberg (2000). doi:10.1007/3-540-44618-4_29
19. Jürjens, J.: Modelling audit security for smart-card payment schemes with UMLsec. In: Dupuy, M., Paradinas, P. (eds.) Trusted Information: The New Decade Challenge, pp. 93–108 (2001). Proceedings of the 16th International Conference on Information Security (SEC 2001). http://www.jurjens.de/jan
20. Jürjens, J.: Model-based security engineering with UML. In: Aldini, A., Gorrieri, R., Martinelli, F. (eds.) FOSAD 2004-2005. LNCS, vol. 3655, pp. 42–77. Springer, Heidelberg (2005). doi:10.1007/11554578_2
21. Jürjens, J.: Secure Systems Development with UML. Springer, Heidelberg (2005)
22. Kalloniatis, C., Kavakli, E., Gritzalis, S.: Addressing privacy requirements in system design: the PriS method. Requirements Eng. 13(3), 241–255 (2008)
23. Kerschbaum, F.: Privacy-Preserving Computation, pp. 41–54. Springer, Heidelberg (2014)
24. Object Management Group (OMG): UML 2.5 Superstructure Specification (2011)
25. Pearson, S.: Taking account of privacy when designing cloud computing services. In: Proceedings of the 2009 ICSE Workshop on Software Engineering Challenges of Cloud Computing, pp. 44–52, CLOUD 2009. IEEE Computer Society (2009)
26. Pearson, S., Allison, D.: A model-based privacy compliance checker. IJEBR 5(2), 63–83 (2009)
27. Schneider, K., Knauss, E., Houmb, S., Islam, S., Jürjens, J.: Enhancing security requirements engineering by organisational learning. Requirements Eng. J. (REJ) 17(1), 35–56 (2012)
28. Spiekermann, S.: The challenges of privacy by design. Commun. ACM 55(7), 38–40 (2012)
29. Spiekermann, S., Cranor, L.F.: Engineering privacy. IEEE Trans. Softw. Eng. 35(1), 67–82 (2009)
30. van Staden, W., Olivier, M.S.: Using Purpose Lattices to Facilitate Customisation of Privacy Agreements, pp. 201–209. Springer, Heidelberg (2007)

Formulating Model Verification Tasks Prover-Independently as UML Diagrams

Martin Gogolla[1]([✉]), Frank Hilken[1], Philipp Niemann[2], and Robert Wille[2,3]

[1] University of Bremen, Bremen, Germany
{gogolla,fhilken}@informatik.uni-bremen.de
[2] Cyber-Physical Systems, DFKI GmbH, Bremen, Germany
philipp.niemann@dfki.de
[3] Johannes Kepler University, Linz, Austria
robert.wille@jku.at

Abstract. The success of Model-Driven Engineering (MDE) relies on the quality of the employed models. Thus, quality assurance through validation and verification has a tradition within MDE. But model verification is typically done in the context of specialized approaches and provers. Therefore, verification tasks are expressed from the viewpoint of the chosen prover and approach requiring particular expertise and background knowledge. This contribution suggests to take a new view on verification tasks that is independent from the employed approach and prover. We propose to formulate verifications tasks in terms of the used modeling language itself, e.g. with UML and OCL. As prototypical example tasks we show how (a) questions concerning model consistency can be expressed with UML object diagrams and (b) issues regarding state reachability can be defined with UML sequence diagrams.

1 Introduction

Software development following the *Model-Driven Engineering* (MDE) paradigm focuses on models in contrast to traditional code-centric approaches. Models are said to offer advantages like a high degree of abstraction or platform-independence. As models become the central artifacts – particular in early stages of the design process – means for model quality assurance in form of validation ("Are we building the right product?") and verification ("Are we building the product right?") become indispensable. In particular, verification techniques get more and more important, since they allow to check whether a system to be realized is described and behaves as intended before a single line of programming code is written.

Nowadays, the UML *(Unified Modeling Language)* and the OCL *(Object Constraint Language)* are frequently applied modeling languages. Correspondingly, a substantial number of verification techniques has been developed for models provided in UML/OCL. The spectrum of approaches ranges from solutions for structural and behavioral verification tasks as well as along the employed verification engines such as theorem provers [8], solvers for *Constraint Satisfaction*

A. Anjorin and H. Espinoza (Eds.): ECMFA 2017, LNCS 10376, pp. 232–247, 2017.
DOI: 10.1007/978-3-319-61482-3_14

Problems (CSP) [9], Petri nets [10], model checkers [18], intermediate languages like *Alloy* or *Kodkod* [1,28], or solvers for *Boolean satisfiability* (SAT) and *SAT Modulo Theories* (SMT) [26,27].

However, these approaches often address the respective verification tasks from their own particular perspective and with respect to their paradigms. For example, solutions based on SAT or SMT require a description of the considered verification tasks in terms of propositional logic or bit-vector logic, respectively. This poses a significant challenge to the designer, since expertise and background knowledge about the employed verification approach and the used tool is needed in order to formulate a verification task. Moreover, this nullifies several of the benefits of using UML/OCL models such as the easy accessibility of a system description also for non-technical stakeholders, the high-degree of freedom, as well as the independence from programming or, in this case, verification languages.

In this work, we propose a solution to this problem by introducing a view on verification tasks in a tool- and approach-independent manner. The main idea is as follows: Instead of formulating the respective verification task in a tool-related language (such as propositional logic or bit-vector logic), we propose to describe them in terms of the used modeling language (such as UML/OCL) itself. To this end, we consider some well-known and frequently applied verification tasks such as consistency or reachability and provide corresponding formulations in UML/OCL.

Overall, this allows designers to formulate additional properties for an existing UML/OCL model which are not explicitly part of the system description, but represent verification tasks. By this, designers can formulate verification tasks with description means they are most familiar with and in which they designed the currently considered model anyway.

The structure of the rest of this paper is as follows. Section 2 introduces central notions and the paper's background. Section 3 shows how a representative verification tool for UML/OCL models currently handles verification tasks. In Sect. 4, the central idea of this work, namely the formulation of structural verification tasks within UML/OCL is introduced and illustrated. Section 5 concentrates on behavioral verification tasks from the developer's point of view and discusses advantages of our proposal. Finally, related work is discussed in Sect. 6 before the paper is concluded in Sect. 7.

2   Preliminaries and Background

Modeling languages such as the UML have been established to specify the design of complex systems. They provide a broad variety of different concepts such as class diagrams, sequence diagrams, or activity diagrams which are expressive enough to formally specify a complex system – especially together with textual constraints, e.g., in terms of OCL. These formal descriptions additionally allow for the verification of the respective specification already in the absence of a specific implementation, i.e., in an early stage of the design where flaws can be eliminated at relatively low costs.

The corresponding verification tasks can be divided into *Structural Verification Tasks*, where single states of the system are considered, as well as *Behavioral Verification Tasks*, where sequences of system states together with the connecting transitions (e.g., described in terms of state charts or operations with pre- and postconditions) are considered, see e.g., [16] for an overview.

A very common structural verification task is to check the *consistency* of a model, i.e., investigating whether the model description is consistent in the sense that an instantiation of the model exists which satisfies all of the model constraints. For behavioral verification, a typical task is to consider the *reachability* of certain good or bad states from a given initial state. As these two are very popular verification tasks, they will be considered as stereotypes in the remainder of the paper to illustrate existing approaches and the proposed concepts. Other verification tasks include, for instance, to check whether (1) the model satisfies certain properties such that corresponding constraints hold for any instantiation of the model, or to check whether (2) the invariants are independent or possibly imply each other (e.g., in order to find a minimal set of invariants or constraints) [13]. Typically either solely structural or solely behavioral aspects are considered, though there are a few works that consider the model structure and behavior at once (e.g., by considering operation contracts in combination with invariants) [15].

For both categories of verification tasks, a variety of automatic solving approaches have been introduced. The main idea of most of these approaches is to encode verification problems in a language that can be passed to a dedicated solving engine and transfer the results (more or less) back to the level of UML and OCL. In this context, different languages and solving engines have been proposed such as approaches (a) using *theorem provers* like Isabelle [8], (b) reformulating the problem as a *Constraint Satisfaction Problem* (CSP) [9], (c) using *Petri nets* [10], (d) addressing *model checkers* [18], (e) using intermediate languages like *Alloy* or *Kodkod* [1,28] though finally resulting in a *SAT* problem, or (f) using a direct encoding in the more general language of *SMT* [26,27].

All these approaches have their very own characteristics and need a high amount of expert knowledge and specific experience in order to be used which cannot be expected from a common developer. And, many approaches often support a single or a small set of verification tasks only, such that a developer would need to familiarize with many of these approaches in order to conduct a reasonable variety of verification tasks. This problem will be illustrated in more detail in Sect. 3 where we will show how two popular verification tasks (consistency and reachability) are formulated in one of these approaches.

In order to show examples for verification tasks and also to illustrate the proposed new concepts, we will make use of a running example as depicted in Fig. 1. The model describes a `CivilStatusWorld` with persons having a gender and a civil status attribute and marriages between persons determined by a reflexive association. Operations for marrying and divorcing are provided as well as a query operation `spouse` determining a (possible) set of persons. Under the assumption that the model is bigamy-free, this operation returns a singleton set.

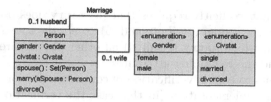

Fig. 1. Example class diagram.

OCL invariants and operation contracts in form of OCL pre- and postconditions as shown in Fig. 2 further restrict the structural and behavioral aspects of the model. More precisely, the query operation spouse is defined in a defensive way as a set-valued operation because the class diagram allows a person to have both a wife and a husband. The aim of the model is to have the empty set or a singleton set as the result for spouse, if all multiplicities and the invariant hold. The invariant establishes a connection between the gender attribute and the marriage role names as well as a connection between the civstat attribute and the spouse operation. We only show the contract for the operation marry, because the divorce contract is formulated analogously. marry has one precondition and a first ordinary postcondition. The second marry postcondition is a

```
spouse():Set(Person)=
  if wife->notEmpty and husband->notEmpty then
    Set{wife,husband} else
  if wife->notEmpty then
    Set{wife} else
  if husband->notEmpty then
    Set{husband}
  else
    Set{}
  endif endif endif

context Person inv traditionalRoles:
  ( gender=#female implies wife->isEmpty ) and
  ( gender=#male implies husband->isEmpty ) and
  ( spouse()->notEmpty = (civstat=#married) )

context Person::marry(aSpouse:Person)
pre unmarriedDifferentGenders:
  self.spouse()->isEmpty and aSpouse.spouse()->isEmpty and
  Set{self.gender,aSpouse.gender}=Set{#female,#male}
post married:
  Set{aSpouse}=self.spouse() and Set{self}=aSpouse.spouse() and
  self.civstat=#married and aSpouse.civstat=#married

post personUnchangedExceptSet:
  let x=self.spouse()->including(self) in
  Person.allInstances@pre=Person.allInstances and
  Person.allInstances->forAll(p|
    (p.gender@pre=p.gender) and
    (x->excludes(p) implies p.civstat@pre=p.civstat) and
    (x->excludes(p) implies p.wife@pre=p.wife) and
    (x->excludes(p) implies p.husband@pre=p.husband))
```

Fig. 2. OCL query operation, invariant, and operation contract.

frame condition that explicitly requires that (a) `marry` does not introduce new objects nor change the gender attribute and (b) except the `spouse` set and except the self object (on which `marry` is called) all other objects are left unchanged w.r.t. the roles and the remaining attributes.

When one wants to enable verification of contract behavior, one must either have an operation implementation (in that case the verification results are relative to the given implementation) or one must say in a declarative, complete way what the effect of an operation is, in particular, which things (attributes or roles from the class diagram) are changed by the operation and which things are left unchanged. In the example, the two postconditions serve this purpose.

3 Manifesting Consistency and Reachability in Tools

We now explain three typical verification tasks for the running example and show how they are realized in one UML and OCL tool. The discussion underpins our claim that specific knowledge and expertise is needed for successfully verifying properties in UML and OCL models. The three verification tasks are as follows.

1. Assume a system state is given with (a) objects possessing partially specified attribute values, (b) one female person participating in a marriage (where the roles wife and husband are left unspecified) and (c) another present male person. The first verification task now asks whether the system state can be completed to a full object diagram. If successful, this would prove consistency of the structural model, i.e., satisfiability of the class diagram including the multiplicities and the invariants.
2. The second verification task asks whether it is possible to construct a system state with a marriage link where both participating persons have the same gender that is however not a priori fixed. If this is not possible, then the fact that in a marriage the participating persons must have different genders is a consequence of the model.
3. The third verification task checks whether it is possible to find a sequence of operation calls that leads from four single persons to four married persons. In case all operations, i.e., both marry and divorce, show up, this would show the satisfiability of the invariants considered together with the operation contracts. It would guarantee the satisfiability of the structural model (class diagram with multiplicities and invariants) considered together with the behavioral model (operation contracts).

We classify tasks (1) and (2) as consistency problems (because they aim at constructing one consistent system state) and task (3) as a property reachability problem (because a particular property must be reached when starting in a given initial situation). A general classification of verification tasks was proposed recently in [16].

USE (Uml-based Specification Environment) is a modeling tool for a subset of UML and for full OCL [11,12]. USE offers options to validate and verify UML and OCL models, in particular by employing a component called model validator that is able to automatically construct object diagrams for UML class diagrams enriched by OCL invariants [12].

The first verification task is realized in USE by expressing the verbally expressed requirements as an additional OCL constraint and by employing the USE model validator. In general, the model validator considers a UML and OCL model with invariants together with a so-called configuration providing bounds for the possible object diagrams that are to be constructed (configuration examples can be found in [12]). The configuration bounds determine finite populations of classes, associations, datatypes and attribute values. The model validator then tries to construct an object diagram satisfying the class diagram and the invariants under the stated bounds. In this case, the additional constraint requires three persons to exist with particular attribute values and particular association participation conditions as stated below.

```
context Person inv VerificationTask1:
Person.allInstances->exists(A,B,C |
  Set{A,B,C}->size=3 and
  A.gender=#female and
  ( (A.husband=B and B.wife=A) or (B.husband=A and A.wife=B) ) and
  C.gender=#male)
```

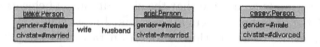

Fig. 3. USE Solution for first verification task.

As shown in Fig. 3, the model validator is successful in finding a fitting object diagram. Thus the first verification task is mastered, and the consistency of the model has been proven.

For the second validation task another OCL invariant is loaded in addition to the present model invariant. The invariant is stated below. In particular, this invariant requires a marriage between two persons which possess the same gender attribute value.

```
context Person inv VerificationTask2:
Person.allInstances->exists(P1,P2 |
  Set{P1,P2}->size=2 and
  (P1.wife=P2 or P1.husband=P2) and
  P1.gender=P2.gender )
```

In this case, the model validator reports that the model is unsatisfiable, i.e., no valid object diagram can be found. From this fact we conclude that the additional requirement involving two persons with the same gender in a marriage cannot be satisfied, and that thus the gender attributes values in a marriage must be different.

For the third verification task, the stated USE model is first transformed into a so-called filmstrip model [14]. In the filmstrip model, additional classes and associations are introduced that serve for representing a sequence of object

238   M. Gogolla et al.

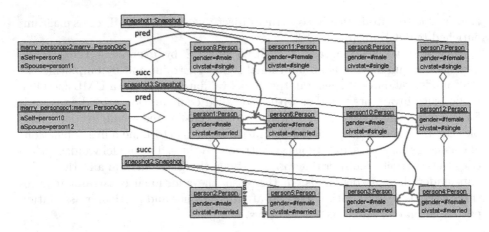

Fig. 4. USE Solution for third verification task (4 persons single to married).

diagrams from the originally stated model within a single object diagram; the original sequence of object diagrams becomes a sequence of (so-called) snapshot objects with operation call objects connecting them, as shown in Fig. 4. Additional OCL constraints guarantee that the filmstrip model behaves properly, for example, that the snapshot objects are not linked in a cyclic way.

The requirements from the third verification task that initially all persons are single and all persons are finally married are expressed as OCL invariants on the filmstrip model as stated below. The subexpressions involving **any** select the first, resp. last snapshot. The configuration for this verification task allows up to four operation calls, either marry or divorce calls, and the four person demand is reflected by appropriate settings for the number of objects in class **Person** (and could be restricted even more by another invariant).

```
context Person inv allInitiallySingle:
  Snapshot.allInstances->any(s | s.pred()=null).person->
    forAll(p | p.civstat=#single)
```

```
context Person inv allFinallyMarried:
  Snapshot.allInstances->any(s | s.succ()=null).person->
    forAll(p | p.civstat=#married)
```

The solution for this verification task is shown in Fig. 4. This filmstrip object diagram with two operation call objects and three snapshot objects corresponds to a sequence diagram in the original (application) model with two operation calls dealing implicitly with three object diagrams: one object diagram before the first call, one between the two calls, and one after the second call. These three (implicit) object diagrams are made explicit in Fig. 4 through the three snapshot objects.

4   Viewing Verification Tasks as UML Diagrams

This section is devoted to the explanation how verification tasks can be developed and represented in a way that is independent from an underlying proving engine.

As good UML "citizens", we believe that UML can be employed for a lot of tasks within the software development process. The main idea of UML is to represent issues and artifacts independent of a needed underlying (proving) engine. The idea that we want to contribute is to allow non-verification experts to phrase requirements and formal properties with UML, the language they use anyway to express their models. Even verification experts may find this attractive.

We will go through the verification tasks and present UML diagrams for them. The first task about UML and OCL model consistency can be graphically shown as the object diagram in Fig. 5. The elements from the verbal explanation are translated into respective UML features, basically objects, links possessing role names and association names as well as attribute values. In some spots, concrete values (as e.g., #female) or concrete items from the class diagram (as e.g., Person or Marriage) are shown. Now, the idea, that we come up with, is not only to allow concrete items in a UML diagram, but to indicate some "open", not yet fixed items that represent placeholders that are to be filled by an underlying engine. Such a UML diagram with placeholders may be seen as a UML query (stealing ideas from QBE [30]) or a verification task expressed in UML. In order to distinguish between concrete items and placeholders, placeholders are syntactically marked with a starting question mark. In principle, every spot in a UML diagram, where some concrete item may be written down, may also be filled with a placeholder. In the example we have used placeholders for attribute values and role names.

The task for the underlying proving engine is now to show substitutions or answers for the placeholders with suitable concrete items. The developer will typically have a particular expectation for the possible answers. In the example, this could be that ?RA can only be substituted with the role wife, whereas ?CC could be replaced by one of #single or #divorced or even #married if it is allowed to add Person objects and Marriage links.

The second verification task can be graphically presented with the object diagram in Fig. 6. Here, the placeholder ?G is used in two different spots, for the gender attribute value of persons P1 and P2 which are required to be connected by a marriage link. This expresses that the two persons in the marriage possess the same gender.

A:Person			B:Person		C:Person
	?RA	?RB			
gender=#female		Marriage	gender=?GB		gender=#male
civstat=?CA			civstat=?CB		civstat=?CC

Fig. 5. First verification task as UML diagram.

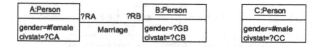

P1:Person			P2:Person
	?R1	?R2	
gender=?G		Marriage	gender=?G
civstat=?C1			civstat=?C2

Fig. 6. Second verification task as UML diagram.

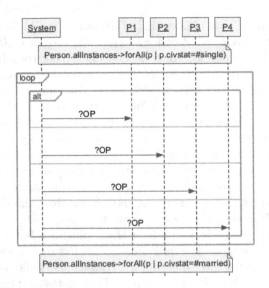

Fig. 7. Third verification task as UML diagram.

The third verification task is represented as a sequence diagram in Fig. 7. Four lifelines represent objects, two OCL constraints express an initial and a final condition and placeholders are used for operation calls. The standard UML sequence diagram features loop and alt (for alternative) are used to formulate that an operation call can go to one of the four objects and that a sequence of such calls is allowed.

In Fig. 8 we show a sequence diagram with a solution for the third task. This solution corresponds to the USE filmstrip object diagram from Fig. 4. Thus in general, it is desirable to see a found solution not only on the level of the employed technology, but it is necessary to transform a found solution onto the level on which the verification task was formulated. In the concrete case, the transformation process from the filmstrip object diagram to the sequence diagram can be automated. The solution for task 1 was already shown as a

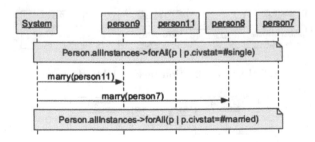

Fig. 8. Solution for third task viewed as UML sequence diagram.

UML object diagram in Fig. 3, whereas for task 2 no UML diagram was shown, because that task was not satisfiable.

Let us shortly wrap up and look back at the verification task formulation in UML and the proposed use of placeholders. The above examples employ the following UML diagram and OCL features for task formulation: in the object diagram we had objects, associations, roles, attribute values, and OCL formulas; in the sequence diagram we saw lifelines for objects, operation calls, alternative calls, calls within a loop, and on lifelines closed OCL formulas (or on a lifeline there could be a partial or complete object diagram as well). These language features have a precise meaning for task formulation. The proposed verification tasks can be transformed into prover-specific approaches. For our three example verification tasks, a precise meaning is given by the added OCL constraints before starting the verification process. These constraints can be retrieved from the graphical verification task representation automatically. As said already, in principle, we do not see any reason to restrict UML language features for task formulation as long as a precise task is determined.

Essential for our proposal is the use and role of placeholders and the kind of UML diagram features that placeholders can stand for. Currently we have had in the examples placeholders for the following features: attribute values, roles in associations, association names (not in the running example, as there is only one association in the example class diagram), operation calls and implicit or explicit operation parameters. The intention of placeholders is that they will be replaced by the underlying analysis or proving engine with concrete UML "items". These UML items either may come from the model (e.g., the class diagram) or may be explicitly provided by the developer as currently stated in a USE configuration.

5   A Developer's View on Verification Tasks

So far, we have demonstrated the basic idea of prover-independent verification tasks and sketched how they can be represented with diagrams. We now want to focus on the simplifications for developers in regards to the knowledge required to express verification tasks that can be used in any verification tool. With the tasks being tool-independent, the developer is not required to have any specific further knowledge about the tools. Even complex behavioral verification tasks can be formulated with mostly intuitive UML and OCL language features alone.

In order to illustrate the simplifications for developers, we consider the model of a traffic light which is depicted in Fig. 9. As we will see in the following, the model exhibits significantly more interesting behavioral aspects than the CivilStatusWorld model considered above.

The main component of the traffic light is the Controller which is connected to exactly one (visual) signal for cars and exactly one visual and acoustic signal each for the pedestrians. Two buttons are connected to the controller that can be pushed in order to indicate a pedestrian crossing request to the controller. When one button is pushed, all connected buttons indicate that there is a pending request. The invariant safety states a general safety property for traffic lights,

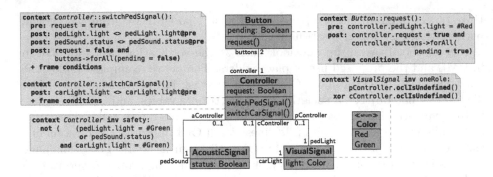

Fig. 9. Traffic light example

i.e., that both the signals for the pedestrians and the signal for the cars must not indicate a safe crossing at the same time. Finally, the invariant oneRole ensures that each visual signal can either serve as a signal for pedestrians or cars, but not both at the same time.

This model allows for instantiating various meaningful states that are vital for operating the system, but also several states that shall never be reached in practice. For instance, the standard idling state of the system in which a green light is shown to the cars while there is no pending request for a pedestrian crossing is shown on the top of Fig. 10. Below it, we can see a (partially defined) state where all visual signals are turned red while the acoustic signal indicates a safe crossing for pedestrians. Though this state is not violating any of the model's invariants, it shall never be entered in practice. Thus, it should just be unreachable by the definition of the operations. As it does not make a difference for the rejection of the state whether there is a pending request or not, unnamed placeholders are used to express that the values of the corresponding attributes are insignificant.

Now, the designer might be interested to find out whether certain states are reachable from the standard idling state. Using the proposed diagram-based approach, this task can be formulated very comfortably by (1) specifying the (partial) system states that shall serve as the start/target of the reachability analysis in terms of object diagrams and (2) employing them in a sequence diagram that allows arbitrary behavior in order to reach the target, i.e., a loop of arbitrary alternative operation calls on arbitrary objects. The corresponding diagram is shown in Fig. 11. Note that lifelines and objects for signals are not shown as no operations can be called on them.

While this formulation will fortunately yield UNSAT (proving that the erroneous state is not reachable within the number of steps that are specified as the upper limit of iterations of the loop), the designer might want to find out whether it is possible to reach a state that enables a safe crossing for pedestrians and, at the same time, allows for returning to the idling state afterwards. This task can be formulated by extending the existing diagram with another loop of arbitrary operation calls (for returning to the initial state) and an intermediate

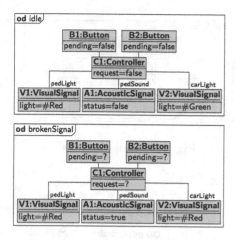

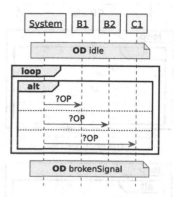

Fig. 10. (Partial) system states for the traffic light model.

Fig. 11. Simple reachability formulation

state (which expresses the safe crossing for pedestrians) as shown in Fig. 12. The corresponding partial object diagram for the intermediate state is shown in Fig. 13. Note that the state only requires the visual signal for the pedestrians to show a green light, while the assignment of all other attributes are left open.

While this formulation will unfortunately also yield UNSAT (proving that there is no possibility to reach a green light for pedestrians and return to the idle state afterwards), the designer may query whether the intermediate state is reachable at all. This can be formulated by simply replacing the target state – more precisely, its object diagram – in the first sequence diagram with this state. Then, the formulation will yield that the intermediate state is indeed reachable from the idle state (e.g., using the operation call sequence B1.request(), C1.switchCarSignal(), C1.switchPedSignal()), but interchanging start and target state will show that this is not true for the way back, i.e., the idle state is not reachable from the intermediate state. One reason for this could be, that the intermediate state – more precisely, all states for which the visual signal for the pedestrians shows a green light – are deadlocks. To verify this property, a formulation as in Fig. 14 can be employed which asks whether any operation can be called in a (partially) given system state at all. In this special case, the operations B1.request() and C1.switchPedSignal() may not be called, since their preconditions are not fulfilled. In addition, calling C1.switchCarSignal() would yield a situation where both the lights for pedestrians and cars are green, which violates the safety invariant. Consequently, the state characterization in Fig. 13 indeed describes a deadlock scenario. Note that, in contrast to the previous diagrams, there is no more loop in Fig. 14 and no restrictions are applied to the succeeding system state.

To summarize, this small case study shows that a wide spectrum of behavioral verification tasks can be formulated independently of a specific prover technology

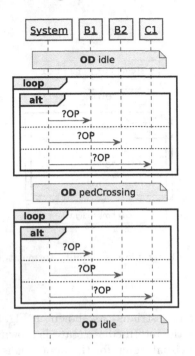

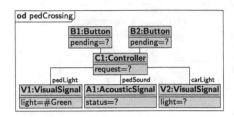

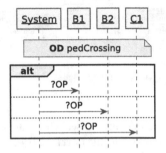

Fig. 13. Deadlock states

Fig. 12. Extended reachability formulation

Fig. 14. Deadlock check

in terms of a modeling language, here UML-like sequence diagrams with some additional, new features.

6   Related Work

There is related work sharing the aim of this paper to improve the usability of UML/OCL verification techniques. Concerning the question of building a user-friendly interface, much work has, e.g., been done in the theorem prover community (see e.g., [2,17,19,20]). There seems to be a high awareness in that community for the need to improve the usability of provers [6]. On the one hand, this is an implicit requirement as using theorem provers requires much interaction by the user. On the other hand, it is recognized that these provers focus on assisting particularly trained and skilled users, while they are difficult to use for non-expert users. Consequently, user-friendly interfaces play an important role in promoting the benefits of the underlying techniques [2].

However, these approaches do not aim at hiding details of the underlying verification technique, but only provide a "nicer", graphical interface. To this end, the potential of using UML diagrams to hide details and, thus, make verification easier accessible, has been recognized. UML diagrams have been used for various purposes so far: many verification approaches present solutions (witnesses found by the prover) back at the level of the model, e.g., in terms of UML diagrams. In contrast, in [23] UML sequence diagrams are used for visualizing patterns of temporal logic as part of a UML-based front-end to a formal verification/model checking toolset. More precisely, the sequence diagrams depict the desired behavior which the user can select from and combine in order to tailor dedicated verification tasks (formulas). In [21], it is suggested to combine UML diagrams and the B formalism in a design flow for hardware. However, the user can hardly specify particular properties to be verified.

The general and nice idea to employ placeholders in query languages is due to QBE [30]. A combination of model checking but having in mind a particular application for business processes is proposed in [3]. Placeholders, partly also with similar notation as here, have been used in the study of class model patterns and anti-patterns [5,7], in the consideration of general model quality [4] and in the context of domain-specific languages [22]. Recently, there has been a proposal for a "user-friendly" interface to Alloy which employs a similar idea to formulate verification tasks by modelling them graphically [29] focusing on structural verification. In [24,25] so-called partial models are put forward, a general framework being less tuned to specific verification tasks as we want to cover.

So far UML diagrams in combination with OCL expressions have not been used as a means for formulating dedicated structural and behavioral verification tasks.

7   Conclusion

This contribution proposed to formulate model verification tasks from the viewpoint of the employed modeling language. We aim to relieve the developer from expressing tasks only on the basis of the used approach and proving engine. Our proposal aims at giving non-verification experts the option to work with formal verification approaches. We have used UML object diagrams to formulate consistency issues and UML sequence diagrams for reachability topics. Central in our approach are so-called placeholders representing open items that can occur in UML diagrams and that should be substituted by model elements. Solutions in terms of substitutions and thus verification task feedback should be given in terms of the employed modeling languages as far as possible, e.g., as UML diagrams.

We have concentrated here on prover-independent task formulation. As one topic for future work we identify the open details for the transformation into prover- and approach-specific task formulation. The expressibility of the approach, i.e., the answer to the question which verification tasks can be formulated by UML diagrams, is bounded on the one hand by the employed verification task features, but on the other hand it is an open question how to enable the formulation of all possible verification tasks in general by the modeling language itself. Our proposal has to be consolidated and validated by an implementation of what has been sketched by the features that we used for task formulation. Other UML diagram kinds than object and sequence diagrams, in particular communication diagrams with communication channels and state machines for attribute, role or

OCL expression evolution have to be studied in more detail. Good explanations in the case of unsatisfiable tasks indicating the "guilty" model parts or at least identifying the "innocent" model parts have to be developed. Guilty model parts, i.e., the parts that essentially contribute to the invalidity could be any model element, e.g., classes, associations, invariants, contracts or even more detailed information, for example, subformulas of constraints. Last but not least, larger case studies should give feedback on the practicability of the proposal.

References

1. Anastasakis, K., Bordbar, B., Georg, G., Ray, I.: UML2Alloy: a challenging model transformation. In: Engels, G., Opdyke, B., Schmidt, D.C., Weil, F. (eds.) MODELS 2007. LNCS, vol. 4735, pp. 436–450. Springer, Heidelberg (2007). doi:10.1007/978-3-540-75209-7_30
2. Arshad, F., Mehmood, H., Raza, F., Hasan, O.: g-HOL: a graphical user interface for the HOL proof assistant. In: Artho, C., Ölveczky, P.C. (eds.) FTSCS 2015. CCIS, vol. 596, pp. 265–269. Springer, Cham (2016). doi:10.1007/978-3-319-29510-7_16
3. Awad, A., Sakr, S.: On efficient processing of BPMN-Q queries. Comput. Ind. **63**(9), 867–881 (2012)
4. Balaban, M., Maraee, A., Sturm, A., Jelnov, P.: A pattern-based approach for improving model quality. Softw. Syst. Model. **14**(4), 1527–1555 (2015)
5. Ballis, D., Baruzzo, A., Comini, M.: A minimalist visual notation for design patterns and antipatterns. In: 5th International Conference on Information Technology: New Generations (ITNG 2008), pp. 51–56 (2008)
6. Beckert, B., Grebing, S.: Evaluating the usability of interactive verification systems. In: Proceedings of 1st International Workshop Comparative Empirical Evaluation of Reasoning Systems, pp. 3–17 (2012)
7. Bottoni, P., Guerra, E., de Lara, J.: A language-independent and formal approach to pattern-based modelling with support for composition and analysis. Inf. Softw. Technol. **52**(8), 821–844 (2010)
8. Brucker, A.D., Wolff, B.: HOL-OCL: a formal proof environment for UML/OCL. In: Fiadeiro, J.L., Inverardi, P. (eds.) FASE 2008. LNCS, vol. 4961, pp. 97–100. Springer, Heidelberg (2008). doi:10.1007/978-3-540-78743-3_8
9. Cabot, J., Clarisó, R., Riera, D.: Verification of UML/OCL class diagrams using constraint programming. In: First International Conference on Software Testing Verification and Validation, ICST 2008, pp. 73–80. IEEE Computer Society (2008)
10. Choppy, C., Klai, K., Zidani, H.: Formal verification of UML state diagrams: a petri net based approach. Softw. Eng. Notes **36**(1), 1–8 (2011)
11. Gogolla, M., Büttner, F., Richters, M.: USE: a UML-based specification environment for validating UML and OCL. Sci. Comput. Program. **69**, 27–34 (2007)
12. Gogolla, M., Hilken, F.: Model validation and verification options in a contemporary UML and OCL analysis tool. In: Oberweis, A., Reussner, R. (eds.) Proceedings of Modellierung (MODELLIERUNG 2016). LNI, GI, vol. 254, pp. 203–218 (2016)
13. Gogolla, M., Kuhlmann, M., Hamann, L.: Consistency, independence and consequences in UML and OCL models. In: Dubois, C. (ed.) TAP 2009. LNCS, vol. 5668, pp. 90–104. Springer, Heidelberg (2009). doi:10.1007/978-3-642-02949-3_8

14. Hilken, F., Hamann, L., Gogolla, M.: Transformation of UML and OCL models into filmstrip models. In: Ruscio, D., Varró, D. (eds.) ICMT 2014. LNCS, vol. 8568, pp. 170–185. Springer, Cham (2014). doi:10.1007/978-3-319-08789-4_13

15. Hilken, F., Niemann, P., Gogolla, M., Wille, R.: Filmstripping and unrolling: a comparison of verification approaches for UML and OCL behavioral models. In: Seidl, M., Tillmann, N. (eds.) TAP 2014. LNCS, vol. 8570, pp. 99–116. Springer, Cham (2014). doi:10.1007/978-3-319-09099-3_8

16. Hilken, F., Niemann, P., Gogolla, M., Wille, R.: Towards a catalog of structural and behavioral verification tasks for UML/OCL models. In: Oberweis, A., Reussner, R. (eds.) Proceedings of Modellierung (MODELLIERUNG 2016). LNI, GI, vol. 254, pp. 115–122 (2016)

17. Homik, M., Meier, A.: Designing a GUI for proofs - evaluation of an HCI experiment. CoRR abs/0903.3926 (2009)

18. Lam, V.S.W.: A formalism for reasoning about UML activity diagrams. Nordic J. Comp. 14(1), 43–64 (2007)

19. Lapets, A., Kfoury, A.J.: A user-friendly interface for a lightweight verification system. Electr. Notes Theor. Comput. Sci. 285, 29–41 (2012)

20. Lüth, C.: User interfaces for theorem provers: necessary nuisance or unexplored potential? ECEASST 23 (2009). http://dblp.uni-trier.de/db/journals/eceasst/eceasst23.html

21. Moisuc, D., Revol, S., Snook, C.F.: UML user interface to a proof-based hardware design flow. In: Forum on Specification and Design Languages, FDL 2006, pp. 337–344. ECSI (2006)

22. Pescador, A., Garmendia, A., Guerra, E., Cuadrado, J.S., de Lara, J.: Pattern-based development of domain-specific modelling languages. In: 18th ACM/IEEE MoDELS 2015, pp. 166–175 (2015)

23. Remenska, D., Willemse, T.A.C., Templon, J., Verstoep, K., Bal, H.: Property specification made easy: harnessing the power of model checking in UML designs. In: Ábrahám, E., Palamidessi, C. (eds.) FORTE 2014. LNCS, vol. 8461, pp. 17–32. Springer, Heidelberg (2014). doi:10.1007/978-3-662-43613-4_2

24. Salay, R., Chechik, M.: A generalized formal framework for partial modeling. In: Egyed, A., Schaefer, I. (eds.) FASE 2015. LNCS, vol. 9033, pp. 133–148. Springer, Heidelberg (2015). doi:10.1007/978-3-662-46675-9_9

25. Salay, R., Chechik, M., Famelis, M., Gorzny, J.: A methodology for verifying refinements of partial models. J. Object Technol. 14(3), 3:1–3:31 (2015)

26. Soeken, M., Wille, R., Drechsler, R.: Verifying dynamic aspects of UML models. In: Design, Automation and Test in Europe, DATE 2011, pp. 1077–1082. IEEE (2011)

27. Soeken, M., Wille, R., Kuhlmann, M., Gogolla, M., Drechsler, R.: Verifying UML/OCL models using Boolean satisfiability. In: Design, Automation and Test in Europe, DATE 2010, pp. 1341–1344. IEEE (2010)

28. Straeten, R., Pinna Puissant, J., Mens, T.: Assessing the Kodkod model finder for resolving model inconsistencies. In: France, R.B., Kuester, J.M., Bordbar, B., Paige, R.F. (eds.) ECMFA 2011. LNCS, vol. 6698, pp. 69–84. Springer, Heidelberg (2011). doi:10.1007/978-3-642-21470-7_6

29. Wang, X., Rutle, A., Lamo, Y.: Towards user-friendly and efficient analysis with alloy. In: Model-Driven Engineering, Verification and Validation, MoDeVVa@MoDELS 2015, pp. 28–37 (2015)

30. Zloof, M.M.: QBE/OBE: a language for office and business automation. IEEE Comput. 14(5), 13–22 (1981)

Modeling and Formal Analysis of Probabilistic Complex Event Processing (CEP) Applications

Hichem Debbi$^{(\boxtimes)}$

Department of Computer Science,
Med BOUDIAF University–M'sila, M'sila, Algeria
hichem.debbi@univ-msila.dz

Abstract. Complex Event Processing (CEP) is a powerful technology used in complex and real-time environments. CEP is an Event Driven Architecture (EDA) style consists of processing different events within the distributed enterprise system attempting to discover interesting information from multiple streams of events in timely manner. In real world, the streams of events are uncertain, which means that is not guaranteed that an event has actually occurred, this uncertainty is due mainly to imprecise content from the event sources (Sensors, RFID,...). As a result, probabilistic CEP has become an important issue in complex environments that require a real-time reaction given streams of probabilistic events.

It is evident that building probabilistic CEP applications is not a trivial task, which makes the description of these applications and the analysis of their behavior a necessary task. In this paper, we propose a formal verification approach for probabilistic CEP applications based on probabilistic model checking. To this end, we use the probabilistic Timed Automata (PTA) for describing the probabilistic CEP applications, and the Probabilistic Timed CTL (PTCTL) logic for specifying probabilistic timed properties.

Keywords: Complex Event Processing (CEP) · Probabilistic CEP · Event Processing Network (EPN) · Probabilistic model checking · PRISM

1 Introduction

Complex Event Processing (CEP) is defined by its founder Luckham as a set of tools and techniques for analyzing and controlling the complex series of inter-related events that drive modern distributed information systems [1]. CEP is a style of Event Driven Architecture (EDA) that refers to generation, reaction, detection and consumption of events that represent notable changes in the state of enterprise's activities. CEP applications are based on decoupling principle, which means that the events are sent or received over publish/subscribe bus, where the events providers and events consumers are independent components.

© Springer International Publishing AG 2017
A. Anjorin and H. Espinoza (Eds.): ECMFA 2017, LNCS 10376, pp. 248–263, 2017.
DOI: 10.1007/978-3-319-61482-3_15

CEP is considered as a promising complementary technique for many existing techniques. CEP was proposed to support Business Process Management (BPM), where business processes are continuously reacting with simple or complex events, CEP can give the ability to discover patterns within the events cloud providing the business manager by interesting information [2]. CEP was also proposed as a support for Business Activity Monitoring (BAM) to take place in complex monitoring environments [3]. CEP can also support Business Intelligence (BI) tools to extract information from continuous events not just from historical data, thus enabling real-time intelligence [4]. It has been shown that CEP can play a crucial role in many domains such as sensor and RFID networks [5], and health care systems [6].

In real world the streams of events are uncertain, this uncertainty is due mainly to imprecise content from the event sources (Sensors, RFID,...). As a result, probabilistic CEP has become an important issue to deal with in complex and uncertain environments. There are two main challenges for implementing probabilistic CEP applications, the first concerns the huge number of events incoming from different sources that we should to deal with in real-time constraints, and the second concerns the assignment of probabilities measures to complex events aggregated from probabilistic basic events.

Probabilistic CEP has attracted recently a great attention. Chuanfei et al. [7] proposed an infrastructure for event detection and triggering with noisily input data from sensors and delivered a probabilistic inference system using Bayesian networks. Li and Ge [8] have studied the problem of windowed sub-sequences from probabilistic sequences of events, providing optimization algorithms that perform in real time. Mainly focusing on RFID networks, Re et al. [9] proposed a set of algorithms and probabilistic processing engine *Lahar* that acts on probabilistic RFID events. The authors in [10] proposed a model for representing materialized events with Bayesian and sampling algorithm for correctly specifying the probabilities of complex events from events history. Another interesting work that addressed many issues related to probabilistic CEP is presented in [11]. Based on probabilistic nondeterministic finite automaton and active instance stacks, they proposed a method for processing probabilistic events over distributed probabilistic event streams, enhanced with query plan optimization method to enable hierarchical complex event detection. In [12], Cugola et al. introduced *CEP2U*, an engine for CEP under uncertainty, which has been built based on TELSA language [13] and the T-Rex CEP engine [14]. *CEP2U* does not just consider uncertainty in basic events and how it propagates, but also it considered uncertainty in rules. The issue of uncertain data processing is not exclusive for CEP, but it has its origins in databases community [15].

The analysis of CEP applications using formal methods has been addressed before. Ericsson et al. [16] introduced an approach based on transforming CEP rules into timed automata to be verified using timed model checker UPPAAL, through a proposed tool REX. However, they did not describe in detail how to perform the verification process. A formal verification approach was also proposed among other approaches proposed by [17] for analyzing CEP applications.

They used Discreet Transition System (DTS) as a verification model and the Property Specification Language (PSL) sequences for specifying temporal properties.

In this paper, we propose a novel approach for analyzing probabilistic CEP applications based on probabilistic model checking. While analyzing CEP applications has been investigated before, and not really in depth, to our knowledge, this is the first attempt to analyze probabilistic CEP. Probabilistic model checking has appeared as an extension of model checking for modeling and analyzing systems that exhibit stochastic behavior. Several case studies in several domains have been addressed from randomized distributed algorithms and network protocols to biological systems and cloud computing environments. These systems are described usually using Discrete-Time Markov Chains (DTMC), Continuous-Time Markov Chains (CTMC), Probabilistic Timed Automata (PTA) or Markov Decision Processes (MDP), and verified against properties specified in Probabilistic Computation Tree Logic (PCTL) [18], Continuous Stochastic Logic (CSL) [19,20] or the extension of Timed CTL (TCTL) the probabilistic TCTL (PTCTL) [21].

The rest of this paper is organized as follows. In Sect. 2 we present some preliminaries and definitions, Probabilistic Timed Automata (PTA) and Probabilistic Timed Computation Tree Logic (PTCTL) are presented in this section. Section 3 introduces some basic definitions related to CEP. In Sect. 4, we introduce our approach for probabilistic CEP verification. Finally, conclusion and future works are presented.

2   Preliminaries and Definitions

2.1   Clocks and Zones

We denote by R the domain of time (non-negative reals), and by N the naturals. Let X be a set of finite variables called clocks which take values from R. We denote by $v(x)$ the clock valuation function that assigns a value $v \in R^X$, where R^x represents the set of all clock valuations of X. For any $v \in R^X$ and $t \in R$, $v + t$ denotes the clock valuation defined as $(v + t)(x) = v(x) + t$ for all $x \in X$.

The set of zones (clock constraints) of X, denoted $Z(X)$ is defined by the syntax

$$\zeta ::= x \leq d \mid c \leq x \mid x + c \leq y + d \mid \neg \zeta \mid \zeta \vee \zeta$$

where $x, y \in X$ and $c, d \in N$. We say that a clock valuation v satisfies a zone ζ, denoted $v \triangleright \zeta$ if and only if ζ resolves to true after substituting each clock x with $v(x)$. Other constraints can be easily derived, for example, $x > 1 \equiv \neg(x \leq 2)$ and equality can be written as a conjuction of constraints,for example $x = 2 \equiv (x \geq 2 \wedge x \leq 3)$.

2.2   Probabilistic Timed Automata

While the formalism of Clocks and Zones is the same for classical timed automata, PTA are extended with discrete probability distributions over edges.

A probabilistic timed automaton is a tuple $(L, l_0, X, inv, prob)$ where: L is a finite set of locations with l_0 is the initial location. X is a finite set of clocks. $inv : L \longrightarrow Z(x)$ maps to each location an invariant condition. $prob \subseteq S \times Z(X) \times Dis(L \times 2^x)$ is the probabilistic edge relation.

A state of PTA is a pair $(l, v) \in L \times R^X$ such that $\triangleright inv(l)$. An edge of PTA is (l, g, a, p, l', Y) where l' is the destination location and and Y is the set of clocks to be reset and (l, g, a, p) is a probabilistic edge of PTA where l is source location, g is a guard, a is an action and p is the destination distribution. In l_0 all clocks are initialized to zero. For any state (l, v), there is a non-deterministic choice between making a discrete transition and letting time pass, the transition is enabled if $v \triangleright g$ and probability to moving to destination location l' resulting in resetting the set Y of clocks equals to $p(l', Y)$. Letting the time passes in the current location l is provided by the invariant condition $inv(l)$, which is continuously satisfied while time elapses.

2.3   Probabilistic Timed CTL (PTCTL)

The Probabilistic Timed Computation Tree Logic (PTCTL) has appeared as an extension of CTL for the specification of probabilistic timed systems. We use the PTCTL for defining quantitative and timing properties of PTAs. Like TCTL, we use a set of clock variables for expressing timing properties, this set is denoted by Z disjoint from X, where $\xi : Z \to R$ is a formula clock valuation that assigns values to such clocks. TPCTL state formulas are formed according to the following grammar:

$$\phi ::= true|a|\zeta|z.\phi|\phi_1 \wedge \phi_2|\neg\phi|\mathbf{P}_{\sim p}(\varphi)$$

where $a \in AP$ is an atomic proposition, ζ is a zone over $X \cup Z$, $z.\phi$ is reset quantifier, φ is a path formula, $\mathbf{P}$ is a probability threshold operator, $\sim \in \{<, \leq, >, \geq\}$ is a comparison operator, and p is a probability threshold. The path formulas φ are formed according to the following grammar:

$$\varphi ::= \phi_1\mathbf{U}\phi_2|\phi_1\mathbf{W}\phi_2|\phi_1\mathbf{U}^{\leq n}\phi_2|\phi_1\mathbf{W}^{\leq n}\phi_2$$

where ϕ_1 and ϕ_2 are state formulas and $n \in N$. As in CTL, the temporal operators ($\mathbf{U}$ for strong until, $\mathbf{W}$ for weak (unless) until and their bounded variants) are required to be immediately preceded by the operator $\mathbf{P}$. The PTCTL formula is a state formula, where path formulas only occur inside the operator $\mathbf{P}$. The operator $\mathbf{P}$ can be seen as a quantification operator for both the operators $\forall$ (universal quantification) and $\exists$ (existential quantification), since the properties are representing quantitative requirements.

With TPCTL we can express properties such as, with a probability at least 0.98, the packet is eventually delivered within 5 time units, which is expressed using TPCTL as follows: $P_{\geq 0.98}[(true\mathbf{U}PacketDelivered \wedge (z = 5)]$.

2.4   PRISM Language

A model in PRISM consists of one or several modules that interact with each other. The module is specified using PRISM language as a set of guarded commands.

$[< action >] < guard > \longrightarrow < updates >$

Where the guard is a predicate over the variables of the system and the updates describe probabilistic transitions that the module can make if the guard is true. These updates are defined as follows:

$< prob >:< atomicupdate > +.....+ < prob >:< atomicupdate >$

PRISM also supports rewards which are real values associated with states or transitions of the model. Where state rewards can be specified as: $g : r$, and transition rewards are represented as: $[a]g : r$.

PTA is modeled in PRISM as an MDP [22]. The entire model is represented as a parallel composition of different modules and can be synchronized. PRISM defines the action *time* to label the transitions corresponding to time passing for each module. Thus, for time passing, all the modules will be synchronized on this action. The *time* transitions are defined in term of clocks, which are represented by bounded integer-valued variables. Suppose that we have an invariant $(x < 5)$ a location l, where x is a clock. The time elapse transition (duration 1) can be modeled as follows:

$[time]l = 1 \& x < 4 \longrightarrow (x' = min(x + 1, kx + 1))$

For the case of discrete transitions, they are enabled based on the value of the clock x. For instance, in the location l when the value of x becomes in the interval $4 \leq x \leq 6$, the enabling condition is satisfied, and discrete transitions are enabled. For the following guarded command, two transitions are enabled from location l by performing an action a, the first leads to a location $(l = 2)$ with probability 0.25, and the second leads to a location $(l = 3)$ with probability 0.75, and the clock x is reset.

$[a]l = 1 \& x >= 4 \& x <= 6 \longrightarrow 0.25 : (l' = 2) + 0.75 : (l' = 3) \& (x' = 0)$

3   Complex Event Processing (CEP)

Any CEP application regardless of the technique employed for processing events: query-based, rule-based, etc., can be described using the Event Processing Network (EPN) [1,23]. EPN is a conceptual model that enables us to build a CEP application in reliable way by describing the event execution flow, from sources passing by processing modules to destinations. We call the modules responsible for the processing, Event Processing Agents (EPAs). EPAs are simply a set of objects that monitor event execution to detect such patterns. For each pattern found there is a set of actions to be performed. The EPN we use for modeling CEP applications consists of four main components:

Event producer: the entity responsible for generating the stream of events
Event consumer: the final entity that consumes the outcome of EPAs
EPA: is the component that given set of input events, it generates output events to be consumed by applying such logic that must expresses time constraints (Fig. 1).

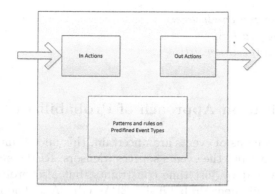

Fig. 1. An EPA

Event Type: represents the event object structure that consists of specified attributes, where the time-stamp is a present attribute in any event type.

The output of an EPA is either consumed by event consumer, or it feeds another EPA (Fig. 2). We notice that EPA is the central component in EPN, in way we can say that an EPN is a set of EPAs communicating between each other by exchanging events asynchronously. Roughly speaking, EPA employs such rules that consist of two parts: pattern called the trigger and a set of actions. By executing these rules, output events are generated. In CEP applications, EPAs nature varies according to the engine used (rule-based, query-based,..) [1]. For example, we can express an EPA as an Event Processing Language (EPL) query, the language used by ESPER [24] engine for processing events as follows:

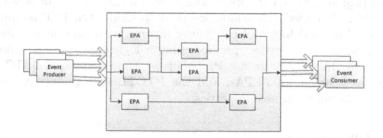

Fig. 2. An EPN

[insert into insert_into_def]
select select_list
from stream_def[as name] [, stream_def[as name] [,...]
[where search_conditions]
[within time_period_expression]
[group by grouping_expression_list]

[having grouping_search_conditions]
[output output_specification]
[order by order_by_expression_list]
[limit num_rows]

4   The Verification Approach of Probabilistic CEP

In real world the streams of events are uncertain, this uncertainty is due mainly to imprecise content from the events sources (Sensors, RFID, etc.). As a result, the EPAs will not employ just time constraints, but also probabilistic thresholds, and thus we call them Probabilistic EPAs (PEPAs). The major challenge for employing probabilities, is how PEPAs derive and output complex events aggregated from probabilistic basic events. Feeding the events from a PEPA to another is subjected to a probability threshold called the *confidence threshold*. Most of the approaches proposed for probabilistic CEP use the confidence threshold [11,12]. We present here an example of query language structure of a PEPA with confidence threshold [11].

[EVENT < eventpattern >]
[WHERE < qualification >]
[WITHIN < time_window >]
[GROUP BY < attribute_set >]
[HAVING < confidence_qualification >]

This paper does not consider the inference of the probabilistic complex events, but rather it reveals the way of analyzing probabilistic CEP application by focusing only on the confidence threshold despite the inference technique in use. The analysis of probabilistic CEP applications relies on the analysis of how PEPAs behave as it is intended. Therefore, we need to model the PEPAs and their interaction using modeling tool capable of dealing with time and probability and verified against properties specified using a logic that expresses time and probability. In this paper, we use Probabilistic Timed Automaton (PTA) for modeling the behavior of PEPAs, and the PTCTL as specification logic for specifying probabilistic timed properties.

4.1   Modeling Phase

In our approach we argue that probabilistic timed automaton is the best choice for verifying CEP applications under uncertainty. To this end, we have to show the correspondence between EPN that describes the event execution flow and PTA.

Using PTA, we model the PEPAs as locations where the initial location is represented by an PEPA that acts on events generated from event producers and the final location is represented by an PEPA that delivers final events to event consumers. We associate to each location an invariant that represents in CEP the time window defined by the PEPA for such type of events. Each out action from an PEPA is enabled with respect to a guard which is specified by the PEPA source itself, where each action leads to other PEPAs with new event types is subjected to such a probability threshold. That is, probabilistic edges from an PEPA source will lead to possible PEPAs with respect to the probabilistic output events types. By moving to new PEPAs, previous clocks could be reset.

We introduce below the formalization of PEPAs as PTA, and how we can model their behavior in PRISM language. For the seek of simplicity, we refer to the PTA representing the entire EPN as PTAofPCEP.

- **Locations:** Each location in PTAofPCEP represents a specific type of event. Moving from an PEPA to another is subjected to time constraint, which is represented by the clock valuation. As long as the clock does not reach the specified bound, the time is still elapsing in the current location. This time interval is usually called in CEP literature as *time window*.
- **Initial state:** The PTAofPCEP starts in the initial state, where all clocks are set to zero, and only the basic events types can be represented, no complex events can be expressed in the initial state.
- **Final state:** The final state in PTAofPCEP is the state in which there is no transition enabled. These states represent the final complex events to be delivered to the different destinations.
- **Transition Probability:** In the PTAofPCEP, every location with enabled action has exactly two transitions. The first leads to a new PEPA with a probability equals to the confidentiality threshold (CT), the second is a self transition with a probability $1 - CT$.
- **Non-deterministic Choice:** There is always a non-deterministic choice of either making a transition to another PEPA or letting time pass. In addition, moving from a PEPA to another is also based on non-deterministic choice. For instance, in case of moving from one PEPA to two other PEPAs, two actions should take place, each one with two enabled transitions as described before.
- **Parallel Composition:** In case of having different sources of events, we should not restrict ourself to one PTAofPCEP, but rather we can use a parallel composition of PTAofPCEP, where each PTAofPCEP refers to exactly one event source.
- **PRISM Language:** In PRISM, we will introduce the types of events as Boolean variables. A variable being true, means that the current PEPA represents this event. In the case of many variables being true, this means that the current PEPA represents a complex event that requires these events being true. In PRISM language, each PTAofPCEP is represented as a module, the parallel composition of these modules form the entire model.

4.2 Specification Phase

After modeling probabilistic CEP application as a PTAofPCEP or a parallel composition of PTAofPCEP, we can use TPCTL logic to specify temporal and probabilistic properties, to verify if the model meets the specification. The type of properties that can be specified for probabilistic CEP are not much different from the standard types defined by [21]. We present here the main types of probabilistic timed properties that can be used to specify probabilistic CEP applications as follows:

Reachability: The application can produce an output event with a given probability. For example, with probability 0.99 or greater, a deliver alert is received by a client.

$$P_{\geq 0.99}[true\mathbf{U}\,AllertDelivered]$$

Time bounded reachability: The application can produce an output event within a certain time deadline with a given probability. For example, with probability 0.975 or greater, an alert is received by a client within 5 time units.

$$P_{\geq 0.975}[true\mathbf{U}\,(AllertDelivered \wedge (z < 5))]$$

Invariance: Certain type of events are not produced with a given probability. For example, with probability 0.75 or greater, error event is never generated.

$P_{\geq 0.75}[true\mathbf{U}\neg error]$

We can also specify such properties using PTCTL for complex events. For example, eventC must not appear until eventA and eventB have already occurred with probability 0.9 or greater.

$P_{\geq 0.9}[\neg EventC\mathbf{U}\,EventA \wedge EventB]$

5   Case Study

In this section we will apply our approach to a case study. The case study concerns a system equipped with different RFID readers, sensors and radars for tracking vehicles and detecting overspeed and accidents, and delivering all interesting events in real-time. This case study has been shown as a good example for probabilistic CEP in [11], where it has been used to express different PEPAs.

5.1   Model

Suppose that we have three RFID readers, installed in three different locations (A, B and C), each reader reports two main types of events, Accident denoted X and Over-speed denoted O, together with the type of the vehicle detected (we consider here two types: *Car* and *Truck*). Thus, the CEP engine will have three events sources with respect to each RFID. These sources of events are often called input streams. After receiving these basic events, which are themselves uncertain, they will be passed to different PEPAs for inferring complex events. An example of complex event is an event composed of *overspeed (O)* and *accident (X)*. Below, we present a PRISM model for this probabilistic CEP system. PRISM supports mainly three types of models: DTMs, CTMSc and MDPs. PTAs are expressed in PRISM as MDPs [22]. MDP is a model that extends DTMC by allowing the non-deterministic choice.

```
1    mdp
2
3        //Time window
4        const int TimeWindow;
5        // Used in properties
6        const int T;
7        // probability Overspeed
8        const double OvSpeed;
9        const double NotOvSpeed = 1-OvSpeed;
10       // Probability Accident
11       const double Accident;
12       const double NotAccident = 1-Accident;
13       // Probability Car accident
14       const double CarAccident;
15       const double NotCarAccident = 1-CarAccident;
16       // Probability Truck Accident
17       const double TruckAccident;
18       const double NotTruckAccident = 1-TruckAccident;
```

Fig. 3. Global variables

```
1        module RfidA
2        // OverSpeed
3        Oa: [0..1];
4        // Accident
5        Xa: [0..1];
6        // Veihcle type : Car or Truck
7        CarTypeA: [0..1];
8        // clock up to time window
9        x : [0..TimeWindow];
10
11       [time] Oa=0 & x<TimeWindow -> (x'=min(x+1,TimeWindow+1));
12       [] Oa=0 & x=TimeWindow -> OvSpeed : (Oa'=1)+
13       NotOvSpeed : (Oa'=Oa) & (x'=0);
14       [] Oa=0 & Xa=0 & x =TimeWindow  -> Accident : (Xa'=1)+
15       NotAccident : (Oa'=Oa) & (Xa'=Xa) & (x'=0);
16
17       [time] Oa=1 & x<TimeWindow -> (x'=min(x+1,TimeWindow+1));
18       [] Oa=1 & Xa=0 & x =TimeWindow -> Accident : (Xa'=1)+
19       NotAccident : (Oa'=Oa) & (Xa'=Xa) & (x'=0);
20
21       [time] Xa=1 & x <TimeWindow -> (x'=min(x+1,TimeWindow+1));
22       [] Xa=1 & x =TimeWindow  -> CarAccident : (CarTypeA'=0) +
23       NotCarAccident : (Xa'=Xa) & (x'=0);
24
25       [time] Xa=1 & x <TimeWindow -> (x'=min(x+1,TimeWindow+1));
26       [] Xa=1 & x =TimeWindow -> TruckAccident : (CarTypeA'=1)+
27       NotTruckAccident: (Xa'=Xa) & (x'=0);
28       endmodule
```

Fig. 4. Module

Since our system consists of three different sources, our model will be represented as a parallel composition of three modules, each one refers exactly to one RFID reader. Each module consists of three main variables, which represent the types of events (O, X and $CarType$), in addition to the clock variable, which is responsible for estimating time elapsing that should not exceed the timewindow specified by the user, where timewindow is declared as a global variable. The other constants declared globally are the confidence probability thresholds defined by the user, these constants represent the probabilities of leaving a PEPA to another, while the value (1-Confidence threshold) represents the probability of remaining in the same PEPA, or in other words the probability of not leaving to the other PEPA, where new event type is emerged. Figure 3 shows the declared constants that should be defined by the user while building the model.

Figure 4 identifies the main module of this MDP model. We start by defining a module for RFID A. It starts by introducing the three local variables (Oa, Xa and $CarTypeA$) that represent the event types, as well as the clock x. The clock x is always reset when the time window elapses.

The commands in lines (11, 17, 21 and 25) represent the time window defined by each PEPA. For seek of simplicity, we consider that all the PEPAs define the same time window. The rest of commands define the probabilities of going from a PEPA to another. For instance, from received events, with confidence probability threshold $OvSpeed$, output event $overspeed$ will be generated. The same thing is applied to $Accident$ event. We modeled here the two possibilities, $accident$ with no overspeed (line 14) and the other complex event where there exist overspeed with $accident$ (line 18). The rest of commands represent the probability correspondent to the type of vehicle, when an $accident$ has already occurred. Here a confidence probability threshold must be identified for each type (Car or $Truck$).

Figure 5 represents the parallel composition of the module RfidA with the two others ($RfidB$ and $RfidC$). It's performed by renaming the local variables. Figure 6 shows the reward structure of the transition $time$ that represents time elapsing until time window is reached. It could be helpful for the analysis of expected reward or cost properties. Figure 7 represents some labels that will be used for specifying the probabilistic properties.

```
1    // Two other RIFDs (Parallel Composition)
2    module RfidB=RfidA[Oa=Ob,Xa=Xb,CarTypeA=CarTypeB,x=y]  endmodule
3    module RfidC=RfidA[Oa=Oc,Xa=Xc,CarTypeA=CarTypeC,x=z]  endmodule
```

Fig. 5. Module duplication

The model generated by PRISM consists of 2592 states and 12312 transitions. The entire model is resulted from the parallel composition of the modules, and thus each state is determined simply by the values of all the variables of the three modules.

```
1    //reward structures
2    // time
3    rewards "time"
4    [time] true : 1;
5    endrewards
```

Fig. 6. Time reward

```
1      // Labels
2      label "No_Accident" = Xa=0 & Xb=0 & Xc=0;
3      label "Accident" = Xa=1 | Xb=1| Xc=1;
4      label "OvSpeed_All" = Oa=1&Ob=1&Oc=1;
```

Fig. 7. Labels

5.2   Model Analysis

After building the model, we can specify different probabilistic properties. Since the model is represented as an MDP, we use *Pmin* and *Pmax* for estimating the minimum and the maximum probabilities respectively, over all the possible resolutions of non-determinism. PRISM not only offers the maximum and the minimum probabilities, but also the maximum and minimum reward for cost analysis. In addition, it offers simulation framework aiding the user to interpret the results, which we will use it for plotting the graphs of probability estimation based on time variable T. For the model to be built and verified against the probabilistic properties, we must define all the constants. The window in which these values are defined is shown in Fig. 8. We present the values that we should use for the model analysis. Different values would absolutely lead to different results. We cite below a set of different properties.

Please define the following constants:

Model Constants

Name	Type	Value
TimeWindow	int	5
T	int	5
OvSpeed	double	0.7
Accident	double	0.9
CarAccident	double	0.65
TruckAccident	double	0.85

Fig. 8. Defining constants by the user

We can estimate the probability of an event not occurring until some other events have already occurred. For instance, an *accident* does not happen at location C until an *overspeed* is detected at all the locations (A, B and C), which is defined by the label *OvSpeed_All*.

$Pmax =?[(!Xc = 1)\mathbf{U}(\text{``}OvSpeed\_All\text{''})]$

Prism renders the value 0.63 as a maximum probability. We can rewrite this property to be a property with lower threshold as follows:

$P <= 0.64[(!Xc = 1)\mathbf{U}(\text{"}OvSpeed\_All\text{"})]$

The interpretation of this property becomes: the probability of an *accident* at location C after an *overspeed* has been detected at all locations should not exceed the probability threshold 0.64.

Another property can be used to estimate the maximum probability of having an *overspeed* at all locations, but with no accident.

$Pmax =?[(true)\mathbf{U}(\text{"}OvSpeed\_All\text{"}\&\text{"}No\_Accident\text{"})]$

Prism renders the value 0.36 as a maximum probability. We can rewrite this property to be a reachability property with lower threshold as follows :

$P <= 0.37[(true)\mathbf{U}(\text{"}OvSpeed\_All\text{"}\&\text{"}No\_Accident\text{"})]$

We can also need properties with upper threshold. These invariance properties can be used to express that an event should not occur with such probability threshold. For instance, the probability of an event of *truck accident* is generated where actually no accident has been reported should be practically zero. However, we can express this property as a property with upper threshold as follows:

$P >= 0.999[trueU!(\text{"}No\_Accident\text{"}\&CarTypeA = 1)]$

Now, we are going to present some time bounded properties, which are based on the time variable T. For instance, we can use the following property to measure the probability of generating an event of *overspeed* with *accident* at location A during a period of time T.

$Pmax =?[F <= T(Oa = 1\&Xa = 1)]$

A graph plotting the probability estimated as a function of T is shown in Fig. 9. It shows that the probability of the complex event *overspeed* with *accident* at location A increases over time. Another graph is presented in Fig. 10 for the following property.

$Pmax =?[F <= T(\text{"}OvSpeed\_All\text{"}\&Xc = 1)]$

This property estimates the probability of generating the complex event that indicates that *overspeed* has been detected at all locations with *accident* at location C. By comparing the two graphs, we observe that the maximum probability of the first property is reached in shorter period of time than in the previous one. For instance, for the first property the probability reaches 0.9 at $T = 30$, while in the second property, it is reached at $T = 40$.

We can generate a graph for the property $Pmax =?[F <= T(\text{"}OvSpeed\_All\text{"}\&\text{"}No\_Accident\text{"})]$ (See Fig. 11). Here we see that the probability increases until it reaches its maximum value at $T = 20$.

Another interesting aspect of analysis provided by PRISM is the expected reward analysis. It might be useful for probabilistic CEP applications when we want to reason about the time reward for generating such event. For instance, the following property estimates the minimum reward of having overspeed in all locations, where the value rendered by PRISM is 10.083.

$R\text{"}time\text{"}min =?[F(\text{"}OvSpeed\_All\text{"})]$

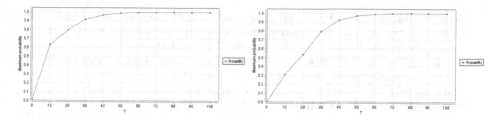

Fig. 9. Probability of overspeed with accident at location A

Fig. 10. Probability of overspeed all with accident at location C

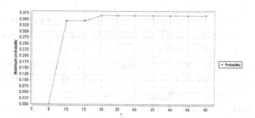

Fig. 11. Overspeed all with no accident

6 Conclusion

Probabilistic CEP applications have known a great success as a technological paradigm to deal with the high processing of events in real time under uncertainty. Therefore, delivering analysis techniques to ensure the correctness of these systems has become a great challenge. In this paper, we proposed a formal verification framework for probabilistic CEP based on probabilistic model checking. We showed how TPCTL logic can be useful for specifying timed probabilistic properties to analyze the behavior of PEPAs.

As a future work, we aim to investigate in depth manner the constraints that should be put on adopting the probabilistic timed automata (PTA) as a description model for probabilistic CEP, and we aim also to investigate the extension of TPCTL for specifying more special properties of probabilistic CEP. We aim also to deliver a tool that allows the description of EPN of PEAPs in graphical simple language, and then generates the corresponding PRISM model automatically.

References

1. Luckham, D.: The Power of Events: An Introduction to Complex Event Processing in Distributed Enterprise Systems. Addison-Wesley, Boston (2002)
2. Ammon, R., Emmersberger, C., Springer, F., Wolff, C.: Event-driven business process management and its practical application taking the example of DHL. In: The 1st International Workshop on Complex Event Processing for the Future Internet (iCEP), pp. 1–26 (2008)

3. Sen, S.: Business activity monitoring based on action-ready dashboards and response loop. In: The 1st International Workshop on Complex Event Processing for the Future Internet (iCEP), pp. 46–57. IEEE (2008)

4. Laha, A.: Rap: a conceptual business intelligence framework. In: Proceedings of the 1st Bangalore Annual Compute Conference (2008)

5. Zang, C., Fan, Y.: Complex event processing in enterprise information systems based on RFID. J. Enterp. Inf. Syst. 01(01), 3–23 (2007)

6. Yao, W., Chu, C., Li, Z.: Leveraging complex event processing for smart hospitals using RFID. J. Netw. Comput. Appl. 34(03), 799–810 (2011)

7. Chuanfei, X., Shukuan, L., Lei, W., Jianzhong, Q.: Complex event detection in probabilistic stream. In: 12th International Asia-Pacific Web Conference, pp. 361–363 (2010)

8. Li, Z., Ge, T.: Online windowed subsequence matching over probabilistic sequences. In: Proceedings of the 2012 ACM SIGMOD International Conference on Management of Data, pp. 277–288 (2012)

9. Re, C., Letchner, J., Balazinska, M., Suciu, D.: Event queries on correlated probabilistic streams. In: Proceedings of the 2008 ACM SIGMOD International Conference on Management of Data, pp. 715–728 (2008)

10. Wasserkrug, S., Gal, A., Etzion, O., Turchin, Y.: Complex event processing over uncertain data. In: Proceedings of the Second International Conference on Distributed Event-Based Systems, pp. 253–264 (2008)

11. Wang, Y., Cao, K., Zhang, X.: Complex event processing over distributed probabilistic event streams. Comput. Math. Appl. 66(10), 1808–1821 (2015)

12. Cugola, G., Margara, A., Matteucci, M., Tamburrelli, G.: Introducing uncertainty in complex event processing: model, implementation, and validation. Computing 97(02), 103–144 (2015)

13. Cugola, G., Margara, A.: TESLA: a formally defined event specification language. In: Proceedings of the Fourth International Conference on Distributed Event-Based Systems 2010, pp. 50–61 (2010)

14. Cugola, G., Margara, A.: Complex event processing with T-Rex. Comput. Math. Appl. 85(08), 1709–1728 (2012)

15. Dalvi, N., Suciu, D.: Efficient query evaluation on probabilistic databases. VLDB J. 16(04), 523–544 (2007)

16. Ericsson, A., Pettersson, P., Berndtsson, M., Seirio, M.: Seamless formal verification of complex event processing applications. In: Proceedings of the International Conference on Distributed Event Based Systems (DEBS), pp. 50–61 (2007)

17. Rabinovich, E., Etzion, O., Ruah, S.: Analyzing the behavior of event processing applications. In: Proceedings of the Fourth ACM International Conference on Distributed Event-Based Systems, pp. 223–234 (2010)

18. Hansson, H., Jonsson, B.: Logic for reasoning about time and reliability. Formal Aspects Comput. 6(05), 512–535 (1994)

19. Aziz, A., Sanwal, K., Singhal, V., Brayton, R.: Model-checking continuous-time markov chains. ACM Trans. Comput. Logic 1(1), 162–170 (2000)

20. Baier, C., Haverkort, B., Hermanns, H., Katoen, J.P.: Model checking algorithms for continuous-time markov chains. IEEE Trans. Softw. Eng. 29(07), 524–541 (2003)

21. Kwiatkowska, M., Norman, G., Segala, R., Sproston, J.: Automatic verification of real-time systems with discrete probability distributions. Theor. Comput. Sci. 282(01), 101–150 (2002)

22. Kwiatkowska, M., Norman, G., Parker, D., Sproston, J.: Performance analysis of probabilistic timed automata using digital clocks. Formal Methods Syst. Des. **29**, 33–78 (2006)
23. Etzion, O., Niblett, P.: Event Processing in Action. Manning, Greenwich (2010)
24. ESPER. http://www.espertech.com/

Experience Reports, Case Studics, and New Application Scenarios

Example-Driven Web API Specification Discovery

Hamza Ed-douibi[1]([⊠]) [iD], Javier Luis Cánovas Izquierdo[1] [iD],
and Jordi Cabot[1,2] [iD]

[1] UOC, Barcelona, Spain
{hed-douibi,jcanovasi}@uoc.edu
[2] ICREA, Barcelona, Spain
jordi.cabot@icrea.cat

Abstract. REpresentational State Transfer (REST) has become the dominant approach to design Web APIs nowadays, resulting in thousands of public REST Web APIs offering access to a variety of data sources (e.g., open-data initiatives) or advanced functionalities (e.g., geolocation services). Unfortunately, most of these APIs do not come with any specification that developers (and machines) can rely on to automatically understand and integrate them. Instead, most of the time we have to rely on reading its ad-hoc documentation web pages, despite the existence of languages like Swagger or, more recently, OpenAPI that developers could use to formally describe their APIs. In this paper we present an example-driven discovery process that generates model-based OpenAPI specifications for REST Web APIs by using API call examples. A tool implementing our approach and a community-driven repository for the discovered APIs are also presented.

Keywords: REST web APIs · Discovery process · OpenAPI · Repository

1 Introduction

Web APIs are becoming the backbone of Web, cloud, mobile applications and even many open data initiatives. For example, as of February 2017, PROGRAM-MABLEWEB lists more than 16,997 public APIs. REST is the predominant architectural style for building such Web APIs, which proposes to manipulate Web resources using a uniform set of *stateless operations* and relying only on simple URIs and HTTP verbs.

Despite their popularity, REST Web APIs do not typically come with any precise specification of the functionality or data they offer. Instead, REST "specifications" are typically simple informal textual descriptions [11] (i.e., documentation pages), which hampers their integration in third-party tools and services. Indeed, developers need to read documentation pages, manually write code to assemble the resource URIs and encode/decode the exchanged resource representations. This manual process is time-consuming and error-prone and affects not only the

© Springer International Publishing AG 2017
A. Anjorin and H. Espinoza (Eds.): ECMFA 2017, LNCS 10376, pp. 267–284, 2017.
DOI: 10.1007/978-3-319-61482-3_16

adoption of APIs but also its discovery so many web applications are missing good opportunities to extend their functionality with already available APIs.

Actually, languages to formalize APIs exist, but they are barely used in practice. Web Application Description Language (WADL) [6], a specification language for REST Web APIs was the first one to be proposed. However, it was deemed too tedious to use and alternatives like Swagger[1], API Blueprint[2] or RAML[3] quickly surfaced. Aiming at standardizing the way to specify REST Web APIs, several vendors (e.g., Google, IBM, SmartBear, or 3Scale) have recently announced the OpenAPI Initiative[4], a vendor neutral, portable and open specification for providing metadata (in JSON and YAML) for REST Web APIs.

This paper aims to improve this situation by helping both API builders and API users to interact with (and discover) each other by proposing an approach to automatically infer OpenAPI-compliant specifications for REST Web APIs, and, optionally, store them in a community-oriented directory. From the user's point of view, this facilitates the discovery and integration of existing APIs, favouring software reuse. For instance, API specifications can be used to generate SDKs for different frameworks (e.g., using APIMATIC[5]). From the API builder's point of view, this helps increase the exposure of the APIs without the need to learn and fully write the API specifications or alter the API code, thus allowing fast-prototyping of API specifications and leveraging on several existing toolsets featuring API documentation generation (e.g., using Swagger UI[6]) or API monitoring and testing (e.g., using Runscope[7]).

Our approach is an example-driven approach, meaning that the OpenAPI specification is derived from a set of examples showing its usage. The use of examples is a well-known technique in several areas such as Software Engineering [8,10] and Automatic Programming [5]. In our context, the examples are REST Web API calls expressed in terms of API requests and responses.

We follow a metamodeling approach [1] and create an intermediate model-based representation of the OpenAPI specifications before generating the final OpenAPI JSON Schema definition[8] for two main reasons: i) to leverage the plethora of modeling tools to generate, transform, analyze and validate our discovered specifications (as existing JSON schema tools are limited and may produce contradictory results [12]); and ii) to enable the integration of APIs into model-driven development processes (for code-generation, reverse engineering,..). For instance, we envision designers being able to include API calls in the definition of web-based applications using the Interaction Flow Modeling Language (IFML) [2].

---

[1] http://swagger.io/.

[2] https://apiblueprint.org/.

[3] http://raml.org/.

[4] https://openapis.org.

[5] https://apimatic.io/.

[6] http://swagger.io/swagger-ui/.

[7] https://www.runscope.com/.

[8] https://github.com/OAI/OpenAPI-Specification/blob/master/schemas/v2.0/schema.json.

The remainder of this paper is structured as follows. Section 2 show the running example used along the paper. Section 3 presents the overall approach and then Sects. 4, 5 and 6 describe the OpenAPI metamodel, the discovery process and the generation process, respectively. Section 7 describes the validation process and limitations of the approach. Section 8 presents the related work. Section 9 describes the tool support, and finally, Sect. 10 concludes the paper.

2 Running Example

This section introduces the running example used along the paper together with the main elements of a REST Web API. The example is based on the Pet-store API, a REST Web API for a pet store management system, released by the OpenAPI community as a reference. This API allows users to manage pets (e.g., add/find/delete pets), orders (e.g., place/delete orders), and users (e.g., create/delete users). Figure 1 shows an excerpt of this API specification, an API access request and a possible response document for that call request.

Figure 1a shows the request to retrieve the pet with the id 123 while Fig. 1b shows the returned response with that pet information. A request includes a method (e.g., GET), a URL (e.g., http://petstore.swagger.io/v2/pet/123) and optionally a message body (empty for this example). The URL in turn includes: (i) the transfer protocol, (ii) the host, (iii) the base path, (iv) the relative path and (v) the query (indicated by the first question mark "?", empty for this example). The relative path and the query are optional. A response includes a status code (e.g., 200) and optionally a JSON response message. Figure 1c shows an excerpt of the OpenAPI-compliant specification for this example call in JSON

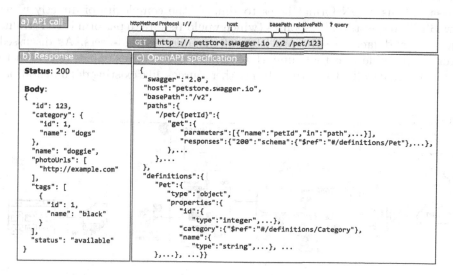

Fig. 1. API call example of the Petstore API: (a) the request, (b) the response, and (c) an excerpt of the corresponding OpenAPI specification.

format. This document includes fields to specify properties such as the host, the base path, the available paths (i.e., the field **paths**), the supported operations for each path (e.g., the field **get**), and the data types produced and consumed by the API (i.e., the field **definitions**). The specification indicates that the GET operation of the path **/pet/{petId}** allows retrieving a pet by his ID.

3   Approach

We define a two-step process to discover OpenAPI-compliant specifications from a set of REST Web API call examples. Figure 2 shows an overview of our approach.

The process takes as input a set of API call examples. For the sake of simplicity, we assume examples are provided beforehand and later in Sect. 9 we describe how we devised a solution to provide them both manually and relying on other sources. These examples are used to build an OpenAPI model (see Fig. 2a) in the first step of the process. Each example is analyzed with two discoverers, namely: (1) behavioral and (2) structural targeting the corresponding elements of the API definition. The output of these discoverers is merged and added incrementally to an OpenAPI model, conforming to the OpenAPI metamodel presented in the next section. The second step transforms these OpenAPI models to valid OpenAPI JSON documents (see Fig. 2b).

To represent the API call examples themselves, we rely on a JSON-based representation of the request/response details. Both, the request sent to the server and the received response message, are represented as JSON objects (i.e., **request** and **response** fields in left upper box of Fig. 2). The request object includes fields to set the method, the URL and the JSON message body; while the response object includes fields for the status code and the JSON response message. This JSON format helps to simplify the complexity of directly using raw HTTP requests and responses (which would require to perform HTTP traffic analysis) and facilitate the provision of examples by end-users. As discussed later, we provide also tool support to provide API call examples and even to (semi)automatically derive them from other sources, like existing documentation.

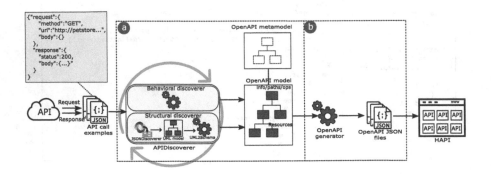

Fig. 2. Overview of the approach.

As a final step, the resulting OpenAPI-compliant specifications may optionally be added to HAPI, our community-driven hub for REST Web APIs, where developers can search and query them. In the following sections we describe our OpenAPI metamodel, the discoverers, and the OpenAPI generator. The example providers, APIs importers, and HAPI will be explained in Sect. 9.

4   The OpenAPI Metamodel

This section presents the OpenAPI metamodel to specify REST Web APIs. In a nutshell, a metamodel describes the set of valid models for a language, specifying how the different elements of the modeling language can be used and combined [1].

This model-based approach to define and store internally OpenAPIs facilitates the integration of our approach with model-based development methods and facilitates the manipulation of such OpenAPI specifications before the final generation of the corresponding JSON documents. Such features are not provided by the JSON Schema definition of OpenAPI[9], which is limited to be used to validate documents against the original specification; or existing implementations (e.g., the Java model for OpenAPI[10]), which generally consist of a set of *POJOs* to serve as parsing facilities.

The metamodel is derived from the concepts and properties described in the OpenAPI specification document. Next we explain the main parts of this metamodel, namely: (1) behavioral elements, (2) structural elements, and (3) serialization/deserialization elements. The metamodel also includes support for metadata (e.g., description or version) and security aspects. The complete metamodel, comprised of 29 different metaclasses, is available in our repository[11].

4.1   Behavioral Elements

Figure 3 shows the behavioral elements of the OpenAPI metamodel. A REST Web API is represented by the API element, which is the root element of our metamodel. This element includes attributes to specify the version of the API (swagger attribute), the host serving the API, the base path of the API, the supported transfer protocols of the API (schemes attribute) and the list of MIME types the API can consume/produce. It also includes references to the available paths, the data types used by the operations (definitions reference) and the possible responses of the API calls.

The Path element contains a relative path to an individual endpoint and the operations for the HTTP methods (e.g., get and put references). The description of an operation (Operation element) includes an identifier operationId, the MIME types the operation can consume/produce, and the supported transfer

---

[9] https://github.com/OAI/OpenAPI-Specification/blob/master/schemas/v2.0/schema.json.

[10] https://github.com/swagger-api/swagger-core.

[11] https://github.com/SOM-Research/APIDiscoverer/tree/master/metamodel.

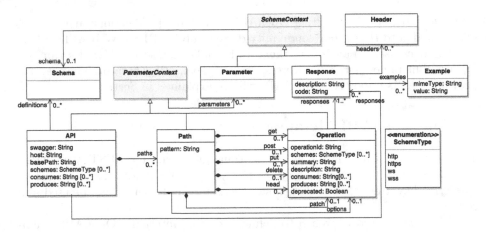

Fig. 3. Behavioral elements of the OpenAPI metamodel.

protocols for the operation (`schemes` attribute). An operation includes also the possible responses returned from executing the operation (`responses` reference).

API, `Path` and `Operation` elements inherit from `ParameterContext`, which allow them to define parameters at API level (applicable for all API operations), path level (applicable for all the operations under this path) or operation level (applicable only for this operation).

The `Response` element defines the possible responses of an operation and includes the HTTP response code, a description, the list of headers sent with the response, and optionally an example of the response message. `Response` and `Parameters` elements inherit from `SchemaContext` thus allowing them to add the definition of the response structure and the data type (`schema` reference) used for the parameter, respectively. `Parameter` and `Schema` elements will be explained in Sect. 4.2.

4.2   Structural Elements

Figure 4 describes the structural elements used in a REST Web API, namely: the `Schema` element, which describes the data types; the `Parameter` element, which defines an operation parameter; the `ItemsDefiniton` element, which describes the type of items in an array; and the `Header` element, which describes a header sent as part of a response. These elements use an adapted subset of the JSON Schema Specification defined in the super class `JSONSchemaSubset`[12].

A parameter includes a name, and two flags to specify whether either the parameter is required or empty.

The location of the parameter is defined by the `location` attribute. The possible locations are: (i) `path`, when it is part of the URL (e.g., `petId` in

---

[12] More information about the schema information can be found at http://json-schema. org/latest/json-schema-validation.html.

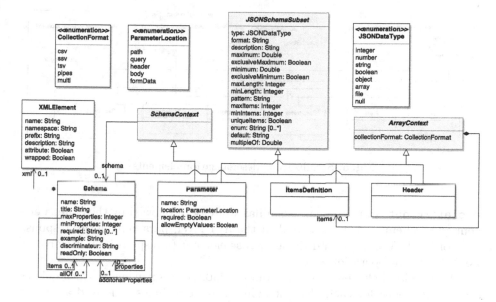

Fig. 4. Structural elements of the OpenAPI metamodel.

/pet/petId); (ii) query, when it is appended to the URL (e.g., status in /pet/findByStatus?status="sold"); (iii) header, for custom headers; (iv) body, when it is in the request payload; and (v) formData, for specific payloads[13].

Parameter and Header elements inherit from ArrayContext to allow them to specify the collection format and the items definition for attributes of type array. Additionally the Parameter element inherits from the SchemaContext to define the data structure when the attribute location is of type body (Schema reference).

The Schema element defines the data types that can be consumed and produced by operations. It includes a name, a title, and an example. Inheritance and polymorphism is specified by using the allOf reference and the discriminator attribute, respectively. Furthermore, when the schema is of type array, the items reference makes possible to specify the values of the array.

4.3   Serialization/Deserialization Support

Figure 5 shows the elements of the metamodel to support serialization and deserialization of OpenAPI models in JSON (or YAML) format. As said before, a parameter can be defined at the API level, path level, or operation level. To specify this, API, Path, and Operation elements inherit from the ParameterDeclaringContext element which is referenced in each parameter

---

[13] application/x-www-form-urlencoded or multipart/form-data.

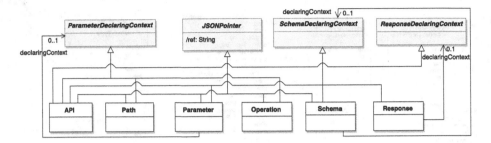

Fig. 5. Serialization/deserialization elements

(`declaringContext` reference). A similar strategy is followed by the `Schema` element (the schema can be declared in the API level, parameter level, response level, or inside a schema) and the `Response` element (a response can declared at the API level or operation level).

All behavioral elements inherit from the `JSONPointer` element which defines a JSON reference for each element. This element includes a derived attribute called `ref` which is dynamically calculated depending on its declaring context. This attribute specifies the path of the element within a JSON document following RCF 6901[14] which can be used to reference a JSON object within the JSON document.

5   The Discovery Process

The discovery process takes as input a set of API call examples and incrementally generates an OpenAPI model conforming to our OpenAPI metamodel using two types of discoverers: (1) behavioral and (2) structural. The former generates the behavioral elements of the model (e.g., paths, operations) while the latter focuses on the data types elements. In the following we explain the steps followed by these two discoverers.

5.1   Behavioral Discoverer

This discoverer analyzes the different elements of the API example calls (i.e., HTTP method, URL, request body, response status, response body) to discover the behavioral elements of the metamodel.

Table 1 shows the applied steps. *Target elements* column displays the created/updated elements in the OpenAPI model while *Source* column shows the elements of an API call example triggering those changes (see Fig. 1a and b). The *Action* column describes the applied action at each step and the *Notes* column displays notes for special cases. These steps are applied in order and repeated for each API call example. A new element is created only if such element does not exist

---

[14] https://tools.ietf.org/html/rfc6901.

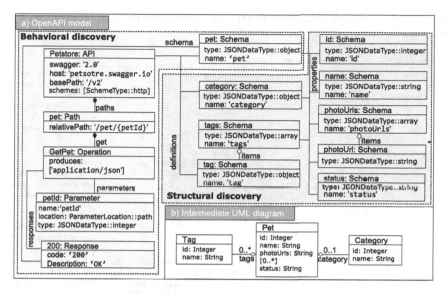

Fig. 6. The discovered OpenAPI model from the Petstore API example.

already in the OpenAPI model. Otherwise, the element is retrieved and enriched with the new discovered information. Note that the discovery of the schema structure will be assessed by the structural discoverer (see step 6).

Figure 6a shows the generated OpenAPI model for the API call example shown in Fig. 1. The discovery process is applied as follows. Step 1 creates an API element and set its attributes (i.e., `schemes` to *SchemeType::http*, `host` to *petstore.swagger.io*, and `basePath` to */v2*). Step 2 creates a `Path` element, sets its only attribute `realtivePath` to */pet/{petId}* (the string '*123*' was detected as identifier), and adds it to the `paths` references of the API element. Step 3 creates an `Operation` element, sets its `produces` attribute to *application/json*, and adds it to the `get` reference of the previously created `Path` element. Step 4 creates a `Parameter` element, sets its attributes (i.e., `name` to *petId*, `location` to *path*, and `type` to *JSONDataType::integer*), and adds it to the `parameters` reference of the previously created `Operation` element. Step 5 creates a `Response` element, sets its attributes (i.e., `code` to *200* and `description` to *OK*), and adds it to the `response` reference of the previously created `Operation` element. Finally step 6 creates a `Schema` element, sets only its name to `Pet`, and adds it to the `definitions` reference of the API element. The rest of the `Schema` element will be completed by the structural discoverer.

5.2 Structural Discoverer

This discoverer instantiates the part of the OpenAPI model related to data types and schema information. This process is started after the behavioral discovery when the API call includes a JSON object either in the request body or the

Table 1. Steps of the behavioral discoverer applied for each REST Web API call example.

STEP	Source	Target elements	ACTION	NOTES
1	$<host>$, $<basePath>$, $<protocol>$	a:API	-a.schemes= $protocol$ -a.host= $host$ -a.basePath= $basePath$	If the path contains many sections (e.g., /one/two/...) the base path is set to the first section (e.g., /one) otherwise it is set to "/".
2	$<relativePath>$	pt:Path	-Add pt to a.paths -pt.relativePath= $relativePath$.	If *relative path* contains an identifier, it is replaced with a variable in curly braces to use path parameters. A pattern-based approach is used to discover identifiers.[a]
3	$<httpMethod>$, $<RequestBody>$, $<ResponseBody>$	o:Operation	-pt.{httpMethod}= o -If *requestBody* is of type JSON then add "application/json" to o.consumes otherwise keep o.consumes empty. -If *responseBody* is of type JSON then add "application/json" to o.produces o.produces otherwise keep o.consumes empty	{*httpMethod*} is the reference of pt which corresponds to $<httpMethod>$ (e.g., *get* or *post*).
4	$<query>$, $<relativePath>$, $<requestBody>$	pr:Parameter	-Add pr to o.parameters -Set pr.type to the inferred type[b] -Set pr.location to: (i) path if parameter is in *relativePath* (ii) query if parameter is in *query* (iii) body if parameter is in *requestBody*	Apply this rule for all the detected parameters. The discovery of the schema of the body parameter is launched in step 6
5	$<ResponseCode>$	r:Response	-Add r to o.responses -r.code= *responseCode* -r.description= correspondent description of the response	The discovery of the schema of the response body is launched in step 6.
6	$<RequestBody>$, $<ResponseBody>$	s:Schema	-Add s to a.definitions. -Set the s.name= the last meaningful section of the path. -If the schema is in $<RequestBody>$, set pr.schema to s where pr is the body parameter created in step 4. -If the schema is in $<ResponseBody>$, set r.schema to s where r is the response created in step 5. -Launch the structural discoverer	We apply this rule only if *requestBody* or *responseBody* contains a JSON object.

[a] We apply an algorithm which detects if a string is a UID (e.g., hexadecimal strings, integer).
[b] When a conflict is detected (e.g., a parameter was inferred as integer and then as string), the most generic form is used (e.g., string).

response body that will be used to enrich the definition of the discovered Schema elements.

We devised a two-step process where we first obtain an intermediate UML-based representation from the JSON objects and then we perform a model-to-model transformation to instantiate the actual schema elements of the OpenAPI metamodel. This intermediate step allows us to benefit from JSONDiscoverer [4], which is the tool used to build a UML class diagram, and to use this

Table 2. Transformation rules from UML to Schema

SOURCE	TARGET: CREATE	TARGET: UPDATE	ATTRIBUTES INITIALIZATION
Class	c: Schema	- Add c to the api.definitions.	- c.type = Object - c.name = The corresponding class name
Attribute (1)	a: Schema	-Add a to c.properties where c is the correspondent schema of the class containing the attribute.	- a.type = the JSONDataType correspondent to the type of the attribute - a.name = the attribute name
Attribute (*)	a: Schema, i: Schema	-Add a to c.properties where c is the correspondent schema of the class containing the attribute	- a.type = array - a.items= i - i.type= the JSONDataType correspondent to the type of the attribute - i.name = the attribute name
Association (1)	-	-Add tc to c.properties where c is the correspondent schema of the source class of the association and tc the correspondent schema of the target class of the association	-
Association (*)	a: Schema	-Add a to sc.properties where sc is the correspondent schema of the source class of the association	- a.type = array - a.items= tc where tc is the correspondent schema of the target class of the association

UML-based representation to bridge easily to other model-based tools if needed. Then, classes, attributes, and associations of the UML class model are transformed to Schema elements. Table 2 shows the transformation rules applied to transform UML models to Schema elements. *Source* column shows the source elements in a UML model while *Target: create* and *Target: update* columns display the created/updated elements in the OpenAPI model. The *Attribute initialization* column describes the transformation rules.

Note that elements are updated/enriched when they already exist in the OpenAPI model. This particularly happens when different examples represent the same schema elements, as JSON schema allows having optional parts in the examples.

Figure 6b shows the UML class model discovered by JSONDiscoverer for the API response shown in Fig. 1b. This class model is transformed to actual schema elements applying the discovery process as follows. Tag, Pet, and Category classes are transformed to schema elements of type Object. Single-valued attributes (e.g., name, id) are transformed to Schema elements where type is set to the corresponding primitive type. The photoUrls multivalued attribute and tags multivalued association are transformed to Schema elements of type array having as items a Schema element of type String and Tag element, respectively. Finally, attributes and associations are added to the properties reference of the corresponding Schema element.

6   The Generation Process

The generator creates a OpenAPI-compliant JSON file from an OpenAPI model by means of a model-to-text transformation. The root object of the JSON file is the `API` model element, then each model element is transformed to a pair of name/value items where the type for the value is (1) a string for primitive attributes, (2) a JSON array for multivalued element or (3) a JSON object for references. Serialization/deserialization model elements are used to resolve references. As said in Sect. 4, elements such as `Schema`, `Parameter`, and `Response` can be declared in different locations and reused by other elements. While the `declaringContext` reference is used to define where to declare the object, the `ref` attribute (inherited form `JSONPointer` class) is used to reference this object from another element. By default the discovery process sets the declaring context to the containing class of the element (e.g., parameters in operations).

Figure 7 shows the generated JSON file for the OpenAPI model shown in Fig. 6a. Note that the declaring context of the `Pet` schema element is set to *API*, which resulted in listing the `Pet` element in the `definitions` object. Consequently, the attribute `ref` is set to `#/definitions/Pet` and will be used to reference `Pet` from any another element (as in the `response` object).

```
1  { "swagger":"2.0",
2      "info":{  },
3      "host":"petstore.swagger.io","basePath":"/v2",
4      "tags":[ "pet" ],"Schemes":[ "http" ],
5      "paths":{
6          "/pet/{petId}":{
7              "get":{
8                  "produces":["application/json"],
9                  "parameters":[{"name":"petId","in":"path","type":"integer"}],
10                 "responses":{
11                     "200":{
12                         "description":"OK",
13                         "schema":{"$ref":"#/definitions/Pet"
14                     }}}}
15     }},
16     "definitions":{
17         "Pet":{
18             "type":"object",
19             "properties":{
20                 "id":{"type":"integer"},
21                 "category":{"$ref":"#/definitions/Category"},
22                 "name":{"type":"string"},
23                 "photoUrls":{"type":"array","items":{"type":"string"}},
24                 "tags":{"type":"array","items":{"$ref":"#/definitions/Tag"}},
25                 "Status":{"type":"string"}},
26             }}}
```

Fig. 7. The generated OpenAPI specification of the Petstore API example.

7   Validation and Limitations

To ensure the quality of the OpenAPIs we generate, we have first enriched the OpenAPI metamodel with a set of well-formedness constraints written using the Object Constraint Language (OCL) [3] (e.g., to guarantee the uniqueness of the parameters in a call). These constraints are checked during the discovery process to validate the generated OpenAPI specification against the constraints published in the last official OpenAPI specification document. Note that this is in itself a useful contribution with regard to other syntax checkers for API documents that offer a limited support in terms of constraint checking.

Additionally, we have validated our approach by manually comparing the results of our generated OpenAPI with the original specification for a number of APIs providing already such information. This has been an iterative process but we would like to highlight the latest test, comprising the following five APIs: (1) Refuge Restrooms[15], a web application that seeks to provide safe restroom access for transgender; (2) OMDb[16], an API to obtain information about movies; (3) Graphhopper[17], a route optimization API to solve vehicle routing problems; (4) Passwordutility[18], an API to validate and generate passwords using open source tools; and finally (5) the Petstore API. Several factors influenced the choice of these APIs to serve for our testing purposes. Beside having an OpenAPI specification, these APIs did not involve fees or invoke services (e.g., SMS APIs), they managed JSON format (to test our structural discoverer) and were concise (to keep limited the number of examples required).

For the chosen APIs, our approach was able to generate on average 80% of the required specification elements and did not generate any incorrect result. Mainly, the missing information was due to the structure of the call examples which cannot cover advanced details such as: (i) the enumerations used for some parameters, (ii) the optionality or not of the parameters, (iii) form parameters, and (iv) the headers used in some operations. Furthermore, the quality of the results depend on the number and the variety of the API call examples used to discover the specification. Our experience so far shows that the number of examples should be higher than the number of operations of an API covering all the parameters. However, more experiments are required to identify the ideal balance between the quality of the result and the number of needed experiments.

Note that even if the result is not complete, it can still be useful. Even for APIs that do provide an OpenAPI as starting point. For instance, for Refuge Restrooms, we were able to discover both the operations and data model of the API even if the latter was not part of the original specification. The complete set of examples and generated APIs are available in our repository.

8   Related Work

Several tools supporting the OpenAPI initiative have recently appeared[19], e.g., able to generate documentation and code (e.g., client SDKs, server skeletons) from OpenAPI-compliant specifications making OpenAPIs a more valuable artefact. Third party companies like Lucybot[20] or ReDoc[21], provide similar

---

[15] http://www.refugerestrooms.org/api/docs/.
[16] http://www.omdbapi.com/.
[17] https://graphhopper.com/.
[18] http://passwordutility.net.
[19] http://swagger.io/tools/.
[20] https://lucybot.com/.
[21] http://rebilly.github.io/ReDoc/.

capabilities while others as Restlet Studio[22] and stoplight[23] add also the feature of helping developers manually design such APIs with visual tools. Our approach can join this tool ecosystem by inferring the OpenAPIs to be used as input for all these tools out of the box.

Regarding the discovery process itself, there is a limited number of related efforts and barely any targeting specifically REST or Web APIs in general. Some research efforts (i.e., [9,17]) focus on the analysis of service interaction logs to discoverer message correlation in business processes. Other works (i.e., [13,14,16]) are more proactive and try to suggest possible compositions based on a WSDL (or similar) description of the service. Nevertheless, they all focus on the interaction patterns and do not generate any description of Web APIs specification (or the initial WSDL document for previous approaches) themselves. SpyREST [18] is a closer work to ours. It proposes a Proxy server to analyze HTTP traffic involved in API calls to generate API documentation. Still, the generated documentation is intended to be read by humans and therefore does not adhere to any formal API specification language.

Other research efforts limit themselves to discover the data model underlying an API, specially by analysing the JSON documents it returns. For instance, the works in [7] and [15] analyze JSON documents in order to generate their (implicit) schemas. However, they are specially bounded to NoSQL databases and are not applicable for Web APIs. On the other hand, JSONDiscoverer [4] generates UML class diagrams from the JSON data returned after calling a Web API. We use this tool in our structural discoverer phase.

9   Tool Support

Figure 8 shows the underlying architecture of our discovery tool. Our tool includes a front-end, which allows users to collect and run API call examples (see *APIDiscoverer UI*) to trigger the launch of the core API discoverer process; and a back-end, which all the components to parse the calls and responses, generate the intermediate models, etc. Our tool has been implemented in Java and is available as an Open Source application[24].

More specifically, *APIDiscoverer* is a Java Web application that can be deployed in any Servlet container (e.g., Apache Tomcat). The application relies on JavaServer Faces (JSF), a server-side technology for developing Web applications, and Primefaces[25], a UI framework for JSF applications. Figure 9 shows a screenshot of the APIDiscoverer interface. The center panel of APIDiscoverer contains a form to provide API call examples either by sending requests or using our JSON-based representation format. The former requires providing the request and obtaining a response from the API. As result, a JSON-based API

---

[22] https://studio.restlet.com.
[23] http://stoplight.io/platform/design/.
[24] https://github.com/SOM-Research/APIDiscoverer.
[25] http://www.primefaces.org.

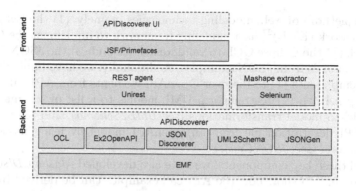

Fig. 8. Tool architecture.

call example is shown on the right. The latter only requires providing the JSON-based API call example. API call examples are then used by APIDiscoverer to obtain/enrich the corresponding OpenAPI model. The examples history is shown on the left panel and an intermediate OpenAPI model is shown on the right panel. The OpenAPI model is updated after each example with the new information discovered by the last request. Finally, a button in the top panel allows the user to download the final OpenAPI description file.

The main components of the back-end are (1) a REST agent and (2) the core APIDiscoverer. The REST agent relies on unirest[26], a REST library to send requests to APIs to build and collect API call examples. The APIDiscoverer

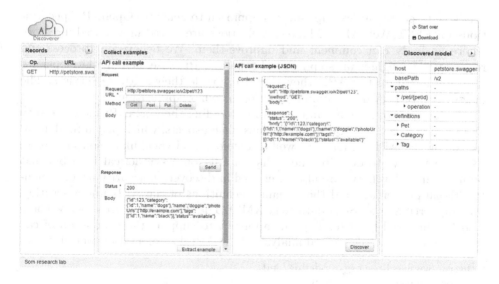

Fig. 9. Screenshot of the discoverer UI.

---

[26] http://unirest.io.

relies on a plethora of web/modeling technologies, namely, (1) the Eclipse Modeling Framework (EMF)[27] as a modeling framework to implement the OpenAPI metamodel, (2) the Eclipse OCL to validate models and (3) the JSONDiscoverer to discover models from JSON examples. Additionally, we have implemented the required components (1) to discover OpenAPI elements from API call examples (see *Ex2OpenAPI*), (2) to transform UML models to a list of schema elements using model-to-model transformations (see *UML2Schema*), and (3) to generate an OpenAPI description file from an OpenAPI model by using model-to-text transformations (see *JSONGen*).

Beyond these key components, we have also developed *MashapeDiscoverer*, a proof-of-concept to show how the API call examples can be derived from other sources like available examples in the API documentation (in this specific case, from APIs in the Mashape marketplace[28], a documentation portal with over 2,000 APIs) by using Selenium[29] to crawl the documentation pages and extract the relevant examples information (i.e., entrypoints, parameters, response examples).

Additionally, we have created HAPI[30], a public REST Web API directory and an open source community-driven project, which stores the discovered Web APIs. Besides allowing users to download the Web API specifications, this directory invites developers to contribute using the well-known pull-request model of GitHub. In order to enrich *HAPI*, we have also created two OpenAPI importers for APIs.GURU and APIs.IO that use their dedicated Web APIs[31]. This allows easily adding to HAPI APIs already with a predefined specification.

10   Conclusion

We have presented an example-driven approach to generate OpenAPI specifications for REST Web APIs. These specifications are stored in a shared directory where anybody can comment and improve them. We believe our process and repository is a significant step forward towards API reuse, helping developers to find and integrate the APIs they need to provide their software services. The discovery tool is available online as an open source application.

As further work, we are interested in extending the OpenAPI metamodel to add Quality of Service (QoS) and business plan aspects, which play a fundamental role in the API economy, as well as ontology and vocabulary concepts (e.g., FOAF ontology) to describe the APIs not only on a syntactical level but also on a semantic level. We are also interested in discovering security aspects, non-functional properties, and the semantic definitions of the APIs under scrutiny, and supporting non-JSON data (e.g. XML). The discovery process per se could also be improved by extending our approach to support the generation of call examples based on the textual analysis of the API documentation websites, this

---

[27] http://www.eclipse.org/modeling/emf/.
[28] https://market.mashape.com.
[29] http://docs.seleniumhq.org/projects/webdriver/.
[30] https://github.com/SOM-Research/hapi.
[31] https://apis.guru/api-doc/ and http://www.apis.io/apiDoc.

way speeding up the process of interacting with the API to infer its specification. Finally, we plan to systematically apply our process to a large number of APIs (linked from other directories or repositories) in order to expand HAPI.

Acknowledgment. This work has been supported by the Spanish government (TIN2016-75944-R project).

References

1. Brambilla, M., Cabot, J., Wimmer, M.: Model-Driven Software Engineering in Practice. Morgan & Claypool Publishers, San Rafael (2012)
2. Brambilla, M., Fraternali, P., et al.: The Interaction Flow Modeling Language (IFML). Technical report, Object Management Group (OMG) (2014)
3. Cabot, J., Gogolla, M.: Object constraint language (OCL): a definitive guide. In: Bernardo, M., Cortellessa, V., Pierantonio, A. (eds.) SFM 2012. LNCS, vol. 7320, pp. 58–90. Springer, Heidelberg (2012). doi:10.1007/978-3-642-30982-3_3
4. Cánovas Izquierdo, J.L., Cabot, J.: JSONDiscoverer: visualizing the schema lurking behind JSON documents. Knowl.-Based Syst. **103**, 52–55 (2016)
5. Frankle, J., Osera, P.M., Walker, D., Zdancewic, S.: Example-directed synthesis: a type-theoretic interpretation. In: ACM Symposium on Principles of Programming Languages, pp. 802–815 (2016)
6. Hadley, M.J.: Web Application Description Language (WADL). Technical report (2006)
7. Klettke, M., Störl, U., Scherzinger, S., Regensburg, O.: Schema extraction and structural outlier detection for JSON-based NoSQL data stores. In: Conference on Database Systems for Business, Technology, and Web, pp. 425–444 (2015)
8. López-Fernández, J.J., Cuadrado, J.S., Guerra, E., de Lara, J.: Example-driven meta-model development. Softw. Syst. Model. **14**(4), 1323–1347 (2015)
9. Motahari-Nezhad, H.R., Saint-Paul, R., Casati, F., Benatallah, B.: Event correlation for process discovery from web service interaction logs. Inter. J. Very Large Data Bases **20**(3), 417–444 (2011)
10. Nierstrasz, O., Kobel, M., Girba, T., Lanza, M.: Example-driven reconstruction of software models. In: European Conference on Software Maintenance and Reengineering, pp. 275–286 (2007)
11. Pautasso, C., Zimmermann, O., Leymann, F.: RESTful web services vs. "Big" web services. In: International Conference on World Wide Web, pp. 805–814 (2008)
12. Pezoa, F., Reutter, J.L., Suarez, F., Ugarte, M., Vrgoč, D.: Foundations of JSON schema. In: International Conference on World Wide Web, pp. 263–273 (2016)
13. Quarteroni, S., Brambilla, M., Ceri, S.: A bottom-up, knowledge-aware approach to integrating and querying web data services. ACM Trans. Web **7**(4), 19–33 (2013)
14. Rodriguez Mier, P., Pedrinaci, C., Lama, M., Mucientes, M.: An integrated semantic web service discovery and composition framework. IEEE Trans. Serv. Comput. **9**(4), 537–550 (2015)
15. Ruiz, D.S., Morales, S.F., Molina, J.G.: Inferring versioned schemas from NoSQL databases and its applications. In: International Conference on Conceptual Modeling, pp. 467–480 (2015)
16. Schmidt, C., Parashar, M.: A peer-to-peer approach to web service discovery. In: International Conference on World Wide Web, pp. 211–229 (2004)

17. Serrour, B., Gasparotto, D.P., Kheddouci, H., Benatallah, B.: Message correlation and business protocol discovery in service interaction logs. In: Bellahsène, Z., Léonard, M. (eds.) CAiSE 2008. LNCS, vol. 5074, pp. 405–419. Springer, Heidelberg (2008). doi:10.1007/978-3-540-69534-9_31
18. Sohan, S., Anslow, C., Maurer, F.: SpyREST: automated RESTful API documentation using an HTTP proxy server (N). In: International Conference on Automated Software Engineering, pp. 271–276 (2015)

Technology-Preserving Transition from Single-Core to Multi-core in Modelling Vehicular Systems

Alessio Bucaioni[1,2（✉)], Saad Mubeen[1,2], Federico Ciccozzi[1],
Antonio Cicchetti[1], and Mikael Sjödin[1]

[1] School of Innovation, Design and Engineering,
Mälardalen University, Västerås, Sweden
{alessio.bucaioni,saad.mubeen,federico.ciccozzi,
antonio.cicchetti,mikael.sjodin}@mdh.se
[2] Arcticus Systems AB, Järfälla, Sweden
{alessio.bucaioni,saad.mubeen}@arcticus-systems.com

Abstract. The vehicular industry has exploited model-based engineering for design, analysis, and development of single-core vehicular systems. Next generation of autonomous vehicles will require higher computational power, which can only be provided by parallel computing platforms such as multi-core electronic control units. Current model-based software development solutions and related modelling languages, originally conceived for single-core, cannot effectively deal with multi-core specific challenges, such as core-interdependency and allocation of software to hardware. In this paper, we propose an extension to the Rubus Component Model, central to the Rubus model-based approach, for the modelling, analysis, and development of vehicular systems on multi-core. Our goal is to provide a lightweight transition of a model-based software development approach from single-core to multi-core, without disrupting the current technological assets in the vehicular domain.

Keywords: Model-based engineering · Metamodelling · Multi-core · Vehicular domain · Embedded systems · Real-time systems

1 Introduction

Software is ubiquitous in our society. In automotive, vehicles have transitioned from being mechanics-intensive to software-intensive systems [12]. For instance, the throttle control system of a modern vehicle is realised by means of Electronic Control Units (ECUs), sensors, and actuators, connected by several networks, and run by software, which replace the mechanical linkage between the accelerator pedal and the throttle. The current trend in the vehicular domain is towards vehicles capable of autonomously driving. While most of the current vehicular systems still employ single-core ECUs, the tendency is to switch to ECUs

© Springer International Publishing AG 2017
A. Anjorin and H. Espinoza (Eds.): ECMFA 2017, LNCS 10376, pp. 285–299, 2017.
DOI: 10.1007/978-3-319-61482-3_17

equipped with multi-core microprocessors. In fact, next generation vehicles, particularly autonomous ones, are expected to require higher computational power, which can only be provided by multi-core solutions.

On the one hand, the shift to multi-core impacts the way vehicular software is designed, analysed and developed. Current model-based solutions, specifically tailored to single-core, are not as effective when dealing with multi-core specific challenges, such as core-interdependency and allocation of software to hardware. On the other hand, the vehicular industry cannot prescind from the current technological assets for many reasons, among which:

Legacy. It has been estimated that up to 90% of the software in a new vehicle release can be reused from previous releases when using model-based engineering [38].

Organisation. Original Equipment Manufacturers (OEMs) suppliers define their technological assets based on decennial contracts with Tier-1 and Tier-2 suppliers. Changes to these assets shall not affect these contracts.

Certified run-time support. Functional safety [36] is paramount for the safety criticality in vehicles [37]. Current model-based solutions rely on certified development environments and real-time operating systems [1]. Typically, the certification process adds a development cost overhead between 25 and 100%, and it lasts for several years [29].

We have investigated the extension of Rubus [4], a commercial model-based approach for vehicular single-core systems, to multi-core with the intent of not disrupting the current vehicular technological assets related to it. Our hypothesis is two-fold. (H1) Abstraction provided by models and automation provided by model transformations can be a game changer in the development of multi-core applications. Abstraction permits to detach software functional modelling from multi-core hardware modelling and software/hardware allocation modelling. Automation can support the developer in taking important decisions, such as how to allocate tasks to available cores in order to maximise a specific quality aspect [13]. (H2) A lightweight transition of a model-based approach from single-core to multi-core which does not affect critical aspects such as certified run-time support and lastingness of legacy applications is possible.

In model-based engineering, metamodels play a pivotal role as they define the set of available modelling entities and relationships for representing the software architecture and its quality attributes. Moreover, they enable automation via model transformations. However, it is essential that metamodels effectively prescribe the type system, the structure, and the behaviour of domain-specific applications [34]. In [24] we have discussed some modelling languages (among which Rubus Component Model) used for single-core vehicular applications and highlighted the issues arising when using them for modelling multi-core applications. In particular, existing structural hierarchies lack concepts for representing multi-core aspects (e.g., cores and partitions) and do not provide explicit support for core-interdependency and allocation of software to hardware.

In this paper, we propose an extension to the Rubus Component Model (RCM) [18], core of the Rubus approach, to support multi-core. This represents the first crucial step in the transition from single-core to multi-core. The contribution of the proposed extension is two-fold. We provide a modelling language able to prescribe type system, structure, and behaviour of multi-core applications (C1). In particular, the proposed extension comprises modelling elements for representing the software architecture, the hardware platform, and the software to hardware allocation. We ensure backward compatibility with legacy single-core applications modelled with RCM and do not entail any modification to the Rubus run-time layer, the Rubus Kernel (C2).

The remainder of the paper is structured as follows. Section 2 introduces RCM and motivates its selection as well as its extension. Section 3 presents a comparison between existing related approaches documented in the literature and our solution. Section 4 describes the proposed solution in all its constituents. Section 5 describes the application of the proposed solution to an industrial vehicular application. Sections 6 and 7 discuss the benefits and limitations of our solution and conclude the paper, respectively.

2   The Rubus Component Model

There are several modelling languages used in the vehicular domain, such as RCM, AUTOSAR [3], ProCom [35], COMDES [21], AADL [16], to name a few. These languages were not conceived to deal with the complexity of predictable vehicle software specifically developed to run on multi-core platforms.

We focus on RCM and its extension for multi-core due to the following reasons. RCM is a good candidate to overcome the issues related to predictability thanks to its statically synthesised communication as well as its predictable and fine-grained execution model [25]. RCM uses pipe-and-filter communication and distinguishes between the control and data flows among its software components. In [26], we showed that these two features are central for providing early timing verification of the modelled system, e.g., by supporting end-to-end timing analysis [15]. Another reason for focusing on RCM is the small run-time footprint of the developed software (automatically generated from RCM models) as compared to other languages [26].

RCM is developed by Arcticus Systems AB[1] in collaboration with Mälardalen University. Through the years, RCM has been adopted by several OEM, Tier-1 and Tier-2 companies (e.g., Volvo Construction Equipment, BAE Systems Hägglunds, Hoerbiger and Knorr Bremse) for the development of embedded real-time software. RCM provides the Rubus Kernel, a dedicated real-time operating system, which is available for different processor architectures and certified according to the ISO 26262 [1] standard ASIL D (Road vehicle – Functional Safety) from Safety Integrity AB[2].

RCM was originally thought for providing modelling purposes, but it did not feature model-based mechanisms, i.e. automation in terms of model transformation. In order to achieve a full-fledge model-based approach, in [9] we

---

[1] https://www.arcticus-systems.com.
[2] http://www.safetyintegrity.se.

reverse-engineered the RCM specification in order to express it in a more canonical form, a metamodel, which we called RubusMM. RubusMM included concepts for expressing software architectures and concepts for describing timing information of vehicular single-core applications. In this paper, we extend RubusMM to enable modelling of software applications for multi-core.

3   Related Work

AUTOSAR [3] is an industrial initiative to provide a standardised software architecture for the development of vehicular software systems. Since the emergence of AUTOSAR 4.0, multi-core support is part of the standard. Similar to RCM, AUTOSAR describes the application software by means of self-contained units called software components which are mapped to the ECUs. At the application software level, AUTOSAR does not distinguish between the control and the data flows. In [26], we discussed how this feature is central for providing early timing verification of the modelled system. AUTOSAR does not provide means for modelling the execution platform [33]. Recently, several works on the use of AUTOSAR for multi-core have been proposed both from industry and academia. However, their main focus is on the adaptation of the AUTOSAR runtime support rather than on specific modelling challenges such as, e.g., allocation of the software components. In [30], the authors investigated the use of AUTOSAR for virtualised architecture and they identified some challenges on the use of AUTOSAR for multi-core. They concluded that additional features for the dynamic allocation of the software were needed. In [7,23], the authors evaluated AUTOSAR systems realised with a centralised architecture where the layered architecture was entirely allocated to one of the available cores only. Both the approaches were able to demonstrate that the behaviour of the multi-core software system and its footprint did not significantly vary from the corresponding single-core configuration. However, in both approaches, the uneven distribution of the workload among the cores led to performance and timing verification issues. In [31,32] the authors described AUTOSAR systems based on virtualised architectures where hypervisors coordinate multiple software systems with same or different real-time operating system(s). The use of hypervisors complicates early timing verification as it introduces additional complexity. From a footprint point of view, the virtualised architecture may lose its efficiency as each software system can carry a different real-time operating system. Both approaches rely on certified versions of AUTOSAR systems. In the AMALTHEA project [2], AUTOSAR standardised software architecture and methodology are used as a base for a development methodology aiming at reducing the effort in exchanging dtata.

Besides technologies specific to the vehicular domain, several works have discussed the use of the UML language and its profile MARTE [5]. Being general-purpose, these technologies are often used as complementary to domain-specific languages as, e.g., AUTOSAR and RCM. In [22], the authors present the VERTAF/Multi-core UML-based framework for the development of multi-core software. Within VERTAF/Multi-core, the software system is described by means of UML class diagrams, timed state machines and sequence diagrams. Model transformations are used for generating extensions to these models for checking the viability of the design with respect to schedulability and conformance to the specifications. In [14,27] MARTE is used for representing the high-level architecture of the software system and as enabler for code-generation. In the first approach, UML is used for modelling the software components while MARTE is used for modelling hardware and software to hardware allocations. Starting from these models, code is automatically generated and timing verification through simulation is run. The second approach focuses on the system deployment of component-based systems. MARTE is used for modelling high level description models from which different models representing allocations of components are generated by means of code generation. In [13], MARTE is used for describing a task model and the allocations of tasks to cores for combined simulation- and execution-based task allocation optimisation. In [17] the authors introduce a MARTE-based framework, named GASPARD, for the design of parallel embedded systems. Herrera et al. [19] discuss a framework for the design space exploration of embedded systems based on MARTE. The framework, called COMPLEX, uses MARTE for describing the different architecture solutions composing the design space.

AADL [16] is an architecture description language developed for the avionic domain, but currently used for modelling embedded systems in general. Similarly to RCM, AADL provides multi-core support and a clear separation of concerns between software and hardware elements. However, unlike to RCM, the software architecture is described at a lower level of abstraction in terms of, e.g., *Processes* and *Threads*.

4 Extending Rubus Component Model for Multi-core

In this section, we describe the extension to RCM for modelling vehicle software on multi-core. The extension is formalised by means of metamodelling. We compare the extended RCM with its previous definition, given in [9], thus highlighting differences and commonalities. The extension comprises the addition of modelling packages, classifiers, features, and relations as well as the modification of some hierarchical structures.

With respect to the previous definition, we have introduced packages for ensuring a better separation of concerns, improving the understandability of the metamodel, and simplifying future extensions. The RubusMM packages involved in the extension are *RCM_COMMON*, *RCM_HW* and *RCM_SW*[3]. *RCM_HW* contains the elements for modelling the hardware platform: *Target*, *Allocator*, *Core*, and *Partition*. *RCM_SW* contains the elements for modelling the software architecture: *Allocatable*, *Mode*, *Assembly*, and *Software Circuit*. *RCM_COMMON* contains elements which are common to different packages as, for instance, *System* and port elements. Figure 1 shows a fragment of

---

[3] The complete explanation of RubusMM is not in the scope of this work. The interested reader may refer to [9].

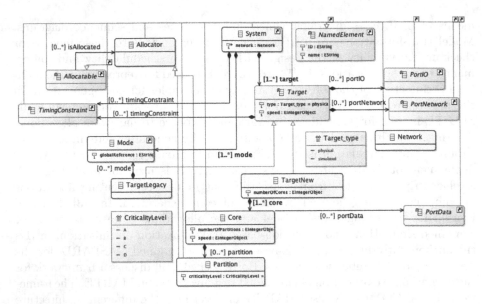

Fig. 1. Fragment of the *RCM_HW* package for modelling the hardware platform.

RubusMM containing elements from *RCM_HW* for modelling the hardware platform. *System* represents the system under development. As all the elements in RubusMM, it inherits from the abstract metaclass *NamedElement* which provides two attributes: *name* and *ID*. We extended *System* with the reference *timingConstraint* for enabling the specification of timing constraints, occurrences and events which are used for timing verification.[4] These constraints are used for running timing analysis, but we employed them for automatically generating the set of RCM models satisfying a given set of timing requirements too [8].

A *System* contains one *Network*, one or more *Target* elements, and one or more *Mode* elements. A *Network* element models all the messages exchanged among the *Node* elements. It has two attributes, *protocol* and *speed*, which specify the protocol (e.g., Controlled Area Network (CAN) [20]) and the speed of the network in Kbit/s, respectively. A *Target* is a hardware-specific element which represents a processor architecture. The definition of *Target* has been extended with the references *timingConstraint*, *portIO*, and *portNetwork*. *portIO* and *portNetwork* model the peripherals and the inter-node communication, respectively.

In the previous definition of RubusMM, *Target* contained *Mode*, representing the software application. However, the containment relation between *Target* and *Mode* was too restrictive for modelling multi-core applications. Such a containment prescribed in fact that *Mode* elements, representing software, were structurally contained by hardware, represented by *Target* elements. Although

---

[4] *TimingConstraint* and other elements from different RCM packages are not part of this extension. However, they are put in relation to the extension as they contribute to a holistic view of the language and its peculiarities.

not providing a clear separation between software and hardware, this structural containment suited the single-core case, since allocation of software to hardware was not variably split across different cores. Modelling for multi-core demanded more flexibility, since allocation of software to hardware is a variability point, which can hardly be represented by a structural containment.

In order to provide such a flexibility, while ensuring backward compatibility with legacy RubusMM models, we have modified the existing hierarchy as follows. We have added the metaclasses *TargetLegacy* and *TargetNew*, both inheriting from the abstract metaclass *Target*. *TargetLegacy* represents a legacy (single-core) ECU and it contains one or more *Mode* elements. This containment is specified through the reference *mode*. *TargetNew* represents a single- or multi-core ECU and contains one or more *Core* elements, which in turn can contain *Partition* elements. Both *Core* and *Partition* elements inherit from the abstract metaclass *Allocator*, representing hardware elements to which software elements, represented by the metaclass *Allocatable*, can be allocated. The metaclasses *Allocator* and *Allocatable*, together with the reference *isAllocated*, provide the flexible mechanism for the allocation of software to hardware that we needed, without any structural containment.

The metaclass *Target* provides the following attributes: *speed*, which specifies its speed in MHz, and *type*, which specifies whether it is a *physical* or a *simulated* target. A simulated target represents the simulation of the actual target processor in a host environment such as Windows or Linux.

Both *TargetLegacy* and *TargetNew* inherit *speed* and *type*. Moreover, *TargetNew* provides additional multi-core specific attributes. *numberOfCores* specifies the number of cores composing the *TargetNew* and it is used by the model-based timing analysis and to automatically allocate software to hardware. The reference *core* links *Core* elements to their respective *TargetNew*. *Core* may contain *Partition* elements. The attribute *numberOfPartitions* specifies the number of partitions within a *Core* and the reference *partition* links them to the *Core*. The attribute *criticalityLevel* specifies the safety criticality level according to the ISO 26262 standard. There are four criticality levels (A to D) in this standard. A is the lowest criticality level, whereas D is the highest criticality level (the Rubus Kernel supports and is certified for all of them). Hence, the *Partition* element allows to develop multi-criticalitysoftware systems, where some parts of the software architecture are more critical than the others. *Target*, *TargetLegacy*, *TargetNew*, *Core*, *Partition*, *Allocator*, *Allocatable*, as well as their attributes and related references were not part of the previous RubusMM definition.

Figure 2 shows a fragment of the RubusMM containing elements from the *RCM_SW* and the *RCM_COMMON* packages for modelling the software architecture. In RCM a software circuit, represented in RubusMM by *SWC*, is the lowest-level hierarchical element that encapsulates basic software functions. A *SWC* contains one *Interface* which groups all its ports. As RubusMM distinguishes between the data and control flows, an *Interface* contains*PortData* and *PortTrig* elements. The *PortData* elements manage the data communication

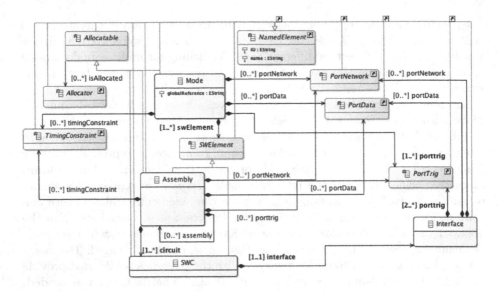

Fig. 2. Fragment of the *RCM_SW* package for modelling the software architecture.

among *SWC* deployed on the same *Target*. The *PortTrig* elements manage the activation of the *SWC* elements.

A *PortNetwork* is a port for the data communication of *SWC* elements deployed on different *Target* elements. The *PortData* elements of a *Core* are referenced to the *PortData* elements of the *SWC*s allocated on that *Core*. Similarly, the *PortNetwork* elements of a *Node* are referenced to the *PortNetwork* elements at *SWC* level. An *Assembly* groups *SWC* and *Assembly* elements in a hierarchical fashion.

Its reference *timingConstraint* enables the specification of timing constraints, occurrences and events which are used for timing verification. With respect to the previous definition, *SWC* and *Assembly* have been extended with the inheritance relation from the abstract metaclass *Allocatable*. A *Mode* groups *Assembly* and *SWC* elements and it is used for modelling a specific application of the software architecture (e.g., start-up or error mode). The attribute *globalReference* serves for creating a reference among all the *Mode* elements contributing to the same application. With respect to its previous definition, *Mode* has been extended with the inheritance relation from the abstract metaclass *Allocatable*. The metaclasses *Allocatable* and *Allocator* together with the reference *isAllocated* enable the specification of the allocation of software to hardware. More precisely, an *Allocatable* element can be deployed to an *Allocator* element by setting the *isAllocated* reference. *Allocatable*, *Allocator*, and related references were not part of the previous RubusMM definition.

5   Modelling the Brake-By-Wire System

In this section, we leverage the extended RubusMM for modelling the Brake-by-wire (BBW) vehicular application. The BBW system is a stand-alone braking system equipped with an anti-lock braking (ABS) function, which allows to control the brakes through electronic means. To this end, it does not employ any mechanical connection between the brake pedal and the brake actuators. Figure 3 depicts the block diagram of the BBW system.

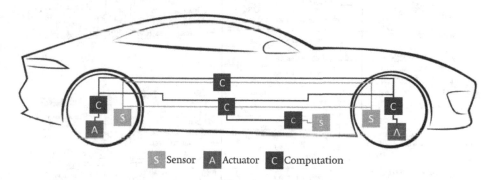

Fig. 3. Block diagram of the BBW system.

A sensor, attached to the brake pedal, acquires the signal expressing the position of the pedal. The signal is sent to a computational unit which translates it into a brake torque. A sensor on each wheel acquires the signal expressing the speed of the wheel. The speed of each wheel, together with the computed brake torque, is sent to a computational unit which calculates the brake torque for each wheel. Also, the speed of each wheel is sent to a computational unit which calculates the speed of the vehicle. The speed of the vehicle and the brake torque of each wheel are used from the ABS units for calculating the optimal brake torque for each wheel for avoiding locking the brakes. Finally, the actuators on the wheels produce the actual brake. Figure 4 shows a RubusMM model depicting the software architecture of the BBW system.

The model consist of 16 software circuits where (i) *Brake_Pedal* models the software operating the sensor on the brake pedal, (ii) *Speed_FR*, *Speed_FL*, *Speed_RR*, and *Speed_RL* model the software operating the speed sensors on the wheels, (iii) *Brake_Torque*, *Brake_Controller*, *Speed_Estimator*, *ABS_FR*, *ABS_FL*, *ABS_RR*, and *ABS_RL* model the software on the computational units and (iv) *Brake_FR*, *Brake_FL*, *Brake_RR*, and *Brake_RL* model the software operating the actuators on the wheels.

In order to show how the extended RubusMM supports the modelling of multi-core applications (H1), while ensuring backward compatibility with legacy single-core applications (H2), we propose two different deployment configurations. In the first configuration, the BBW system is deployed to a MPC5744P

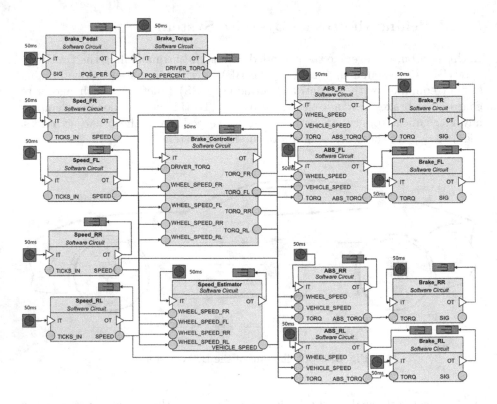

Fig. 4. RubusMM model representing the software architecture of the BBW system.

microcontroller, which is a 32-bit unicore microcontroller designed for vehicular applications.

Figure 5 shows an Ecore serialisation of such a configuration. Note that, according to what described in Sect. 4 regarding the modelling of legacy applications, the deployment on single-core is expressed leveraging the containment relation between the 'TargetLegacy' *MPC574xP* and the 'Mode' element *Operational*.

In the second configuration, the BBW system is deployed to an Infineon SAK-TC299TP-128F300S BBmicrocontroller, which is a tri-core microcontroller developed for applications with high demands of performance and safety.

Figure 6 shows an Ecore serialisation of this configuration. In this case, the deployment information is modelled by means of the 'isAllocated' reference expressed between 'Allocatable' and 'Allocator' elements. More precisely, the software circuits modelling the sensors, the computation units and the actuators of the two front wheels (*WheelSpeed_FR, WheelSpeed_FR, Abs_FR, Abs_FL, Brake_FR, Brake_FL*) are allocated to *Core 1* of the *SAK-TC299TP-128F300S BB* target, as shown by the arrow in the top-right corner of Fig. 6. Similarly, the SWCs modelling the sensors, the computation units and the actuators of the two rear wheels (*WheelSpeed_RR, WheelSpeed_RR, Abs_RR, Abs_RL, Brake_RR,*

▼ ✦ **System BBW**
   ▼ ✦ **Target Legacy MPC574xP**
      ▼ ✦ **Mode Operational**

✦ Circuit BrakePedal	✦ Circuit AbsFR
✦ Circuit BrakeTorque	✦ Circuit AbsFL
✦ Circuit WheelSpeedFR	✦ Circuit AbsRR
✦ Circuit WheelSpeedFL	✦ Circuit AbsRL
✦ Circuit WheelSpeedRR	✦ Circuit BrakeFR
✦ Circuit WheelSpeedRL	✦ Circuit BrakeFL
✦ Circuit BrakeController	✦ Circuit BrakeRR
✦ Circuit SpeedEstimator	✦ Circuit BrakeRL

Fig. 5. Serialisation of the BBW system deployed to a unicore microcontroller.

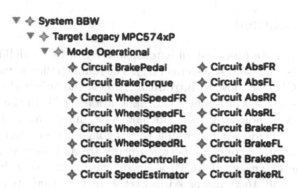

Fig. 6. Serialisation of the BBW system deployed to a tri-core microcontroller.

Brake_RL) are allocated to *Core 2* of the *SAK-TC299TP-128F300S BB* target. The remaining SWCs modelling the computational units are allocated to *Core 3* of the *SAK-TC299TP-128F300S BB* target. As discussed in Sect. 4, the extended RubusMM leverages a clearer separation of concerns between software and hardware elements as well as an explicit and more flexible allocation mechanism. Let us suppose that the allocation specified in Fig. 6 does not satisfy a given set of fault-tolerance requirements. One way of addressing this would be to model a lockstep [28] configuration of the BBW system where each core runs a copy of the complete software, in parallel. In order to model such an allocation with the extended RubusMM, it is sufficient to allocate all software circuits composing a 'Mode' to each single 'Core'.

6   Lesson Learned

In this paper, we have proposed an extension to RCM for modelling next generation of vehicular multi-core systems (H1). The main challenge faced during the extension of RCM was how to introduce the new modelling elements without affecting the lastingness of legacy RCM applications (H2). In the first definition of RCM, pragmatic choices for more efficient modelling and analysis of single-core applications were made when defining the language. In addition to not providing clear separation of concerns between hardware and software, these choices complicated the extension of RCM, as in the case of the containment relation between *Target* and *Mode* discussed in Sect. 4. In fact, that structural containment, although dramatically simplifying model navigation for analysis and code generation purposes in case of single-core applications, did not suit variability of software to hardware allocation in the multi-core case. In this respect, the proposed extension prescribes an allocation mechanism which is more flexible and apt to be automated by means of model transformations. Please note that, we have previously provided RubusMM with support for variability modelling [10]. This feature can be very valuable for representing sets of allocations of software components to multiple cores, all in a single model with variability points representing allocations.

To maximise backward compatibility, we introduced the new modelling elements as leaves in the metamodel hierarchy, as in the case of, e.g., *Core* and *Partition*. This choice could demand additional modelling effort as the engineer can be required to model the entire hierarchy in order to design valid models from scratch. This can be mitigated by tooling features, allowing the modeller to directly model a leaf, while automatically generating the path to the model root populated with a set of default values.

In Sect. 2, we have pointed out early timing verification as one of the main reasons which made RCM very appreciated in the vehicular domain and its extension for multi-core compelling. In this respect, when extending RCM, we have explicitly addressed timing verification by allowing the specification of timing constraints, occurrences and events at several levels of the structural hierarchy by means of the references *timingConstraint*. This ensures full compatibility with the existing model-based timing analysis provided by Rubus. Moreover, it enables the use of the most recent timing analysis for vehicular embedded systems on multi-core [11]. Without the extension provided in this paper, the timing analysis for multi-core would not have been possible in Rubus due to the missing structural and timing information.

Functional safety is paramount for the safety criticality of vehicular systems. For being adopted in the vehicular domain, model-based solutions must provide certified run-time support, e.g., real-time operating system, along with modelling languages able to capture all the characteristics of a vehicular application. The Rubus Kernel is certified according to the ISO 26262 standard ASIL D while Rubus ICE (i.e., the development environment supporting Rubus) is undergoing the same certification. In this respect, we have extended RCM according to the virtualisation design option, as described in [6], which enables the reuse of the certified Rubus Kernel. On the one hand, the reuse of the Rubus Kernel makes also the explicit modelling of the memory not necessary since the mapping of data ports to physical memory is handled by the Rubus Kernel itself. On the other hand, this makes the current definition of RCM not suited for approaches where explicit modelling of the memory is pivotal. Moreover, despite the Rubus Kernel footprint is significantly small, the virtualised design option increases the overall footprint of the developed vehicular application since each core or partition can host a separate instance of the Rubus Kernel.

7   Conclusion and Future Work

In this paper, we have discussed the extension of the Rubus Component Model for modelling vehicular multi-core applications while ensuring backward compatibility with legacy single-core applications. The proposed extensions also support the modelling of multi-criticality applications on single- as well as multi-core platforms. We have leveraged an industrial vehicular application to validate the proposed extension, also in terms of backward compatibility.

One line of future work will investigate how to support the analysis and verification of vehicular embedded systems with multi-criticality levels on multi-core with respect to predictable timing behaviour. Moreover, we will investigate how to adapt the certified Rubus Kernel for providing run-time support to these systems on multi-core. Another line of future work will investigate how to provide automatic support for the allocation of software to hardware. In particular, we are developing model transformations that, starting from a model with no modelled allocations and a set of timing constraints, produce a set of models featuring the set of different allocations of software to hardware optimised for satisfying the set of timing constraints. We are planning to represent the set of generated models by means of the compact notation presented in [10]. Such a notation uses modelling with variability for representing a multitude of models with one single model with variability points.

Acknowledgments. The work in this paper is supported by the Swedish Knowledge Foundation (KKS) through the PreView and MOMENTUM projects, and by the Swedish Research Council (VR) through the SynthSoft project. We thank our industrial partners Arcticus Systems, Volvo Construction Equipment and BAE Systems Hägglunds, Sweden.

References

1. ISO 26262-1:2011: Road Vehicles in Functional Safety. http://www.iso.org/
2. AMALTHEA Project Profile, April 2017. http://www.amalthea-project.org
3. AUTOSAR Techincal Overview, Version 4.3, The AUTOSAR Consortium, December 2016. http://autosar.org
4. Rubus ICE-Integrated Development Environment. http://www.arcticus-systems.com

5. The UML Profile for MARTE: Modeling and Analysis of Real-Time and Embedded Systems. OMG Group, January 2010
6. Becker, M., Dasari, D., Nélis, V., Behnam, M., Miguel, P.L., Nolte, T.: Investigation on AUTOSAR-compliant solutions for many-core architectures. In: 18th Euromicro Conference on Digital System Design, vol. 18, August 2015
7. Böhm, N., Lohmann, D., Schröder-Preikschat, W.: A comparison of pragmatic multi-core adaptations of the AUTOSAR system. In: 7th annual Workshop on Operating System Platforms for Embedded Real-Time Applications (OSPERT), pp. 16–22 (2011)
8. Bucaioni, A., Cicchetti, A., Ciccozzi, F., Eramo, R., Mubeen, S., Sjödin, M.: Anticipating implementation-level timing analysis for driving design-level decisions in EAST-ADL. In: International Workshop on Modelling in Automotive Software Engineering, September 2015
9. Bucaioni, A., Cicchetti, A., Ciccozzi, F., Mubeen, S., Sjödin, M.: A metamodel for the rubus component model: extensions for timing and model transformation from EAST-ADL. J. IEEE Access 5(1), 1–16 (2016)
10. Bucaioni, A., Cicchetti, A., Ciccozzi, F., Mubeen, S., Sjödin, M., Pierantonio, A.: Handling uncertainty in automatically generated implementation models in the automotive domain. In: 42nd Euromicro Conference series on Software Engineering and Advanced Applications, September 2016
11. Burns, A., Davis, R.: Mixed Criticality Systems - A Review, 8th edn. Technical report, Department of Computer Science, University of York (2016). https://www-users.cs.york.ac.uk/burns/review.pdf
12. Charette, R.N.: This car runs on code. IEEE Spectr. 46(3), 3 (2009)
13. Ciccozzi, F., Feljan, J., Carlson, J., Crnković, I.: Architecture optimization: speed or accuracy? both!. Softw. Qual. J. 22, 1–24 (2016)
14. Ciccozzi, F., Seceleanu, T., Corcoran, D., Scholle, D.: UML-based development of embedded real-time software on multi-core in practice: lessons learned and future perspectives. IEEE Access 4, 6528–6540 (2016)
15. Feiertag, N., Richter, K., Nordlander, J., Jonsson, J.: A compositional framework for end-to-end path delay calculation of automotive systems under different path semantics. In: Proceedings of the IEEE Real-Time System Symposium? Workshop on Compositional Theory and Technology for Real-Time Embedded Systems (2008)
16. Feiler, P.H., Gluch, D.P., Hudak, J.J.: The architecture analysis & design language (AADL): an introduction. Technical report, DTIC Document (2006)
17. Gamatié, A., Le Beux, S., Piel, É., Ben Atitallah, R., Etien, A., Marquet, P., Dekeyser, J.L.: A model-driven design framework for massively parallel embedded systems. ACM Trans. Embed. Comput. Syst. (TECS) 10(4), 39 (2011)
18. Hänninen, K., Mäki-Turja, J., Sjödin, M., Lindberg, M., Lundbäck, J., Lundbäck, K.L.: The rubus component model for resource constrained real-time systems. In: 3rd IEEE International Symposium on Industrial Embedded Systems, June 2008
19. Herrera, F., Posadas, H., Peñil, P., Villar, E., Ferrero, F., Valencia, R., Palermo, G.: The COMPLEX methodology for UML/MARTE modeling and design space exploration of embedded systems. J. Syst. Architect. 60(1), 55–78 (2014)
20. ISO 11898-1: Road Vehicles Interchange of Digital Information Controller Area Network (CAN) for high-speed communication, ISO Standard-11898, November 1993

21. Ke, X., Sierszecki, K., Angelov, C.: COMDES-II: a component-based framework for generative development of distributed real-time control systems. In: 13th IEEE International Conference on Embedded and Real-Time Computing Systems and Applications (RTCSA), pp. 199–208, August 2007
22. Lin, C.S., Hsiung, P.A., Chang, C.H., Hsueh, N.L., Koong, C.S., Shih, C.H., Yang, C.T., Chu, W.C.C.: Model-driven multi-core embedded software design (2011)
23. Morgan, G., Borg, A.: Multi-core automotive ECUs: Software and hardware implications. Technical report, ETAS Group (2009)
24. Mubeen, S., Bucaioni, A.: Modeling of vehicular distributed embedded systems: transition from single-core to multi-core. In: 14th International Conference on Information Technology: New Generations. Springer, Switzerland (2017)
25. Mubeen, S., Mäki-Turja, J., Sjödin, M.: Communications-oriented development of component- based vehicular distributed real-time embedded systems. J. Syst. Architect. 60(2), 207–220 (2014)
26. Mubeen, S., Nolte, T., Sjödin, M., Lundbäck, J., Lundbäck, K.L.: Supporting timing analysis of vehicular embedded systems through the refinement of timing constraints. Softw. Syst. Model., 1–31 (2017)
27. Nicolas, A., Posadas, H., Peñil, P., Villar, E.: Automatic deployment of component-based embedded systems from UML/MARTE models using MCAPI. In: 2014 Conference on Design of Circuits and Integrated Circuits (DCIS), pp. 1–6. IEEE (2014)
28. Poledna, S.: Fault-Tolerant Real-Time Systems: The Problem of Replica Determinism, vol. 345. Springer, New York (2007)
29. Pop, P., Scholle, D., Hansson, H., Widforss, G., Rosqvist, M.: The SafeCOP ECSEL project: safe cooperating cyber-physical systems using wireless communication. In: 2016 Euromicro Conference on Digital System Design (DSD), pp. 532–538. IEEE (2016)
30. Reinhardt, D., Kaule, D., Kucera, M.: Achieving a scalable E/E-architecture using AUTOSAR and virtualization. SAE Int. J. Passeng. Cars Electron. Electr. Syst. 6, 489–497 (2013). (2013-01-1399)
31. Reinhardt, D., Kucera, M.: Domain controlled architecture-a new approach for large scale software integrated automotive systems. PECCS 13, 221–226 (2013)
32. Reinhardt, D., Morgan, G.: An embedded hypervisor for safety-relevant automotive E/E-systems. In: Proceedings of the 9th IEEE International Symposium on Industrial Embedded Systems (SIES 2014), pp. 189–198. IEEE (2014)
33. Sangiovanni-Vincentelli, A., Di Natale, M.: Embedded system design for automotive applications. Computer 40(10), 42–51 (2007)
34. Schmidt, D.C.: Guest editor's introduction: model-driven engineering. Computer 39(2), 25–31 (2006)
35. Sentilles, S., Vulgarakis, A., Bures, T., Carlson, J., Crnković, I.: A component model for control-intensive distributed embedded systems. In: Chaudron, M.R.V., Szyperski, C., Reussner, R. (eds.) CBSE 2008. LNCS, vol. 5282, pp. 310–317. Springer, Heidelberg (2008). doi:10.1007/978-3-540-87891-9_21
36. Smith, D., Simpson, K.: Functional Safety. Routledge, London (2004)
37. Storey, N.R.: Safety Critical Computer Systems. Addison-Wesley Longman Publishing Co., Inc., Boston (1996)
38. Thorngren, P.: keynote talk: Experiences from east-adl use. In: EAST-ADL Open Workshop, Gothenberg (2013)

On the Opportunities of Scalable Modeling Technologies: An Experience Report on Wind Turbines Control Applications Development

Abel Gómez[1]([✉])(iD), Xabier Mendialdua[2], Gábor Bergmann[3](iD),
Jordi Cabot[1,4](iD), Csaba Debreceni[3](iD), Antonio Garmendia[5],
Dimitrios S. Kolovos[6], Juan de Lara[5], and Salvador Trujillo[2]

[1] IN3, Universitat Oberta de Catalunya, Barcelona, Spain
`agomezlla@uoc.edu`
[2] IK4-IKERLAN Research Center, Arrasate, Spain
`{xmendialdua,strujillo}@ikerlan.es`
[3] MTA-BME Lendület Research Group on Cyber-Physical Systems,
Budapest University of Technology and Economics, Budapest, Hungary
`{bergmann,debreceni}@mit.bme.hu`
[4] ICREA, Barcelona, Spain
`jordi.cabot@icrea.cat`
[5] Universidad Autónoma de Madrid, Madrid, Spain
`{Antonio.Garmendia,Juan.deLara}@uam.es`
[6] Department of Computer Science, University of York, York, UK
`dimitrios.kolovos@york.ac.uk`

Abstract. Scalability in modeling has many facets, including the ability to build larger models and domain specific languages (DSLs) efficiently. With the aim of tackling some of the most prominent scalability challenges in Model-based Engineering (MBE), the MONDO EU project developed the theoretical foundations and open-source implementation of a platform for scalable modeling and model management. The platform includes facilities for building large DSLs, for splitting large models into sets of smaller interrelated fragments, and enables modelers to construct and refine complex models collaboratively, among other features.

This paper reports on the improvements provided by the MONDO technologies in a software development division of IK4-IKERLAN, a Medium-sized Enterprise which in recent years has embraced the MBE paradigm. The evaluation, conducted in the Wind Turbine Control Applications development domain, shows that scalable MBE technologies give new growth opportunities to Small and Medium-sized Enterprises.

Keywords: Model-Based Engineering (MBE) · Scalability · Experience report

This work has been supported by the MONDO (EU ICT-611125) project.

© Springer International Publishing AG 2017
A. Anjorin and H. Espinoza (Eds.): ECMFA 2017, LNCS 10376, pp. 300–315, 2017.
DOI: 10.1007/978-3-319-61482-3_18

1   Introduction

IK4-IKERLAN is a Spanish private Technology Centre focused on innovation and comprehensive product development, with 40 years of experience in combining and applying mechanics, electronics and computer science in industry. With a staff headcount of nearly 250 employees and a turnover of €18.5 million in 2015 [10], IK4-IKERLAN is a Medium-sized Enterprise [6] that has carried out advanced technology transfer for a wide variety of domains, including transportation (railway and elevators), energy (wind and solar power, and storage systems), automation, industrial, health and home appliances among others. IK4-IKERLAN has been working for the last 10 years in the development of supervisory and control platforms for wind turbines for one of the world's leading companies in the field of renewable energy.

Wind turbines, as Sect. 2 describes, are complex systems where hardware and software components need to interact in intricate ways. To tackle this complexity, Model-based Engineering (MBE) [16] technologies were introduced in 2009 in IK4-IKERLAN for the engineering of the supervisory and control systems. The goal for adopting and investing in MBE was to improve productivity and competitiveness of its industrial customers by enhancing their software development processes using, as Sect. 3 sketches, Domain Specific Languages (DSL) [7,11] and code generators [4]. The experiences reported by customers showed significant productivity increases, indicating that MBE has been critical in the development of new software products faster, cheaper and with fewer errors than previous projects.

However, too often, MBE tools and methodologies have targeted the construction and processing of small models in non-distributed environments. This focus neglects common scalability challenges [13], considering that a more typical scenario involves different engineers working in collaboration at distributed locations. Handling these issues is a challenging task that requires specific solutions that foster scalability as we will discuss in Sect. 4.

In 2013, the MONDO project was launched with the aim of tackling some of the most prominent challenges of scalability in MBE by developing the theoretical foundations and open-source implementation of a platform for scalable modeling and model management. Among the technologies developed, Sect. 5.1 focuses on the ones that can provide IK4-IKERLAN the opportunity to offer its customers software development methodologies in geographically distributed scenarios where multiple users can work collaboratively; and Sect. 5.2 describes, specifically, the different solutions developed in IK4-IKERLAN using the MONDO platform.

Section 6 describes how the scalable MONDO technologies have been evaluated in IK4-IKERLAN and the results obtained. In a scenario where the 99% of all businesses in the EU are Small and Medium-sized Enterprises (SME), Sect. 7 draws the conclusions and discusses this experience on the application of scalable modeling technologies in a company like IK4-IKERLAN.

2 Wind Turbines

A wind turbine is a complex system composed of a set of physical subsystems whose aim is to convert wind energy into electrical energy. The *Wind Turbine Control System* (WTCS) [1] is the system which monitors and controls all the subsystems that make up the wind turbine. Its aim is to maximize the generation of electrical energy, always ensuring the correct operation of the turbine and avoiding any problem which can cause any damage to it. It monitors the status of the wind turbine and the environmental conditions, making decisions to get the highest energy production. The WTCS is a HW/SW system that runs on a dedicated hardware platform. This is connected to the wind turbine through assorted communications to receive information from inputs (sensors, device state signals, etc.) and to actuate on outputs (device actuators).

The HW/SW architecture of the WTCS is shown in Fig. 1. The two lower layers refer to the HW and the Operating System. The software layer is composed of the following components:

The Execution Engine is the component which cyclically executes the algorithms to monitor and control the Wind Turbine.

The Control Units Library is a set of reusable control algorithms. These are basic blocks, with well defined interfaces, which can be instantiated and interconnected to implement the *Wind Turbine Control Application.*

A Wind Turbine Control Application (WTCA) comprises the set of algorithms that must be executed in order to ensure the correct operation of the wind turbine the WTCS is monitoring and controlling. The control algorithms of the wind turbine are specified by instantiating control units available in the *Control Units Library* and by combining those instances.

In this software architecture, the *Execution Engine* is a stable software component which does not vary from one wind turbine to another. The *Control Units Library* is also a stable component which, generally, does not vary either, unless some new device is used in a wind turbine and a custom control unit has

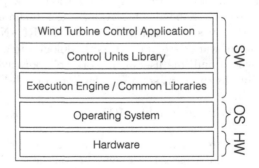

Fig. 1. HW/SW architecture of a Wind Turbine Control System

to be implemented to control it. Finally, the WTCA is the part of the software in a WTCS that is customized for each wind turbine, depending on the specific requirements that WTCS must met.

3   Model-Based Engineering for Offshore Wind Turbine Control System Development

The development of a WTCS is a process where a multidisciplinary team of hardware, software and telecommunications engineers, as well as electrical, mechanical and other engineers work in collaboration. Due to the complexity of such scenario—even considering only the software development, which comprises the three software layers described above—this paper will focus on the development of the top layer (WTCA), because the WTCA is the only part that is specific for each different wind turbine.

In recent years, IK4-IKERLAN has implemented the MBE paradigm to develop the Control Applications for Wind Turbines. This development process exploits a domain-specific modeling tool, the so-called *Wind Turbine Control Modeler* (WTCM), developed in Eclipse [19] and based on Eclipse Modeling Framework (EMF) [17]. The WTCM provides the catalogue of available *control units* that engineers can use to develop the algorithms to monitor and control the subsystems of the wind turbine.

The control system of a wind turbine is typically composed of nearly 2000 basic control units, involving nearly about 2000 inputs and up to 1000 outputs, depending on the specific model configuration. A control unit is a basic and reusable control algorithm which may be combined with other control units to build more complex algorithms. The control system is structured into logical subsystems, each controlling different physical subsystems or parts of them. The control of a wind turbine is built through the aggregation of basic control units in order to specify those complex algorithms.

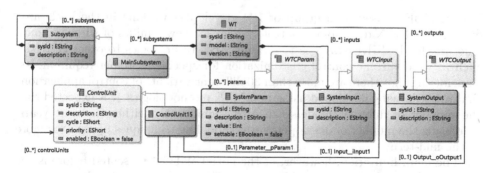

Fig. 2. Metamodel of the Wind Turbine DSL

Figure 2 shows an excerpt of the metamodel which describes the abstract syntax of the DSL provided by the WTCM. As the figure shows, a wind turbine (*WT*) contains a set of *Subsystems* which in turn contain *ControlUnits*.

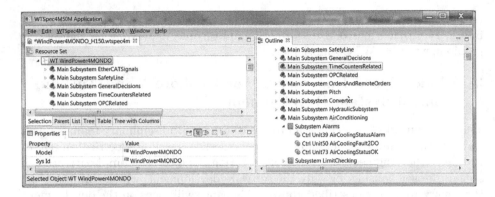

Fig. 3. Screenshot of Wind Turbine Control Modeler

ControlUnits—which may be parameterised—implement the algorithms which process a set of inputs to provide a set of outputs. For the sake of simplicity, Fig. 2 only shows the *ControlUnit15*, which processes a single input receiving a single param, and produces a single output.

Figure 3 shows what the initial implementation of the WTCM—which implements the Wind Turbine DSL—looks like. As it can be seen, the initial WTCM is an Eclipse application, which enables engineers to edit WTCS models using a regular EMF tree editor.

Once a model has been created using the WTCM, the actual C++ code for monitoring and controlling the physical subsystems can be generated using model-to-text transformations expressed in the Epsilon Generation Language [12].

4   Challenges

Today, MBE is used by a group of 10+ developers working in the R&D area of IK4-IKERLAN developing control systems for new families of wind turbines. The aim for IK4-IKERLAN is to extend MBE technologies to other activities such as wind turbine control customization for specific customer requirements. Considering that there are more than 30 different variants of control applications that are still being developed using non-MBE methodologies, it is expected that the number of different models can grow significantly within the next years, increasing the number of developers using modeling techniques up to 20 or more in the mid-term.

The main limitation, however, of the initial WTCM presented before is the lack of features that would enable a team of engineers to work collaboratively: each engineer has to work with his own copy of the model, and model merging operations—e.g., to include changes performed by others—need to be carried out manually. This manual process is a complex, tedious and error prone activity that can take more than half an hour depending on the amount and type of changes made.

Another important limitation is that engineers do not have mechanisms to work with a subset of the model. That means that all engineers must always work with the whole model, although a small subset of elements of the model can be sometimes enough to perform a specific modeling or validation activity.

Considering these limitations for the modeling solution, the following challenges have been identified to improve the development of WTCAs:

1. The **first challenge** is to move from a single-user modeling tool built for an engineer to work in an isolated way, to a modeling tool which enables several engineers to work collaboratively sharing models located in a central repository.
2. The **second challenge** is the ability to edit partial models or model fragments. Such a feature allows each engineer to work with a specific part of the model (as opposed to the whole model), thereby easing modeling activities. Additionally, the use of model fragments allows minimising the volume of data transferred over the network and limits the number of merge conflicts.
3. The **third challenge** is to graphically display and edit WTCS hierarchical models. Graphical models are more expressive for this domains as they ease the identification of relationships between model elements. This is an important enhancement with respect to the initial tree-based editor, where relationships have to be found using auxiliary views of the editor. Scalable graphical editors should include additional features like filtering facilities, hierarchies of diagrams, etc. Figure 4 shows a mockup of what a graphical WTCM would look like.
4. Finally, the **fourth challenge** is to enable model editing using a lightweight mobile device—instead of a laptop—to perform the modeling activities on site in the wind farm.

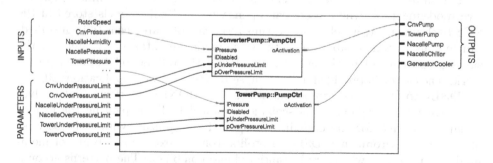

Fig. 4. Wind Turbine Control graphical modeling conceptual mock-up

5   Towards a Scalable MBE Development Process

The goal of IK4-IKERLAN joining the MONDO project was twofold: (i) to provide a real-world scenario where the scalable modeling technologies can be tested and evaluated; and (ii) to improve their development processes by introducing such techniques. In this section we first present the main MONDO technologies employed, and second, the solutions implemented in IK4-IKERLAN using these technologies.

5.1   The MONDO Platform

The MONDO platform is the open-source solution for scalable modeling and model management developed within the MONDO project. Its main purpose is to address the shortage of scalable and collaborative support in state-of-the art technologies within the MBE landscape. It is composed by several components for the development of scalable Eclipse-based editors and DSLs, collaborative modeling, model indexing and scalable model transformations and queries. The MONDO components that have been introduced in the IK4-IKERLAN development process are presented next.

The **MONDO Collaboration Framework** [3] is the MONDO component which enables collaboration both in *offline* and *online* scenarios.

In an *offline collaboration scenario*, as described in [22], models are stored in the so-called *gold repository* of a *version control system* (VCS) which is inaccessible to the actual users. VCS servers instead host separate *front repositories* dedicated to each user, that contain a copy of the gold repository, with complete version history, filtered according to the read access privileges of that user. Users are given access to a dedicated front repository so that they can read the current or historical contents of the model files (up to their read privileges) and commit their changes (which may be denied based on write permissions). In their normal day-to-day workflow, users interact with their front repository using standard VCS protocols and off-the-shelf VCS client software.

For an *online collaboration scenario*, MONDO provides an online collaborative modeling tool, where users can open, view and edit models stored in the VCS backends using a web browser, thus no client software needs to be installed. Multiple users can collaborate on the same model simultaneously, enjoying the same access control mechanism that underlies the offline collaboration framework. The editor is provided as an Eclipse RAP-based web application [20].

DSL-tao [15] is the component within the MONDO platform that enables the systematic development of scalable graphical DSLs, exploiting the idea of reusing patterns (for the domain concepts, the graphical syntax, the services of the final environment). DSL-tao profits from an extensible library of metamodeling patterns, which are instantiated and combined. The patterns account for recurring domain concepts, concrete syntax representation, semantics and services for the DSL environment. In particular, patterns have been developed to define modularization strategies for DSLs—using the **EMF-Splitter** [8] component—which result in graphical modeling environments with built-in fragmentation capabilities, and services for scoping, element visibility and filtering, among others. Using this technology, models are no longer monolithic, but split into fragments and organized similarly to programming projects. The generated environment relies on Sirius for graphical model editing, while **Hawk** [2]—the

MONDO model indexer—is used for efficient look-up of model element across fragments.

5.2 MONDO Solutions for Offshore Wind Power

Using the previous core MONDO infrastructure, three modeling solutions have been implemented in IK4-IKERLAN, which are described next.

The Online Concurrent WTCS Modeling Solution is a web modeling application which allows multiple modelers to share a modeling session. All modelers can work concurrently with the same WTCS model versioned in a model repository. All changes performed by a modeler are automatically propagated to all other modelers, having all of them an updated version of the model.

Besides allowing concurrent modeling activities, this solution also supports working with partial models. It means that each modeler can work with a different view of the same model, thus editing a different fragment of it. This is achieved by creating a custom model view containing only the model elements a user is allowed to see and edit, hiding all other elements in the model. Unauthorized editing of model elements is also prevented. The *Online Concurrent WTCS Modeling solution* allows modelers to commit the changes performed in the model to the model repository.

The Offline Collaborative WTCS Modeling Solution is an Eclipse application which runs locally. It enables several engineers to work with a shared model, but unlike the solution presented above, collaborative modeling is done asynchronously, i.e., each modeler working with the shared model edits a local copy of the shared WTCS model, which is checked out (or updated) from a model repository. When model editing has finished—or whenever the user decides—a commit operation is requested and the MONDO Collaboration Framework carries out the operation.

This asynchronous way of working with a WTCS model may lead to conflicts when several engineers make changes to the model and try to commit them. However, to avoid this, the MONDO Collaboration Framework will assist the modeler to resolve the conflicts by merging the remote and local changes consistently using an automated search-based model merge [5] before the commit succeeds.

As aforementioned, in MONDO, the management of partial models in an offline manner is handled by the MONDO Collaboration Framework which performs the synchronization between all the front repositories and the gold repository. In the case of the *Offline Collaborative WTCS Modeling solution*, there exists a different front repository for each different user type which contains the partial model for that user type.

Apart from collaboration related operations, the way a model user will work with the *Offline Collaborative WTCS Modeling solution* is quite similar to the way the modeler was working with the tree-based single user modeling tool introduced in Sect. 3.

The Offline Graphical Collaborative WTCS Modeling Solution is a Sirius-based editor which allows editing WTCS models graphically. As mentioned above, WTCS models edited by the offline modeling solution are built with the Wind Power domain specific tree editor, but, as mentioned in Sect. 4, an important challenge is the capability of editing WTCS models graphically, with an editor which provides advanced features like drill-down, element filtering, layers, custom views, different diagrams, etc.

This Offline Graphical Collaborative editor addresses this challenge by exploiting DSL-tao. DSL-tao was used to define the graphical syntax by instantiating the pattern for concrete syntax using its dedicated wizard, and to generate the Sirius-based editor. It is noteworthy that a wind turbine model can be edited either using the classical EMF-based tree editor or the graphical editor based on Sirius.

6   Evaluation

In order to assess the success of the MONDO technologies in the IK4-IKERLAN MBE processes, an evaluation has been performed. This evaluation—whose details are extensively covered in the project deliverables [22]—is reported next.

6.1   Evaluation Framework

Three realistic scenarios, which express the four challenges presented in Sect. 4, are used for the validation of the MONDO technologies:

Scenario S1: Wind turbine control design — Three system engineers work concurrently on a single model, modeling different subsystems. Each system engineer works on a partial model or submodel and MONDO technologies shall merge all the partial models into a unified model.

Scenario S2: Wind turbine commissioning — A system engineer works on a partial submodel of a model during the commissioning of a subsystem. Transformations for code generation will only take into account the artefacts contained in (and referenced from) the submodel the engineer is working on.

Scenario S3: Maintenance activities in the wind farm using mobile devices — A maintenance operator of a wind farm detects a malfunction of a non-critical element in a wind turbine. This causes the wind turbine to be out of operation. The engineer makes a minor change in the control model and obtains new code to put the wind turbine into operation in a degraded mode. These minor changes are made using a tablet or a mobile device.

The solutions presented in Sect. 5.2 support the three aforementioned scenarios:

Scenario S1 can be supported by two MONDO solutions: the *Online Concurrent WTCS Modeling Solution* and the *Offline Collaborative WTCS Modeling Solution*. Although in a different way, both solutions allow several engineers to work in parallel on the algorithms for the different subsystems of a wind turbine. Likewise, both solutions manage all changes performed by each engineer merging them in a single WTCS model.

Scenario S2 is supported by the *Offline Collaborative WTCS Modeling Solution*. A specific subsystem manager is allowed to load only a fragment of the entire WTCS model. Thus she can only edit the part of the model for the subsystem under her responsibility. The subsystem manager also has the ability to generate code for the subsystem.

Scenario S3 is supported by the *Online Concurrent WTCS Modeling Solution*. As this is a web based solution deployed on a web server, it can be accessed using a tablet. Thus, on-site modeling operations related to maintenance activities can be performed by the maintenance operator.

In order to better measure the impact of the MONDO technologies in the development of a WTCA, the following top-level indicators have been identified: (i) *time for committing model changes*; (ii) *impact on performance derived from using MONDO Collaboration technology*; and (iii) *time reduction for building graphical domain specific modeling editors*. These generic indicators have been materialized into a set of quantitative and qualitative measures, which are summarized in Tables 1 and 2. Based on the expertise of IK4-IKERLAN in the domain, different criteria have been defined to measure the success of the quantitative measures. On the other hand, the qualitative evaluation is carried out amongst the engineers participating in the evaluations using the questions in Table 2. In their answers, a four point scale (i.e., *fully*, *largely*, *partially*, *none*) is used together with the opportunity for respondents to provide comments and clarifications regarding their assessment.

Table 1. Quantitative measures and evaluation criteria

Id	Description	Sufficient	Good	Excellent
QN1	Increase in time for loading a model on a tablet instead of on a PC	25%	15%	10%
QN2	Number of concurrent users working with a model	2	3	5+
QN3	Time for change propagation and notification among concurrent users	<5 s	<3 s	<1 s
QN4	Maximum number of elements that can be displayed in a diagram	25	50	>50
QN5	Time for loading a diagram having 25 elements to be displayed	2 s	1 s	<1 s
QN6	Time for committing model changes	<5 s	<3 s	<1 s
QN7	Performance impact caused by the MONDO Collaboration Framework	<5%	<2%	<1%
QN8	Time reduction for building graphical domain specific modeling editors	25%	50%	75%

Table 2. Qualitative measures

Id	Description
QL1	Is there a methodology which specifies how a large DSL should be constructed?
QL2	Is there a tool support for the methodology, which guides the user on the construction of a large DSL?
QL3	Does this tool provide a way to create a basic but fully functional collaborative domain specific modeling tool?
QL4	Is MONDO technology mature enough to be used in industrial solutions?
QL5	Does MONDO technology allow concurrent editing of a model?
QL6	Does MONDO technology allow partial loading of models?
QL7	Does MONDO technology allow progressive loading of a model?
QL8	Does MONDO technology allow working with several modeling languages in a single tool?
QL9	Can a model be edited using a tablet?

6.2   Evaluation Results

In order to perform the evaluation, a test environment was set up as described in [22]. This environment consisted of a group of 6 different types of domain engineers—with different privileges—working together in collaborative modeling tasks using state-of-the-art tablets, desktop and laptop PCs.

Quantitative Measures

QN1 — The *Online Concurrent WTCS Modeling solution* has been used to evaluate this measure. Analyzing the data collected, we observe that the increase of time for loading the model on a tablet instead of on a PC, is between 11% and 13% for model fragments and goes up to 20% when full model is loaded.

QN2 — This measure has been evaluated using the *Online Concurrent WTCS Modeling solution*. The modeling solution has been successfully executed— i.e., without performance loss—by five different users on the same shared modeling session.

QN3 — Time needed to propagate changes and notifying them among concurrent users has been evaluated using the *Online Concurrent WTCS Modeling solution*. The solution has been executed by five different users, four of them were working with a desktop PC, while fifth one worked on a tablet. Each time a modification was made by one user, the time required for notifying other users has been measured. Less than one second was needed to propagate the modifications with a standard network equipment.

QN4 — The *Offline WTCS Graphical Modeling solution* has been used to evaluate this measure. In this evaluation, several diagrams have been loaded in this editor with scalable capabilities such as drill-down and filtering. Their sizes ranged from 5–15 elements to nearly 450 elements. All the diagrams were successfully loaded.

QN5 — The *Offline WTCS Graphical Modeling solution* has been used to evaluate this measure. The measurements show that loading and displaying a diagram with 25 elements takes between two and three seconds. However, although the target measure is not met, the result achieved is very close to the target result. It is also noteworthy that the largest diagram (with 452 elements) can be loaded in less than 7 s. As a consequence, although the target result has not been met, the overall results achieved in this evaluation are considered sufficient.

QN6 — This measure has been evaluated with the *Offline Collaborative WTCS Modeling solution*. When a commit operation is performed in an offline scenario, model changes are committed to the gold repository and propagated to the front repositories for the different engineer types who are working in collaboration.

The first conclusion after the evaluation is that the number of changes to be committed to the repository has no significant impact on the time needed to commit them. Specifically, the times collected for committing changes and updating the front repositories range from two to three seconds for every front repository, regardless of the number of changes. It is important to highlight that model merging was a hand-made and error prone activity which could take up to half an hour before the introduction of the MONDO technologies [5].

QN7 — Impact on performance has been evaluated using the *Offline Collaborative WTCS Modeling solution*. The solution designed and developed for offline collaboration does not penalize the performance of features that were already available in the solution. In this sense, an engineer gets the same performance for the modeling activities she was used to carry out, but with the addition of the collaborative modeling capabilities.

QN8 — The process of construction of the *Offline WTCS Graphical Modeling solution* has been considered for the evaluation of this measure. The aim of this measure is to compare the time required to create a graphical wind turbine control system modeling editor using MONDO technology (concretely DSL-tao and its design patterns), and time required to create the graphical modeling editor using the design tool provided by Sirius. Specifically, a graphical WTCS modeling editor prototype can be constructed using the Sirius graphical specification in nearly two hours by an expert developer on this technology. The equivalent graphical modeling editor has been constructed using DSL-tao in no more than half an hour by the same developer with basic—but sufficient—knowledge of DSL-tao.

Table 3 summarizes the rates achieved in the different quantitative measures according to the criteria specified in Table 1.

Table 3. Quantitative measures Results

Id	Rating	Id	Rating	Id	Rating	Id	Rating
QN1	Sufficient	QN3	Excellent	QN5	Sufficient	QN7	Excellent
QN2	Excellent	QN4	Excellent	QN6	Good	QN8	Excellent

Qualitative Measures. Besides the quantitative measures presented above, a set of qualitative measures were also planned. The fulfillment of this set of measures is explained below, in Table 4, where the level of compliance for each measure is presented along with some additional comments. The level of compliance is set using a four point scale with the following values: (i) *fully*, the expected target measure has been achieved for the Wind Power domain; (ii) *largely*, although the target measure has not been fully been reached, the achieved result is very close to the expected result; (iii) *partially*, some interesting results have been achieved for the Wind Power domain thanks to MONDO technology, although the target measure has not been reached; (i) *none*, no result related to the target measure has been obtained with the MONDO technology.

Table 4. Qualitative measures results

Id	Fulfillment	Comments
QL1	Fully	DSL-* tools provide a step by step process for designing large DSLs.
QL2	Fully	The tool supporting large DSL construction is DSL-tao. It provides a set of design patterns to design the DSL and to build its modeling tool
QL3	Largely	A functional domain specific modeling tool can be created using DSL-tao, but collaboration features are not fully supported
QL4	Largely	Components like the MONDO Collaboration Framework are ready to use. Setting up of the collaboration environments, however, should be automated
QL5	Fully	This feature is provided by MONDO Online Collaboration Framework, which has been used to build the *Online Concurrent WTCS Modeling solution*
QL6	Fully	This feature is provided by the MONDO Collaboration Framework. EMF-Splitter provides also this feature, enabling to split a model into different physical files that can be loaded separately on demand
QL7	Fully	Progressive loading can be achieved by EMF-Splitter where each model fragment can be loaded on demand, when modularity pattern is applied
QL8	Fully	Although this requirement has not been validated in the previous use cases, the MONDO technology has been tested to confirm that there is no constraint to combine two different modelling languages in a single modelling tool
QL9	Fully	The MONDO Collaboration Framework allows users to edit a model concurrently using a web modeling application run on a tablet

Table 5. Scenarios, solutions and evaluated measures

Scenario	MONDO solution	Measure id
S1	Online concurrent	QN2, QN3, QL5, QL6, QL4
S1	Offline collaborative	QN4, QN5, QN6, QN7, QN8, QL1, QL2, QL3, QL4, QL6, QL7, QL8
S2	Offline collaborative	QN6, QN7, QL1, QL2, QL3, QL4, QL6
S3	Online concurrent	QN1, QL4, QL9

Scenario Coverage. Table 5 summarises the relationship among the evaluation scenarios described in Sect. 6.1, the MONDO solutions used for each scenario, and the measures evaluated by the solution in each scenario.

7 Discussion

Scalable modeling technologies can provide new opportunities to SME to grow their software development teams. In this document we have reported on the experience at IK4-IKERLAN after implementing the technologies developed in the MONDO project. The experience has been extremely positive, and the evaluation shows that five out of eight quantitative measures scored excellent—one of them scored good and two others scored sufficient—while seven out of nine qualitative measures were fully fulfilled—the two remaining were largely fulfilled.

From this experience, we can also learn that **continuous compliance** with existing development processes is a key factor for success. The MONDO scalable technologies do not impose a big change on the processes and tools that were already implemented in the company. In this sense, the new solutions enable teamwork in the offline scenario in such a way that can be integrated without changing the pre-existing single-user modeling tools. This way developers continue working in the same way they used to work, and collaboration features only come into play to automate operations that were manual before (e.g., model merging).

Part of this success has been due to, not only the technology itself, but to the **methodological guidance** provided by MONDO. Specifically, the methodology supported by DSL-tao can be easily followed to construct large scale DSLs. In this sense, it is important that this methodology provides a wide set of predefined design patterns, which DSL designers can take advantage of to build their custom modeling solutions.

Another important contribution of the scalable technology is the capability for **concurrent model editing using web technology**, enabling real-time collaboration with secure access control, even using mobile devices. While there are several emerging modeling frameworks to support web-based collaborative modeling such as AToMPM [18], WebGME [14], Web Modeling Framework [21]—see [9] for an overview—security and scalability remains a major challenge for them.

As demonstrated by *Online Graphical Collaborative WTCS Modeling Solution* the Eclipse RAP platform [20] is not mature enough.

Finally, this experience also evidences that web-based solutions are not best suited to carry out modeling activities in handheld mobile devices, since they present usability issues. In this sense, another possible avenue for research is the development of **dedicated domain-specific modeling environments for mobile devices** [23].

Acknowledgements. We would like to thank István Ráth, Dániel Varró, and all the MONDO researchers for their contributions to the project.

References

1. Ackermann, T., Söder, L.: Wind energy technology and current status: a review. Renew. Sustain. Energy Rev. **4**(4), 315–374 (2000). doi:10.1016/S1364-0321(00)00004-6
2. Barmpis, K., Kolovos, D.: Hawk: towards a scalable model indexing architecture. In: Proceedings of the Workshop on Scalability in Model Driven Engineering, pp. 6:1–6:9, BigMDE 2013, NY, USA (2013). doi:10.1145/2487766.2487771
3. Bergmann, G., Debreceni, C., Ráth, I., Varró, D.: Query-based access control for secure collaborative modeling using bidirectional transformations. In: Proceedings of the ACM/IEEE 19th International Conference on Model Driven Engineering Languages and Systems, Saint-Malo, France, 2–7 October 2016, pp. 351–361 (2016).doi:10.1145/2976767.2976793
4. Czarnecki, K., Eisenecker, U.W.: Generative Programming: Methods, Tools, and Applications. ACM Press/Addison-Wesley Publishing Co., New York (2000). ISBN:0-201-30977-7
5. Debreceni, C., Ráth, I., Varró, D., Carlos, X., Mendialdua, X., Trujillo, S.: Automated model merge by design space exploration. In: Stevens, P., Wąsowski, A. (eds.) FASE 2016. LNCS, vol. 9633, pp. 104–121. Springer, Heidelberg (2016). doi:10.1007/978-3-662-49665-7_7
6. European Commission: What is an SME? http://ec.europa.eu/growth/smes/business-friendly-environment/sme-definition_es. Accessed Feb 2017
7. Fowler, M.: Domain Specific Languages, 1st edn. Addison-Wesley Professional, Upper Saddle River (2010)
8. Garmendia, A., Guerra, E., Kolovos, D.S., de Lara, J.: EMF splitter: a structured approach to EMF modularity. In: Proceedings of XM@MODELS. CEUR Workshop Proceedings, vol. 1239, pp. 22–31. CEUR-WS.org (2014). http://ceur-ws.org/Vol-1239/xm14_submission_3.pdf
9. Gray, J., Rumpe, B.: The evolution of model editors: browser- and cloud-based solutions. Softw. Syst. Model. **15**(2), 303–305 (2016). doi:10.1007/s10270-016-0524-2
10. IK4-IKERLAN: Efficiency in service innovation for companies—IK4-IKERLAN. http://www.ikerlan.es/en/ikerlan/. Accessed Feb 2017
11. Kleppe, A.: Software Language Engineering: Creating Domain-Specific Languages Using Metamodels, 1st edn. Addison-Wesley Professional, Upper Saddle River (2008). ISBN:0321553454, 9780321553454
12. Kolovos, D.S., Paige, R.F., Polack, F.A.C.: The epsilon transformation language. In: Vallecillo, A., Gray, J., Pierantonio, A. (eds.) ICMT 2008. LNCS, vol. 5063, pp. 46–60. Springer, Heidelberg (2008). doi:10.1007/978-3-540-69927-9_4

13. Kolovos, D.S., Rose, L.M., Matragkas, N., Paige, R.F., Guerra, E., Cuadrado, J.S., De Lara, J., Ráth, I., Varró, D., Tisi, M., Cabot, J.: A research roadmap towards achieving scalability in model driven engineering. In: Proceedings of the Workshop on Scalability in Model Driven Engineering, pp. 2:1–2:10. BigMDE 2013, NY, USA (2013).doi:10.1145/2487766.2487768

14. Maróti, M., Kecskés, T., Kereskényi, R., Broll, B., Völgyesi, P., Jurácz, L., Levendovszky, T., Lédeczi, Á.: Next generation (meta)modeling: web- and cloud-based collaborative tool infrastructure. In: Proceedings of the 8th Workshop on Multi-Paradigm Modeling (MPM) co-located with MODELS 2014, pp. 41–60 (2014). http://ceur-ws.org/Vol-1237/paper5.pdf

15. Pescador, A., Garmendia, A., Guerra, E., Cuadrado, J.S., de Lara, J.: Pattern-based development of domain-specific modelling languages. In: 18th ACM/IEEE International Conference on Model Driven Engineering Languages and Systems, MoDELS, pp. 166–175. IEEE Computer Society (2015). doi:10.1109/MODELS.2015.7338247

16. Selic, B.: The pragmatics of model-driven development. IEEE Softw. 20(5), 19–25 (2003). doi:10.1109/MS.2003.1231146

17. Steinberg, D., Budinsky, F., Paternostro, M., Merks, E.: EMF: Eclipse Modeling Framework 2.0, 2nd edn. Addison-Wesley Professional, Amsterdam (2009). ISBN:0321331885

18. Syriani, E., Vangheluwe, H., Mannadiar, R., Hansen, C., Mierlo, S.V., Ergin, H.: AToMPM: a web-based modeling environment. In: Joint Proceedings of MODELS 2013 Invited Talks, Demonstration Session, Poster Session, and ACM Student Research Competition, pp. 21–25 (2013). http://ceur-ws.org/Vol-1115/demo4.pdf

19. The Eclipse Foundation: Eclipse The Eclipse Foundation open source community website. https://eclipse.org/ Accessed Feb 2017

20. The Eclipse Foundation: Remote Application Platform (RAP). http://eclipse.org/rap/. Accessed Feb 2017

21. The Eclipse Foundation: Web Modeling Framework (previously genmymodel.com). https://projects.eclipse.org/proposals/web-modeling-framework/. Accessed Feb 2017

22. The MONDO Project: Work Package 4 - Scalable Collaborative Modelling. Deliverable 4.4: Prototype Tool for Collaborative Modeling. http://hdl.handle.net/20.500.12004/1/P/MONDO/D4.4

23. Vaquero-Melchor, D., Garmendia, A., Guerra, E., de Lara, J.: Towards enabling mobile domain-specific modelling. In: Proceedings of the 11th International Joint Conference on Software Technologies - Volume 2: ICSOFT-PT, (ICSOFT 2016), pp. 117–122 (2016).doi:10.5220/0006002501170122

Author Index

Printed in the United States
By Bookmasters